Human Chromosomes

Third Edition

Eeva Therman   Millard Susman

Human Chromosomes
Structure, Behavior, and Effects

Third Edition

With 105 Figures

Springer-Verlag
New York Berlin Heidelberg London Paris
Tokyo Hong Kong Barcelona Budapest

Eeva Therman
Department of Medical Genetics
University of Wisconsin
Madison, WI 53706 USA

Millard Susman
Medical School
University of Wisconsin
Madison, WI 53706 USA

Cover illustration: Human chromosomes visualized following hybridization with six different chromosome-specific libraries: #1 (green), #2 (violet), #4 (white), #8 (yellow), #14 (red), and #X (orange). Images were taken with an epifluorescence microscope coupled to a CCD-camera, and processed using custom computer software. Courtesy of Dr. Thomas Ried and Dr. David Ward, Department of Medical Genetics, Yale University.

Library of Congress Cataloging-in-Publication Data
Therman, Eeva.
    Human chromosomes : structure, behavior, and effects / Eeva Therman,
Millard Susman.—3rd ed.
      p. cm.
    "Springer study edition"—p. i
    Includes bibliographical references and index.
    ISBN 0-387-97871-2.—ISBN 3-540-97871-2
    1. Human chromosomes. 2. Human cytogenetics. 3. Human chromosome
abnormalities. I. Susman, Millard. II. Title.
    [DNLM: 1. Chromosomes, Human. 2. Cytogenetics. QH 600 T411h]
QH431.T436 1992
611'.01816—dc20
DNLM/DLC
for Library of Congress   92-2335

Printed on acid-free paper.

Production managed by Henry Krell; manufacturing supervised by Jacqui Ashri.
Typeset by Best-set Typesetter, Ltd., Hong Kong.
Printed and bound by Arcata Graphics/Halliday, West Hanover, MA.
Printed in the United States of America.

9 8 7 6 5 4 3 2 1

ISBN 0-387-97871-2 Springer-Verlag New York Berlin Heidelberg
ISBN 3-540-97871-2 Springer-Verlag Berlin Heidelberg New York

For Barbara Susman

Preface

This book, like the two previous editions, was written as an introduction to human cytogenetics, but it could also be used as a text for a general cytogenetics course, since chromosome structure and behavior are similar in all eukaryotes. Many examples in this book are from organisms other than humans, reflecting our combined backgrounds of molecular and bacterial genetics, and plant and animal cytogenetics. In the rapidly expanding field of human cytogenetics, certain subjects, for instance clinical and cancer cytogenetics, are now covered in recently published, thousand-page volumes. In this book, such subjects are presented only in outline. The enormous growth of information has also made the choice of topics and of examples to illustrate them even more arbitrary and subjective than in the previous editions. Apart from a few pages here and there, the text has been rewritten. Major parts, especially those on molecular matters, have been added.

This book would not exist without the dedicated participation of Mrs. Barbara Susman. She has been involved in the project from the planning stages to the final proofreading. She has done the extensive literature research, designed most of the tables and illustrations, and edited and typed the text.

For discussions and suggestions we are indebted to many colleagues. We wish especially to mention Drs. Lassi Alvesalo, Evelyn M. Kuhn, and Renata Laxova, who have critically read selected parts of the book, and Dr. Carter Denniston, who has read the whole text.

We are grateful to the colleagues and editors who have generously permitted the use of published and unpublished pictures. We would especially like to thank Dr. Thomas Ried for the use of the lovely cover photo. Dr. Carolyn Trunca has allowed us to use her unpublished analysis of the segregation of human translocations, and Dr. Andrew Drewry has given us unpublished data. The photographic work has been done by Mr. Walter Kugler, Jr. Our excellent editor is Dr. Ilse Riegel.

Madison, Wisconsin   Eeva Therman
January, 1992   Millard Susman

Contents

1
Origins and Directions of Human Cytogenetics

Before 1956 two "facts" were known about human cytogenetics. The human chromosome number was believed to be 48, and the XX–XY mechanism of sex determination was assumed to work in the same way as it does in *Drosophila*. Studies of the fruit fly had shown that the *ratio* of the number of X chromosomes to the number of sets of autosomes determines the sex of the organism. Both of these fundamental notions about human chromosomes were eventually proved wrong.

The year 1956 is often given as the beginning of modern human cytogenetics. Indeed, the technical improvements that allowed Tjio and Levan (1956) to discover that the human chromosome number is 46, instead of 48, provided the starting point for subsequent spectacular developments in human chromosome studies. The difficulties of writing about even fairly recent history are well demonstrated by the very different accounts of this discovery related by the two participants themselves (Tjio, 1978; Levan, 1978).

The history of human cytogenetics has been reviewed at length several times; for instance, by Makino (1975) and by Hsu (1979). Hsu's delightful book relieves us of the responsibility of giving a detailed description of past developments in the field. (The terms used here are explained in the appropriate chapters). Hsu (1979) divides human cytogenetics conveniently into four eras: the dark ages before 1952, the hypotonic period from 1952 to about 1958, the trisomy period between 1959 and 1969, and the chromosome banding era that started in 1970 and still continues. To these should be added prophase or high-resolution banding, which has opened completely new avenues in human cytogenetics (Yunis, 1976). Finally, there is the convergence of molecular and cytogenetic techniques, which makes it possible to look for the chemical nature of structures and behaviors visible through the light microscope. In the following discussion only a few highlights of these various developments will be recounted.

The Dark Ages

The difficulties faced by the early cytogeneticists are illustrated by a comparison of Fig. 3.1 with the other photomicrographs of human chromosomes in this book. Despite the lack of clarity, the lymphocyte mitosis in Fig. 3.1 shows the chromosomes considerably better than did the slides of paraffin-sectioned testes, stained with hematoxylin, that were used during the first quarter of this century. Of these studies, only the paper by Painter (1923) is mentioned here, since it determined the ideas in this field for the next 33 years. Even though Painter's report that the human chromosome number was 48 was worded quite cautiously, the more often it was quoted the more certain the finding seemed to become.

Despite the primitive techniques available, the groundwork for future studies was laid during these dark ages. The first satisfactory preparations of mammalian chromosomes were obtained by squashing ascites tumor cells of the mouse (Levan and Hauschka, 1952, 1953) and of the rat (Makino, 1975). The first successful treatment with chemical substances to improve visibility was performed on mouse tumor cells by Bayreuther (1952). Early studies with these crude techniques confirmed that human chromosomes, like those of other organisms, show reproducible segmental differences in staining. This pattern of darkly stained *euchromatin* and lightly stained *heterochromatin* made it possible to distinguish some of the chromosomes from one another. Later, colchicine or its derivatives, which arrest cells in *division*, were used to make it easier for researchers to collect data on large numbers of dividing cells. During this era, mammalian tissue culture techniques were developed.

The Hypotonic Era

Prefixation treatment with hypotonic salt solution, which swells the cells and thus separates the chromosomes, was a decisive improvement in cytological techniques. The hypotonic treatment was launched by Hsu (1952), although other laboratories were experimenting with similar treatments at the same time.

The simultaneous use of a number of new techniques made it possible to establish the correct chromosome number in man. They were the tissue culture and squash techniques, combined with treatments with colchicine and hypotonic solution prior to fixation. Before the end of 1956, the finding of Tjio and Levan in embryonic lung cells was confirmed in human spermatocytes by Ford and Hamerton (1956), whose photo-micrographs also showed that the X and Y chromosomes are attached end to end by their short arms in meiosis. During the hypotonic era the analysis of the human karyotype, which led to the ability to distinguish each of the human chromosomes from the others, was also begun.

The Trisomy Period

The new techniques were soon applied to chromosome analyses of individuals who were mentally retarded or had other congenital anomalies, or both. The first autosomal trisomy was described by Lejeune et al. (1959), who found that Down syndrome was caused by the presence of three copies, as opposed to the normal two, of one of the smallest human chromosomes. During the same year it was reported that females with the abnormal sexual development called Turner syndrome were characterized by an abnormal sex chromosome constitution: they had only one X , and no Y, chromosome in each cell (Ford et al., 1959). That same year, it was found that abnormal males with Klinefelter syndrome had two X chromosomes *and* a Y in each cell (Jacobs and Strong, 1959). In addition, the first XXX woman was described (Jacobs et al., 1959). These observations on the Turner and Klinefelter syndromes showed that sex determination in humans occurs by a mechanism entirely different from that in *Drosophila*. The male sex, in human beings, is determined by the presence of the Y chromosome. Later it was established that the Y chromosome is effective in determining male sex, even if it is combined with four X chromosomes; individuals with the XXXXY sex chromosome constitution are males, although abnormal.

The following year, D_1 trisomy (now known to be 13 trisomy) (Patau et al., 1960) and 18 trisomy (Edwards et al., 1960; Patau et al., 1960; Smith et al., 1960) were described. With these discoveries the viable autosomal trisomies—apart from mosaics—seemed to be exhausted, and chromosome studies turned to structural aberrations and their phenotypic consequences.

These developments coincided with an important innovation in cell culture technique. Nowell (1960) and Moorhead et al. (1960) launched the short-term culture technique, using peripheral lymphocytes from blood samples. The effectiveness of the technique was based on the mitosis-inducing ability of phytohemagglutinin, a bean extract. Such cultures, combined with the trick of drying the fixed chromosomes directly on microscope slides (Rothfels and Siminovitch, 1958), are still the most important source of human and mammalian chromosomes.

Chromosome Banding Era

The first attempts to differentiate the human chromosomes sorted them into seven groups on the basis of length and morphology. Despite claims to the contrary, the chromosomes within five of these groups (B, C, D, F, and G) could not be identified individually (Patau, 1960); the numbers attached to the paired-off chromosomes in prebanding karyotypes represented sheer guesses. Although autoradiography had allowed the accurate identification of some chromosomes (Patau, 1965), the degree of precision was increased by orders of magnitude with the introduction of chromosome banding techniques. In 1970, Caspersson et al. applied fluorescence microscopy, which they had originally used to study plant chromosomes, to the analysis of the human karyotype. They discovered that the chromosomes consist of differentially fluorescent cross-bands of various lengths. Careful study of these bands made possible the identification of all human chromosomes. This discovery was followed by a flood of different banding techniques that utilized either fluorescent dyes or the Giemsa stain (Drets and Shaw, 1971). Later, the banding of prophase chromosomes made it possible to determine chromosome segments and breakpoints even more accurately (Yunis, 1976).

Another milestone was the discovery that chromosomes incorporating 5-bromodeoxyuridine (BrdU) instead of thymidine into their DNA have different staining properties. This phenomenon has been successfully used to reveal the late-replicating chromosomes and chromosome segments (Latt, 1974), as well as the replication order of chromosome bands. It also provides the basis for the study of sister chromatid exchanges (Latt, 1973).

It is much more difficult to obtain satisfactory chromosome preparations of male meiosis—not to mention female meiosis—in humans than in the mouse, for instance. But more recently these difficulties have been overcome to some extent. The early stages of meiosis have been analyzed successfully in the oocytes (for instance, Therman and Sarto, 1977; Hultén et al., 1978), whereas work on the spermatocytes has yielded clear photomicrographs of the later stages (for instance, Stahl et al., 1973).

Human Sex Chromosomes

Throughout the four eras described by Hsu (1979), our understanding of the function and behavior of mammalian sex chromosomes increased steadily. One of the first important observations was that the neural nuclei of the female cat had a condensed body, missing in the male nuclei (Barr and Bertram, 1949). This body is called sex chromatin, the *Barr body*, or X chromatin.

The single-active-X hypothesis of Lyon (1961; Russell, 1961) had a decisive influence on the entire field of mammalian sex chromosome studies. According to the Lyon hypothesis, as it is called, one X chromosome in mammalian female cells is inactivated at an early embryonic stage. The original choice of which X is inactivated is random, but in all the descendants of a particular cell the same X remains inactive. If a cell has more than two X chromosomes, all but one are turned off. The Barr body is formed by the inactive X chromosome (Ohno and Cattanach, 1962), which is out of step with the active X chromosome during the cell cycle.

Evolution of Human Chromosomes

The phylogeny of human chromosomes, see Seuánez (1979), has been studied intensively in recent years. A comparison of human chromosomes with those of our closest relatives—the chimpanzee, gorilla, and orangutan—shows that 99 percent of the chromosome bands are shared by the four genera. This similarity extends even to the prophase bands (Yunis and Prakash, 1982). The most prominent differences in banding patterns occur in the heterochromatic regions (Seuánez, 1979).

The similarity of the chromosome banding pattern in the four genera demonstrates that most of the individual bands have retained their identity for more than 20 million years, and many of them for considerably longer. A number of chromosomes in man and the great apes are identical. The most conserved of these chromosomes is the X, which has not changed in morphology between monkeys and man. Its gene content is assumed to have remained the same throughout mammalian development, or for some 125 million years (Ohno, 1967; Seuánez, 1979).

Nomenclature of Human Chromosomes

As the number of laboratories involved in the analysis of human chromosomes grew, so did the number of systems used to name the chromosomes. In an effort to create order out of potential chaos, several conferences on chromosome nomenclature were held: in Denver (1960), London (1963), Chicago (1966), and Paris (1971) (Makino, 1975; Paris Conference: 1971 [1972]). These produced a universally accepted nomenclature. The recommendations of later conferences in Stockholm and Paris (ISCN, 1978, 1981) include the designations of metaphase and prophase chromosome bands (Chapter 4).

The Molecular Era

Although chromosomes are extremely large and molecularly complex objects, it has now become possible to deal with them in the laboratory in much the same way as one deals with viruses. Chromosomes can be isolated from other cellular components, "sorted" into relatively pure preparations of individual chromosomes, and fractionated into their molecular components. The DNA molecules can be fragmented, and the fragments can be cloned and sequenced. Treatments have been discovered that distinguish between "active" and "inactive" segments of chromosomes; these methods make it possible to search for the molecular mechanisms of gene regulation. The centromeres, where spindle fibers attach to pull chromosomes to the poles during cell divisions, and the telomeres, which stabilize the ends of the linear DNA molecules of chromosomes, have now been cloned and sequenced. More and more of the proteins that bind to DNA are being purified and studied in controlled, in vitro systems. Highly specific antibodies are available to identify and localize proteins bound to DNA molecules. New methods of electron microscopy are making it possible to study chromosome ultrastructure at higher and higher levels of resolution. The concerted efforts of hundreds of scientists in the Human Genome Project will, in the near future, produce complete chromosome maps and DNA sequences for *Homo sapiens* and several other genetically important organisms ranging from the bacterium, *Escherichia coli*, to the roundworm, *Caenorhabditis elegans*. We can confidently forecast a deluge of new information on the molecular structure of genes and chromosomes and on the molecular mechanisms that regulate the expression and behavior of chromosomes.

Ultrastructure of Eukaryotic Chromosomes

The gap that existed for a long time between our knowledge of DNA and of chromosome structure on the level of the light microscope is finally being bridged (Chapter 8). Although some of the steps still are hypothetical, we now have a fairly good idea how a several-centimeter-long DNA double helix is packed to form a few-micra-long chromatid. Interestingly, the structure as found in the giant lampbrush and polytene chromosomes seems in principle to apply to all eukaryotic chromosomes. Even gene action in lampbrush chromosomes is directly visible in the electron microscope (Chapter 8).

In addition, "recombination nodules" are being studied in the electron microscope. These seem to mark the crossing-over sites in meiosis (Chapter 18). Obviously, many of the mysteries surrounding chromosome pairing and crossing-over will be solved with similar studies. Actually much remains to be done on the early meiotic stages, even at the level of the light microscope.

Microspread and silver staining techniques have brought the synaptonemal complexes within reach of light microscopic examination, offering interesting possibilities for the analysis of the pairing of both normal and structurally aberrant chromosomes.

Functional Structure of Human Chromosomes

For the first 10 years after its discovery, chromosome banding was used mostly to identify individual chromosomes or segments. However, gradually the significance of the bands themselves has come under study (Chapter 7). It has been obvious for a long time that the Q-dark bands (bands that do not fluoresce when stained with the dye quinacrine) contain more genes than the Q-bright bands. Now it is accepted that all housekeeping genes (and most, if not all, tissue-specific genes) are situated in the Q-dark bands. Other differences between the two types of bands are emerging. Thus, the Q-dark bands are characterized by the presence of short, interspersed elements (SINES), whereas the Q-bright bands contain long, interspersed elements (LINES). An accurate gene map will further add to our understanding of the function of the various chromosome segments (Chapters 6 and 7).

The role of heterochromatin is still completely mysterious. DNA in the regions called "constitutive heterochromatin" is never transcribed. These chromosome regions therefore contain no genetic information that is used for making metabolically active RNAs or proteins. So far, not even a plausible hypothesis of its possible function exists.

Eukaryotic chromosomes also contain large amounts of untranscribed DNA that is not heterochromatin; i.e., the regions containing this silent DNA do not stain differently from other segments of the chromosomes. The possible role of this apparently inert chromatin is a challenge to future studies.

Structure of Interphase Nuclei

Although the arrangement of chromosomes in interphase nuclei attracted attention as early as the 1880s, only recently have techniques been developed that allow us to follow the chromosomes throughout the mitotic cycle (Chapter 14). One of these is cell fusion, which causes the condensation of the chromosomes in the interphase nucleus. Such studies have demonstrated that chromosomes occupy the same relative positions from one metaphase to the next within the lineage of a particular cell. However, with the exception of Diptera and some other special cases, the arrangement of the chromosomes appears to vary randomly when one compares cells that are not in the same lineage.

In addition to the old technique of determining the sites of heterochromatic segments in interphase nuclei, recent methods of hybridizing chromosome-specific DNA to nuclei have yielded important information on the spatial arrangement of chromosomes.

Somatic Cell Cytogenetics

A branch of mammalian cytogenetics that is only beginning is the analysis of what happens in the nuclei during development (Chapters 15 and 16). Important results in developmental cytology were achieved in plants and insects during the 1930s and 1940s. In mammals, however, mitotic modifications and their effects have been studied almost exclusively in liver, bone marrow, and malignant cells. Recently the cells of the normal trophoblast as well as of hydatidiform moles have also been analyzed. In addition to spectrophotometry, in use for more than 30 years, new techniques such as flow cytometry, analysis of prematurely condensed chromosomes in cells fused at different stages of the cell cycle, and differential staining are being applied to the analysis of interphase nuclei. Studies like these may shed light on the role that nuclear changes play in differentiation. Important information might be gained by the above-mentioned hybridization of chromosome-specific DNA to differentiated nuclei.

At least the following phenomena seem to be correlated with cell differentiation (although their relationships are still unclear): ploidy of the nuclei, the mechanisms creating polyploidy, amplification–under-replication of various chromosome segments, arrangement of the chromosomes in the nuclei, and inactivation of various chromosome segments through heterochromatic condensation.

Sex Chromosomes and Sex Determination

The ongoing discovery and mapping of X-linked genes, and the determination of their behavior on the active and inactive X chromosomes, have confirmed and helped in the understanding of earlier observations (Chapters 21–23). The existence of an inactivation center on the long arm of the X (called Xq) and of an always-active region on the distal end of the short arm (Xp) are firmly established. Under study are other possible always-active regions, especially in short regions on either side of the centromere. The Xq contains a "critical region." A break there causes ovarian dysgenesis in the carrier. We do not know the basis for this phenotypic effect, nor do we know how to explain the surprising observation that Xp and Xq deletions cause the same symptoms. The molecular structures of the important pairing regions of the tip of Yp and Xp are under intensive study. The identity of the *testis-determining factor* (SRY, sex-determining region Y), the region of the Y chromosome that causes male sexual development, seems finally to have been established (Chapter 20).

The molecular basis of X inactivation remains to be discovered. The reactivation of a few genes on the inactive X chromosome was accomplished some 15 years ago (Chapter 21). Trophoblastic genes show a special tendency to be turned on, and even the whole inactive X has been reactivated. What causes the absence of Barr bodies in many female cancers is still an unsolved question.

Mutagenesis Studies

Chromosome breakage has been used for a long time as an indicator of the mutagenic effects of various agents (Chapters 9 and 10). The resolution of such studies has been greatly increased by chromosome banding. Chromosome breaks occur nonrandomly along the chromosomes: the breaks are localized mainly in the Q-dark bands, some of which constitute veritable "hot spots."

The introduction of sister chromatid exchanges as a test system has improved the accuracy of mutagenesis testing (Chapter 12). Sister chromatid exchanges are not only a more sensitive indicator of mutagenic activity than chromosome breaks, but they are also easier to score unambiguously. However, in spite of these advances, trying to make sense of the mutagenesis literature is almost impossible. Apart from the main phenomena, for practically every claim there is a counterclaim, and a choice between them often seems impossible. If the vast amount of work in this important field is not to go to waste, standardization of the methodology is urgently needed (Chapters 10 and 12).

Chromosome Instability Syndromes

The main chromosome instability syndromes—Fanconi anemia, ataxia telangiectasia, and Bloom syndrome—have been studied since the 1960s (Chapters 11 and 12). These syndromes are rare, and the interest in them has been inspired by the chromosome aberrations characterizing each of them and the resulting high risk for malignant disease. Geneticists always hope that the study of exceptional cases in which mechanisms have gone awry will shed light on how normal processes are controlled. Presumably the functions that have gone awry in these syndromes are the processes that control chromosome repair and recombination.

A special feature in Bloom syndrome is a greatly increased tendency of exchanges between homologous chromosome segments, which expresses itself in high rates of sister chromatid exchanges and mitotic crossing-over (meiotic crossing-over has not been studied). This allows us to study phenomena, such as mitotic crossing-over, which otherwise are very rare. Unequal exchanges apparently play an important role in gene amplification, in the variation of heterochromatic segments, and in the development of homogeneously stained regions and of a special class of abnormal chromosomes called "double minutes."

The genes causing these diseases are under study, and the Fanconi anemia and ataxia genes have been mapped. Several other conditions in which chromosomal instability has been reported should be analyzed in more detail.

Mapping of Human Chromosomes

The development of an accurate gene map is one of the main goals of cytogenetic studies in any organism. The localization of genes to specific chromosomes and chromosome segments is one of the most rapidly advancing branches of human cytogenetics (Chapter 31). The methodology includes linkage studies, the use of marker chromosomes in family studies, in vitro fusion of human cells with cells of other species, and the determination of minute deletions or single breaks. Previously it was possible to localize repeated genes by hybridizing their DNA on the chromosomes. This has also now become one of the most important techniques for mapping single genes. The Human Genome Project hopes to provide ultimately a complete gene map.

Chromosomes and Cancer

The field of cytogenetics in which the most spectacular successes have been achieved during the last few years is the study of cancer chromosomes (Chapters 28–30). The old idea that, if the same chromosome aberration is consistently found in a certain type of malignant disease, it probably is its cause has finally proven itself. Observations on these constant chromosome aberrations, combined with virology and molecular biology, resulted in the discovery of oncogenes, and this finding has given an insight into the origin of cancer. Proto-oncogenes, which are present in all eukaryotic cells, can be activated through various processes, one of which is rearrangement of the chromosome so that the level of activity of the oncogene is increased or decreased. High-resolution banding of rearranged chromosomes has played a major role in the mapping of oncogenes. One of the most interesting discoveries, so far made only in a few malignant tumors, is that the full development of a cancer needs a series of definite steps, such as gene mutations, deletions and/or duplications, and chromosome structural changes.

Homogeneously stained regions and double minutes, which consist of one or more genes amplified hundreds of times, are in some cases a step in carcinogenesis itself; in others, they play a role in the progression of tumors (Chapter 28).

An interesting though still unanswered question is what causes the ubiquitous and similar mitotic aberrations found in different human cancers, as well as in those of other mammals.

Clinical Cytogenetics

The vast amount of work done in clinical cytogenetics has led to the description of syndromes caused by partial trisomy (three doses of a short chromosomal region) and monosomy (one dose) for each of the chromosome arms (Chapters 25 and 26). Prophase banding and molecular techniques, which have helped to determine accurate breakpoints, have also resulted in the discovery of syndromes caused by minute deletions. Such discoveries can safely be predicted to continue.

Chromosome analyses of defined populations have uncovered the causes of many birth defects and spontaneous abortions. Examples of such populations are: spontaneous abortuses, newborn infants, mentally retarded individuals, infertile men, women with gonadal dysgenesis, and couples with repeated abortions. Studies of such populations are producing more accurate empirical risk figures for different types of translocations and other chromosome aberrations (Chapters 26 and 27). Segregation in males heterozygous for chromosome aberrations can now be directly studied by using the technique of fertilizing hamster eggs with the sperm of such men or by direct molecular studies of single sperm cells. Genetic counseling is further helped by the placental biopsy technique, which allows the diagnosis of chromosomally or biochemically abnormal fetuses at an early stage. Molecular techniques to identify single-gene abnormalities are also being applied to genetic counseling.

The causes of the highly nonrandom participation of the human acrocentric chromosomes in whole-arm transfers (Robertsonian translocations) might become clear through molecular studies of the pericentric regions of these chromosomes (Chapter 27).

The interesting observations that some genes may have different effects depending on the parent from whom they are inherited and that two homologous chromosomes may come from the same parent should be studied more extensively, both to find out how frequently such events occur and what the range of their effects may be.

The following problems still await solution. Do extreme heterochromatic variants ever affect the phenotype of carriers or the nondisjunction rate of the chromosome involved? Robertsonian translocations, as a rule, do not exert interchromosomal effects; in other words, they do not affect the behavior of unrelated chromosomes. However, it is unclear whether heterochromatic variants, reciprocal translocations, and other structurally abnormal chromosomes have such effects (Chapter 27). Finally, are there genes in the human that increase nondisjunction, and, if so, through what pathways do they act?

The Future of Human Cytogenetics

The expansion of human cytogenetics in somewhat more than 35 years is little short of miraculous; by now, from the viewpoint of cytogenetics, man is by far the most extensively studied organism. During its early stages, human cytogenetics was a more-or-less applied science: phenomena previously described in plants and animals were being observed in man. However, human cytogenetics has come of age, and advances in this field have inspired studies in other branches of human genetics. Indeed, it is the coordination of different approaches that has led to the most interesting results in this field. During the "dark ages," human cytogeneticists borrowed techniques from plant and animal studies. Now the opposite is often true, and both animal and plant chromosome studies owe a debt to the work done on humans.

Predictions of future developments in a scientific field can be based only on its present state, and thus it does not take second sight to claim that the next era in human cytogenetics belongs to molecular biology, and especially to the joint application of molecular and cytogenetic techniques to problems.

References

Barr ML, Bertram EG (1949) A morphological distinction between neurones of the male and female, and the behaviour of the nucleolar satellite during accelerated nucleoprotein synthesis. Nature 163:676–677

Bayreuther K (1952) Der Chromosomenbestand des Ehrlich-Ascites-Tumors der Maus. Naturforsch 7:554–557

Caspersson T, Zech L, Johansson C (1970) Differential banding of alkylating fluorochromes in human chromosomes. Exp Cell Res 60:315–319

Drets ME, Shaw MW (1971) Specific banding patterns in human chromosomes. Proc Natl Acad Sci USA 68:2073–2077

Edwards JH, Harnden DG, Cameron AH, et al. (1960) A new trisomic syndrome. Lancet i:787–790

Ford CE, Hamerton JL (1956) The chromosomes of man. Nature 178:1020–1023

Ford CE, Jones KW, Polani PE, et al. (1959) A sex-chromosome anomaly in a case of gonadal dysgenesis (Turner's syndrome). Lancet i:711–713

Hsu TC (1952) Mammalian chromosomes in vitro. I. The karyotype of man. J Hered 43:167–172

Hsu TC (1979) Human and mammalian cytogenetics. An historical perspective. Springer, Heidelberg

Hultén M, Luciani JM, Kirton V, et al. (1978) The use and limitations of chiasma scoring with reference to human genetic mapping. Cytogenet Cell Genet 22:37–58

ISCN (1978) An international system for human cytogenetic nomenclature. Birth defects: original article series, XIV: 8. National Foundation, New York; also in Cytogenet Cell Genet 21:309–404

ISCN (1981) An international system for human cytogenetic nomenclature—high resolution banding. Birth defects: original article series, XVII: 5. National Foundation, New York; also in Cytogenet Cell Genet 31:1–84

Jacobs PA, Strong JA (1959) A case of human intersexuality having a possible XXY sex-determining mechanism. Nature 183:302–303

Jacobs PA, Baikie AG, Court Brown WM, et al. (1959) Evidence for the existence of the human "super female." Lancet ii:423–425

Latt SA (1973) Microfluorometric detection of deoxyribonucleic acid replication in human metaphase chromosomes. Proc Natl Acad Sci USA 70:3395–3399

Latt SA (1974) Microfluorometric analysis of DNA replication in human X chromosomes. Exp Cell Res 86:412–415

Lejeune J, Gautier M, Turpin R (1959) Etude des chromosomes somatiques de neuf enfants mongoliens. Compt Rend 248:1721–1722

Levan A (1978) The background to the determination of the human chromosome number. Am J Obstet Gynecol 130:725–726

Levan A, Hauschka TS (1952) Chromosome numbers of three mouse ascites tumors. Hereditas 38:251–255

Levan A, Hauschka TS (1953) Endomitotic reduplication mechanisms in ascites tumors of the mouse. J Natl Cancer Inst 14:1–43

Lyon MF (1961) Gene action in the X-chromosome of the mouse (*Mus musculus* L.). Nature 190:372–373

Makino S (1975) Human chromosomes. Igaku Shoin, Tokyo

Moorhead PS, Nowell PC, Mellman WJ, et al. (1960) Chromosome preparations of leucocytes cultured from human peripheral blood. Exp Cell Res 20:613–616

Nowell PC (1960) Phytohemagglutinin: an initiator of mitosis in cultures of normal human leukocytes. Cancer Res 20:462–466

Ohno S (1967) Sex chromosomes and sex-linked genes. Springer, Heidelberg

Ohno S, Cattanach BM (1962) Cytological study of an X-autosome translocation in *Mus musculus*. Cytogenetics 1:129–140

Painter TS (1923) Studies in mammalian spermatogenesis. II. The spermatogenesis of man. J Exp Zool 37:291–336

Paris Conference:1971 (1972) Standardization in human cytogenetics. Birth defects: original article series, VIII: 7. New York: The National Foundation

Patau K (1960) The identification of individual chromosomes, especially in man. Am J Hum Genet 12:250–276

Patau K (1965) Identification of chromosomes. In: Yunis JJ (ed) Human chromosome methodology. Academic, New York, pp 155–186

Patau K, Smith DW, Therman E, et al. (1960) Multiple congenital anomaly caused by an extra autosome. Lancet i:790–793

Rothfels KH, Siminovitch L (1958) An air-drying technique for flattening chromosomes in mammalian cells grown in vitro. Stain Technol 33:73–77

Russell LB (1961) Genetics of mammalian sex chromosomes. Science 133:1795–1803

Seuánez HN (1979) The phylogeny of human chromosomes. Springer, Berlin

Smith DW, Patau K, Therman E, et al. (1960) A new autosomal trisomy syndrome: multiple congenital anomalies caused by an extra chromosome. J Pediatr 57:338–345

Stahl A, Luciani JM, Devictor-Vuillet M (1973) Etude chromosomique de la meiose. In: Boué A, Thibault C (eds) Les accidents chromosomiques de la reproduction. Paris: I.N.S.E.R.M., Centre International de l'Enfance, pp 197–218

Therman E, Sarto GE (1977) Premeiotic and early meiotic stages in the pollen mother cells of *Eremurus* and in human embryonic oocytes. Hum Genet 35:137–151

Tjio JH (1978) The chromosome number of man. Am J Obstet Gynecol 130:723–724

Tjio JH, Levan A (1956) The chromosome number in man. Hereditas 42:16

Yunis JJ (1976) High resolution of human chromosomes. Science 191:1268–1270

Yunis JJ, Prakash O (1982) The origin of man: A chromosomal pictorial legacy. Science 215:1525–1530

2
Structure of the Eukaryotic Chromosome and the Karyotype

Metaphase Chromosome

Higher organisms are *eukaryotes* in contrast to bacteria and blue-green algae, which are *prokaryotes*. The eukaryotic chromosome is a complicated structure that contains DNA and several different types of proteins. Chromosomes of higher organisms are studied most frequently at mitotic metaphase. This is the stage at which the chromosomes reach their greatest condensation. Microscopic study of chromosomes generally utilizes cells that have been treated with a *fixative* to preserve the structure of chromosomes and other cell components. Then the chromosomes are *stained* with one or more of a variety of dyes. Because these treatments can alter the structure of cellular components, it may be necessary to study cells treated with several different fixatives and stains in order to ascertain that features seen under the microscope are real. The natural condensation of mitotic chromosomes is increased by a prefixation treatment with various drugs, for example, colchicine. During mitotic metaphase, the condensed chromosomes appear in identifiable shapes (the *karyotype*) characteristic of the species being studied.

Primary Constriction

A typical metaphase chromosome consists of two arms separated by a *primary constriction*, which is made more clearly visible by treatment with colchicine. This constriction marks the location of the *centromere* or *spindle attachment*, which is essential for the normal movements of the chromosomes in relation to the spindle. A chromosome without a centromere is an *acentric* fragment and either is lost or drifts passively when the other chromosomes are drawn to the poles, by the action of the spindle, during anaphase.

In the plant genera of rushes (*Juncus*) and sedges (*Carex*), as well as in certain insects and the scorpions, the centromere is diffuse or multiple, and the chromosomes lack a primary constriction. This means that a small chromosomal fragment, even when separated from the rest of the chromosome, acts like a complete chromosome and displays normal anaphase movements.

A metaphase chromosome consists of two *sister chromatids* that separate in mitotic anaphase. The genetic constituent of a chromatid is a double helix of DNA. Cytologists have long disputed whether a chromatid consists of one double helix of DNA or of several parallel ones. It was formerly assumed that the latter situation prevailed, especially in organisms with large chromosomes. However, recent observations show con-

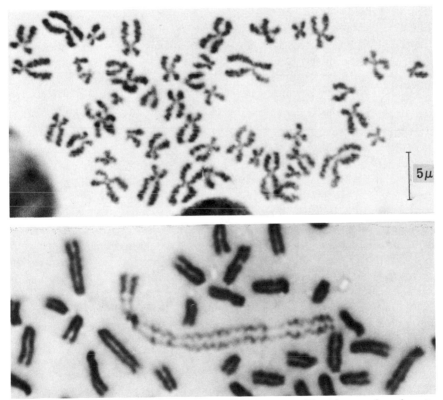

Figure 2.1. Spiralization of metaphase chromosomes. Top: human lymphocyte. Bottom: mouse cancer cell treated with 1-methyl-2-benzylhydrazine (Therman, 1972).

vincingly that each chromatid of a mitotic eukaryotic chromosome contains one double helix of DNA continuous from one end of the chromosome to the other. In other words, a chromatid is a *unineme* structure.

Through a series of coils within coils, the chromosome strands, or *chromonemata*, shorten greatly between interphase and metaphase. The largest coil is sometimes visible in the light microscope, as in a mouse cancer chromosome treated with 1-methyl-2-benzylhydrazine (Fig. 2.1), which displays segments with distinct coiling interspersed with condensed regions (Therman, 1972). In addition to DNA, eukaryotic chromosomes contain nonhistone proteins, together with five types of histones (Ris and Korenberg, 1979), all of which seem to play a role in the condensation and coiling of chromosomes (Chapter 8).

Secondary Constrictions

A chromosome may also contain a *secondary constriction*, which appears as an unstained gap in the chromosome. Usually a secondary constriction (Fig. 2.2) contains a *nucleolar organizer* (see Chapter 6), and may be situated anywhere along the chromosome. However, these secondary constrictions are most often near a chromosome end, separating a small segment, a *satellite*, from the main body of the chromosome. In such cases, the secondary constriction is called a *satellite stalk*.

Characterization of Metaphase Chromosomes

In the early literature, a metaphase chromosome is characterized morphologically both by its total length and by the position of the centromere, which determines the relative lengths of its arms. A secondary constriction also helps in the identification of a particular chromosome. Nowadays, chromosomes are usually identified by means of banding techniques (Chapters 6 and 7).

A chromosome in which the centromere is near the middle is called *metacentric*. A chromosome in which the centromere is at the very end is *telocentric*. Chromosomes intermediate between these two are *submetacentric* and *subtelocentric*. Chromosomes with markedly unequal arms are also called *acrocentric*. Truly telocentric chromosomes are almost nonexistent in natural populations, but they have been found in some unusual individuals of various species, including humans.

In human chromosomes, the short arm is designated p (petite) and the long arm q (the next letter in the alphabet). Chromosomes are usually characterized by one of two parameters. The *arm ratio* (q/p) is the length of the long arm divided by that of the short arm. The *centromere index* expresses the length of the short arm as a percentage of the total chromo-

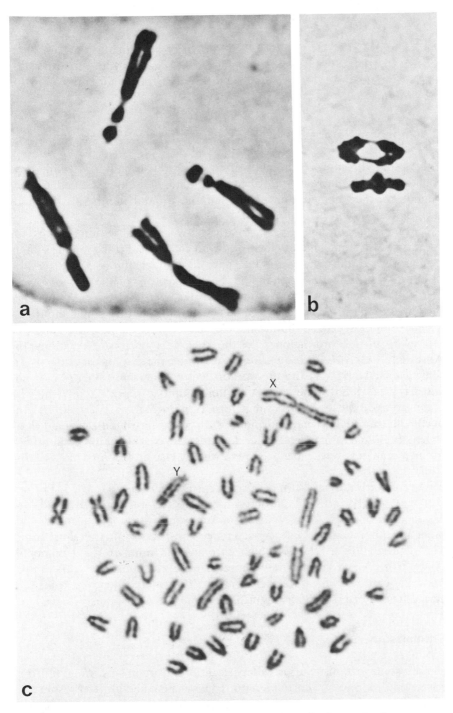

Figure 2.2. (a) Metaphase of *Haplopappus* with two subtelocentric chromosomes (secondary constrictions in the short arms) and two submetacentric chromosomes; (b) two bivalents in I meiotic metaphase of *Haplopappus* (a and b, courtesy of RC Jackson); (c) metaphase of male reindeer (*2n* = 76) showing X and Y chromosomes.

some length $[(p/p + q) \times 100]$. The length of a particular chromosome relative to others in the same metaphase cell, together with the arm ratio or centromere index, is sometimes sufficient to permit identification of the chromosome.

Chromosome Number

The diploid chromosome number of an organism, usually determined by counting the chromosomes in dividing somatic cells, is indicated by the symbol *2n*. The gametes have one-half the diploid number (a haploid set), indicated by *n*.

Chromosome numbers vary greatly between and within groups of organisms. Chromosome numbers show no clear trend of becoming either higher or lower during evolution. A haploid number of $n = 2$ is extremely rare, the best known example being the compositous plant, *Haplopappus* (Fig. 2.2), which grows in the southwestern United States. In mammals, the lowest haploid number, $n = 3$, has been found in the female muntjac, a small Indian deer (the diploid female has 6 chromosomes; the male 7). However, the record belongs to the members of a single colony of Australian ants (*Myrmecia pilosula*), in which the haploid number is 1. The males have $n \, (= 1)$ and the workers $2n \, (= 2)$ chromosomes (Crosland and Crozier, 1986). The largest haploid number reported in a higher organism is about $n = 630$, in a fern (*Ophioglossum reticulatum*). In mammals, the highest haploid number, $n = 46$, has been observed in a rodent (*Anotomys leander*). The chromosome complements established for mammalian species have been reviewed by Hsu and Benirschke (1967– 1977).

The haploid numbers of most organisms are between 6 and 25. In Fig. 2.2, two widely different chromosome constitutions are illustrated. In *Haplopappus* ($2n = 4$) one pair of chromosomes is submetacentric; the other is subtelocentric, with a secondary constriction in the short arm. The reindeer has a relatively high chromosome number for a mammal ($2n = 76$). Apart from a few subtelocentric chromosome pairs, most reindeer chromosomes are acrocentric. The metacentric X and the acrocentric Y are clearly distinguishable from the autosomes.

Chromosome Size

Chromosome size also varies widely in different organisms, ranging from a fraction of a micron (μm) in length, which is near the limit of resolution of the light microscope, to more than $30 \, \mu$m. Very small chromosomes are found in the fungi and green algae, whereas the largest ones have been observed in some amphibians and liliaceous plants. Most grasshoppers also have large chromosomes.

Although the chromosome complements of closely related organisms tend to be similar, there are striking exceptions to this rule. One of the classic examples of a great size difference in the chromosomes of two related species with the same diploid number (*2n* = 12), is provided by the leguminous plants *Lotus tenuis*, in which the mean length of the chromosomes is 1.8 μm, and *Vicia faba*, in which the corresponding value is 14.0 μm (Stebbins, 1971).

In general, higher organisms tend to have larger chromosomes than do lower organisms. However, exceptions to this rule are numerous among all organisms.

The chromosomes within the same chromosome complement usually fall into a fairly limited size range; in other words, they all tend to be either large or small. Yet in some animal groups, such as birds and lizards, the chromosome complements consist of a number of large chromosomes and a larger number of very small microchromosomes. In metaphase, the small chromosomes usually lie in the middle of the plate, with the large ones forming a circle around them.

Shape of Chromosomes

In addition to the number and size of the chromosomes, the chromosome complement of a species is characterized by the shape of the chromosomes. They may all be of one type or a combination of different types.

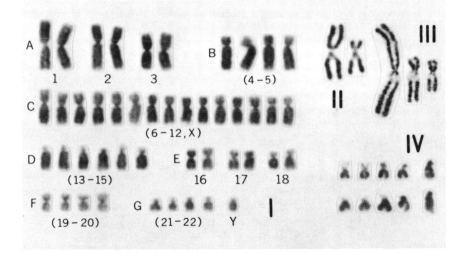

Figure 2.3. (I) Normal human male karyotype from a lymphocyte. (II) Chromosomes 1 and 9 showing fuzzy regions, which now are known to represent heterochromatin. (III) Chromosomes 1, 9, and 16 showing fuzzy regions. (IV) G and Y chromosomes from father and son (orcein staining).

For instance, in the mouse, all the chromosomes are acrocentric (Fig. 10.1); in man, the chromosomes range from metacentric to acrocentric (Figs. 2.1 and 2.3). Within a group, the more highly developed species tend to have more asymmetric chromosomes (the two arms are unequal), which have evolved from species with more metacentric complements (Stebbins, 1971).

DNA Content of Nuclei

The DNA content of a nucleus is determined by the number and size of the chromosomes of the organism. In the animal kingdom, the values range, per diploid nucleus, from 0.2 picograms (pg) in *Drosophila* to 168.0 pg in the very large chromosomes of the salamander *Amphiuma*, an almost 1000-fold difference. In plants, the differences are almost as great, with values ranging from 1.4 pg in the flax (*Linum usitatissimum*) to 196.7 pg in the liliaceous plant *Fritillaria* (Rees and Jones, 1977). In humans, the DNA content of a diploid nucleus is 6.4 pg (Rees and Jones, 1977). The values in other mammals deviate surprisingly little from this, especially when we consider the variations shown in their chromosome numbers and sizes.

Human Chromosome Complement

Humans have 44 autosomes (nonsex chromosomes) and two sex chromosomes (two X chromosomes in the female, and one X and one Y chromosome in the male). Human chromosomes range in size from less than 1 μm to somewhat larger than 5 μm; however, the range varies between cells. With respect to both chromosome number and size, man stands in the middle range of higher organisms.

The term *karyotype* signifies a display of the chromosomes of an organism in which they are lined up, starting with the largest, with the shorter arm of each chromosome pointing to the top of the page. An *idiogram* is a diagrammatic karyotype based on chromosome measurements in many cells. Figure 2.3 illustrates the karyotype of a normal human male. Morphological identification is based on the relative sizes of the chromosomes and their arm ratios. According to these criteria, chromosomes 1, 2, 3, 16, 17, 18, and the Y can be individually distinguished. Chromosome 9 (C′ in prebanding karyotypes) sometimes shows a fuzzy region next to the centromere on the long arm and can be identified on that basis. The rest of the chromosomes can be classified only as belonging to the groups B, C (which contains the X chromosome), D, F, and G. Chromosomes 1 and 3 are typically metacentric; chromosome 2 is on the borderline between metacentric and submetacentric; the B chromosomes represent the subtelocentric type. The D and G chromosomes are acrocentric and usually display satellites on the short arms. The sizes of both short arms and satellites vary in different persons. Sometimes satellites are so small that they are invisible in the light microscope.

Banded Human Karyotype

A G-banded human karyotype is presented in Fig. 2.4. Banding techniques and their uses will be discussed in detail in Chapters 4 and 7. The chromosomes are numbered according to Caspersson et al. (1971; see also Paris Conference: 1971 [1972]), who first published a banded human karyotype. The chromosomes are arranged numerically according to length, with one exception; chromosome 22 is actually longer than 21. Since the chromosome that in the trisomic state causes Down syndrome had long been called 21 in the literature, it was thought impractical and confusing to reverse the numbers. Thus, chromosome 21 is defined by the syndrome it causes. As seen in Fig. 2.4, each human chromosome can be distinguished by its banding pattern. Most of the individual arms can also be unambiguously identified.

In Table 2.1 the lengths of human chromosome arms are expressed as a percentage of the length of the haploid autosomal set or genome. The values are averages based on the compilation of a large number of measurements by different authors, with certain systematic errors corrected (K Patau, unpublished). The lengths of the short arms of the acrocentric chromosomes are not given, both because they vary between individuals and because any measurement less than 1 μm (which would be about 1 percent of the haploid karyotype) is only about twice the wavelength of visible light; therefore, the measurement of the much smaller short arms would be of dubious value.

Euploid Chromosome Changes

An interesting question is: how have the widely different karyotypes diverged from each other during evolution? Evolution is based on changes that occur in the genetic material. These changes are of two kinds: *neutral* changes, which are fixed by chance, and *selective* changes, which are fixed by natural selection. The genetic material may undergo qualitative gene changes, i.e., *gene mutations*. However, the evolution of karyotypes depends mainly on changes in the quantity or arrangement of the genes. These larger changes constitute the so-called *chromosome mutations*.

Changes in the number of whole sets of chromosomes, or *euploid* changes, usually lead to *polyploidy*. As a rule, *haploidy* is not a viable condition. Polyploidy can be inferred when the chromosome number of an organism is a multiple of the haploid chromosome number of a related species. A chromosome complement containing three haploid sets is

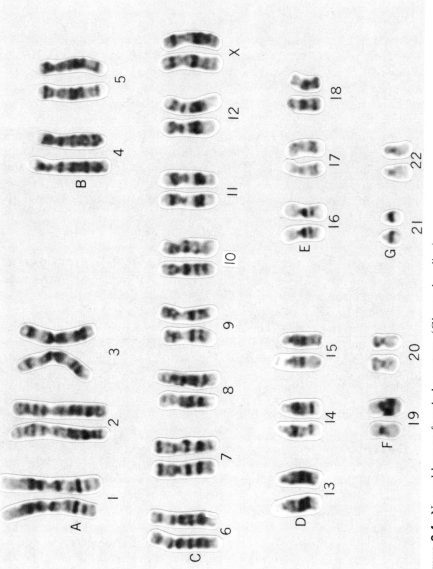

Figure 2.4. Normal human female karyotype (Giemsa-banding).

Table 2.1. Relative lengths of human chromosomes[a]

Chromosome		Average length (in % of autosomal genome) of:		Chromosome		Average length (in % of autosomal genome) of:	
Group	No.	Long arm	Short arm	Group	No.	Long arm	Short arm
A	1	4.68	4.57	D	13	3.29	—
	2	5.28	3.35		14	3.12	—
	3	3.80	3.32		15	2.89	—
B	4	4.85	1.84	E	16	1.93	1.34
	5	4.66	1.75		17	2.07	0.96
					18	2.04	0.76
C	6	3.87	2.36	F	19	1.32	1.11
	7	3.54	2.04		20	1.30	1.05
	8	3.45	1.63				
	9	3.23	1.72	G	21	1.26	—
	10	3.22	1.54		22	1.38	—
	11	2.90	1.88				
	12	3.38	1.32				
				Total autosomes		100.00	
				X		3.26	2.02
				Y		1.64	—

— Short arms not measurable.
[a] Revised by K Patau (unpublished).

called *triploid* (*3n*). Four sets constitute a *tetraploid* chromosome complement (*4n*). It is estimated that about one-half of higher plants have
chromosome numbers that are multiples of those of other related species.
In certain plant families, such as grasses (*Graminae*) or roses (*Rosaceae*),
three-fourths of the species are polyploid. For example, in the genus
Rubus of the rose family, the following multiples of the basic number 7
are found: 14, 21, 28, 35, 42, 49, 56, 63, and 84. In the compositous genus
Chrysanthemum (*n* = 9), the chromosome numbers range from 18 to 198
(Darlington and Wylie, 1955).

In plant evolution, polyploidy is often combined with hybridization
between different species. When the chromosome number of a hybrid is
duplicated, we may see, in one step, the emergence of a new species
combining the diploid complements of the parents. A well-known cultivated plant of this type is *Triticale*, a hybrid of wheat and rye, with the
combined "diploid" chromosome complements of both species (*2n* = 56).
However, one of the parents, the cultivated wheat, is a hexaploid with six
sets of 7 chromosomes (one of the basic numbers in the grasses). Rye, on
the other hand, is a diploid with *2n* = 14 chromosomes.

Polyploidy, which has been very important in plant evolution, seems to
have played almost no role in animal evolution. However, in fishes and
lizards there are indications, and in amphibians definite proof, of poly-

ploidy (Beçak et al., 1967). Polyploidy in animals usually upsets the sex determination mechanism, and this has generally been assumed to block the successful establishment of polyploidy. Indeed, most polyploid animal species are *asexual*; they produce offspring *without* meiosis or fertilization. As a rule, such offspring are uniform and genetically identical with the parent. Because asexual reproduction takes place without meiosis or fertilization, the results of the process naturally lack the variability created by meiotic crossing-over and segregation.

From an evolutionary point of view, asexual species have reached a dead end, no matter how successful they may be under specific prevailing conditions. Polyploid parthenogenetic forms are found in shrimp, earthworms, and some insect groups (Darlington, 1958). In plants, asexual reproduction through rhizomes, bulbs, runners, and other organs is common, especially in polyploid species. Apomictic asexual seed formation corresponds to parthenogenesis in animals. However, all organisms reproducing asexually can be said to have sold their future for a present advantage (Darlington, 1958).

Aneuploid Chromosome Changes

Chromosome mutations also include changes in the number of individual chromosomes, as opposed to the number of sets of chromosomes. These changes in the number of normal chromosomes, leading to unequal numbers of different chromosomes, are referred to as *aneuploidy*. The absence of one chromosome from the diploid complement is *monosomy*; the presence of an extra one is *trisomy*. A chromosome complement with two identical extra chromosomes is *tetrasomic*.

Structural Changes in Chromosomes

The third type of chromosome mutation occurs as a result of chromosome breakage and rejoining in such a way that the chromosomes are structurally reorganized. The details of chromosome rearrangements are discussed in Chapter 9. Such changes may sometimes result in an increase or decrease in the number of chromosome segments, as well as in changes in their arrangement. Usually, different mutation processes play a role in the evolution of a taxonomic group, although one of them may predominate, as polyploidy does in many plant taxa. In closely related strains of the ant *Myrmecia*, mentioned above, the diploid numbers 2, 3, and 4 have been found (Imai and Taylor, 1987). (Other numbers in this species are $2n = 9, 10, 15, 17-32$). One might expect that the $2n = 4$ chromosome number would be a tetraploid derivative of $2n = 2$. However, a detailed analysis has shown that the chromosome complement $2n = 2$ has developed from $2n = 4$, through several structural changes, including inversion, insertion, and fusion of chromosome ends.

Various changes in chromosome number and structure have created the multitude of karyotypes observed in plants and animals. However, the selective advantage bestowed on a given species by the type of its chromosome complement, which may contain few or numerous, large or small, symmetric or asymmetric chromosomes, is a much discussed, but still unresolved question (Stebbins, 1971).

References

Beçak ML, Beçak W, Rabello MN (1967) Further studies on polyploid amphibians (*Ceratophrydidae*). I. Mitotic and meiotic aspects. Chromosoma 22:192–201

Caspersson T, Lomakka G, Zech L (1971) 24 fluorescence patterns of human metaphase chromosomes—distinguishing characters and variability. Hereditas 67:89–102

Crosland MWJ, Crozier RH (1986) *Myrmecia pilosula*, an ant with only one pair of chromosomes. Science 231:1278

Darlington CD (1958) The evolution of genetic systems. Basic Books, New York

Darlington CD, Wylie AP (1955) Chromosome atlas of flowering plants. Hafner, New York

Hsu TC, Benirschke K (1967–1977) An atlas of mammalian chromosomes, Vol 1–10. Springer, Heidelberg

Imai HT, Taylor RW (1989) Chromosomal polymorphisms involving telomeric fusion, centromeric inactivation and centromere shift in the ant *Myrmecia* (*pilosula*) $n = 1$. Chromosoma 98:456–460

Paris Conference:1971 (1972) Standardization in human cytogenetics. Birth defects: original article series, VIII: 7. New York: The National Foundation

Rees H, Jones RN (1977) Chromosome genetics. University Park Press, Baltimore

Ris H, Korenberg JR (1979) Chromosome structure and levels of chromosome organization. In: Goldstein L, Prescott DM (eds) Cell biology, Vol 2. Academic, New York, pp 268–361

Stebbins GL (1971) Chromosomal evolution in higher plants. Addison-Wesley, Menlo Park, California

Therman E (1972) Chromosome breakage by 1-methyl-2-benzylhydrazine in mouse cancer cells. Cancer Res 32: 1133–1136

3
Mitotic Cycle and Chromosome Reproduction

Significance of Mitosis

In mitosis the genetic material of a cell is divided equally and exactly between two daughter cells. Each chromosome replicates in interphase, then divides into two daughter chromosomes, which segregate in anaphase and, with the other chromosomes of the set, form two daughter nuclei. In other words, the cells undergo a regular alternation of chromosome replication and segregation. The main features of mitosis are strikingly universal and may be observed throughout eukaryotes, from unicellular organisms to man. Figure 3.1 illustrates mitosis in untreated human lymphocytes. (Nowadays, only a few cytogeneticists have even seen human chromosomes that have not been treated with colchicine and hypotonic solution.) For comparison, Fig. 17.1 shows the last premeiotic mitosis in untreated pollen mother cells of the liliaceous plant, *Eremurus* ($2n = 14$).

Interphase

The mitotic cycle consists of the mitotic stages—prophase through telophase—and the interphase. In interphase the chromosomes are despiralized threads that form so-called domains. The structure of interphase and differentiated nuclei is reviewed in Chapter 14. In the light microscope, interphase nuclei appear more or less evenly stained, with certain condensed chromosome segments, the so-called chromocenters, standing out (Chapter 6). The shapes and sizes of chromocenters vary greatly, not only among species but also in different tissues of the same organism (Fig. 6.2c–e). One or more nucleoli are usually visible in an interphase nucleus

(Fig. 6.2a). Since the nucleoli tend to fuse, the largest number observed reflects the true number of active nucleolar organizers (see Chapter 6) in the organism.

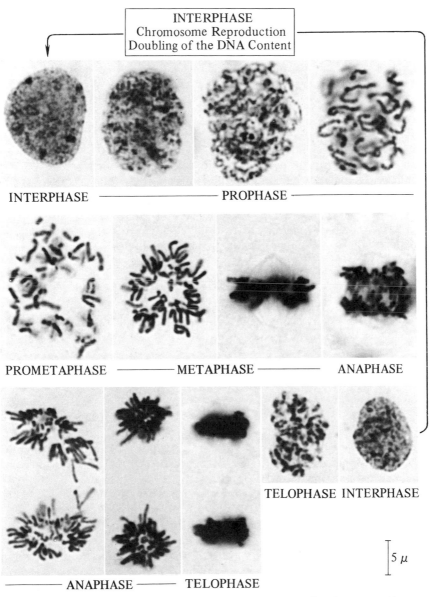

Figure 3.1. Mitotic cycle in cultured human lymphocytes (Feulgen squash).

Prophase

In prophase, the chromosomes first become visible as long thin threads that gradually shorten and thicken as the diameter of the chromosome coil increases (Figs. 3.1 and 17.1). At the same time that the threads are shortening, the nucleoli vanish.

Prometaphase

Prophase is followed by a short prometaphase. During this period, the nuclear membrane dissolves and the chromosomes, which are nearing their maximum condensation, collect on a metaphase plate.

Metaphase

Outside the nucleus, an organelle, called the *centriole* or *centrosome*, has divided, and the mitotic spindle develops between the centrioles. The centromeres of the chromosomes collect halfway between the poles (centrioles) to form a metaphase plate (Fig. 3.1). Long chromosome arms may stick out of the plate. Even though plants do not possess defined centrioles, the spindle arises between two polar areas.

Anaphase

The centromeres divide and the spindle fibers drag the sister chromosomes to opposite poles (Figs. 3.1 and 17.1).

Telophase

Nuclear membranes are formed around the two chromosome groups. Gradually the chromosome coils loosen; the individual chromosomes become indistinguishable (Figs. 3.1 and 17.1); and the nucleoli reappear. Telophase is usually followed by cytoplasmic division, after which the nuclei revert once more to interphase.

Nondisjunction and Loss of Chromosomes

For various reasons, the orderly segregation of daughter chromosomes in anaphase may sometimes fail. Like other biological processes, it is more likely to go wrong in older persons. The inclusion of *both* daughter chromosomes in the *same* nucleus, whatever the mechanism or reason, is called *nondisjunction*. As a result, one daughter cell gains an extra chromosome, becoming trisomic, whereas the other loses a chromosome and ends up being monosomic.

One daughter chromosome—or sometimes both—may lag behind in its division and not reach either pole. Such laggard chromosomes form micronuclei in interphase. These nuclei usually do not divide, and consequently the chromosomes included in them are lost from the complements of both daughter cells.

If the trisomic and monosomic cells arising in somatic tissues through nondisjunction or chromosome loss are viable, the result is *mosaicism*—the presence in one individual of "patches" of cells with differing genotypes. Mosaicism may occur in a tissue or, if nondisjunction takes place very early in development, the entire organism may be mosaic. Actually, we are all mosaics to some degree.

Mitotic Cycle

The duration of the mitotic cycle varies greatly in different organisms and in different tissues. A cleavage division of a toad egg takes 15 minutes, whereas the same process in mouse ear epidermis lasts more than 40 hours (White, 1973). The general rule seems to be that the larger the amount of nuclear DNA, the longer the duration of the mitotic cycle. Thus, organisms that are polyploid or have an otherwise high nuclear DNA content display the longest cycles. The relative lengths of the individual phases also vary, although less than the variability in the duration of the whole cycle.

Interphase, which usually lasts much longer than mitosis, is itself divided into stages. Of the interphasic stages, Gap 1 (G_1), which lies between the end of telophase and the beginning of the Synthesis (S) periods, is the longest; DNA synthesis (chromosome replication) takes place during the S period. This stage is succeeded by Gap 2 (G_2), which lasts until prophase. A chromosome is made up of one chromatid during G_1 and two in the G_2 phase. The molecular biology of the mitotic cycle has been reviewed in *Science* (November 3, 1989).

As already mentioned, the number of haploid chromosome sets in a cell is indicated by the symbols *n*, *2n*, *3n*, and so on. The symbol for the amount of DNA, as opposed to the number of chromosome sets, is C. The haploid nucleus of a gamete has the DNA content of 1C. A diploid nucleus from anaphase through G_1 has a 2C amount of DNA. This is doubled during the S period, so that from G_2 to metaphase the DNA content of the cell is 4C. It is more practical to talk about 2C and 4C nuclei than about diploid and tetraploid cells, since 4C represents both the G_2 phase of a diploid nucleus and the G_1 stage of a tetraploid one (Patau and Das, 1961).

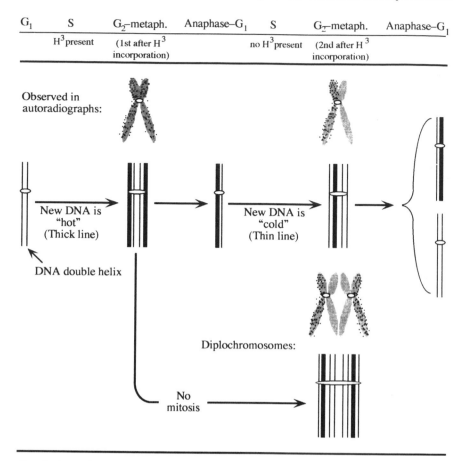

Conclusions: 1. at least one double helix per chromatid; replication is semiconservative
2. strand continuity is not interrupted at the centromere
3. in diplochromosomes, the "oldest" strands are in the inner pair of chromatids

Figure 3.2. Semiconservative replication of eukaryotic chromosomes demonstrated with tritiated thymidine and autoradiography.

Chromosome Replication

The mechanisms of chromosome reproduction can be studied by autoradiography, in which radioactivity in microscope preparations can be detected by spreading photographic emulsion over the microscope slide. Radiographic decay of isotopes in the specimen causes silver grains to appear in the emulsion after photographic development. (See Chapter 5 for more discussion of autoradiography.) In studies of chromosome replication, cells are grown for one S period in medium containing a

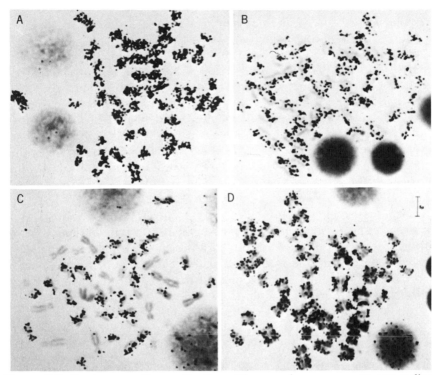

Figure 3.3. Semiconservative replication of human chromosomes corresponding to Fig. 3.2 (see text).

radioactive constituent of DNA, usually [³H]thymidine, and are then transferred back to normal nonradioactive medium. The results of such an experiment can be seen in Figs. 3.2 and 3 (Taylor, 1963). Before the S period, the chromosome consists of one double helix of DNA. During the S period, in radioactive medium, each strand acts as a template for a new radioactive strand. In autoradiographs of the subsequent metaphase, each chromatid, which now has one "cold" and one "hot" DNA strand, is covered with silver grains. In the next S period, in nonradioactive medium, both hot and cold strands act as templates for new cold strands. Then, in metaphase autoradiographs, one chromatid of each chromosome displays silver grains, the other does not. In *diplochromosomes*, which have undergone the same two syntheses without an intervening mitosis and chromatid segregation, the outer chromatids are radioactive (Fig. 3.2). This shows that the "oldest" DNA strands in the diplochromosome are in the inner pair of chromatids. In the third diploid metaphase (after the last anaphase-G₁ shown in Fig. 3.2) following [³H]thymidine treatment, the hot and the cold chromatids are distributed at random among the chromosomes.

This type of chromosome reproduction, in which each chromatid contains one old strand of DNA and one new, is called *semiconservative*.

In Fig. 3.3, semiconservative replication of human chromosomes corresponding to Fig. 3.2 is shown. Figure 3.3A illustrates a metaphase after one S period in "hot" medium. In Fig. 3.3B, the chromosomes have been, for one S period, in "hot" medium, and for another in "cold" medium. Figure 3.3.C again illustrates a metaphase after one cycle in "hot" and two cycles in "cold" medium, and finally, Fig. 3.3D shows diplochromosomes in which the outer chromatids are labeled.

Another characteristic feature in the replication of human and other eukaryotic chromosomes is that the DNA synthesis starts at several points along the chromosome. This can be demonstrated by giving the cells a short pulse of [^{3}H]thymidine, after which they are grown in cold medium. In metaphase, the chromosome shows labeling over separate short stretches. The various chromosome segments start their replication at different times during the S period, with the heterochromatic segments of chromosomes being the last to replicate. However, the replication of chromosome segments can be studied more accurately by the more recent 5-bromodeoxyuridine techniques (Latt, 1979; see also Chapter 12).

References

Latt SA (1979) Patterns of late replication in human X chromosomes. In: Vallet HL, Porter IH (eds) Genetic mechanisms of sexual development. Academic, New York, pp 305–329

Patau K, Das NK (1961) The relation of DNA synthesis and mitosis in tobacco pith tissue cultured in vitro. Chromosoma 11:553–572

Science (1989) Frontiers in biology: The cell cycle (3 November 1989 issue). Science 246:537–724

Taylor JH (1963) The replication and organization of DNA in chromosomes. In: Taylor JH (ed) Molecular genetics I. Academic, New York, pp 65–111

White MJD (1973) Animal cytology and evolution, 3rd edn. University Press, Cambridge, England

4
Methods in Human Cytogenetics

In this chapter various human chromosome techniques are reviewed. For the detailed descriptions the reader is referred to Darlington and La Cour (1975), to *Human Chromosome Methodology* (Yunis, 1965, 1974), to Dutrillaux and Lejeune (1975), to Yunis (1981b), and to Verma and Babu (1989). The book by Verma and Babu (1989) surveys the enormous increase in the number and variety of cytogenetic techniques in recent years, of which only the most important can be discussed here.

Direct Methods

In the 1920s and earlier, work on human chromosomes was done mostly on testicular tissue, by use of paraffin-sectioned preparations stained with hematoxylin. One can only admire the fact that with these relatively primitive techniques the human cytologists came as close to the right chromosome number as 48.

In the late 1940s the Feulgen squash technique came into general use (Darlington and La Cour, 1975). It was an excellent method for studying unusual mitoses; for instance, mitotic aberrations in cancer cells. The chromosome constitution can also be analyzed in Feulgen squash preparations if the number of chromosomes is not too large and the metaphase plate not too crowded. The root tips and pollen mother cells of many plants, as well as the testicular tissue of animals, have been studied successfully by this method.

The squash technique was greatly improved by the added step of treating the cells with drugs before fixation. These drugs, particularly colchicine, shorten the chromosomes, destroy the mitotic spindle, and as a result spread the chromosomes around the cell. Colchicine also prevents cells from entering anaphase; this leads to an accumulation of metaphases, a distinct advantage in cytological work. The most common fixative for Feulgen preparations, as well as for cells in tissue culture, is acetic acid–ethanol.

Tissue Culture Techniques

The real breakthrough in human cytogenetics came when tissue culture was combined with colchicine and hypotonic solution treatments before fixation. Thus, Tjio and Levan (1956) were able to report that in cultured embryonic lung cells the human chromosome number was 46. It should be pointed out that, to the chagrin of everyone who had already been working on human chromosomes, this technical "breakthrough" should have been obvious before 1956. Colchicine had been used to spread plant chromosomes and to produce polyploidy in plant breeding for two decades, and it had been known since the last century that hypotonic solutions swell animal cells.

Until 1960, when Moorhead et al. launched the short-term lymphocyte culture technique, human chromosomes were studied mainly in cultured fibroblasts and in bone marrow cells. The essential agent in lymphocyte cultures is a natural product of plants that stimulates cell divisions. These are known as *phytohemagglutinins*, the most widely used being an extract of kidney beans. Leukemic lymphocytes divide in vitro without "phyto", as it is usually called, whereas normal lymphocytes do not. Short-term lymphocyte cultures provide an important tool in human chromosome studies and have also found wide use in cytogenetic studies of diverse animals. It takes only 48–72 h to obtain chromosome preparations with this easy method, whereas weeks of growth are needed before chromosomes can be studied in fibroblast cultures.

Drying of the cells on the microscope slide was a further improvement, in that the flattened chromosomes are more easily stained and photographed. The most common chromosome stains have been orcein and Giemsa, but azure A and Feulgen, as well as a few others, have also been used.

At present, cultured lymphocytes and fibroblasts are the main sources of cells for human chromosome studies. However, both types of cultured cells have the disadvantage that they do not reveal what happens in vivo; this can be seen in mitoses from direct bone marrow biopsies, which, however, usually do not yield chromosome preparations as beautiful as those from cultured cells.

Prenatal Studies

Amniocentesis, an important tool in genetic counseling, involves taking a sample of amniotic fluid, usually during the second trimester of pregnancy.

This fluid contains floating cells from the fetus. The sex of the fetus can be determined directly from such cells (which is important when counseling is done for diseases caused by X-linked genes), or tissue culture for chromosome studies can be initiated from these cells. Certain metabolic diseases can also be determined by biochemical tests of fetal cells. If the analysis reveals a chromosome or biochemical anomaly that would lead to serious phenotypic consequences, an abortion can be performed. The various issues in the prenatal diagnosis of genetic diseases have been reviewed by Epstein et al. (1983).

A recent technique, still under development, that may finally replace amniocentesis is based on biopsies of trophoblastic villi. A catheter guided by ultrasound is inserted through the vagina into the uterus, and a villus sample is aspirated. Chromosomes (or enzymes) can be studied directly from such a biopsy or from a tissue culture grown from it. A great advantage of this method, compared with amniocentesis, is that it can be done during the first trimester and is less hazardous (Simoni et al., 1983; Gustavii, 1983); moreover, abortions induced early in a pregnancy are less risky and more acceptable than those done later.

Meiotic Studies

Meiosis has been studied far more extensively in the human male than in the female. Initially male meiosis was analyzed in biopsies prepared by the Feulgen squash technique. A more recent method has been to extract the meiocytes from testicular tubules and to swell them in hypotonic solution, after which they are fixed and dried on a slide in the same way as lymphocytes.

With these techniques, elegant studies on the frequency and location of chiasmata (chromatid exchange points) in the human male (Fig. 18.8) have been made by Hultén and her colleagues (Hultén, 1974; Hultén et al., 1978, 1982).

Synaptonemal complexes (Chapter 18) were originally studied solely by means of electron microscopy. However, microspreading of the chromosomes (Solari, 1980), combined with silver staining (Pathak and Hsu, 1979), has made their analysis possible also in the light microscope (Fig. 18.4).

Female mammalian meiosis has been analyzed especially in the mouse. Similar attempts have been made in the human (Edwards, 1970; Jagiello et al., 1976), but so far the results have not been as satisfactory as those obtained in the mouse. Meiotic chromosome preparations of the mouse and other animals can be improved by an injection of colchicine into the animal a few hours before it is sacrificed. Meiotic prophase stages have been studied successfully in human embryonic oocytes (Therman and Sarto, 1977). A special technique for the dictyotene (diplotene, see Chapter 18) stage in humans has been developed by Stahl et al. (1976).

The results of meiosis in the human male can now be analyzed by fertilizing hamster eggs, which have been freed from the zona pellucida, with human sperm and studying the haploid chromosome set in the male pronucleus (Rudak et al., 1978). This technique permits the determination of the type and frequency of chromosome aberrations in the sperm (see, for example, Martin et al., 1987; Brandriff et al., 1988). Furthermore, in carriers with abnormal chromosome constitutions, such as balanced translocations, segregation can be directly analyzed with this technique (Martin, 1989).

Sex Chromatin Techniques

Since all the human cell types that are generally cultured are of mesodermal origin, practically the only information on the ectoderm comes from studies on sex chromatin. This includes the X chromatin (Barr body), which consists of the inactive X, and the Y chromatin body, which represents the distal end of Yq. These are most often determined in cell smears made from the buccal mucosa. Barr bodies are usually stained with orcein, acid fuchsin, or Feulgen (Fig. 21.1), but the fluorochrome acridine orange also gives excellent results (Fig. 2 in Dutrillaux, 1977). Because the Y body is too small to be distinct in the light microscope, it is usually stained with quinacrine and studied with fluorescence microscopy (Fig. 20.1c) The fluorescent Y body is also visible in Y-carrying sperm. In addition to buccal smears, X chromatin has been analyzed in cultured fibroblasts, hair-root cells, and cells of the vaginal epithelium.

Banding Techniques

A decisive step forward in human cytogenetics was the invention of chromosome banding techniques that reveal reproducible patterns of transverse bands of different lengths. With these methods, all the chromosomes of man and many other organisms, and even the breakpoints in most structural rearrangements, can be identified. The banding techniques and what they reveal about chromosome structure have been reviewed in many articles, for example, Arrighi (1974), Latt (1976), Evans (1977), Sanchez and Yunis (1977), Dutrillaux (1977), Ris and Korenberg (1979), Bickmore and Sumner (1989), and Sumner (1990).

When human chromosomes are stained with quinacrine HCl (Atebrine) or quinacrine mustard and studied with a fluorescence microscope, they show bands of differing brightness (Caspersson et al., 1970). These are called Q-bands (quinacrine or QFQ bands) (Fig. 24.3). Slides stained with quinacrine are not permanent, and after a couple of photomicrographic exposures the fluorescence fades too much to be usable.

The other type of banding technique involves various pretreatments and staining with Giemsa or certain fluorochromes; Giemsa bands (G-bands or GTG bands) are obtained when the chromosomes are pretreated with a salt solution at 60°C or with proteolytic enzymes, usually trypsin (Drets and Shaw, 1971). Giemsa banding yields essentially the same information as Q-banding, only the brightly fluorescent Q-bands are now darkly stained, whereas the Q-dark regions are light (Fig. 2.4). Each method has its advantages. With Q-banding the chromosomes are stained without any pretreatment, and their morphology is retained. This makes measurements of bands more accurate. Also, the relative brightness of the bands can be estimated (Kuhn, 1976). However, the chromosomes can be analyzed only from photographs.

The G-banded slides, on the other hand, are permanent and are therefore more suitable for routine work. By means of these two techniques, some 300 bands have been described in the human chromosomes (Figs. 4.1 and 2) (Paris Conference:1971 [1972]). However, in most metaphase plates only a fraction of this number of bands can actually be seen.

Prophase chromosomes, which are much longer than metaphase chromosomes, can also be banded. By studying such chromosomes, the number of visible bands has been increased to 1000–2000 (see below).

Reverse banding (R-banding) involves pretreatment with hot (80–90°C) alkali and subsequent staining with Giemsa (RHG bands) or with a fluorochrome such as acridine orange (RFA bands). As the name indicates, the RHG banding pattern is the reverse of G-banding; in other words, the bands that are dark with R-banding are light with G-banding and vice versa (Fig. 6.1f). Similarly, fluorescent R-banding (RFA) is the reverse of Q-banding. Although this banding reveals nothing new compared with Q-banding and G-banding, it complements them, especially when chromosome ends are studied, as in distal deletions and translocations. A modification of R-banding, called T-banding, brings out mainly the tips of chromosomes.

Another technique, which also utilizes the Giemsa stain, has given additional information about chromosome structure. Centric banding (C-banding), for which chromosomes are usually first treated in acid and then in alkali (barium hydroxide, for example) prior to Giemsa staining, brings out the heterochromatic regions around the centromere (Fig. 6.1f and g) and at the distal end of the Y chromosome (Arrighi and Hsu, 1971). With a modification of the C-banding technique (G-11), it is possible to stain the centric heterochromatin in human chromosome 9 specifically.

The banding technique used most successfully in plants corresponds to C-banding, and the resulting darkly stained bands probably represent constitutive heterochromatin (Chapter 6).

New banding techniques, often combining two or more stains, appear frequently. A variety of fluorochromes, including Hoechst 33258, a number of antibiotics, and so-called DAPI and DIPI stains, have found use in the detailed analysis of chromosome bands (Schweizer, 1981). A recent

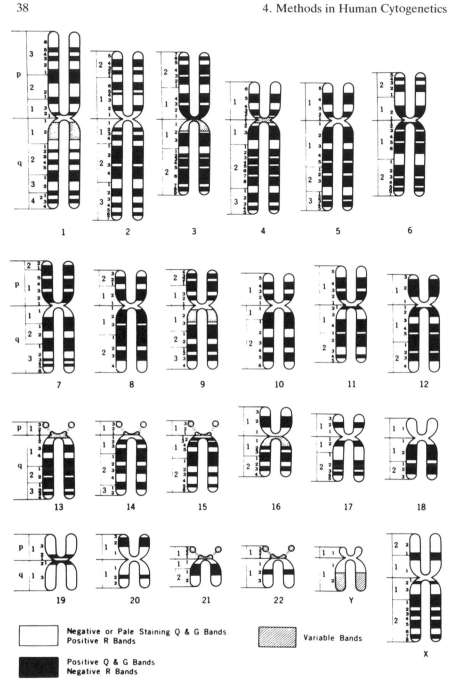

Figure 4.1. Diagram of a banded human karyotype (Paris Conference:1971 [1972]).

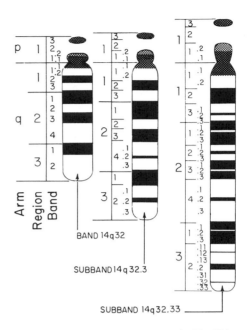

Figure 4.2. Schematic representation of chromosome #14 at the 320- (left), 500-(center), and 900-band (right) stages, illustrating the use of the Paris nomenclature to designate with decimals the sub-bands seen in the 500-band stage, and with decimals and digits the sub-bands observed in the 900-band stage (Yunis, 1980).

list of fluorochromes and their uses is found in Verma and Babu (1989).

With a special Giemsa method it is possible to differentially stain nucleolar organizers, and a silver (NOR) staining technique reveals the organizers that are active (Fig. 6.1c and e) (Bloom and Goodpasture, 1976).

So-called Cd banding stains active centromeres, but not inactive ones (Eiberg, 1974). Special centromere techniques are based on the observation that the sera of scleroderma (CREST syndrome) patients contain an autoantibody to centromeric regions (Moroi et al., 1980; Brenner et al., 1981). The tagged centromeres are made visible with various immuno-fluorescent techniques. This method also distinguishes between active and inactive centromeres (Earnshaw and Migeon, 1985).

Prophase Banding

One of the most important developments in cytogenetic techniques is the prophase or high-resolution banding (Yunis, 1976). Whereas the usual Q-, G-, or R-banding techniques reveal some 300 bands, prometaphase or prophase chromosomes show from 500 to 2000 bands (Yunis et al., 1979; Yunis, 1981a). For high-resolution banding, dividing cells are blocked at the S stage with amethopterin (methotrexate). When the block is released with thymidine-rich medium, a large proportion of the cells are synchronous and can be fixed at the required stage. Prophase chromosomes show natural banding with Giemsa or Wright's stain, or the banding can be enhanced with G-banding techniques.

The longer the chromosomes are, the more bands they show. However, with more bands, more overlap; and the analysis becomes more tedious. The most important uses of prophase banding have been the exact determination of breakpoints in cases in which the general area of the breaks is already known, and the mapping of genes with molecular methods (Chapter 5).

Replication Studies

Chromosomes and chromosome segments replicate at different times during the S period. This phenomenon has been extensively studied both for itself and for its implications for chromosome structure and function. Initially, the main technique for such studies involved feeding the cells with a radioactive chromosome constituent and analyzing the results with autoradiography (Chapter 5). Recent methods, however, are based on the important discovery that chromosomes and chromatids that have incorporated BrdU, instead of thymidine, have a different structure and consequently different staining properties from those containing thymidine. Substitution with BrdU has also been successful in demonstrating the late-labeling X chromosome and other individual chromosomes and segments that replicate in the latter part of the S period (Latt, 1973, 1974). This can be done, for instance, by growing lymphocytes for 40–44 h in a medium containing BrdU and, thereafter, feeding them thymidine for 6–7 h. When stained with a suitable fluorochrome, the late-replicating X chromosome fluoresces more brightly than the other chromosomes or is darker than the others when Giemsa staining is used. An example of this technique is seen in Fig. 21.3, in which the late-replicating X chromosomes stand out.

This technique can also be done in reverse, in that the cells are first grown in thymidine-containing medium and then with BrdU. The late-replicating chromosomes, including the inactive X chromosome, are now darkly fluorescent with quinacrine and faintly stained with Giemsa.

Chromosome banding, comparable to that achieved with other banding techniques, can also be induced with the BrdU method (Zakharov and Egolina, 1976). An important application is the analysis of the replication order of the bands (Camargo and Cervenka, 1982), which has shown that the Q-dark bands replicate during the first half of the S period and the Q-bright bands during the latter half. Moreover, the individual bands show

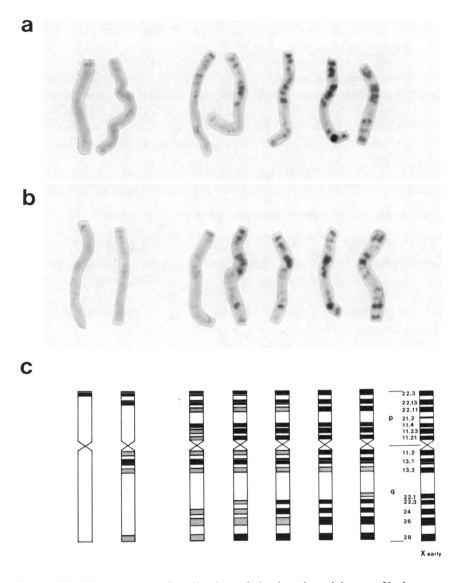

Figure 4.3. Time courses of replication of the inactivated human X chromosomes, R-bands obtained by BrdU treatment and Giemsa staining (RBG), (a) from female cells (46,XX) and (b) from cells of a Klinefelter male (47,XXY). (c) A diagramatic representation of the time course. The replication bands that are clearly visible are shown as *solid bars*; those sites that have started to develop and are only faintly visible are shown as *shaded bars*. The RBG replication pattern for the early (active) X according to ISCN (1981) is given at the right for comparison. Note that there are several segments escaping inactivation, especially the pseudoautosomal segment Xp22.3 and the postulated inactivation center Xq13.l (Schempp and Meer, 1983).

a constant replication order. Schempp and Meer (1983) have utilized the above techniques to study the order of replication for the human inactive X chromosome (Fig. 4.3).

Another application of this technique involves the study of cells grown under conditions that cause one chromatid to contain BrdU, whereas the other contains thymidine. Sister chromatid exchanges, the existence of which was already revealed by autoradiography, can be studied with much greater accuracy with this technique (Latt, 1973). For the analysis of sister chromatid exchanges, the fluorochromes—Hoechst 33258, acridine orange, and coriphosphine O—as well as the Giemsa stain after heat treatment have been used (Korenberg and Freedlender, 1974).

Nomenclature of Human Chromosomes

As a continuation of previous agreements on the nomenclature of human chromosomes, at the Paris Conference:1971 (1972) a system was proposed for identifying human chromosome bands and indicating various chromosome abnormalities. Figure 4.1 shows a diagram of a banded human karyotype according to this system. Telomeres, centromeres, and a number of prominent bands are used as "landmarks." A section of a chromosome between two landmarks is called a region, and these regions are numbered 1, 2, 3, and so on, in both directions, starting from the centromere. The bands within the regions are numbered according to the same rule. Thus, the first band in the second region of the short arm of chromosome 1 is 1p21 (ISCN, 1978).

A corresponding system for prophase bands has been presented by Yunis (1980) and is illustrated in Fig. 4.2 for chromosome 14 (see also ISCN, 1981). For instance, 14q32 (Fig. 4.2 left) indicates chromosome 14, long arm region 3, band 2. For a sub-band, a decimal point is placed after this, followed by the number of the sub-band (they are numbered sequentially from the centromere). The last sub-band in chromosome 14 (Fig. 4.2 middle) is thus 14q32.3. When the sub-band is further subdivided (Fig. 4.2 right), an additional digit is added, the last sub-sub-band thus being 14q32.33.

For the designation of chromosome abnormalities, two systems—one short and one detailed—were put forward. For the actual use of both systems the reader is referred to the Paris Conference:1971 (1972), and to Sanchez and Yunis (1977). In the following discussion only a few basic examples of the short system are given.

An extra or a missing chromosome is denoted with a plus or a minus sign, respectively, before the number of the chromosome. Thus, the chromosome constitution of a female with trisomy for chromosome 13 would be 47,XX,+13, and a male with monosomy for 21 would have the formula 45,XY,−21.

A plus or minus sign after the symbol of the chromosome arm means that a segment is added to or missing from it. For example, a female with the cri du chat syndrome, caused by a deletion in the short arm of chromosome 5, would have the chromosome formula 46,XX,5p−, and a male with an abnormally long 4q would be designated as 46,XY,4q+. The karyotype of a female with a Robertsonian translocation (centric fusion) between chromosomes 13 and 14 would be 45,XX,t(13q14q). The formula for a male carrier in whom chromosome arms 3p and 6q have exchanged segments, the breakpoints being 3p12 and 6q34, would be 46,XY,t(3;6)(p12;q34).

Unfortunately, the lengths of chromosome bands in Fig. 4.1 (Paris Conference:1971 [1972]) are not based on actual measurements, although a realistic banded diagram would be most useful. Furthermore, only a small fraction of metaphase plates reveal all the bands illustrated in this diagram. Therefore, it is often difficult, if not impossible, to determine the exact breakpoints in, say, a reciprocal translocation. Despite this, most authors feel obliged to specify the breakpoints, even when they are based only on guesses. Obviously, it is now possible to determine breakpoints more accurately, since the banding of prophase chromosomes has come into wide use (Sanchez and Yunis, 1977).

Quantitative Methods

One of the most important applications of quantitative methods in cytogenetics has been the measuring of the DNA content of nondividing nuclei; for instance, in differentiated or malignant cells or in sperm. In spectrocytophotometry, which has been used for over 30 years, the light absorption of nuclei or chromosomes is determined (Patau, 1952). This has been done most successfully on stained nuclei, and the stain most often used has been Feulgen (Mendelsohn, 1966). The light absorption of individual chromosomes or chromosome bands can be done in the same way (Drets and Seuanez, 1973; Drets, 1978). That automated computerized scanning methods will play an increasingly important role in the analysis of nuclear and chromosome structure is convincingly demonstrated by Drets and Monteverde (1987) and Drets et al. (1990).

Another recent method, flow cytometry, which for many purposes has replaced cytophotometry, will be discussed in Chapter 5.

References

Arrighi FE (1974) Mammalian chromosomes. In: Busch H (ed) The cell nucleus. Academic, New York, pp 1–32
Arrighi FE, Hsu TC (1971) Localization of heterochromatin in human chromosomes. Cytogenetics 10:81–86

Bickmore WA, Sumner AT (1989) Mammalian chromosome banding—an expression of genome organization. Trends Genet 5:144–148

Bloom SE, Goodpasture C (1976) An improved technique for selective silver staining of nucleolar organizer regions in human chromosomes. Hum Genet 34:199–206

Brandriff BF, Gordon LA, Moore D II, et al. (1988) An analysis of structural aberrations in human sperm chromosomes. Cytogenet Cell Genet 47:29–36

Brenner S, Pepper D, Berns MW, et al. (1981) Kinetochore structure, duplication, and distribution in mammalian cells: analysis by human autoantibodies from scleroderma patients. J Cell Biol 91:95–102

Camargo M, Cervenka J (1982) Patterns of DNA replication of human chromosomes. II. Replication map and replication model. Am J Hum Genet 34:757–780

Caspersson T, Zech L, Johansson C (1970) Differential binding of alkylating fluorochromes in human chromosomes. Exp Cell Res 60:315–319

Darlington CD, La Cour LF (1975) The handling of chromosomes, 6th edn. Wiley, New York

Drets ME (1978) BANDSCAN—a computer program for on-line linear scanning of human banded chromosomes. Computer Programs Biomed 8:283–294

Drets ME, Monteverde FJ (1987) Automated cytogenetics with modern computerized scanning microscope photometer systems. In: Obe G , Basler A (eds) Cytogenetics. Springer, Berlin, pp 48–64

Drets ME, Seuanez H (1973) Quantitation of heterogeneous human heterochromatin: microdensitometric analysis of C- and G-bands. In: Coutinho EM, Fuchs F (eds) Physiology and genetics of reproduction, Part A. Plenum, New York, pp 29–52

Drets ME, Shaw MW (1971) Specific banding patterns of human chromosomes. Proc Natl Acad Sci USA 68:2073–2077

Drets ME, Folle GA, Monteverde FJ (1990) Quantitative detection of chromosome structures by computerized microphotometric scanning. In: Obe G, Natarajan AT (eds) Chromosomal aberrations: Basic and applied aspects. Springer, Berlin, pp 1–12

Dutrillaux B (1977) New chromosome techniques. In: Yunis JJ (ed) Molecular structure of human chromosomes. Academic, New York, pp 233–265

Dutrillaux B, Lejeune J (1975) New techniques in the study of human chromosomes: methods and applications. In: Harris H, Hirschhorn K (eds) Advances in human genetics, Vol 5. Plenum, New York, pp 119–156

Earnshaw WC, Migeon BR (1985) Three related centromere proteins are absent from the inactive centromere of a stable isodicentric chromosome. Chromosoma 92:290–296

Edwards RG (1970) Observations on meiosis in normal males and females. In: Jacobs PA, Price WH, Law P (eds) Human population cytogenetics. Williams and Wilkins, Baltimore, pp 10–21

Eiberg H (1974) New selective Giemsa technique for human chromosomes, Cd staining. Nature 248:55

Epstein CJ, Cox DR, Schonberg SA, et al. (1983) Recent developments in the prenatal diagnosis of genetic diseases and birth defects. Annu Rev Genet 17:49–83

Evans HJ (1977) Some facts and fancies relating to chromosome structure in man. In: Harris H, Hirschhorn K (eds) Advances in human genetics, Vol 8. Plenum, New York, pp 347–438

Gustavii B (1983) First-trimester chromosomal analysis of chorionic villi obtained by direct vision technique. Lancet ii:507–508

Hultén M (1974) Chiasma distribution at diakinesis in the normal human male. Hereditas 76:55–78

Hultén M, Luciani JM, Kirton V, et al. (1978) The use and limitations of chiasma scoring with reference to human genetic mapping. Cytogenet Cell Genet 22:37–58

Hultén MA, Palmer RW, Laurie DA (1982) Chiasma derived genetic maps and recombination fractions: Chromosome 1. Ann Hum Genet 46:167–175

ISCN (1978) An international system for human cytogenetic nomenclature. Birth defects: original article series, XIV: 8. National Foundation, New York; also in Cytogenet Cell Genet 21:309–404

ISCN (1981) An international system for human cytogenetic nomenclature—high resolution banding. Birth defects: original article series, XVII: 5. National Foundation, New York; also in Cytogenet Cell Genet 31:1–84

Jagiello G, Ducayen M, Fang J-S, et al. (1976) Cytogenetic observations in mammalian oocytes. In: Pearson PL, Lewis KR (eds) Chromosomes today, Vol 5. Wiley, New York, pp 43–63

Korenberg JR, Freedlender EF (1974) Giemsa technique for the detection of sister chromatid exchanges. Chromosoma 48:355–360

Kuhn EM (1976) Localization by Q-banding of mitotic chiasmata in cases of Bloom's syndrome. Chromosoma 57:1–11

Latt SA (1973) Microfluorometric detection of deoxyribonucleic acid replication in human metaphase chromosomes. Proc Natl Acad Sci USA 70:3395–3399

Latt SA (1974) Microfluorometric analysis of DNA replication in human X chromosomes. Exp Cell Res 86:412–415

Latt SA (1976) Optical studies of metaphase chromosome organization. Annu Rev Biophys Bioeng 5:1–37

Martin RH (1989) Invited editorial: segregation analysis of translocations by the study of human sperm chromosome complements. Am J Hum Genet 44:461–463

Martin RH, Rademaker AW, Hildebrand K, et al. (1987) Variation in the frequency and type of sperm chromosomal abnormalities among normal men. Hum Genet 77:108–114

Mendelsohn ML (1966) Absorption cytophotometry. Comparative methodology for heterogeneous objects and the two-wavelength method. In: Wied GL (ed) Introduction to quantitative cytochemistry. Academic, New York, pp 201–237

Moorhead PS, Nowell PC, Mellman WJ, et al. (1960) Chromosome preparations of leukocytes cultured from human peripheral blood. Exp Cell Res 20:613–616

Moroi Y, Peebles C, Fritzler MJ, et al. (1980) Autoantibody to centromere (kinetochore) in scleroderma sera. Proc Natl Acad Sci USA 77:1627–1631

Paris Conference:1971 (1972) Standardization in human cytogenetics. Birth defects: original article series, VIII: 7. The National Foundation, New York

Patau K (1952) Absorption microphotometry of irregular shaped objects. Chromosoma 5:341–362

Pathak S, Hsu TC (1979) Silver-stained structures in mammalian meiotic prophase. Chromosoma 70:195–203

Ris H, Korenberg JR (1979) Chromosome structure and levels of chromosome organization. In: Goldstein L, Prescott DM (eds) Cell biology, Vol 2. Academic, New York, pp 268–361

Rudak E, Jacobs PA, Yanagimachi R (1978) Direct analysis of the chromosome constitution of human spermatozoa. Nature 274:911–913

Sanchez O, Yunis JJ (1977) New chromosome techniques and their medical applications. In: Yunis JJ (ed) New chromosomal syndromes. Academic, New York, pp 1–54

Schempp W, Meer B (1983) Cytologic evidence for three human X-chromosomal segments escaping inactivation. Hum Genet 63:171–174

Schweizer D (1981) Counterstain-enhanced chromosome banding. Hum Genet 57:1–14

Simoni G, Brambati B, Danesino C, et al. (1983) Efficient direct chromosome analyses and enzyme determinations from chorionic villi samples in the first trimester of pregnancy. Hum Genet 63:349–357

Solari AJ (1980) Synaptonemal complexes and associated structures in microspread human spermatocytes. Chromosoma 81:315–337

Stahl A, Luciani JM, Gagne R, et al. (1976) Heterochromatin, micronucleoli, and RNA containing body in the pachytene and diplotene stages of the human oocyte. In: Pearson PL, Lewis KR (eds) Chromosomes today, Vol 5. Wiley, New York, pp 65–73

Sumner AT (1990) Chromosome banding. Unwin Hyman, London

Therman E, Sarto GE (1977) Premeiotic and early meiotic stages in the pollen mother cells of *Eremurus* and in human embryonic oocytes. Hum Genet 35: 137–151

Tjio JH, Levan A (1956) The chromosome number in man. Hereditas 42:1–6

Verma RS, Babu A (eds) (1989) Human chromosomes: manual of basic techniques. Pergamon, New York

Yunis JJ (ed) (1965, 1974) Human chromosome methodology, 1st and 2nd edns. Academic, New York

Yunis JJ (1976) High resolution of human chromosomes. Science 191:1268–1270

Yunis JJ (1980) Nomenclature for high resolution human chromosomes. Cancer Genet Cytogenet 2:221–229

Yunis JJ (1981a) Mid-prophase human chromosomes. The attainment of 2000 bands. Hum Genet 56:293–298

Yunis JJ (1981b) New chromosome techniques in the study of human neoplasia. Hum Pathol 12:540–549

Yunis JJ, Ball DW, Sawyer JR (1979) G-banding patterns of high-resolution human chromosomes 6–22, X, and Y. Hum Genet 49:291–306

Zakharov AF, Egolina NA (1976) Correlation between patterns of DNA replication and chromosome banding. Biol Zbl 95:327–334

5
Molecular Methods

Study of the molecular structure of human chromosomes began in 1869, when Miescher first described "nuclein" extracted from the nuclei of pus cells. Miescher's description of the new substance lacked biochemical resolution, but the discovery that "nuclein" was found to be universally present in nuclei from a variety of sources led to speculation, even before the turn of the century, that nucleic acid might be the bearer of genetic information (Sturtevant, 1965). Biochemists have been working steadily ever since to discover the molecular components and architecture of chromosomes. The work proceeded relatively slowly until the explosive growth of molecular genetics in the 1970s suddenly provided a kit of tools for disassembling DNA into small fragments and then replicating (cloning) the fragments to yield enough material for chemical analysis down to the level of nucleotide sequence. Thanks to these techniques, new information on the molecular structure of chromosomes now flows so rapidly that no one can keep up with it. This chapter describes some of the most important molecular methods used in studying chromosome structure and function. The literature on molecular methodology is growing even more rapidly than the literature on chromosome structure. Useful reviews can be found in Alberts et al. (1989), Darnell et al. (1990), Freifelder (1987), and a variety of "how to" manuals (e.g., Ausubel et al., 1991; Buckler and Housman, 1991; Wu et al., 1989; Zyskind and Bernstein, 1992).

Fragmentation of DNA

Many microorganisms manufacture DNA-cutting enzymes that serve as a primitive immunity mechanism to defend against invasion by foreign DNA molecules (such as the genomes of viruses). These *restriction endo-*

Table 5.1. Representative restriction endonucleases.

Enzyme	Target Sequence	Class of Enzyme
*Alu*I	5′...AG$\downarrow$CT...3′	II
*Bam*HI	5′...G$\downarrow$GATCC...3′	II
*Eco*RI	5′...G$\downarrow$AATTC...3′	II
*Fok*I	5′...GGATG(N)$_{9/13}$$\downarrow$...3′	I
*Hpa*II	5′...C$\downarrow$CGG...3′	II
*Sma*I	5′...CCC$\downarrow$GGG...3′	II

Only one strand of the DNA is shown. The cleavage sites are indicated by arrows. The cut site for the type I enzyme, *Fok*I, is located 9 to 13 bases beyond the recognition sequence. The cut sites for the type II enzymes, *Alu*I and *Sma*I, are centered in the target sequence and produce flush ends rather than sticky ends. *Bam*HI, *Eco*RI, and *Hpa*II produce off-center cuts that leave single-stranded tails on the cleavage fragments.

nucleases, so called because they restrict the expression of the invading DNA molecules, are highly specific; they recognize a sequence of four to eight nucleotides on the target DNA and cleave the DNA backbone either within the recognition sequence (type II nucleases) or near it (type I nucleases). For example, *Hin*dIII, a type II nuclease isolated from *Haemophilus influenzae*, recognizes the following nucleotide sequence:

$$5'...A\overset{\downarrow}{}A\ G\ C\ T\ T...3'$$
$$3'...T\ T\ C\ G\ A\underset{\uparrow}{}A...5'$$

and cuts the single strands at the positions indicated by the arrows. (Table 5.1 shows a few other restriction enzymes and their cut sites.) This target sequence has the properties of most cut sites recognized by type II restriction endonucleases: first, it is symmetrical in the sense that the two strands are identical if read from 5′ to 3′ and, second, that the cuts are staggered so that, when the DNA fragments separate, each will end with a short single-stranded tail of DNA reading 5′AGCT3′. These single-stranded tails are all Watson-Crick complements of one another so that *Hin*dIII fragments can hybridize to one another by their *cohesive* (or *sticky*) *ends* if the temperature is low enough to stabilize hydrogen bonding over a segment of just four complementary base pairs.

The wide variety of commercially available restriction enzymes allows a researcher to choose enzymes with specificities that serve the particular needs of an experiment. For example, the longer the recognition sequence of the endonuclease, the larger the fragments produced from the "restricted" DNA. In DNA containing equal amounts of the four bases, the probability that any given sequence of four bases would occur at random is $(1/4)^4 = 1/256$. Such a restriction endonuclease would cut the DNA

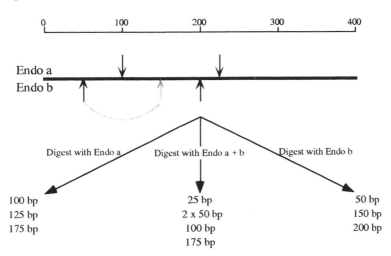

Figure 5.1. An illustration of the use of restriction endonucleases in mapping DNA. The dark arrows show the actual positions of restriction endonuclease sites on a DNA molecule 400 base pairs long. The bottom of the figure shows the results of a restriction experiment in which the DNA is cut with endonuclease a, endonuclease b, or a combination of the two. The restriction fragment sizes, given in base pairs (bp), are measured by gel electrophoresis. The data shown are not sufficient to derive an unambiguous map of the cut sites on the original DNA molecule. The data are compatible either with the actual map, as shown by the dark arrows, or a map in which the first endonuclease b cut site is moved from its position 50 bp from the left end of the DNA molecule to the alternative position (gray arrow) at 150 bp from the left.

molecule of *E. coli* into about 15,000 fragments—or the DNA of a human gamete into 11.3 *million* fragments—with an average length of approximately $0.087\,\mu$m. An endonuclease that recognized a sequence of eight bases would cut the *E. coli* chromosome into about 60 fragments—or a human genome into 44,000 fragments—with an average length of approximately $22.3\,\mu$m.

A homogeneous preparation of DNA can be restriction mapped by digestion with single endonucleases and combinations of endonucleases and use of gel electrophoresis to measure the sizes of the fragments produced by each treatment. The map resulting from such analysis shows the locations of the restriction target sites on the DNA molecule. An example is shown in Figure 5.1.

Cloning

The *cloning* of a gene or other DNA fragment is simply the production of many identical copies from a single original. See Figure 5.2 for an over-

Donor human cell   *E. coli* with plasmid

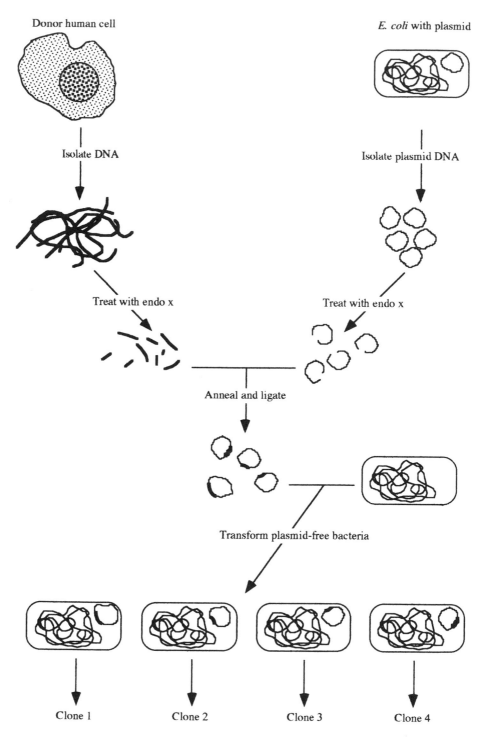

Isolate DNA   Isolate plasmid DNA

Treat with endo x   Treat with endo x

Anneal and ligate

Transform plasmid-free bacteria

Clone 1   Clone 2   Clone 3   Clone 4

view of the process. The production of a clone yields a homogeneous preparation of the desired DNA in sufficient quantity for chemical analysis. Many systems are now available for preparing clones of DNA, most of them with either *E. coli* or yeast as the cell providing the energy and biosynthetic enzymes for production of the DNA. The production of a clone requires a *vector*, a small DNA molecule that serves as a carrier for the cloned gene or gene fragment. A vector may be a virus, such as phage λ, or a plasmid, such as the colicin factors or drug-resistance factors of *E. coli*, or a laboratory-manufactured combination of bits and pieces from several such biological elements. The essential features of vectors are that they are small and easily manipulated in the test tube, that they can replicate in a host cell to yield large quantities of DNA, and that they produce some sort of biological signal that makes it possible to distinguish cells containing vectors from cells that do not. In the case of phage λ, the biological signal is the formation of a plaque. In the case of a bacterial plasmid, it is usually a plasmid-borne gene for drug resistance. In the case of yeast plasmids, it is often a gene for a biosynthetic enzyme that allows the cell carrying the plasmid to grow on medium lacking a nutrient required by the plasmid-free cells.

Generally, DNA to be cloned is purified from donor (e.g., human) cells, treated with a restriction endonuclease to produce short fragments (generally with sticky ends), and mixed with vector DNA that has been

Figure 5.2. A diagram of the cloning of human DNA in a bacterial plasmid vector. The human DNA is shown as a heavy line, the bacterial DNA as a thin line. The bacterial plasmid, shown as a small circle of DNA in the bacterium, can be isolated free of DNA from the chromosome, which is shown as a large tangle of DNA. Plasmids are engineered to contain restriction cut sites at convenient locations. The plasmid shown has just one such site, so that digestion with the restriction enzyme opens the circle but does not cut out any DNA. Treatment of the human DNA and the plasmid DNA with the same restriction endonuclease ensures that the fragments of DNA from the human source will have sticky ends matching those of the broken plasmid. The plasmids and the fragments of human DNA are mixed at a temperature low enough to stabilize hydrogen bonding between the short sticky ends. The DNA ligase then closes the circles covalently. Each plasmid in this diagram will contain a different fragment of human DNA. When the recombinant plasmids are introduced into host bacteria, the plasmids— and the human DNA inserts—will replicate along with the bacteria. Each transformed bacterium shown at the bottom of the figure will give rise to a culture containing a clone of a specific human DNA insert. Collectively, the plasmids in all of the transformed bacteria constitute a library of human DNA fragments. The number of plasmid clones needed to ensure a comprehensive library containing at least one copy of every bit of human DNA would depend on the size of the fragments produced by the restriction endonuclease (see text). Such a library would include at least several hundred thousand clones.

cut with the same endonuclease so it will have complementary sticky ends able to hybridize with the fragments of donor DNA. The unstable hybridization between donor DNA and vector is then stabilized by treating the mixture with DNA ligase, an enzyme that joins the sugar phosphate backbones of donor and vector DNA with covalent phosphodiester linkages. The vector, which has now become a "recombinant DNA" molecule, is then introduced into an appropriate host cell and replicated. In the case of phage λ, the recombinant DNA is packaged in vitro into a phage coat, and the phages are used to infect *E. coli* cells on which they form plaques. Each plaque can be used to initiate the growth of a clonal phage culture—a culture grown from a *single* initial phage particle. In the case of a bacterial plasmid, the recombinant plasmid is introduced into calcium-shocked host bacteria, which are rendered permeable to exogenous DNA by the shock, and individual plasmid-transformed cells are used to initiate the growth of clonal cultures of bacteria—cultures that originate from single plasmid-bearing cells and that, therefore, contain identical copies of a single plasmid forebear.

The recombinant phage or plasmid DNA purified from these cultures contains the cloned gene or gene fragment, which can be released from the vector by treatment with the restriction endonuclease that was used to create the fragment in the first place. This procedure yields homogeneous preparations of DNA molecules that can be analyzed to determine their DNA sequence, labeled to serve as probes for molecules having similar or identical sequences, or subjected to deliberate sequence modifications and then introduced back into host cells so that the effects of the *directed mutations* can be assessed.

The challenge in cloning DNA fragments is to identify the clone containing the desired fragment. In the experimental procedure described above, the investigator ends up with a collection of phages or plasmids each of which contains a cloned fragment of donor DNA. Such a collection is called a library of DNA fragments. The approach to finding the particular items of interest in a *library* will depend on how the library was assembled in the first place. For example, it would be easier to find clones corresponding to a particular sex-linked gene in a library of X chromosome fragments than in a library of total human DNA. A general discussion of the methods for isolating clones of desired DNA fragments is beyond the scope of this book, but the following section discusses a method that is of particular interest to students of cytogenetics.

Flow Cytometry and Chromosome Sorting

The flow cytometer is a machine that converts a suspension of cells or chromosomes into a stream of small droplets. The cells or chromosomes are stained with a fluorescent dye, and the cytometer shoots the droplets through a detector containing a laser light source to excite the fluorescent dye and a photocell to measure the fluorescence drop by drop. A computer connected to this detector records the measurements and provides a statistical summary or profile. Dual-beam machines are available that use two different excitatory lasers and two photomultiplier cells. By choosing appropriate dyes and fluorescence "windows," the investigator can gather information on the distribution of cell (or chromosome) sizes in the population, on the DNA content of cells, or on the presence of *any* cell component that is specifically stainable with a fluorescent dye.

A fluorescence-activated cell sorter is a flow cytometer equipped to introduce an electrical charge into droplets that conform to pre-set fluorescence criteria. These charged drops are then passed through an electrical field that draws them out of the stream of uncharged droplets and directs them toward a separate collection tube. In practice, it is possible to differentially charge two different populations of droplets and to separate them from the bulk population. High speed machines can examine and sort about 20,000 drops per second.

This method can be used to sort suspensions of human chromosomes (Van Dilla et al., 1986). The single-chromosome preparations are sufficiently pure to be used in the production of chromosome-specific libraries of cloned DNA. It has been possible to prepare probes for repetitious DNA sequences that are specific to single chromsomes. When these are hybridized to chromosomes on a microscope slide (see the following section), they label localized bands of DNA on the chromosomes bearing the specific DNA sequence. Probes for repetitive DNA on at least 12 different human chromosomes are commercially available at the time of this writing. It is likely that probes specific for the other 12 will be available by the time these words are read.

In Situ Hybridization

Cloned DNAs can be used as *probes* to identify DNA (or RNA) molecules with complementary base pair sequences. This use of cloned DNA is based on the ability of single strands of nucleic acid to find their Watson-Crick complements in solution and to *renature* (or *hybridize*) into a perfect, hydrogen-bonded double helix. Cloned DNA can be labeled either radioactively or with some readily detectable chemical side-group. It is then denatured (i.e., heated to separate the two strands) and mixed with denatured target nucleic acid, which may be bound to a filter membrane of some sort or fixed in its original location in a cell or tissue. The mixture of nucleic acids is then *annealed*. This means that it is maintained at a temperature just below the melting temperature of the native double helix so that bonds formed between imperfectly paired sequences will be short-lived, but bonds between perfectly paired sequences will be stable.

Renaturation proceeds at a rate dependent on the frequency of collision between complementary sequences, which in turn depends on the concentrations of the complementary sequences. The high concentration of the cloned, labeled probe DNA makes it possible to detect complementary nucleic acid sequences in the target preparation with high speed and sensitivity.

In situ hybridization can be used to identify whole chromosomes or short regions on chromosomes directly on a microscope slide. Cells fixed on the microscope slide are annealed with probe DNA and then washed to remove the excess probe. The method used to detect the probe depends on the label used. If the probe is radioactively labeled (generally with tritium, ^3H, which decays to yield a low energy β particle), the slide is coated with photographic emulsion and stored in the dark to allow the radioactive marker to expose silver grains in the emulsion. The photographic emulsion is then developed and the dark silver grains mark the location of the probe DNA bound to the target. Resolution of the target by this sort of autoradiographic procedure is limited because the β^- particle from the decaying ^3H atom may travel some distance before striking a silver grain. Normally, silver grains are found in a halo with a radius of about 0.5 μm around the labeled site.

Much better resolution is provided by probes that can be detected by fluorescence. One such probe is DNA in which the thymine is replaced by biotinylated uracil. The biotin side groups on this modified DNA do not affect its pairing properties, but they make it a target for the protein avidin, a biotin-specific binding protein found in high concentration in egg white (or for streptavidin, a similar protein made by the bacterium *Streptomyces avidinii*). After the biotinylated DNA has hybridized to complementary sequences in the chromosomes, fluorescein-labeled avidin is added. This binds to the biotinylated segments of DNA and makes them fluorescent. The fluorescence can be augmented by adding fluorescein-labeled antibody specific for avidin, a treatment that builds up a thicker layer of fluorescent molecules around the biotin-labeled DNA. The labeled segments of the chromosome can then be visualized in a fluorescence microscope.

Methods for studying chromosomes by using non-radioactive probes are increasing rapidly (Trask, 1991; Lichter and Ward, 1990). DNA probes containing bromodeoxyuracil, digoxigenin, dinitrophenol, and other side-groups can be detected by highly specific fluorescent antibodies. New probes are now being developed in which fluorescent side-groups are attached directly to the probe DNA, thus eliminating the need to add a fluorescent molecule that binds to the probe. These techniques are making it possible to prepare chromosome-specific probe sets that "paint" different chromosomes or different parts of chromosomes in different colors (Sasavage, 1992). The picture on the cover of this book illustrates the power and beauty of these new techniques.

Polymerase Chain Reaction (PCR)

The polymerase chain reaction (Erlich et al., 1989; Reiss and Cooper, 1990) is a recently developed method that has become one of the most widely used techniques for preparing homogeneous samples of specific segments of DNA. PCR amplifies selected segments of template DNA with only small quantities of crude extract as the starting material. The method uses short pieces of synthetic DNA—oligonucleotides—as primers for DNA synthesis (see Figure 5.3). By selecting oligonucleotide sequences corresponding to unique DNA segments flanking the region of interest, an investigator can produce many copies of the DNA between the two primers. The sensitivity of this technique is so great that it can be used to characterize DNA from a single cell. For example, it has been used to detect recombination in short segments of DNA from individual human sperm cells (Li et al., 1988).

It would be impossible to survey here the wide variety of ingenious uses that have been invented for PCR. Clearly, however, it can be used to prepare homogeneous DNA samples for DNA sequencing, and it can facilitate chromosome "walking" in which successive overlapping segments of DNA are isolated in order to move toward a target sequence of particular interest. Regions beyond the oligonucleotide primers can be prepared by fragmenting DNA with restriction endonucleases that cut to the left and right of a specific pair of PCR primers. The long DNA fragment produced can then be circularized with DNA ligase and amplified using a pair of primers that are the Watson-Crick complements of the original pair. The product of the chain reaction in this case will be the arc of the circle that includes the DNA sequences just outside of the region amplified in the first reaction.

Yeast Artificial Chromosomes (YACs)

Research on the molecular properties of eukaryotic chromosomes has depended to a large extent on the use of prokaryotic models and on the cloning of eukaryotic genes in prokaryotic systems. However, one eukaryotic system is as amenable to genetic engineering as *E. coli*. The system is *Saccharomyces cerevisiae*, common baker's yeast, and much of what we know about eukaryotic chromosomes we have learned from experiments on "artificial chromosomes" in that organism. Yeast has been thoroughly studied by geneticists for many years. A large collection of useful mutations has been accumulated and exhaustively mapped. Furthermore, yeast, like *E. coli*, harbors extrachromosomal DNA circles, plasmids, that can be isolated and purified, genetically engineered in vitro, and then introduced back into the host cell. The behavior of these genetically engineered plasmids has shed much light on the structure and

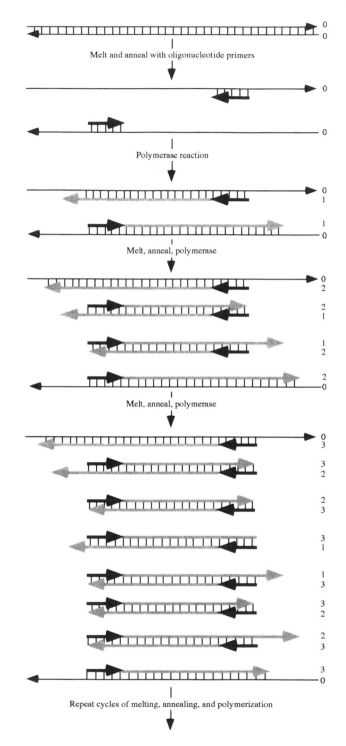

Melt and anneal with oligonucleotide primers

Polymerase reaction

Melt, anneal, polymerase

Melt, anneal, polymerase

Repeat cycles of melting, annealing, and polymerization

function of specialized structures in eukaryotic chromosomes in general.

In a typical experiment, a selectable marker is inserted into a yeast plasmid, and the plasmid is then introduced into host cells unable to grow unless the gene on the plasmid is expressed. This provides a sensitive system in which to assay the ability of the plasmid to replicate in the host cell and to segregate in parallel with the chromosomes. The ability of the plasmids to replicate turns out to be dependent on *cis*-acting elements called autonomous replication sequences (or ARS), which appear to be the origins of DNA replication. Plasmids lacking an ARS are unable to replicate at all in the host cell. Fragments of yeast chromosomal DNA can be inserted into a replication-deficient plasmid to determine whether they render the plasmid capable of independent replication. Such cloning experiments show that the yeast genome contains several hundred ARS (Stinchcomb et al., 1979).

Figure 5.3. The polymerase chain reaction. The DNA molecule shown at the top of the figure represents a specific chromosomal region that has been selected for study. The short heavy arrows represent synthetic oligonucleotide primers that are added in large excess to a crude DNA preparation containing the segment to be amplified. When the DNA is heated to separate the two strands and annealed with the synthetic primer molecules, the primers hybridize to template molecule at positions flanking the selected chromosomal segment. Polymerization of new DNA, shown in gray, produces strands that, like the original DNA, can serve as template in the next cycle of DNA melting/annealing/polymerization. The starting points for DNA synthesis in this reaction are determined by the primers, which are present in large molar excess. The end points for the new DNA depend on the length of the DNA template. The original template, whose strands are labeled **0** so that they can be followed through the entire diagram, will produce daughter strands extending well beyond the defined region of interest. The same is true of the long daughter strands produced from this original template molecule (for example, those produced in the first round of replication and labeled **1** in the diagram). However, the exponential increase in the number of daughter strands containing the synthetic oligonucleotide primer quickly swamps out the extra-length templates and sets the pattern for the later stages of polymerization, in which the beginnings and ends of the daughter strands are defined by the 5′ ends of the two primers. In the last round of replication shown in the diagram, six of the eight new single strands (labeled **3**) begin and end at the exact locations desired.

In practice, the cycles of melting, annealing, and polymerization take place in a single test tube. The DNA polymerase used is a heat-stable enzyme from a thermophilic bacterium. It is not inactivated at the temperatures needed for melting of the DNA. Cycling of the reaction is accomplished by heating the reaction mixture to separate the DNA strands, cooling it to allow hybridization with the oligonucleotide primers and synthesis of new strands of DNA, heating again, cooling again, and so forth until enough cycles of replication have passed to provide the required amplification of the target sequence.

The presence of an ARS in a plasmid is not sufficient, however, to make it a stable hereditary unit. Although the plasmids can replicate in the host cell, they do not segregate regularly at cell division, and plasmid-free daughter cells are produced. The introduction of a centromere (CEN) sequence *does* ensure the inheritance of the plasmid by all daughter cells, apparently by making it possible for the plasmid to attach to spindle fibers at cell division (Clarke and Carbon, 1985).

Yeast plasmids, unlike chromosomes, are closed circles of DNA. Linearized plasmids do not survive in the cell, even if they contain both ARS and CEN sequences. If, however, telomere (TEL) sequences are attached to the ends of the linearized plasmids, the plasmid becomes perfectly stable and behaves exactly as if it were a normal yeast chromosome (Zakian, 1989). These small pieces of DNA containing ARS and CEN and TEL sequences are called *yeast artificial chromosomes* (YACs). The ease with which they can be isolated and modified makes them ideal tools for studying the molecular mechanisms of eukaryotic chromosome behavior.

Finally, it should be noted that large, megabase-long segments of double-stranded DNA can be inserted into YACs and propagated in host yeast cells. Such long segments of cloned DNA are typically unstable in bacterial cloning systems. Thus, the YAC provides a cloning vector that promises to be especially useful in the ambitious Human Genome Project, which aims to determine the DNA sequence of the entire complement of human chromosomes.

References

Alberts B, Bray D, Lewis J, et al. (eds) (1989) Molecular biology of the cell, 2nd edn. Garland, New York

Ausubel FM, Brent R, Kingston RE, et al. (eds) (1991) Current protocols in molecular biology. Greene Publ and Wiley-Liss, New York

Buckler AJ, Housman DE (1991) Methods of genome analysis: a gene hunter's guide. Freeman, Salt Lake City, Utah

Clarke L, Carbon J (1985) The structure and function of yeast centromeres. Annu Rev Genet 19:29–56

Darnell J, Lodish H, Baltimore D (1990) Molecular cell biology, 2nd edn. Scientific American Books, Freeman, New York

Erlich HA, Gibbs R, Kazazian HH Jr (1989) Current communications in molecular biology: polymerase chain reaction. Cold Spring Harbor Laboratory, New York

Freifelder D (1987) Molecular biology, 2nd edn. Jones and Bartlett, Boston

Li H, Gyllensten UB, Xui X, et al. (1988) Amplification and analysis of DNA sequences in single human sperm and diploid cells. Nature 335:414–417

Lichter P, Ward DC (1990) Is non-isotopic *in-situ* hybridization finally coming of age? Nature 345:93–94

Reiss J, Cooper DN (1990) Application of the polymerase chain reaction to the diagnosis of human genetic disease. Hum Genet 85:1–8

Sasavage N (1992) Painting by the chromosome numbers. J NIH Res USA 4:44–46

Stinchcomb DT, Struhl K, Davis RW (1979) Isolation and characterisation of a yeast chromosomal replicator. Nature 282:39–43

Sturtevant AH (1965) A history of genetics. Harper and Row, New York

Trask BJ (1991) Fluorescence in situ hybridization: applications in cytogenetics and gene mapping. Trends Genet 7:149–154

Van Dilla MA, Deaven LL, Albright KL, et al. (1986) Human chromosome-specific DNA libraries: construction and availability. Bio/Technology 4:537–552

Wu R, Grossman L, Moldave K (eds) (1989) Recombinant DNA methodology. Academic, New York

Zakian VA (1989) Structure and function of telomeres. Annu Rev Genet 23:579–604

Zyskind JW, Bernstein SI (1992) Recombinant DNA laboratory manual, revised edn. Academic, New York

6
Longitudinal Differentiation of Eukaryotic Chromosomes

Longitudinal Differentiation of Chromosomes

Longitudinal differentiation of chromosomes is expressed at several levels. However, there are still gaps in the information gained by different methods, and the goal of future studies will be to close these gaps. Observations on nonbanded chromosomes have been replaced to a large extent by studies on variously banded chromosomes. Molecular studies have shown that chromosomes consist of repetitive, middle repetitive, and unique DNA sequences; a picture of the fine structure of the eukaryotic chromosome is finally emerging (Chapter 8).

Molecular Differentiation of Chromosomes

On the molecular level, the genome of eukaryotes consists of highly repeated sequences ($>10^5$ copies), middle repeated sequences (ca. 10^2–10^4 copies) and unique sequences (one, or a few copies) (Hood et al., 1975). The distinctions between these classes are somewhat arbitrary.

In the highly repeated sequences, the repeated units vary in length from 2 to at least 2350 base pairs (Miklos, 1982). In *simple sequence* DNAs, such as the DNA of constitutive heterochromatin, short base sequences are repeated over and over again to make long, meaningless stretches of DNA. These simple DNAs show limited sequence variation within species, but extensive variation between species—even closely related species. Simple sequence DNA may have a buoyant density distinctly different from that of the bulk DNA of the organism, so that it forms satellite bands in density gradient centrifugation—hence the term *satellite DNA*.

In human chromosomes there are two major families of interspersed, highly repeated sequences that may have spread through the genome by some sort of transposition process. These have been identified by looking for scattered stretches of DNA that can pair with one another to form a double helix (Singer, 1982; Singer and Skowronski, 1985). One family, SINES (short, interspersed elements), is about 300 base pairs long and is characterized by the presence of cleavage sites recognized by the restriction endonuclease, *Alu*I. Thus, SINES, identified by DNA hybridization, and the so-called *Alu* sequences, identified by the presence of *Alu*I cleavage sites, are closely related if not identical. SINES are repeated half a million to one million times in the human chromosomes, mainly in the Q-dark bands (Korenberg and Rykowski, 1988). The other family consists of LINES (long, interspersed elements). In humans, there are about 100,000 copies per nucleus. The full length of the element is about five kilo-base pairs, but many truncated copies are found. They are mainly situated in the Q-bright bands (Korenberg and Rykowski, 1988).

Multigene families, which code, for instance, for ribosomal RNA or histones, represent middle repeated DNA. These genes, which code for products needed in large quantity in the cell, are repeated hundreds of times in the genome. Furthermore, transposable elements, which do not have a fixed location on the chromosomes, make up a considerable proportion of the middle repeated DNA in such organisms as yeast and *Drosophila* (Finnegan et al., 1982), and this may be true elsewhere.

Other informational multigene families, of which globin and immunoglobulin genes are typical examples, bridge the gap between unique sequences and middle repeated sequences. Characteristic of genes in such multigene families is multiplicity, close linkage, sequence homology, and similar or overlapping functions (Hood et al., 1975).

Unique sequences can be divided into transcribed genes and noncoding unique sequences, to which spacers and so-called pseudogenes also belong.

At a cruder level, chromosomal DNA can be sorted into *isochores* (Bernardi, 1989), which are long (±300 kilo-base pairs) fragments of DNA separated from one another on the basis of their buoyant density (and, thus, their nucleotide composition). GC-rich isochores come mainly from Q-dark chromosome bands, which contain a high density of genes and are especially rich in housekeeping genes. GC-poor isochores are associated with Q-bright bands, which are relatively poor in genic DNA and contain mostly tissue-specific genes.

Prebanding Studies

Apart from primary and secondary constrictions and satellites, chromosomes of most higher organisms display differential segments, sometimes whole chromosomes, that exhibit a condensation cycle which deviates from the main part of the chromosomes. Heitz (for example, 1933), who made a number of basic studies in this field during the late 1920s and early 1930s, named these chromosome parts *heterochromatic* in contrast to the majority of the chromosomes, which he termed *euchromatic* (Passarge, 1979). Chromosomes that are more condensed than the rest have also been called *positively heteropycnotic*, whereas those that are less condensed are *negatively heteropycnotic*. The same chromosome may at some stages be positively, at others negatively, heteropycnotic. The X chromosome in the spermatocytes of grasshoppers is an example of this.

Being out of step with the rest of the chromosomes, which is one of the characteristics of heterochromatin, is called *allocycly*. In interphase, heterochromatic chromosome segments often appear as more condensed *chromocenters* or *prochromosomes* (Wilson, 1925). As a result of the studies of Heitz, it is known that heterochromatin is genetically inert. The achievements of Heitz would be impressive at any period, but when one considers that his main technique was to fix the chromosomes in hot acetic acid to which the stain, carmine, had been added, they become almost unbelievable.

Banding Studies on Human Chromosomes

Q-banding differentiates the human chromosomes into bands of differing length and relative brightness. These two parameters were determined by Kuhn (1976). An interesting property of the metaphasic Q-bands is that they seem to act as units; for instance, each band replicates within a particular limited time during the S period (Ris and Korenberg, 1979). Interestingly, the Q- and G-bands correspond to the chromomeres, as seen in pachytene. These bands have also shown amazing constancy during evolution, the overwhelming majority of even prophase bands appearing identical in man and the great apes (Yunis and Prakash, 1982).

The most brightly quinacrine-fluorescent bands in the human chromosome complement are the distal end of the Y chromosome and the narrow variable bands at the centromeres of chromosomes 3, 4, and the acrocentrics. Human populations are polymorphic for these bright bands, just as they are for the size and fluorescent properties of the satellites.

G-banding and its reverse, R-banding, give essentially the same information as Q-banding. However, R-banding is often useful for the study of structural changes involving chromosome ends that might go undetected with Q-banding or G-banding.

C-banding reveals a type of chromatin that is, in principle, different from euchromatin. This technique specifically stains constitutive heterochromatin, which is situated at the centric regions of all human chromosomes and at the distal end of the Y chromosome. Particularly prominent blocks of this heterochromatin are found in chromosomes 1, 9, and 16, and these regions show considerable polymorphism in the population. Possibly variation in the centric heterochromatin of these chromosomes is more noticeable than variation in the shorter C-bands; however, variation in many of the shorter bands has also been reported. The constitutive heterochromatin in chromosomes 1, 9, 16, and the Y varies from shorter than average to about three times the average length.

The greatest variability is demonstrated by the satellites and short arms of the acrocentric chromosomes (Verma, 1988). The variation of heterochromatin and the possible mechanisms causing it have been reviewed, for instance, by John (1988) and by Verma (1988).

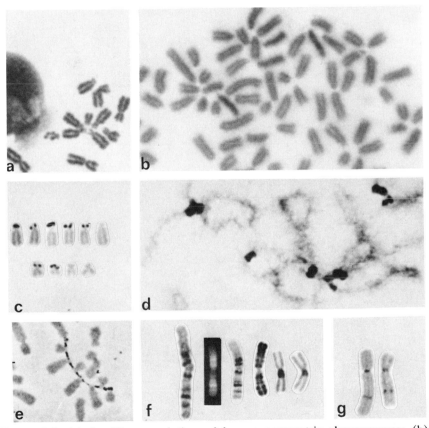

Figure 6.1. (a) Satellite association of human acrocentric chromosomes; (b) centric association of mouse cancer chromosomes; (c) silver-staining of active nucleolar organizers in human D and G chromosomes (courtesy of C Trunca); (d) heterochromatic association of mouse diplotene bivalents; (e) satellite association of silver-stained human acrocentrics (courtesy of TM Schroeder); (f) human chromosome 1 (from the left): prometaphase banding, Q-banding, G-banding, R-banding, C-banding (from a heterozygote for the C-band); (g) C-banded human dicentric chromosomes with one centromere inactivated.

Nucleoli and Chromocenters

The nucleolar organizers, which consist of ribosomal RNA genes, of which the human has about 200, are situated at the satellite stalks of the D and G chromosomes (Miller, 1981). In many organisms these genes are localized in secondary constrictions of one (or more) chromosome pair as in Haplopappus (Fig. 2.2a) and in *Uvularia* (Fig. 14.1). Both satellite stalks and secondary constrictions are usually visible without any banding techniques. That they contain the nucleolar organizers was discovered by Heitz (1931) and verified with in situ hybridization techniques (Henderson

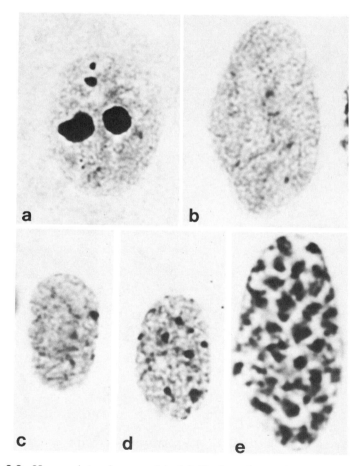

Figure 6.2. Human interphase nuclei. (a) Nucleus from placenta; NOR-silver-staining shows the nucleoli black; (b–e) Feulgen-stained nuclei from cervical cancer: (b) fairly evenly stained nucleus; (c) nucleus showing an X chromatin body; (d) nucleus with several chromocenters; (e) most of the chromatin condensed into chromocenters.

et al., 1972). Active nucleolar organizers can be stained with the NOR silver technique (Fig. 6.1c and e) (Goodpasture and Bloom, 1975), which also stains the nucleoli in interphase nuclei (Fig. 6.2a). Each nucleolar organizer forms a nucleolus in telophase; the nucleoli fuse during interphase and disappear in prophase.

With the Feulgen technique, which does not stain the nucleoli, interphase nuclei may appear fairly evenly stained (Fig. 6.2b), or a Barr body may be visible (Fig. 6.2c). A nucleus may display several chromocenters, also described by Heitz (for example, 1933) (Fig. 6.2d), or most of the chromatin may be condensed into chromocenters (Fig. 6.2e).

Constitutive Heterochromatin

Heterochromatin can be divided into two main categories, *constitutive* and *facultative* (Brown, 1966). Although these two classes behave similarly in many ways, a fundamental structural difference exists between them. The DNA structure that is characteristic of the constitutive heterochromatin is different from that of euchromatic DNA. On the other hand, facultative heterochromatin consists of essentially euchromatic DNA that is specifically inactivated during certain phases of development.

Constitutive heterochromatin, which in man is located in the C-bands and at the distal end of the Y chromosome, consists of simple sequence-repeated DNA. Constitutive heterochromatin contains no Mendelian genes and is never transcribed. This explains the fact that considerable variation in the C-bands does not seem to affect the phenotype, even in extreme cases. Characteristics of constitutive heterochromatin, shared by facultative heterochromatin, are its genetic inertness, its late replication during the S period, and its general allocycly. It has long been known (Vanderlyn, 1949) that heterochromatic segments are "sticky" and tend to fuse in interphase. This is reflected in the satellite association of human acrocentrics (which may be helped by remnants of nucleolar material) and of mouse chromosomes, both in mitotic metaphase and in diplotene (Fig. 6.1a, b, d, and e). Nonhomologous heterochromatic bands often show so-called ectopic pairing in polytene chromosomes (John, 1988).

Constitutive heterochromatin is found in practically all higher organisms, both plants and animals. It is often situated at the centromere, as in the human and the mouse. In many plants it forms blocks at the telomeres, but it can also be intercalary (Fig. 6.3a). Before the invention of banding techniques, the deer mouse *Peromyscus* presented a cytological riddle. Chromosome length and centromere index seemed to vary from animal to animal, and complicated inversion systems were invented to explain this. C-banding revealed that all the short arms consisted of constitutive heterochromatin, the amount varying from animal to animal (Hsu, 1975). Closely related species with the same chromosome number sometimes have very different amounts of DNA per nucleus. This, too,

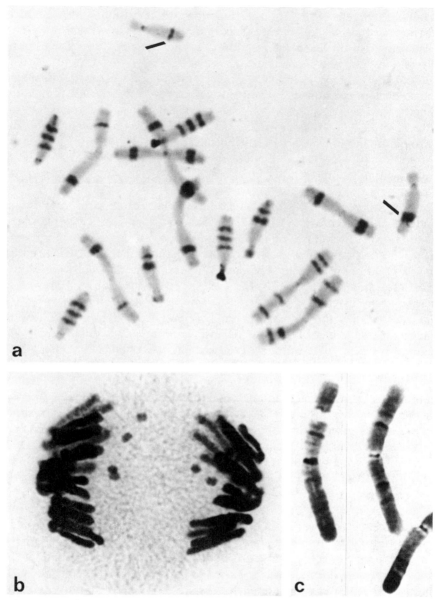

Figure 6.3. (a) C-banding of the chromosomes of *Anemone blanda*; chromosome with heterozygous C-band marked (courtesy of D Schweizer); (b) B-chromosomes segregating irregularly in I meiotic anaphase of *Fritillaria imperialis* (courtesy of M Ulber); (c) Apparently G-banded chromosomes of *Pinus resinosa*; the chromosome on the left has a secondary constriction (courtesy of A Drewry).

has been found to depend on variation in constitutive heterochromatin (Gall, 1981).

The reactions of the different C-bands to the various banding techniques show that their DNA structures are not identical. Thus, although all the constitutive heterochromatin stains dark with C-banding, the distal end of the Y chromosome is brightly fluorescent with Q-banding, whereas the centric heterochromatin of chromosomes 1, 9, and 16 is dark. Also, a specific staining technique (G-11) has been developed for the C-band in chromosome 9. Furthermore, a derivative of the fluorescent dye DAPI (4′,6-diamidino-2-phenylindole) stains the heterochromatin in human chromosomes 9, 15, and Y differentially (Schnedl et al., 1981). The variation in the structure of heterochromatin has been confirmed on the molecular level (Miklos, 1982).

Constitutive heterochromatin seems especially prone to breakage and rearrangement. However, for the most part, the polymorphism of the C-bands is probably the result of unequal pairing and crossing-over. Nevertheless, these changes cannot take place very often, since the C-band variants, as a rule, are constant from one generation to the next and show normal Mendelian inheritance.

In many plants and animals, but not in humans, extra chromosomes, the so-called B chromosomes, have been found (Fig. 6.3b). They occur in addition to the normal chromosome complement and may vary greatly in number from individual to individual within a species, and even from cell to cell within an individual. They appear to be practically inert, since they do not seem to affect the phenotype even when present in considerable numbers (Jones and Rees, 1982). However, they have some effects, especially on viability and chiasma frequency. As a rule, B chromosomes do not show the typical staining of constitutive heterochromatin but appear variably banded, resembling small, normal chromosomes.

Facultative Heterochromatin

One of the best known examples of facultative heterochromatin is the inactive X in the mammalian female (Chapter 21). In the human female, one X in each cell becomes inactivated, at random, during the blastocyst stage. Thereafter, this X behaves as if it consisted of heterochromatin. It is condensed in interphase and shows no transcription. It replicates late during the S period (Figs. 21.2 and 3) and is more condensed than the other chromosomes, even in prophase and prometaphase (Fig. 21.1). Before inactivation, both X chromosomes are active, and the inactive X is turned on again before oogenesis, during which both X chromosomes behave much like the autosomes. During spermatogenesis, on the other hand, neither the X nor the Y chromosome is transcribed. Both chromosomes behave like heterochromatin. The mechanism that determines the behavior of the facultative heterochromatin is still unknown.

Transcription of Chromosomes

In any cell, only a small part of the DNA present is transcribed (Ris and Korenberg, 1979). No condensed parts, whether consisting of constitutive or facultative heterochromatin, produce any proteins. In some cell types, such as sperm or the erythrocytes of certain species, in which the total chromatin is in a condensed state (Ris and Korenberg, 1979), this inactivity applies to the whole chromosome complement. A different type of heterochromatic behavior is seen when chromosomes, or chromosome segments, condense in differentiated cells to form chromocenters of various shapes and sizes (Fig. 6.2d and e). This is probably a mechanism to shut off genes whose activity is not needed at a certain point of development (Ris and Korenberg, 1979). Plants and animals seem to differ in that in animals the condensation of chromatin in interphase acts as a regulating mechanism for gene action, whereas in plants the condensed parts represent constitutive heterochromatin (Nagl, 1982). However, it is not only *condensed* chromatin that is silent; a great part of the *extended* chromatin is also unexpressed in any cell type (Ris and Korenberg, 1979).

Role of Heterochromatin

The various aspects of heterochromatin have been reviewed repeatedly (for instance, John and Miklos, 1979; Babu and Verma, 1987; John, 1988; Sumner, 1990). The characteristics of constitutive and facultative heterochromatin are compared in Table 6.1. The main function of facultative heterochromatin may be the regulation of gene action, since the heterochromatinized segments are inactivated. On the other hand, we are completely in the dark about the role of constitutive heterochromatin, although it is a ubiquitous constituent of eukaryotic chromosomes. Its only established effect, regulation of crossing-over (Miklos and John, 1979), does

Table 6.1. Comparison of constitutive and facultative heterochromatin

Constitutive	Facultative
Consists of highly repeated sequences	Includes other than highly repeated sequences
Corresponds to satellite DNAs	—
Late-labeling in S	Late-labeling in S
C-banding stains the bands in metaphase and the chromocenters in interphase	Orcein and Feulgen stain chromocenters in interphase; Q-, G-, and R-banding, in metaphase
Never transcribed	Parts transcribed when not condensed
No meiotic crossing-over	Meiotic crossing-over
Shows stickiness and ectopic pairing	No corresponding phenomena
No definite function established	Probably acts as gene regulator in mammals

not seem to provide a sufficient explanation for its widespread occurrence. Our ignorance of the true role of heterochromatin has left the field open for a variety of hypotheses ranging from the idea that it is selfish DNA simply perpetuating itself (Doolittle, 1982) to the idea that it has important roles in development or evolution (Flavell, 1982; Miklos, 1982). However, so far none of these ideas has been backed by solid evidence.

References

Babu KA, Verma RS (1987) Chromosome structure: Euchromatin and heterochromatin. Int Rev Cytol 108:1–60

Bernardi G (1989) The isochore organization of the human genome. Annu Rev Genet 23:637–661

Brown SW (1966) Heterochromatin. Science 151:417–425

Doolittle WF (1982) Selfish DNA after fourteen months. In: Dover GA, Flavell RB (eds) Genome evolution. Academic, New York, pp 3–28

Finnegan DJ, Will BH, Bayev AA, et al. (1982) Transposable DNA sequences in eukaryotes. In: Dover GA, Flavell RB (eds) Genome evolution. Academic, New York, pp 29–40

Flavell RB (1982) Sequence amplification, deletion and rearrangement: major sources of variation during species divergence. In: Dover GA, Flavell RB (eds) Genome evolution. Academic, New York, pp 301–323

Gall JG (1981) Chromosome structure and the C-value paradox. J Cell Biol 91:3s–4s

Goodpasture C, Bloom SE (1975) Visualization of nucleolar organizer regions in mammalian chromosomes using silver staining. Chromosoma 53:37–50

Heitz E (1931) Die Ursache der gesetzmässigen Zahl, Lage, Form und Grösse pflanzlicher Nukleolen. Planta 12:775–844

Heitz E (1933) Die Herkunft der Chromocentren. Planta 18:571–635

Henderson AS, Warburton D, Atwood KC (1972) Location of ribosomal DNA in the human chromosome complement. Proc Natl Acad Sci USA 69:3394–3398

Hood L, Campbell JH, Elgin SCR (1975) The organization, expression, and evolution of antibody genes and other multigene families. Annu Rev Genet 9:305–353

Hsu TC (1975) A possible function of constitutive heterochromatin: the bodyguard hypothesis. Genetics 79:137–150

John B (1988) The biology of heterochromatin. In: Verma RS (ed) Heterochromatin: molecular and structural aspects. Cambridge University, Cambridge pp 1–147

John B, Miklos GLG (1979) Functional aspects of satellite DNA and heterochromatin. Int Rev Cytol 58:1–113

Jones RN, Rees H (1982) B chromosomes. Academic, New York

Korenberg JR, Rykowski MC (1988) Human genome organization: Alu, Lines, and the molecular structure of metaphase chromosome bands. Cell 53:391–400

Kuhn EM (1976) Localization by Q-banding of mitotic chiasmata in cases of Bloom's syndrome. Chromosoma 57:1–11

Miklos GLG (1982) Sequencing and manipulating highly repeated DNA. In:

Dover GA, Flavell RB (eds) Genome evolution. Academic, New York, pp 41–68

Miklos GLG, John B (1979) Heterochromatin and satellite DNA in man: properties and prospects. Am J Hum Genet 31:264–280

Miller OJ (1981) Nucleolar organizers in mammalian cells. In: Bennett MD, Bobrow M, Hewitt G (eds) Chromosomes today, Vol 7. Allen and Unwin, London, pp 64–73

Nagl W (1982) Condensed chromatin: species-specificity, tissue-specificity, and cell cycle-specificity, as monitored by scanning cytometry. In: Nicolini C (ed) Cell growth. Plenum, New York, pp 171–218

Passarge E (1979) Emil Heitz and the concept of heterochromatin: longitudinal chromosome differentiation was recognized fifty years ago. Am J Hum Genet 31:106–115

Ris H, Korenberg JR (1979) Chromosome structure and levels of chromosome organization. In: Goldstein L, Prescott DM (eds) Cell biology, Vol 2. Academic, New York, pp 268–361

Schnedl W, Abraham R, Dann O, et al. (1981) Preferential fluorescent staining of heterochromatic regions in human chromosomes 9, 15, and the Y by D287/170. Hum Genet 59:10–13

Singer MF (1982) Highly repeated sequences in mammalian genomes. Int Rev Cytol 76:67–112

Singer MF, Skowronski J (1985) Making sense out of LINES: long interspersed repeat sequences in mammalian genomes. Trends Biochem Sci 10:119–122

Sumner AT (1990) Chromosome banding. Unwin Hyman, London

Vanderlyn L (1949) The heterochromatin problem in cyto-genetics as related to other branches of investigation. Bot Rev 15:507–582

Verma RS (1988) Heteromorphisms of heterochromatin. In: Verma RS (ed) Heterochromatin: molecular and structural aspects. Cambridge University, Cambridge pp 276–292

Vilson EB (1925) The cell in development and heredity, 3rd edn. MacMillan, New York

Yunis JJ, Prakash O (1982) The origin of man: A chromosomal pictorial legacy. Science 215:1525–1530

7
Significance of Chromosome Bands

Chromosome Banding

Even a superficial comparison demonstrates that, apart from C-banding, the different banding techniques reveal the same features in chromosome structure. Thus, the bright Q-bands correspond to the dark G-bands, which in turn appear to be identical with the R-light bands. This does not exclude the possibility that some similar-appearing bands have different properties. Thus, the chromosome ends apparently differ from other Q-dark bands (Ambros and Sumner, 1987; Korenberg and Rykowski, 1988).

The most information exists about Q-banding. Weisblum and de Haseth (1972) and Weisblum (1973) showed in their in vitro studies on polynucleotides of known composition that DNA consisting of repeated adenine–thymine (AT) base pairs fluoresces brightly with quinacrine, whereas guanine–cytosine (GC) pairs quench fluorescence. Quenching is also a function of the degree of the interspersion of GC pairs (AT pairs must occur in uninterrupted stretches of a certain length to cause fluorescence). Two stretches of DNA can have the same base ratio (AT:GC) but fluoresce differently, depending on the sequence of the bases (Sumner, 1986).

Korenberg and Engels (1978), who were the first to determine directly the base ratios of the Q-bands in human chromosomes, demonstrated that the Q-brightness of the bands was positively correlated with the AT:GC ratio. However, the differences in the base ratios between the very bright Y heterochromatin and the dark bands are much less than has often been assumed (Evans, 1977). Interestingly, the longer chromosomes are relatively brighter than the smaller ones. Although the DNA structure is the basis for Q-banding, the chromosomal proteins, both histones and nonhistones, obviously play an important role, especially in the various Giemsa techniques (Ris and Korenberg, 1979; Sumner, 1990).

Korenberg and Rykowski (1988) have elegantly demonstrated that the Q-bright bands have more LINE sequence repeats than the Q-dark bands, which, on the other hand, are characterized by the presence of SINE sequence repeats.

The Q-dark bands replicate early in the S period. This is assumed to be followed by a pause, after which the Q-bright bands (and the C-bands) replicate (John, 1988). The replication order is constant within a tissue, but may vary between tissues (Willard, 1977).

Role of the Bands

The assumption that the Q-bands (and the corresponding G- and R-bands) are the basic building blocks of the mammalian chromosomes is supported by the observation that they have retained their identity through the evolution of the great apes, some 20 million years, and probably much longer (Yunis and Prakash, 1982). Any chromosome breaks that have played a role in evolution must have occurred at the borders of Q-bright and Q-dark bands.

The first indications that most genes are situated in the Q-dark bands came from clinical observations. As early as 1965, Yunis pointed out that the only autosomes (13, 18, and 21) for which trisomy is viable to any appreciable extent are the latest replicating chromosomes in their groups. Now we know that they are also the Q-brightest. Yunis concluded that these chromosomes contained more heterochromatin than did early replicating chromosomes; therefore, their trisomies were better tolerated than trisomies for more gene-rich autosomes. A positive correlation between Q-brightness and the occurrence of liveborn trisomies for all human chromosomes (Table 24.3) has been demonstrated by Kuhn et al. (1987).

Not only are Q-dark bands gene-rich, but some of them appear to be much more so than others. Thus, trisomy for the short Q-dark distal region of chromosome 21 is responsible for all the symptoms characteristic of Down syndrome, whereas trisomy (or even monosomy) for the bright proximal band produces only mild retardation (for example, Hagemeijer and Smit, 1977). Recently, Korenberg et al. (1990) have demonstrated by molecular means that the bands 21q2.2 and 21q2.3 in the trisomic state cause the main Down syndrome symptoms. Similarly, it was found that in 20 cases of trisomy for 11q the symptoms were the same whether almost the whole 11q was trisomic or only the distal end (Pihko et al., 1981). The inevitable conclusion was that the genes causing the trisomy symptoms are concentrated in the region distal to 11q23.

Kuhn (1976) demonstrated that mitotic chiasmata in Bloom syndrome (Chapter 12) are located preferentially in Q-dark regions; the Q-dark regions of 1p, 3p, 6p, 11q, 12q, 17q, 19(p or q), and 22q are especially chiasma-rich. Their behavior in meiosis is not known. A strong negative correlation was found between recombinational hot spots in chromosomes and their involvement in trisomic abortions (Korenberg et al., 1978; Kuhn et al., 1985). In other words, embryos that are trisomic for these chromosomes die too early to be recognized as abortions. The same chromosomes also have a significantly higher number of localized genes than similar-sized control chromosomes (Kuhn et al., 1985, 1987). Korenberg et al. (1978) formulated the hypothesis that the Q-darker chromosome bands have higher gene densities than do the brighter ones and that the chiasma hot spots are especially prominent in this respect. Because they contain active genes, they would be extended in interphase and as a result would be more easily available for mitotic pairing and crossing-over.

Now, more direct methods for the determination of gene distribution are available. Lists of genes (*The Human Genome*, 1990; *New Haven Human Gene Mapping Library: Chromosome Plots*, 1989) show their localization in different chromosome bands, although the sites of many genes are not yet determined very precisely. The evidence shows that the housekeeping genes are concentrated in the Q-dark bands, whereas many of the tissue-specific genes are situated in the Q-bright bands (Goldman et al., 1984; Holmquist, 1989). However, the possibility cannot be excluded that both housekeeping and tissue-specific genes lie in the Q-dark bands (Bickmore and Sumner, 1989; Sumner, 1990).

Future Problems

The characteristics of Q-bright and Q-dark bands are summarized in Table 7.1; however, there are many gaps in our knowledge. It is not clear, as has been stressed by Sumner (1990), how accurately the bands produced by different techniques agree. The use of computerized microphotometric techniques developed by Drets and his colleagues (1990) may help to solve this and other related problems. It is also not known whether the prophase, prometaphase, or metaphase bands are the basic units of chromosome organization. Metaphase bands are supposed to

Table 7.1. Characteristics of human Q-dark and Q-bright chromosome bands.

Q-dark, R-positive bands	Q-bright, R-negative bands
Lower AT:GC ratio	Higher AT:GC ratio
Rich in SINE repeats and *Alu* sequences	Rich in LINE repeats
Early-replicating	Late-replicating
Correspond to pachytene interchromomeres	Correspond to pachytene chromomeres
Contain housekeeping genes	Genes tend to be tissue-specific
Rich in transcribed genes	Sparse genes, simple sequence DNA

arise through fusion of prometaphase bands. However, it seems improbable that a Q-dark band would be able to "swallow" one or more Q-bright bands, whereas the inclusion of dark bands into a bright band is easy to visualize. The status of prophase bands is even less clear. Are they bands in the same sense as metaphase bands or early-coiled segments similar to pachytene chromomeres?

The problem of the basic building blocks of the chromosomes is connected with the question of how clear-cut the differentiation of Q-bright and Q-dark bands is. The activity of the genes in the Q-dark regions is under extensive study. On the other hand, almost nothing is known about the possible function or effects of the Q-bright bands. Not even a satisfactory hypothesis exists on the role of the nontranscribed DNA, which constitutes some 95% of the human genome.

References

Ambros PF, Sumner AT (1987) Correlation of pachytene chromomeres and metaphase bands of human chromosomes, and distinctive properties of telomeric regions. Cytogenet Cell Genet 44:223–228

Bickmore WA, Sumner AT (1989) Mammalian chromosome banding—an expression of genome organization. Trends Genet 5:144–148

Drets ME, Folle GA, Monteverde FJ (1990) Quantitative detection of chromosome structures by computerized microphotometric scanning. In: Obe G, Natarajan AT (eds) Chromosomal aberrations: basic and applied aspects. Springer, Berlin, pp 1–12

Evans HJ (1977) Some facts and fancies relating to chromosome structure in man. In: Harris H, Hirschhorn K (eds) Advances in human genetics, Vol 8. Plenum, New York, pp 347–438

Goldman MA, Holmquist GP, Gray MC, et al. (1984) Replication timing of genes and middle repetitive sequences. Science 224:686–692

Hagemeijer A, Smit EME (1977) Partial trisomy 21. Further evidence that trisomy of band 21q22 is essential for Down's phenotype. Hum Genet 38:15–23

Holmquist GP (1989) Evolution of chromosome bands: molecular ecology of noncoding DNA. J Mol Evol 28:469–486

The Human Genome (1990) J NIH Res USA 2:133–160

John B (1988) The biology of heterochromatin. In: Verma RS (ed) Heterochromatin: molecular and structural aspects. Cambridge University, Cambridge pp 1–147

Korenberg JR, Engels WR (1978) Base ratio, DNA content, and quinacrine-brightness of human chromosomes. Proc Natl Acad Sci USA 75:3382–3386

Korenberg JR, Rykowski MC (1988) Human genome organization: Alu, Lines, and the molecular structure of metaphase chromosome bands. Cell 53:391–400

Korenberg JR, Therman E, Denniston C (1978) Hot spots and functional organization of human chromosomes. Hum Genet 43:13–22

Korenberg JR, Kawashima H, Pulst SM, et al. (1990) Molecular definition of a region of chromosome 21 that causes features of the Down syndrome phenotype. Am J Hum Genet 47:236–246

Kuhn EM (1976) Localization by Q-banding of mitotic chiasmata in cases of Bloom's syndrome. Chromosoma 57:1–11

Kuhn EM, Therman E, Denniston C (1985) Mitotic chiasmata, gene density and oncogenes. Hum Genet 70:1–5

Kuhn EM, Sarto GE, Bates B-J G, et al. (1987) Gene-rich chromosome regions and autosomal trisomy. A case of chromosome 3 trisomy mosaicism. Hum Genet 77:214–220

New Haven Human Gene Mapping Library: Chromosome Plots (1989) Howard Hughes Medical Institute and Yale University, New Haven

Pihko H, Therman E, Uchida IA (1981) Partial 11q trisomy syndrome. Hum Genet 58:129–134

Ris H, Korenberg JR (1979) Chromosome structure and levels of chromosome organization. In: Goldstein L, Prescott DM (eds) Cell biology, Vol 2. Academic, New York, pp 268–361

Sumner AT (1986) Mechanisms of quinacrine binding and fluorescence in nuclei and chromosomes. Histochemistry 84:566–574

Sumner AT (1990) Chromosome banding. Unwin Hyman, London

Weisblum B (1973) Fluorescent probes of chromosomal DNA structure: three classes of acridines. Cold Spring Harbor Symp Quant Biol 38:441–449

Weisblum B, de Haseth PL (1972) Quinacrine, a chromosome stain specific for deoxyadenylate-deoxythymidylate-rich regions in DNA. Proc Natl Acad Sci USA 69:629–632

Willard HF (1977) Tissue-specific heterogeneity in DNA replication patterns of human X chromosomes. Chromosoma 61:61–73

Yunis JJ (1965) Interphase deoxyribonucleic acid condensation, late deoxyribonucleic acid replication, and gene inactivation. Nature 205:311–312

Yunis JJ, Prakash O (1982) The origin of man: A chromosomal pictorial legacy. Science 215:1525–1530

8
Architecture and Function of the Eukaryotic Chromosome

Chromosome Architecture

Viewed from a molecular perspective, the eukaryotic chromosome is an immense structure. Viewed from a physiological perspective, it is not one structure at all, but a family of related structures, differing from one another in form and activity. Even a single chromosome has pronounced structural variation along its length and is changeable from one moment to the next. These factors make the chromosome a difficult object to study, and our understanding of the details of its structure and function remains incomplete. However, in recent years the analytical methods of molecular biology and the discovery of model systems in which to study chromosome function have greatly expanded our understanding of the eukaryotic chromosome. The results have been reviewed in numerous books and articles (for example, Alberts et al., 1983, 1989; Darnell et al., 1990; Jeppesen and Bower, 1987).

Microscopists of the late 19th century observed that material in the nucleus of cells avidly took up certain dyes, and they called this material *chromatin*, which is the name still used for the material of which chromosomes are made. Chromatin is a complex of DNA, some RNA, and a variety of proteins, mainly histones. The entire genome of a haploid human cell contains approximately a meter of DNA; thus, an average chromosome contains about 5 cm of DNA. An average chromatid in a human cell is approximately 5μm long and contains a single continuous DNA double helix. One of the main questions concerning chromosome structure is how a 5 cm-long strand is packaged into a 5μm-long chromatid (Belmont et al., 1990; Klug, 1985; Williams et al., 1986; Woodcock et al., 1991a, b).

At the first level of packaging, the DNA is wound around a protein disk consisting of histones H2A, H2B, H3, and H4. These proteins—especially H3 and H4—display a remarkable similarity of structure throughout all eukaryotes. This evolutionary conservation of structure presumably is related to their crucial importance in the architecture of the chromosome. In view of the structural conservation of the histone proteins, it is interesting to note that the genes encoding the histones show great variability in organization and regulation (Maxson et al., 1983).

Figure 8.1 roughly illustrates current ideas on chromosome structure. The DNA-wound histone disks are called *nucleosomes*. The disk itself is a sandwich, the center consisting of two molecules of H3 and two of H4, with each of the faces consisting of an H2A-H2B complex. The DNA is wound twice around this histone octamer to form a *nucleosome core*. The two coils of DNA containing 146 base pairs (bp) are thus compacted into a length of 5.7 nanometers (nm), which is the thickness of the histone disk. This amounts to about a ninefold compaction of the chromosomal DNA. Running between the successive nucleosome cores are DNA *linkers* of 20–100 nucleotide pairs (Fig. 8.1, second from top). The linker length varies depending on the tissue from which the chromatin is extracted. A nucleosome thus consists of the core and the linker, and the DNA involved in it contains 200 bp (Kornberg and Klug, 1981). When chromatin is unraveled, the chromosome strands appear in electron micrographs as strings of 11-nm disk-like beads (Fig. 8.1).

At the next level of folding, single molecules of histone 1 (H1) attach to the nucleosomes at the position of the linkers, thus bringing together successive nucleosome cores and twisting them into a 30-nm strand in which another sixfold DNA compaction is accomplished. The exact structure of the 30-nm strand remains to be determined (Dimitrov et al., 1990). One possibility is that the strand is a "solenoid"—a simple helical coil of successive nucleosome cores arranged so that each left-handed turn contains about six nucleosome disks. However, the size and complexity of chromatin, even at this level of structure, make it difficult to choose between the solenoid model and other, more elaborate helices known as "twisted ribbon" and "crossed-linker" structures (Dimitrov et al., 1990).

In vitro chromatin assembly has been accomplished in systems that include DNA, histone, and various accessory proteins. It is not enough simply to mix DNA and histones, because that results in a precipitate lacking normal nucleosomal structure. However, the addition of nucleoplasmin, a protein isolated from the oocytes of *Xenopus laevis* (the African clawed toad), potentiates the formation of typical nucleosomal structure. (For a concise review, see Svaren and Chalkley, 1990.)

The formation of the 30-nm strand shortens the DNA double helix 40–50 times. The compactness of a metaphase chromosome can be achieved only by shortening the 30-nm fiber another 250-fold or so. It appears that

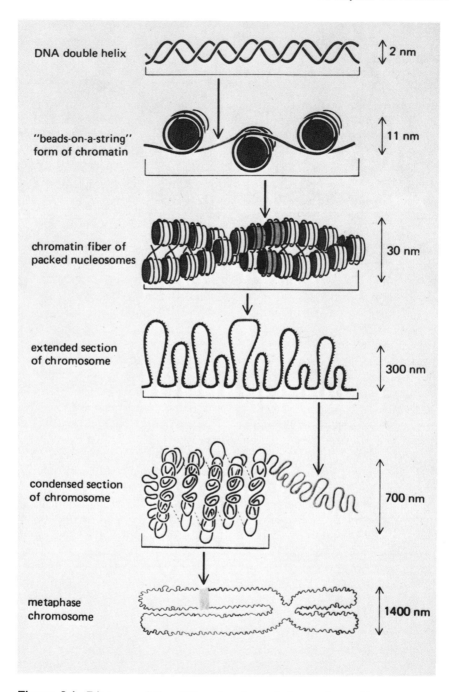

Figure 8.1. Diagram of the different orders of chromatin packing assumed to give rise to a metaphase chromosome. (From Figure 8-24 of Alberts et al., Molecular Biology of the Cell, 1983.)

the next order of packing involves the twisting of the 30-nm structure into a thicker fiber 130–300 nm in diameter. The structure of this thick, contorted fiber is not yet fully understood (Belmont et al., 1990). However, it does appear that these thick fibers are formed into loops, called *domains*, by nonhistone proteins that tie together the segments at either end of each loop. Within the domain, the 130- to 300-nm fiber is folded or twisted or crumpled into a fairly compact lump on the surface of the metaphase chromosome. A domain may contain one or more transcriptional units (i.e., genes). It may be that the 300-nm strand forms a chromatid spiral that sometimes is visible in the light microscope (Fig. 2.1). Apparently, the spiral is tighter in some regions than in others; this may reflect different types of bands, for instance C-bands, in the metaphase chromosome.

When a chromosome is extended, as during the meiotic prophase stages leptotene, zygotene, and pachytene (Fig. 17.3), it appears to consist of different-sized condensed *chromomeres* and less condensed regions between them. Presumably the chromomeres represent folded groups of looped domains (Ris and Korenberg, 1979).

The Chromosome Scaffold

The histones can be removed from metaphase chromosomes under conditions that do not remove the nonhistone proteins. The result is remarkable. The DNA spreads out from the chromosome to form a gossamer halo (Fig. 8.2). At the center is a denser area, a network of heavier fibers that contains the bulk of the nonhistone proteins associated with the chromosome. Evidently, when the domains are stripped of their histones and the loops of DNA are allowed to open out, there remains a *core* or *scaffold* that has nearly the size and structure of the original metaphase chromosome. A major protein component of this core is the enzyme topoisomerase II (gyrase), which can catalyze the passage of one double-stranded DNA molecule through another. It can thus link and unlink circles of DNA. It can also decrease or increase the amount of supercoiling within a single twisted DNA molecule. Whether the topoisomerase in the DNA scaffold plays an important enzymatic role or is simply a DNA-binding molecule that has been put to use as a structural element remains to be seen. Treatment of histone-depleted chromosomes with fluorescent antibody against topoisomerase II results in bright staining of the chromosomal scaffold (Earnshaw and Heck, 1985).

In addition to topoisomerase II, at least two other proteins are found in abundance in the chromosome scaffold, Sc 1 and Sc 2 (Gasser and Laemmli, 1987; Jeppesen and Bower, 1987). These proteins seem to bind to specific sequences, scaffold-associated regions (SARs), on the chromosomal DNA. This binding might be involved not only in the architecture of the chromosome, but also in the regulation of gene function (Gasser and Laemmli, 1987; Grunstein, 1990).

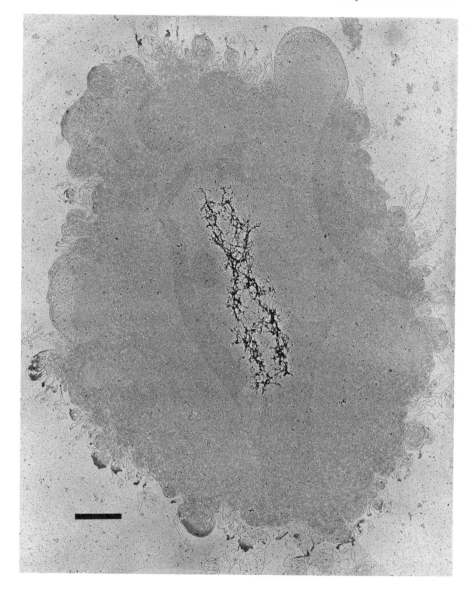

Figure 8.2. Histone-depleted metaphase chromosome showing a portion of the fibrillar halo of DNA surrounding the chromosome and the chromosome-shaped scaffold at the center, bar = $2\,\mu$m. (From Figure 1 of Paulson and Laemmli, 1977, Cell 12: p 819. Copyright 1977 M.I.T.).

Architecture as Related to Regulation of Gene Function

Active regions of the chromosome—regions in which genes are being transcribed—differ structurally from inactive regions. It has been known for a long time that the DNA in active regions is more sensitive to digestion by DNaseI than is the DNA in inactive regions (for review, see Eissenberg et al., 1985). This accessibility to endonucleolytic attack is believed to result from the unfolding of active (or potentially active) DNA. Presumably the DNA loops in active (or inducible) domains are opened out to make them available to RNA polymerases, to regulatory proteins, and, consequently, to DNase I. The DNase I-sensitive regions are not naked DNA. It appears that histone-associated DNA can be activated by *trans*-acting regulatory proteins and transcribed by RNA polymerase. However, histones do play a role in repressing the activity of DNA. *Trans*-acting regulatory proteins cannot bind to target DNA sequences that are wrapped into nucleosomal structures. The activation of genes may depend on the interaction of regulatory proteins with DNA immediately after DNA synthesis, in the short interval between replication of the target site and histone binding. Factors that may influence gene activation include methylation of the DNA, enzymatic modification of histones, tissue-specific domain-activating proteins, and tissue-specific factors that affect the order of replication of domains. (For brief reviews, see Svaren and Chalkley, 1990; Grunstein, 1990.)

Our understanding of the relationship between structure and function of eukaryotic chromosomes has been greatly advanced through studies on specialized chromosome types in which certain architectural features are enormously magnified and therefore amenable to analysis. One example is the *lampbrush chromosome* (Fig. 8.3) found in the growing oocytes of a variety of vertebrates and invertebrates and even in the primary nucleus of the green alga *Acetabularia* (Scheer et al., 1979). The most intensively studied lampbrush chromosomes are those found in the giant oocytes of amphibia.

Lampbrush chromosomes represent a special type of diplotene chromosome. The bivalents are enormously elongated, and pairs of DNA loops extend from the chromomeres, giving the chromosomes their lampbrush appearance. In cross section such a chromosome is star-like, with loops projecting from a dense chromomere core (Scheer et al., 1979).

Transcriptional activity in the loops of lampbrush loops is unusually intense. A very large fraction of the total DNA in the loop is transcribed, and the transcripts produced are longer than normal. As a result the loops are covered with RNA fibrils, which make them thick and therefore visible in a phase contrast microscope (Fig. 8.3). The RNA fibrils are attached to the loop axis via RNA polymerase-containing granules, and the lengths of the fibrils form continuous gradients from the starting point

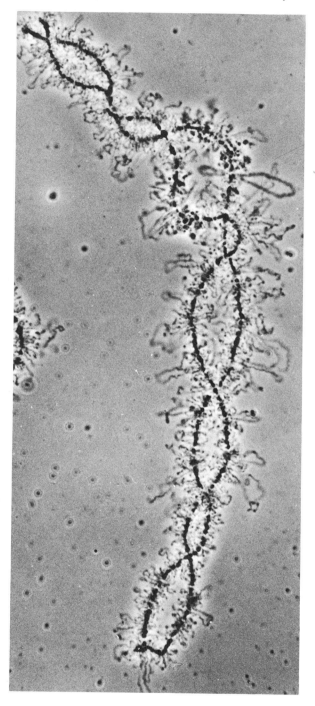

Figure 8.3. The appearance of a lampbrush chromosome bivalent from an oocyte of the salamander *Pleurodeles waltlii* (phase contrast), ×800 (courtesy of U. Scheer).

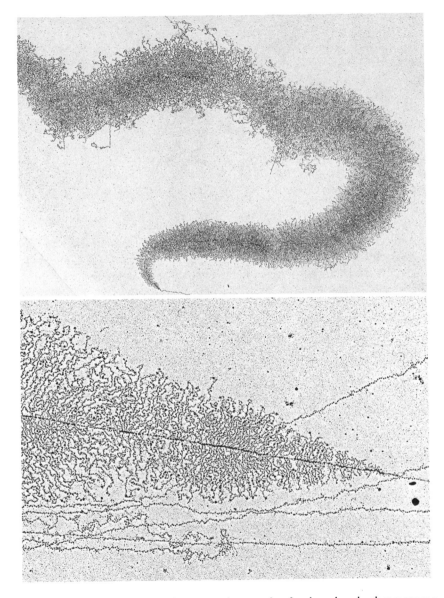

Figure 8.4. Top: low-power electron micrograph of a lampbrush chromosome from *Pleurodeles waltlii*. The central axis is covered with nascent RNA fibrils; the short, naked tail at the bottom is the start of the transcription unit, ×5,000 (courtesy of U. Scheer). Bottom: same preparation as in the above micrograph, showing the start region of a transcribed unit. Densely packed RNA polymerase granules are clearly visible on the central axis. The strands not covered with fibrils represent transcriptionally inactive chromatin showing nucleosomes as little dots, ×20,000 (courtesy of U. Scheer).

of the transcription (Fig. 8.4). A loop may contain one or more transcriptional units.

At the loops involved in synthesis of ribosomal RNA, DNA rings—apparently copies of the loops—are synthesized and extruded into the nucleoplasm. They replicate extrachromosomally through a rolling circle mechanism. In the nucleoplasm the rings form additional nucleoli that may number 200–300 in an amphibian oocyte. In human diplotene oocytes, some 20–30 extra nucleoli are found (Stahl et al., 1975). These processes reflect an enormous amplification of the ribosomal RNA genes to meet the protein-synthesizing needs of the oocyte and ultimately of the growing embryo.

Telomeres

Normal chromosome ends are capped by so-called *telomeres*. These play an important role in chromosome behavior. For example, telomeres prevent normal chromosome ends from joining each other, whereas broken ends lacking telomeres often tend to fuse or recombine. In interphase, telomeres are usually attached to the nuclear envelope, a phenomenon clearly visible during the meiotic bouquet stage (Fig. 17.2). This association with the nuclear envelope may affect both function and segregation of chromosomes.

Our understanding of the molecular structure and function of telomeres has advanced rapidly in the past few years, especially as a result of studies in one-celled eukaryotes such as ciliates and yeasts (Hastie and Allshire, 1989; Zakian, 1989; Blackburn, 1991). Many features in telomere structure have been conserved through eukaryotic evolution. Consequently, it has been possible to transfer telomeres from cells in which study of their molecular properties is relatively difficult—human cells, for example—into cells of simple organisms in which such studies are relatively easy.

Telomeres consist of short nucleotide sequences repeated several hundred times (in yeast) to several thousand times (in vertebrates). In human chromosomes the sequence is TTAGGG (Moyzis et al., 1988) repeated over and over to give a stretch of DNA around 10 kilobase (kb) pairs long at the end of each chromosome. This sequence, the *G-rich strand*, is oriented 5′ to 3′ toward the end of the chromosome (Hastie and Allshire, 1989). The complementary strand, the C-rich strand, ends somewhat short of the G-rich strand so that the latter forms a single-stranded tail at the end of the chromosome. Since DNA synthesis proceeds only in the 5′ to 3′ direction and depends on the presence of a short primer to provide a free 3′-OH group, it might be expected that DNA synthesis at the very end of the chromosome would break down. And it does. Apparently normal chromosome duplication leads to progressive shortening of telomeres until, after a number of cell divisions, the chromosomes become unstable and the cell dies.

Telomeres are maintained in yeast and other organisms by an RNA-containing enzyme called *telomerase*, which can add new repeat units to the 3'-end of the G-rich strand. The enzyme is a reverse transcriptase, synthesizing DNA from an RNA template, in this case the RNA oligonucleotide that is an intrinsic part of the enzyme. The enzyme uses the end of the G-rich strand as its primer, thus replacing the DNA repeat units that are lost during chromosome replication. Cells with defective telomerase suffer progressive shortening of their chromosomes, senesce, and die. Interestingly, human telomerase activity seems to be high in immortal cancer cells (HeLa cells) but low in somatic tissues. It has been hypothesized, therefore, that telomere instability may contribute to aging.

Telomerase is not the only protein that interacts specifically with telomeres (Zakian, 1989). The ends of chromosomes appear to be protected from exonucleases by a protein that binds specifically to the single-stranded tail of the telomere. Other telomere-specific proteins appear to bind to the interior region of the telomere. It is possible that these specialized proteins play a role in the association of telomeres with each other and with the nuclear envelope.

A long-standing question is: Can a broken chromosome "heal" or is a "real" telomere needed to cap an end? On the basis of chromosome behavior, it appears that the answer may depend on which species is being studied. In plants, for example, broken ends of chromosomes tend to fuse. In humans, it appears that broken ends may often heal (Patau, 1965). In the ciliate, *Tetrahymena*, chromosome fragmentation occurs developmentally, and the ends of the fragments are stable. In some cases, there is good evidence that the stabilization of broken ends results from synthesis of new telomeres. This is true, for example, in *Tetrahymena* (Blackburn, 1991). Evidence in human cells is limited, but, in at least one case it was shown that a chromosome 16 terminal deletion was stabilized by the formation of a normal telomere at the point of breakage (Wilkie et al., 1990).

Centromeres and Kinetochores

Biologists generally use the words "centromere" and "kinetochore" interchangeably, but, for clarity of communication, we shall use the terms here as recommended by Brinkley (1990): *centromere* will be used to refer to the DNA at the position of the spindle-fiber attachment, and *kinetochore* to refer to the complex proteinaceous structure associated with the centromere. The microtubules of the spindle fibers attach to the kinetochores.

The centromeres of the budding yeast, *Saccharomyces cerevisiae*, have been cloned and sequenced (see Chapter 5). The elucidation of the structure of the yeast centromere has been possible because there is a simple functional test for the presence of the CEN sequence: autonomously replicating DNA molecules segregate like normal chromosomes if they contain a CEN sequence, but they are easily lost during cell division if they do not. This means that a CEN sequence in *Saccharomyces* can be selected as easily as a drug-resistance marker. The CEN sequences are less than 200 bp long. Although the centromeres of the various chromosomes differ from one another in sequence, they share three highly conserved elements that are indispensable for normal mitotic behavior (Clarke and Carbon, 1985). These are a stretch of about 80 bp with a very high A + T content, flanked on one side by an 8 bp element with the consensus sequence PuTCACPuTG, and on the other by an element about 25 bp long that contains inverted repeat sequences.

Mammalian centromeres are thousands of times larger than those of *Saccharomyces* and, therefore, much more difficult to study. However, the DNA in the region of the centromere is simple-sequence DNA that forms a satellite (called α satellite in DNA from humans and other primates) in density gradient centrifugation. Thus, it has been possible to isolate and analyze DNA that appears to be authentic centromeric DNA. This satellite DNA serves as a molecular probe for centromeric sequences in intact chromosomes.

Tools for studying kinetochore structure have been provided by antibodies from patients with the auto-immune disease called scleroderma CREST. These are specific for several kinetochore proteins. Consequently, fluorescent scleroderma CREST antibodies will "light up" the centromeric regions of both metaphase and interphase chromosomes. Through the use of these antibodies and of α satellite DNA as probes for kinetochore and centromere structures, the molecular biology of chromosome segregation in mammals is beginning to be understood in considerable detail (Brinkley, 1990; Willard, 1990).

Centromeric DNA in human chromosomes is made up of long tandem repeats of a basic monomeric sequence that is approximately 170 bp long. The total length of the centromeric DNA varies from chromosome to chromosome, but all centromeres are very large, ranging from about 300 to 5000 kbp. Thus the 170-bp sequence is repeated over and over some 1700 to 29,000 times to make a centromere. The nucleotide sequence of the 170 bp monomer varies between chromosomes and within chromosomes. Several lines of evidence suggest that the α satellite DNA constitutes the centromere. First, in situ hybridization with DNA complementary to α satellite shows that α satellite DNA is located exclusively at the primary constrictions of the chromosomes. Second, the 170 bp monomer contains a 17 bp "box" which is a specific binding site for the kinetochore structural protein, CENP-B (which stands for *cen*tromeric *p*rotein *B*). The amount of CENP-B protein bound at the primary constriction of the chromosome is reduced when the amount of α satellite DNA is reduced.

The CENP proteins recognized by scleroderma CREST auto-antibodies identify three proteins associated with centromeric DNA:

1. CENP-A appears to be a histone located exclusively in the region of the centromere.
2. CENP-B appears to bind to microtubule-associated protein (MAP), which in turn binds to the microtubules of the spindle.
3. CENP-C is, in a way not yet understood, diagnostic of the presence of an active kinetochore. In a dicentric chromosome, one centromere must be inactivated or the chromosome will be torn apart at cell division. Auto-antibody probes of dicentric chromosomes show that CENP-B is associated with both the active and the inactive centromeres, whereas CENP-C is associated only with the active centromere (Earnshaw et al., 1989).

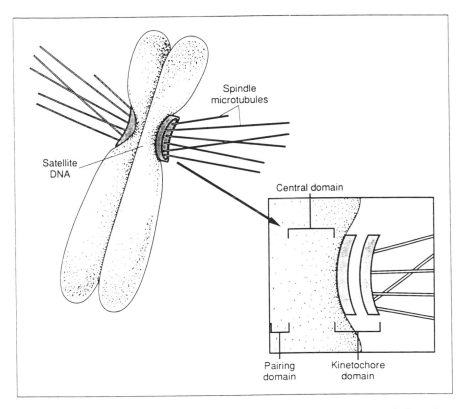

Figure 8.5. A diagram of a chromosome showing the primary constriction, the kinetochore, and the attached spindle fibers. The inset is a sketch of the kinetochore as it appears in an electron micrograph. The labels show the standard terminology for the regions of the kinetochore and centromere (Willard, 1990).

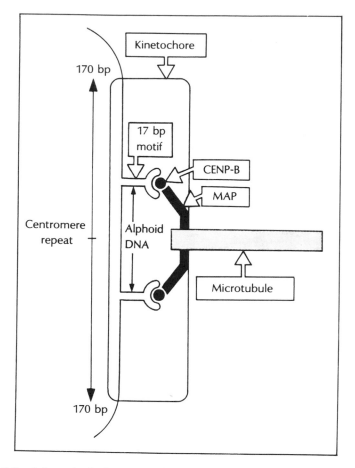

Figure 8.6. A hypothetical structure for one subunit of a kinetochore. This shows the 170-bp repeats of α satellite DNA, the association of CENP-B protein with the 17-bp "box" to which it binds, and the attachment of a microtubule to the kinetochore subunit. According to the subunit model of the kinetochore, the kinetochore plate is a fusion of many of these elementary subunits (Brinkley, 1990).

Auto-antibodies also identify a centromere-associated protein that is found only in cells undergoing mitosis (Hadlaczky et al., 1989).

Other antibodies interact with kinetochores. These include antibodies specific for tubulin, the monomer from which microtubules are assembled, and, for cytoplasmic dynein, an ATPase that provides the motive force for moving materials along microtubules in cells.

Under the electron microscope, the kinetochore appears to be a three-layered plate or disk resting on the surface of the chromatid at the primary constriction (Fig. 8.5). Recent studies (Zinkowski et al., 1991) show that this plate or disk is probably made up of a number of subunits. Cells cultured in the presence of hydroxyurea are unable to synthesize chromosomal DNA. This leads to the accumulation of cells blocked at the transition from G_1 to S phase. When caffeine is added to these cells, they are stimulated to undergo mitosis, despite the fact that the chromosomes have not replicated, and the result is that the chromosomes fall to pieces. Most of the chromatin drifts aimlessly into the cytoplasm. The kineto-chores break up into fragments that behave in an extraordinary way; they line up on the metaphase plate, form attachments to the spindle fibers, and migrate to the spindle poles just as if they were still intact and attached to the chromosomes. It appears, therefore, that kinetochores can be divided into subunits that retain the essential functions of the intact structure. They form attachments to the spindle fibers, and they contain the cytoplasmic dynein that seems to be the "motor" propelling kinetochores and their attached chromosomes to the division poles.

This subunit structure of kinetochores can also be seen when chromosomes are stretched by hypotonic swelling or by mechanical means. Upon stretching, the kinetochores break up into smaller units that look like beads on a string. As the chromosome is stretched more and more, the beads become more numerous and smaller. This suggests that the kineto-chore may not be a single plate-like structure, but may in fact be produced by the fusion of proteinaceous subunits that form on the tandem DNA repeats of the centromere. A hypothetical structure of one "bead" is shown in Figure 8.6. Zinkowski et al. (1991) propose that this basic subunit structure can be arranged in different ways in different eukaryotes to account for the "ball and cup" appearance of the kinetochore in many higher plants and the "holocentric" (diffuse) kinetochores of some roundworms, insects, and monocotyledonous plants.

Relationship between Chromosome Architecture and Nuclear Architecture

The arrangement of chromosomes within the nucleus is not random. Chromosomes seem to occupy relatively separate domains within the interphase nucleus. (The word "domain" is used here to mean a discrete three-dimensional compartment—a distinctly different meaning from that attached to the word earlier in this chapter.) In interphase nuclei, chromosomes and parts of chromosomes may show specific associations that may differ from one cell type to another. For example, heterochromatic regions tend to cluster together in interphase nuclei. In some cells, but not most, homologous chromosomes lie close together. Centromeres and telomeres show specific associations with one another and with the nuclear envelope. The arrangement of chromosomes within the nucleus is likely to affect gene expression, DNA replication, and chromosome movement (Haaf and Schmid, 1991; Pardue and Hennig, 1990).

It has also been suggested that the chromosomes play an active role in organizing the spindle and other structures needed for mitosis and cyto- kinesis (Earnshaw and Bernat, 1991). Some proteins that are associated with the chromosomes—and especially with the centromeric region— during mitotic prophase are later found attached to spindle fibers. Other proteins move from the chromosome and become concentrated in a band under the cell membrane in the region where the cleavage furrow will appear. It is suggested that these proteins may be "passengers" on the chromosomes, which convey the proteins to the locations in the cell where they must perform their roles in cell division.

The availability of new methods for identifying specific DNA sequences, DNA-binding proteins, and gene transcripts within the nucleus should make it possible to resolve the functional compartments of the nucleus and to analyze the mechanisms by which compartmentalization is accomplished.

References

Alberts B, Bray D, Lewis J, et al. (1983) Molecular biology of the cell. Garland, New York

Alberts B, Bray D, Lewis J, et al. (1989) Molecular biology of the cell, 2nd edn. Garland, New York

Belmont AS, Braunfeld MB, Sedat JW, et al. (1990) Large-scale chromatin structural domains within mitotic and interphase chromosomes in vivo and in vitro. Chromosoma 98:129–143

Blackburn EH (1991) Structure and function of telomeres. Nature 350:569–73

Brinkley BR (1990) Centromeres and kinetochores: Integrated domains on eukaryotic chromosomes. Curr Opin Cell Biol 2:446–452

Clarke L, Carbon J (1985) The structure and function of yeast centromeres. Annu Rev Genet 19:29–56

Darnell J, Lodish H, Baltimore D (1990) Molecular cell biology, 2nd edn. Scien- tific American Books, Freeman, New York

Dimitrov SI, Makarov VL, Pashev IG (1990) The chromatin fiber: Structure and conformational transitions as revealed by optical anisotropy studies. J Biomol Struct Dynamics 8:23–35

Earnshaw WC, Bernat RL (1991) Chromosomal passengers: toward an integrated view of mitosis. Chromosoma 100:139–146

Earnshaw WC, Heck MMS (1985) Localization of topoisomerase II in mitotic chromosomes. J Cell Biol 100:1716–1725

Earnshaw WC, Ratrie H, Stetten G (1989) Visualization of centromere proteins CENP-B and CENP-C on a stable dicentric chromosome in cytological spreads. Chromosoma 98:1–12

Eissenberg JC, Cartwright IL, Thomas GH, et al. (1985) Selected topics in chromatin structure. Annu Rev Genet 19:485–536

Gasser SM, Laemmli UK (1987) A glimpse at chromosomal order. Trends Genet 3:16–22

Grunstein M (1990) Nucleosomes: regulators of transcription. Trends Genet 6: 395–400

Haaf T, Schmid M (1991) Chromosome topology in mammalian interphase nuclei. Exp Cell Res 192:325–332

Hadlaczky G, Praznovszky T, Rasko I, et al. (1989) I. Mitosis specific centromere antigen recognized by anit-centromere autoantibodies. Chromosoma 97:282–288

Hastie ND, Allshire RC (1989) Human telomeres: fusion and interstitial sites. Trends Genet 5:326–331

Jeppesen P, Bower DJ (1987) Towards understanding the structure of eukaryotic chromosomes. In: Obe G, Basler A (eds) Cytogenetics. Springer, Berlin/Heidelberg, pp 1–29

Klug A (1985) The higher order structure of chromatin. Proc Robert A Welch Found Conf Chem Res 29:133–160

Kornberg RD, Klug A (1981) The nucleosome. Sci Am 244:52–64

Maxson R, Cohn R, Kedes L, et al. (1983) Expression and organization of histone genes. Annu Rev Genet 17:239–277

Moyzis RK, Buckingham JM, Cram LS, et al. (1988) A highly conserved repetitive DNA sequence, TTAGGG$_n$, present at the telomeres of human chromosomes. Proc Natl Acad Sci USA 85:6622–6626

Pardue ML, Hennig W (1990) Heterochromatin: Junk or collectors item? Chromosoma 100:3–7

Patau K (1965) The chromosomes. In: Birth defects: original article series, I. New York: The National Foundation, pp 71–74

Paulson JR, Laemmli UK (1977) The structure of histone-depleted metaphase chromosomes. Cell 12:817–828

Ris H, Korenberg JR (1979) Chromosome structure and levels of chromosome organization. In: Goldstein L, Prescott DM (eds) Cell biology, Vol 2. Academic, New York, pp 268–361

Scheer U, Spring H, Trendelenburg MF (1979) Organization of transcriptionally active chromatin in lampbrush chromosome loops. In: Busch H (ed) The cell nucleus, Vol 7. Academic, New York, pp 3–47

Stahl A, Luciani JU, Devictor U, et al. (1975) Constitutive heterochromatin and micronucleoli in the human oocyte at the diplotene stage. Humangenetik 26: 315–327

Svaren J, Chalkley R (1990) The structure and assembly of active chromatin. Trends Genet 6:52–56

Wilkie AOM, Lamb J, Harris PC, et al. (1990) A truncated human chromosome 16 with α thalassaemia is stabilized by addition of telomeric repeat (TTAGGG)$_n$. Nature 346:868–871

Willard HF (1990) Centromeres of mammalian chromosomes. Trends Genet 6:410–416

Williams SP, Athey BD, Muglia LJ, et al. (1986) Chromatin fibers are left-handed double helices with a diameter and mass per unit length that depend on linker length. Biophys J 49:233–248

Woodcock CL, Woodcock H, Horowitz RA (1991 a) Ultrastructure of chromatin: I. Negative staining of isolated fibers. J Cell Sci 99:99–106

Woodcock CL, McEwen BF, Frank J (1991 b) Ultrastructure of chromatin: II. Three-dimensional reconstruction of isolated fibers. J Cell Sci 99:107–114

Zakian VA (1989) Structure and function of telomeres. Annu Rev Genet 23:579–604

Zinkowski RP, Meyne J, Brinkley BR (1991) The centromere-kinetochore complex: a repeat subunit model. J Cell Biol 113:1091–1110

9
Chromosome Structural Aberrations

Origin of Structurally Abnormal Chromosomes

Chromosome breaks sometimes occur spontaneously, or they may be induced by a mutagenic agent such as ionizing radiation or DNA-damaging chemicals. Unlike normal chromosome ends, broken ends tend to join together. Usually the broken ends rejoin; in other words, the break heals. However, a break may lead to a deletion or, if more than one break has occurred in a cell, to structural rearrangements of chromosomes.

Chromosomes may break at any stage of the cell cycle—G_1, S, G_2—during mitosis, or during meiosis. Various cell types and stages show very different responses to chromosome-breaking agents even in the same organism. Thus, in *Vicia*, a dose of x-rays that induces one aberration visible at metaphase per 10 cells when irradiation is given in G_1 will produce approximately one aberration per cell if given in G_2 (Evans, 1974). Even greater differences are found when different plant and animal species are compared. In different species of higher plants, the doses of radiation needed to inhibit growth or to cause death were found to vary more than 100-fold (Sparrow, 1965).

The study of chromosome breaks is intimately connected with research on gene mutations, because most mutagens induce both chromosome breaks and gene mutations. Often the same agents are also carcinogenic. We know that the radiations and drugs used in cancer therapy can also cause malignant disease. Various aspects of chromosome breakage are reviewed in numerous books and articles, of which the following reflect a somewhat arbitrary sample: Kihlman, 1966; Rieger and Michaelis, 1967; Gebhart, 1970; Evans, 1962, 1974, 1983; Auerbach, 1976, 1978; Mendelsohn and Albertini, 1990.

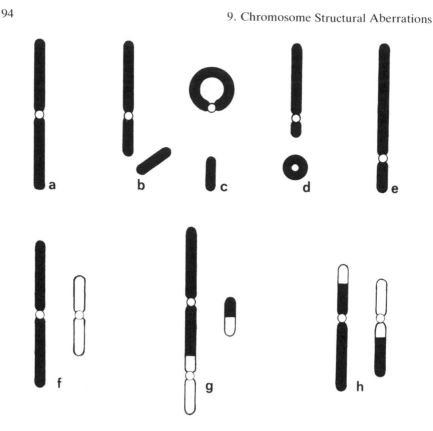

Figure 9.1. Results of G_1 breaks in one chromosome (a), and in two chromosomes (f); (b) broken chromosome; (c) centric ring and acentric fragment; (d) acentric ring and centric fragment; (e) chromosome with pericentric inversion; (g) dicentric chromosome and acentric fragment; (h) balanced reciprocal translocation.

Chromosome Breaks and Rearrangements

If a chromosome breaks during the G_1 stage, when it consists of only one chromatid, the break may be perpetuated in S and affect *both* chromatids in the following metaphase. If a single break does not rejoin, the result will be a deleted chromosome and an acentric fragment (Fig. 9.1b) that may be lost in a subsequent mitosis. Alternatively, the acentric fragment may be included in a daughter nucleus and replicate, so that there will be double fragments in the next metaphase.

Two breaks in the same chromosome may result in the formation of either a centric ring and an acentric fragment or an acentric ring and an interstitial deletion (Figs. 9.1c and d, and Fig. 9.2g). A segment that is deleted interstitially from a chromosome arm may remain as an acentric fragment if its ends fail to join. Very small fragments are called *minutes*.

If the breaks take place in the same arm, another possible result of a two-break intrachange is a *paracentric* inversion, in which the deleted segment rejoins the chromosome in an inverted position. If one break occurs in each arm, a *pericentric* inversion will be formed if the deleted segment rejoins in an inverted position (Figs. 9.1e and 9.2c). The latter

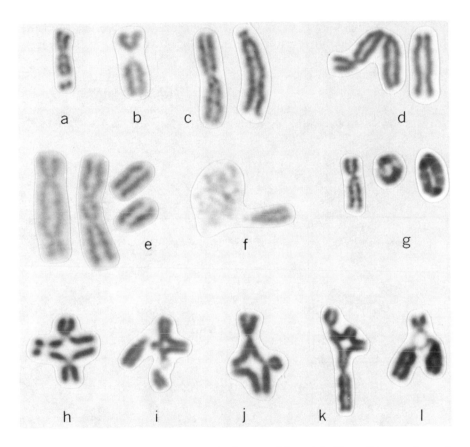

Figure 9.2. Chromosome structural abnormalities. (a) Gap; (b) gap through centromere; (c) normal chromosome 1 and its homologue with a pericentric inversion; (d) dicentric chromosome and acentric fragment; (e) two dicentrics and two acentrics from the same cell (courtesy of EM Kuhn); (f) an interphasic D chromosome in satellite association with a normal D; (g) chromosome 9, ring(9), and double ring(9) (courtesy of ML Motl); (h) mitotic chiasma between hetero-morphic homologues; (i) class II quadriradial between two D chromosomes in satellite association with a D and a G; (j–k) class IVb chromatid translocations; (l) hexaradial chromatid translocation, or a satellite association between two D chromosomes and a G.

rearrangement often shifts the position of the centromere. Many pericentric inversions and all paracentric inversions would be undetectable without banding techniques.

Naturally the first prerequisite for an interchange between two chromosomes is a break in each of them. For the broken ends to fuse, they should not be too far from each other. The period during which broken ends are able to join seems to be limited. An interchange may result in a reciprocal translocation (Fig. 9.1h) or a dicentric chromosome and an acentric fragment (Figs. 9.1g and 9.2d and e). The latter rearrangement is not stable, because the acentric fragment will eventually be lost, and the dicentric will encounter difficulties if the two centromeres are far enough apart for a twist to occur between them.

Multiple breaks in a cell may lead to several reciprocal translocations or other more complicated rearrangements, such as chromosomes with several centromeres. Chromosomes with more than one functional centromere rarely survive more than one mitosis.

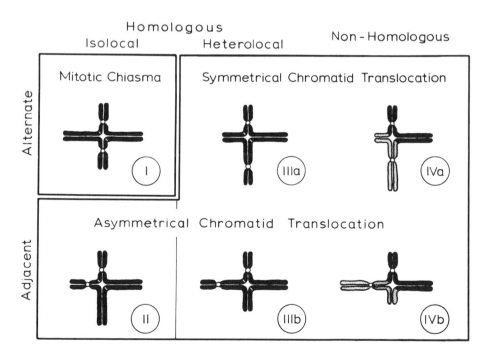

Figure 9.3. The classification of quadriradial configurations (Therman and Kuhn, 1976). In mitotic chiasmata and their adjacent counterparts, the breaks are at homologous points (isolocal); in the other quadriradials, whether homologous or nonhomologous, at nonhomologous points (heterolocal).

Chromatid Breaks and Rearrangements

When a break takes place during G_2, it ordinarily involves only one of the two chromatids. A single break yields a deleted chromatid and an acentric fragment.

Some of the possible consequences of a chromatid break in two chromosomes are shown in Fig. 9.2 i–k. Such configurations, which result from chromatid exchanges between two chromosomes, are called *quadriradials*. They come in two types, depending on whether the centromeres are on opposite sides (alternate) (I, IIIa, and IVa in Fig. 9.3), or next to each other (adjacent) (II, IIIb, and IVb in Fig. 9.3a). The *alternate* type leads to the formation of two chromatids, each with a reciprocal translocation and two unchanged chromatids. The *adjacent* arrangement gives rise to a dicentric and an acentric chromatid and two unchanged chromatids. Mitotic chiasmata (crossing-over between two homologous mitotic chromosomes) (I in Fig. 9.3), which form a special subgroup of the alternate type of quadriradials, are discussed in Chapter 12.

Telomeres

The structure and behavior of telomeres have been described in Chapter 8. The main conclusions are that human chromosomes, to behave normally, must be capped by telomeres, and that cells cannot synthesize extra telomeres. The following observations must be taken into consideration when the function of telomeres is discussed (Patau, 1965).

1. If human chromosomes are broken with x-rays, the sister chromatids do not show a noticeable tendency to join. This differs from the behavior of some plant chromosomes, in which sister chromatid joining leads to the breakage—fusion—bridge cycle. No such cycle has been observed in human cells. However, in Bloom syndrome, broken sister chromatids seem to have an increased tendency to join (Kuhn and Therman, 1979).
2. Cases of terminally deleted chromosomes are too frequent and the breakpoints too consistent for them to be the result of two breaks.
3. In the cri du chat syndrome, which is caused by the deletion of about one-half of the short arm of chromosome 5, the broken ends may appear fuzzy, thus differing from normal chromosome ends (Patau, 1965). In addition, Niebuhr (1978) showed that in 35 cri du chat patients the deletion appeared terminal in 27, interstitial in 4, and capped by a reciprocal translocation in 4 others.
4. Ring chromosomes may sometimes open up and act like normal two-armed chromosomes (for example, Cooke and Gordon, 1965).

One hypothesis that would explain many of these observations is that telomere-like sequences are distributed along the chromosomes and that a break within one of these provides broken ends with telomeres (Hastie and Allshire, 1989).

Telomere Associations

Although the telomere-capped ends of chromosomes do not join non-capped fragments to form translocations, telomeres seem to have a mutual attraction which, in rare cases, leads to reversible or more-or-less stable associations (Drets and Stoll, 1974). Dutrillaux et al. (1977) have described an interesting phenomenon in the Thiberge-Weissenbach syndrome. Unbroken chromosome ends tended to join each other, leading to the formation of chains and rings, sometimes involving all the chromosomes. No acentric fragments were present, indicating that this phenomenon could not be the result of reciprocal translocations. Similar, more-or-less unstable, terminal attachments have been described in mammalian cell lines and in various malignant diseases (for instance, Levan, 1970; Fitzgerald and Morris, 1984; Mandahl et al., 1988; Hastie and Allshire, 1989).

Origin of Dicentric Chromosomes, Including Isodicentrics and Isochromosomes

The structure and function of centromeres have been reviewed in Chapter 8. Isodicentric chromosomes are symmetric, palindromic structures consisting of two homologous chromosomes broken at identical points. Usually one centromere is inactivated. Isochromosomes, on the other hand, which are either monocentric or dicentric, are metacentrics having two homologous arms, which may be genetically homozygous or heterozygous. A dicentric isochromosome corresponds to an isodicentric in which the centromeres are next to each other. Most isodicentrics have been formed by two X chromosomes (Fig. 22.2b and c; Zakharov and Baranovskaya, 1983; Therman and Susman, 1990), and most isochromosomes by X long arms. Isodicentrics consisting of two Y chromosomes have been found repeatedly (Cohen et al., 1973). Dicentrics between various non-homologous chromosomes, with one centromere inactivated, have also been observed (Schwartz et al., 1983), as have many Robertsonian translocations (see Chapter 27) with two centromeres.

Figure 9.4 illustrates two possible modes of origin of isodicentrics and dicentric isochromosomes. (A G_1 break at identical points in two homologous chromosomes is too unlikely an event to need consideration.) In Figure 9.4a, both chromatids of a chromosome are broken and have joined. However, if the breakpoints are at any distance from the centro-

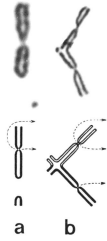

Figure 9.4. Possible origins of isodicentric chromosomes. (a) Isochromatid break and rejoining of the broken chromatids may result in an isodicentric; (b) segregation of an adjacent quadriradial is probably the main mechanism creating isodicentrics.

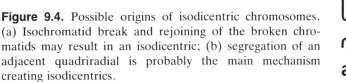

a   b

mere, this mechanism would not lead to an isodicentric, but to a bridge in the next anaphase, since the daughter centromeres would go to opposite poles. If the daughter centromeres are very near each other, they are more likely to go to the same pole, which would give rise to a dicentric isochromosome. The most probable origin of isodicentric chromosomes, including dicentric isochromosomes, is *segregation of an adjacent quadriradial* (type II in Fig. 9.3) when the centromeres of the dicentric chromatid go to the same pole (Fig. 9.4b). Therman and Kuhn (1985) have shown that this is the usual mechanism for creating symmetric dicentrics in Bloom syndrome. Dicentrics between two non-homologous chromosomes arise through segregation of a type IVb quadriradial (Fig. 9.3), or a G_1 break in two non-homologous chromosomes. Molecular studies have shown that in monocentric isochromosomes for Xq and 21q, the two arms may be homozygous or heterozygous (Lorda-Sanchez et al., 1991). The former most probably come about through misdivision of the centromere, the latter through segregation in an adjacent quadriradial between two homologous chromosomes.

A quadriradial may segregate in various ways. However, common to all of them is that the daughter cells are *different from each other*, whereas descendants of a cell in which a G_1 aberration has taken place are identical. Many human mosaics display cell lines with different chromosome constitutions that obviously owe their origin to segregation in a quadriradial (Daly et al., 1977). Good examples of such mosaics are provided by persons having a cell line with an isodicentric X;X chromosome and another with 45,X chromosomes. Although segregation in a quadriradial is the simplest explanation for such mosaics, it has been largely neglected in the literature.

Inactivation of the Centromere

Dicentric chromosomes with any distance between the centromeres will survive only if one centromere is inactivated. This is what has happened in most isodicentrics and dicentrics between homologous chromosomes. Such a chromosome functions like a normal monocentric (Therman et al., 1974). No second primary constriction is visible, but a C-band marks its position (Fig. 22.2b and c).

The same process obviously takes place in monocentric human X chromosomes, which have nonfunctional centromeres and the appearance of acentric fragments. Such chromosomes drift at random in anaphase, giving rise to cells in which one X is missing and to others in which they accumulate (Fig. 22.2a). This obviously is the mechanism that accounts for the increased frequency of 45,X cells in older women (Fitzgerald and McEwan, 1977). This type of centromere inactivation has also been observed in monocentric autosomes (Therman et al., 1986).

In the "acentric" X chromosomes the centromere certainly does not divide prematurely (Nakagome et al., 1984), as has sometimes been assumed; this would create a different configuration, since the centromeres would point towards the poles. However, what is involved at the submicroscopic level in the inactivation of a centromere is not known. The process seems to be irreversible, as demonstrated by the behavior of a 6p;19p translocation, in which the chromosomes were attached at their telomeres (Drets and Therman, 1983), with the centromere of chromosome 6 inactivated. This translocation chromosome had a tendency to break at the fusion point, and in none of the resulting "acentric" chromosomes 6 was the centromere reactivated (Fig. 25.8).

Misdivision

Isochromosomes with one centromere and telocentrics arise through *misdivision of the centromere*. This means that in mitotic or meiotic anaphase the centromere divides transversely instead of longitudinally (Fig. 19.2). Since misdivision most often takes place in the first meiotic anaphase, it will be discussed in Chapter 19.

Centric Fusion

Whole-arm transfers, or Robertsonian translocations as they are called, constitute a special class of reciprocal translocations. In the human, they almost always occur between two acrocentric chromosomes and are the most commonly observed chromosome aberrations.

The origin of Robertsonian translocations has often been assumed to be the fusion of two centromeres that have each broken in the middle.

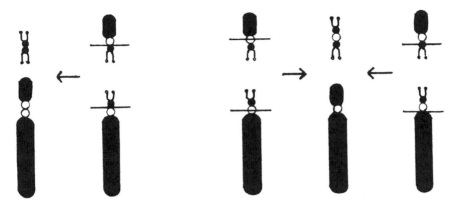

Figure 9.5. Origin of Robertsonian translocations between a G and a D chromosome. Left: Breaks on the short arms resulting in a dicentric and acentric chromosome. Right: Break, either through the centromeres, or one break on the short arm, the other on the long arm, resulting in two monocentric chromosomes. (Note: The centromeres are shown as open circles.)

However, banding studies show that this is not the only, and possibly not even the most common, mechanism. As illustrated in Fig. 9.5, depending on whether the break in the two acrocentrics occurs through the centromere or on the short or the long arm, the result is a monocentric or dicentric (or acentric) translocation chromosome, consisting of two long arms. The reciprocal product, made up of two short arms, is inevitably lost if it does not have a centromere. Neither the absence of these small chromosomes nor their presence as extra units seems to affect the phenotype.

Triradial and Multiradial Chromosomes

Triradial and multiradial chromosome configurations deserve only brief mention because of their extreme rarity and are described here only as examples of the odd ways in which chromosomes may behave. In a triradial, part of the chromosome is duplicated; it has three branches, in contrast to a quadriradial, which has four. Triradials are much rarer than quadriradials; for instance, Stahl-Maugé et al. (1978) found two triradials in 53,000 cells of normal persons. However, they are more frequent in cells of patients with Fanconi anemia and Bloom syndrome and in cells treated with chromosome-breaking substances. The branchpoint in a triradial is often a fragile site.

   Three different mechanisms have been proposed as creating triradial chromosomes: (1) partial endoreduplication (a segment of a chromosome replicates twice, while the rest replicates once); (2) a chromatid fragment

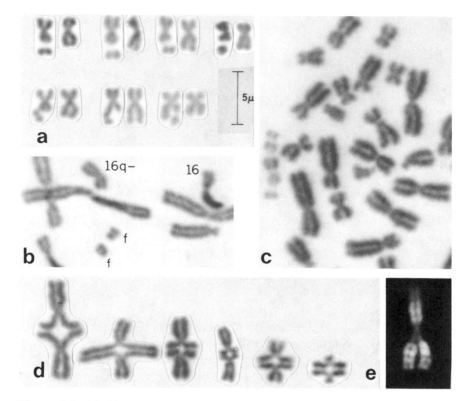

Figure 9.6. (a) Chromosome 16 with a fragile region and its normal homologue, from seven cells; (b) break at the fragile region and the replicated fragment [f]; (c) banded C chromosome left behind in its cycle; (d) mitotic chiasmata involving different human chromosome pairs; (e) triradial chromosome 1 resulting from partial endoreduplication.

remains associated with its sister chromatid in anaphase; (3) a broken chromosome is inserted into a gap formed by a chromatid break (Stahl-Maugé et al., 1978). The last mechanism would be highly unlikely to create symmetrical triradials. That the second mechanism works, at least sometimes, has been shown by studies on differentially stained sister chromatids (Weitkamp et al., 1978). However, the following observations show that most symmetric triradials probably arise through partial endo-reduplication (Fig. 9.6e; Kuhn and Therman, 1982). Sometimes the extra segment joins its intact sister chromatid. It is difficult to imagine duplicate satellites coming about through any other process. The extra segments in a triradial are paired with their sister chromatids and not with each other. Finally, in G_2, x-rays increase the frequency of chromatid fragments but not of symmetric triradials.

Multibranched chromosomes, so far, have been found only in the lymphocytes of a few patients with combined immunodeficiency (Tiepolo et al., 1979; Fryns et al., 1981). These peculiar configurations consist of variable numbers and combinations of short and long arms of chromosomes 1, 9, and 16, in which the exchanges occur at the centric regions.

Fragile Sites

Fragile sites, which appear as unstained or stretched regions, represent weak points in the chromosomes (Figs. 9.6a, b, and 22.2d). Although they resemble secondary constrictions in appearance, they do not contain rRNA genes. Chromosomes have a tendency to break at the fragile sites. This leads to the formation of deletions and translocations (Glover and Stein, 1988). Sister chromatid exchanges also seem to be increased at these sites (Glover and Stein, 1987), and the sites may act as branchpoints in triradial chromosomes (Kuhn and Therman, 1982). Fragile sites are constant features in a person, but are expressed only in a portion of the cells. They are inherited in a Mendelian fashion (Romain et al., 1986) and have been useful as chromosome markers, especially in gene mapping studies. Observations on fragile sites have been reviewed, for instance, by Sutherland and Hecht (1985), and by Ahuja (1990).

Hecht et al. (1990) have surveyed the fragile sites known in 1988. Of the 107 sites, 83 were classified as "common," and the remaining 24 belonged to the "rare" group. The sites are localized in the G-light chromosome bands and are nonrandomly distributed on the different chromosomes. Thus, chromosomes 1 and 2 have 11 fragile sites each, chromosome 3 has 3 sites, and chromosome 21 has none. Lack of folic acid/thymidine in the culture medium induces rare fragile sites, whereas aphidicolin and some other substances, such as distamycin A, 5-azacytidine, and BrdU, increase the expression of the common fragile sites.

As a rule, fragile sites, even in the homozygous condition, do not have any phenotypic effects. Claims that they may induce mental retardation (Sutherland, 1982) and other birth defects (Ahuja, 1990) are in need of confirmation. The only exception seems to be the fragile site at Xq27.3 (Fig. 22.2d), which causes a characteristic mental retardation syndrome. This will be discussed in Chapter 22.

Even more controversial have been claims that the locations of fragile sites coincide with those of the oncogenes and with those of the constant chromosome breaks in malignant disease. A great number of papers have been published both for and against such correlations. The different points of view have been reviewed by Hecht and Sandberg (1988), Sutherland (1988), and Le Beau (1988). This and the following questions still await answers. (1) What is the molecular structure of fragile sites? (2) Do these sites represent one or several fundamentally different phenomena? (3) Apart from the fragile X syndrome, do fragile sites ever cause phenotypic abnormalities? (4) What role do fragile sites play in spontaneous or induced chromosome breakage?

References

Ahuja YR (1990) Fragile site analysis: its significance in environmental mutagenesis. In: Mendelsohn ML, Albertini RJ (eds) Mutation and the environment, Part B. Wiley-Liss, New York, pp 371–384

Auerbach C (1976) Mutation research. Problems, results and perspectives. Chapman and Hall, London

Auerbach C (1978) Forty years of mutation research: a pilgrim's progress. Heredity 40:177–187

Cohen MM, MacGillivray MH, Capraro VJ, et al. (1973) Human dicentric Y chromosomes. J Med Genet 10:74–79

Cooke P, Gordon RR (1965) Cytological studies on a human ring chromosome. Ann Hum Genet 29:147–150

Daly RF, Patau K, Therman E, et al. (1977) Structure and Barr body formation of an Xp+ chromosome with two inactivation centers. Am J Hum Genet 29:83–93

Drets ME, Stoll M (1974) C-banding and non-homologous associations in Gryllus argentinus. Chromosoma 48:367–390

Drets ME, Therman E (1983) Human telomeric 6;19 translocation chromosome with a tendency to break at the fusion point. Chromosoma 88:139–144

Dutrillaux B, Aurias A, Couturier J, et al. (1977) Multiple telomeric fusions and chain configurations in human somatic chromosomes. In: Chapelle A de la, Sorsa M (eds) Chromosomes today, Vol 6. Elsevier/North Holland, Amsterdam, pp 37–44

Evans HJ (1962) Chromosome aberrations induced by ionizing radiations. Int Rev Cytol 13:221–321

Evans HJ (1974) Effects of ionizing radiation on mammalian chromosomes. In: German J (ed) Chromosomes and cancer. Wiley, New York, pp 191–237

Evans HJ (1983) Effects on chromosomes of carcinogenic rays and chemicals. In: German J (ed) Chromosome mutation and neoplasia. Liss, New York, pp 253–279

Fitzgerald PH, McEwan CM (1977) Total aneuploidy and age-related sex chromosome aneuploidy in cultured lymphocytes of normal men and women. Hum Genet 39:329–337

Fitzgerald PH, Morris CM (1984) Telomeric association of chromosomes in B-cell lymphoid leukemia. Hum Genet 67:385–390

Fryns JP, Azou M, Jaeken J, et al. (1981) Centromeric instability of chromosomes 1, 9, and 16 associated with combined immunodeficiency. Hum Genet 57:108–110

Gebhart E (1970) The treatment of human chromosomes in vitro: results. In: Vogel F, Röhrborn G (eds) Chemical mutagenesis in mammals and man. Springer, New York, pp 367–382

Glover TW, Stein CK (1987) Induction of sister chromatid exchanges at common fragile sites. Am J Hum Genet 41:882–890

Glover TW, Stein CK (1988) Chromosome breakage and recombination at fragile sites. Am J Hum Genet 43:265–273

Hastie ND, Allshire RC (1989) Human telomeres: fusion and interstitial sites. Trends Genet 5:326–331

Hecht F, Sandberg AA (1988) Of fragile sites and cancer chromosome breakpoints. Cancer Genet Cytogenet 31:1–3

Hecht F, Ramesh KH, Lockwood DH (1990) A guide to fragile sites on human chromosomes. Cancer Genet Cytogenet 44:37–45

Kihlman BA (1966) Actions of chemicals on dividing cells. Prentice-Hall, Englewood Cliffs, New Jersey

Kuhn EM, Therman E (1979) Chromosome breakage and rejoining of sister chromatids in Bloom's syndrome. Chromosoma 73:275–286

Kuhn EM, Therman E (1982) Origin of symmetrical triradial chromosomes in human cells. Chromosoma 86:673–681

Le Beau MM (1988) Editorial: Chromosomal fragile sites and cancer-specific breakpoints—a moderating viewpoint. Cancer Genet Cytogenet 31:55–61

Levan G (1970) Contributions to the chromosomal characterization of the PTK1 rat–kangaroo cell line. Hereditas 64:85–96

Lorda-Sanchez I, Binkert F, Maechler M, et al. (1991) A molecular study of X isochromosomes: parental origin, centromeric structure, and mechanisms of formation. Am J Hum Genet 49:1034–1040

Mandahl N, Heim S, Arheden K, et al. (1988) Rings, dicentrics, and telomeric association in histiocytomas. Cancer Genet Cytogenet 30:23–33

Mendelsohn ML, Albertini RJ (eds) (1990) Mutation and the environment, Part B. Wiley-Liss, New York

Nakagome Y, Abe T, Misawa S, et al. (1984) The "loss" of centromeres from chromosomes of aged women. Am J Hum Genet 36:398–404

Niebuhr E (1978) Cytologic observations in 35 individuals with a 5p− karyotype. Hum Genet 42:143–156

Patau K (1965) The chromosomes. In: Birth defects: original article series, I. New York: The National Foundation, pp 71–74

Rieger R, Michaelis A (1967) Die Chromosomenmutationen. Gustav Fischer, Jena

Romain DR, Columbano-Green LM, Smythe RH, et al. (1986) Studies on three rare fragile sites: 2q13, 12q13, and 17p12 segregating in one family. Hum Genet 73:164–170

Schwartz S, Palmer CG, Weaver DD, et al. (1983) Dicentric chromosome 13 and centromere inactivation. Hum Genet 63:332–337

Sparrow AH (1965) Comparisons of the tolerances of higher plant species to acute and chronic exposure of ionizing radiation. In: Mechanisms of the dose rate effect of radiation at the genetic and cellular levels. Special suppl. Jpn J Genet 40:12–37

Stahl-Maugé C, Hager HD, Schroeder TM (1978) The problem of partial endoreduplication. Hum Genet 45:51–62

Sutherland GR (1982) Heritable fragile sites on human chromosomes. VIII. Preliminary population cytogenetic data on the folic-acid–sensitive fragile sites. Am J Hum Genet 34:452–458

Sutherland GR (1988) Editorial: Fragile sites and cancer breakpoints—the pessimistic view. Cancer Genet Cytogenet 31:5–7

Sutherland GR, Hecht F (1985) Fragile sites on human chromosomes, Oxford monographs on medical genetics 13. Oxford University Press, New York–Oxford

Therman E, Kuhn EM (1976) Cytological demonstration of mitotic crossing-over in man. Cytogenet Cell Genet 17:254–267

Therman E, Kuhn EM (1985) Incidence and origin of symmetric and asymmetric dicentrics in Bloom's syndrome. Cancer Genet Cytogenet 15:293–301

Therman E, Susman B (1990) The similarity of phenotypic effects caused by Xp and Xq deletions in the human female: a hypothesis. Hum Genet 85:175–183

Therman E, Sarto GE, Patau K (1974) Apparently isodicentric but functionally monocentric X chromosome in man. Am J Hum Genet 26:83–92

Therman E, Trunca C, Kuhn EM, et al. (1986) Dicentric chromosomes and the inactivation of the centromere. Hum Genet 72:191–195

Tiepolo L, Maraschio P, Gimelli G, et al. (1979) Multibranched chromosomes 1, 9, and 16 in a patient with combined IgA and IgE deficiency. Hum Genet 51:127–137

Weitkamp LR, Ferguson-Smith MA, Guttormsen SA, et al. (1978) The linkage relationships of marker sites on chromosomes no. 2 and 10. Ann Hum Genet 42:183–189

Zakharov AF, Baranovskaya LI (1983) X–X chromosome translocations and their karyotype-phenotype correlations. In: Sandberg AA (ed) Cytogenetics of the mammalian X chromosome, Part B: X chromosome anomalies and their clinical manifestations. Liss, New York, pp 261–279

10
Causes of Chromosome Breakage

Mechanisms of Chromosome Breakage

In Chapter 9 the formation of aberrant chromosomes was discussed on a primitive level: chromosomes break, the broken ends join in various ways, and the resulting aberrations can be studied in the next metaphase. However, before this takes place, a series of mechanisms, many of them still unknown, have played a role in the process (Natarajan, 1984; Savage, 1990). The first event is a "lesion", i.e., some sort of DNA damage, the nature of which depends on the agent involved. The DNA strand may break (ionizing radiations, ultraviolet light [UV], bleomycin), or one of the following aberrations may occur: formation of pyrimidine dimers (short-wave UV), base alkylation (alkylating agents), inter- and intra-strand crosslinkage (polyfunctional alkylating agents, psoralen, long-wave UV), and intercalation, an insertion of mutagen between base pairs in the double helix (acriflavine, proflavin, and others). Next, the lesions go through DNA synthesis, which may further affect their behavior. The lesions may undergo repair or misrepair by various repair systems (Natarajan, 1984). The frequency of visible breaks decreases through G_2, since the majority of breaks eventually heal (Hittelman, 1990).

The timing of these events is decisive. This complicates the interpretation of breakage results, since the treatment under study often changes the timing of the various processes, which, in turn, has an effect on the quality and quantity of aberrations. The origin of chromosome breaks has been reviewed, for instance, by Natarajan (1984), Savage (1990), and in several articles in *Mutation and the Environment, Part B* (Mendelsohn and Albertini, 1990).

Spontaneous Chromosome Breaks

Spontaneously broken and rearranged chromosomes are found occasionally in every human being and in every cell culture. Their frequency varies from person to person and from culture to culture. One rule, however, appears to be well established. The incidence of aneuploid cells is known to increase with age, and, similarly, chromosome structural changes become more frequent in older persons. In our laboratory, an analysis of 2324 cells from persons under 40 years of age gave an average of 0.8 percent of cells with chromosome structural aberrations (excluding gaps), whereas in another sample of about the same size from individuals whose average age was 55.8 years, abnormalities were found in 2.4 percent of cells (Kuhn and Therman, 1979). Interestingly, the sensitivity of lymphocytes to alkylating agents increases significantly from newborns to young adults (mean age 23), and again from young adults to old people (mean age 70) (Bochkov and Kuleshov, 1972).

Although the trends are the same, the actual frequencies of chromosome aberrations found in various laboratories show a wide variation. This probably depends mainly on different criteria being used for scoring aberrations, on different degrees of accuracy of the analyses, and on the culture conditions.

Another indication of an age effect is the fact that tissue cultures of normal human fibroblasts can be grown unchanged through only about 50 passages (approximately one year) (Hayflick and Moorhead, 1961). Thereafter, cell growth suffers, and more and more aberrations appear. Finally, the normal cell strains are transformed into permanent cell lines with numerically and structurally aberrant chromosome constitutions (Nichols, 1975). These, in turn, show a greatly increased tendency to become malignant.

When we talk about "spontaneous" chromosome breaks, it means that we can only guess at the actual causes. The genotype of the individual undoubtedly determines the basic level of aberrations. Physiological degeneration in old age probably accounts for the increases in both nondisjunction and in breakage of chromosomes. Exposures to cosmic rays and to medical or occupational radiation constitute other sources of chromosome damage. Various drugs, viral infections, and even high fever may be other sources of damage.

It is well known that chemically induced chromosome breaks do not occur at random among cells; in other words, they do not follow a Poisson distribution. The same seems to be true of spontaneous breaks (Schroeder and German, 1974; Therman and Kuhn, 1976). Furthermore, exceptional rogue cells, with a great number of chromosome aberrations such as acentric fragments (in some cases resembling double minutes), dicentrics, and even tricentrics, have been found in different populations around the world. Awa and Neel (1986) observed 24 such cells among 102,170 cultured lymphocytes from 9818 Japanese individuals. The occurrence of these cells was not correlated with age, sex, year, season, or radiation dose received by the parents of the subjects. No reasonable explanation for the occurrence of such rogue cells has so far been presented.

Part of the evidence for nonrandom breakage comes from individuals with complicated chromosome rearrangements in all cells and is thus incidental. In a population of chromosomally normal grasshoppers, Coleman (1947) found an individual who was heterozygous for three reciprocal translocations and one inversion. Similarly, White (1963) described a grasshopper with a complex translocation involving breaks in four non-homologous chromosomes. In humans, too, complicated rearrangements are occasionally encountered. For example, a child with congenital anomalies had a genotype in which four chromosomes showed a total of six breaks (Seabright et al., 1978). The literature on multiple break cases has been reviewed by Bijlsma et al. (1978) and Pai et al. (1980).

Radiation-Induced Breaks

Ultraviolet light and especially various types of ionizing radiation are powerful chromosome-breaking agents. The effects of a wide range of radiations, such as x-rays, gamma-radiation, alpha and beta particles, and neutrons, have been studied in this respect. Ionizing radiation causes chromosome breaks at any stage of the mitotic cycle or during meiosis, although the vulnerability of different phases and different organisms varies greatly. The results also vary according to whether a given dose of radiation is applied within a short time span or over a longer period, or is fractionated. The tritium in [^{3}H]thymidine, so widely used for autoradiography, emits beta particles that may cause considerable damage when incorporated into the chromosomes.

A great amount of research has been undertaken to elucidate the actual mechanism of radiation-induced chromosome breakage. In the late 1930s the so-called target theory was born. It states that a chromosome is broken when it is hit directly by an ion or an ion cluster. However, because a number of observations cannot be explained on the basis of the target theory, the chemical theory of chromosome breakage was proposed in the 1940s. This theory says that most chromosome breakage is done by substances that result from the chemical reactions induced by radiation. The various radicals that arise from irradiated water molecules seem to be especially active in this respect.

The following are some of the observations that do not agree with the target theory but that can be readily explained by the chemical theory. Chromosomes of many plants are broken with much lower doses of radiation than, for instance, *Drosophila* chromosomes. Chromosome breaks

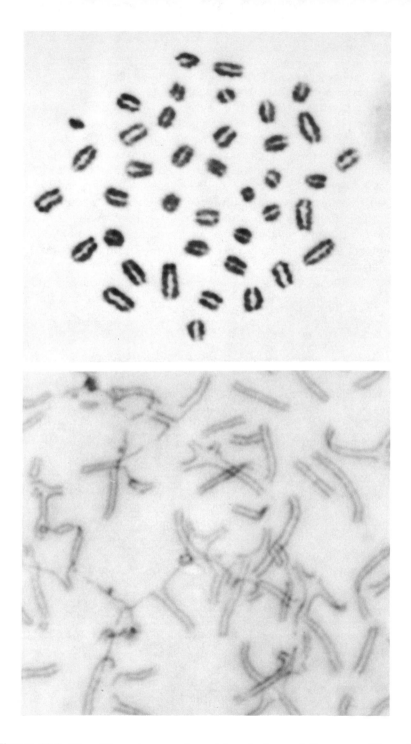

Figure 10.1. Top: Normal spermatogonial metaphase of the mouse (*2n* = 40). Bottom: Chromosome breaks and numerous chromatid translocations in a mouse cancer cell caused by 1-methyl-2-benzylhydrazine. (The cancer chromosomes have been spread by adding water to the fixative and therefore stain differently.)

can be caused by a pre-irradiated medium. One of the most important observations is that oxygen greatly enhances the effects of radiation and, inversely, that a number of reducing substances—especially those containing sulfhydryl groups—counteract radiation damage (Evans, 1974).

Chemically Induced Breaks

The list of substances found to break chromosomes is already very long and is still growing steadily. It includes alkylating agents, purine and pyrimidine derivatives, alkyl epoxides, aromatic amines, nitroso compounds, heavy metals, and a large number of miscellaneous substances (Kihlman, 1966; Rieger and Michaelis, 1967; Auerbach, 1976; Ma, 1982).

Most chemicals induce breaks of the G_2 type, but they have to be present during the preceding S period. As with radiation treatment, different organisms and tissues show a wide range of responses to the same chemical. An example is illustrated in Fig. 10.1. Two anticancer drugs of the methyl-benzyl hydrazine group broke no chromosomes, in either malignant or normal cells in vitro. In vivo, they showed no effect on the chromosomes in normal mouse spleen, bone marrow, or spermatocytes. However, they caused extensive damage in transplantable ascites tumors in the same animal (Therman, 1972; Rapp and Therman, 1977). It seems obvious that the mouse is needed to metabolize and change the drug and that it undergoes a second change in the cancer cells. Apparently, at least two steps are needed to transform the methyl-benzyl hydrazines into chromosome-breaking substances. All the breaks are of the G_2 type and take place in the Q-dark or G-light regions (Rapp and Therman, 1977).

Virus-Induced Breaks

Virus-induced chromosome breaks have been less studied than those caused by radiations or chemical mutagens, and very little is known about the interaction between viruses and chromosomes that is required to bring about chromosome breaks. Viral chromosome breaks may or may not undergo repair. Harnden (1974) and Nichols (1975, 1983) have reviewed the information on chromosome-breaking viruses.

Chromosome damage caused by viral infection varies from single chromosome and chromatid breaks to rearrangements and total pulverization of the chromosome complement. The latter is found especially in lymphocytes of persons with an acute viral infection, such as measles. Cells containing viruses also often fuse, forming syncytia. In subsequent mitoses multipolar spindles appear (Nichols, 1970). What proportion, if any, of spontaneous chromosome aberrations in the human is attributable to viral action is still unknown.

Enzyme-Induced Breaks

Studies on the chromosomal effects of various restriction endonucleases have been reviewed by Bryant (1988). The impermeability of cells to these enzymes has been the main obstacle to their investigation. However, this can be overcome by a treatment with inactivated Sendai virus. Restriction endonucleases especially induce double-strand breaks, which can take place at any stage of the mitotic cycle and can lead to chromosome aberrations, mutations, and cell death. However, it seems unlikely that these enzymes, products of free-living prokaryotes for the most part, have much effect on the breakage of human chromosomes outside the laboratory.

Genetic Causes of Chromosome Breaks

As already pointed out, different persons may show consistently different rates of spontaneous chromosome breakage, these rates probably depending on genetic makeup. In a number of syndromes, most of which are caused by single recessive autosomal genes, the incidence of chromosome breaks and rearrangements is greatly increased. Such chromosome-breakage syndromes are described in Chapters 11 and 12.

Many interspecific plant and animal hybrids display a wide range of chromosome aberrations in their somatic cells (Shaw et al., 1983).

Nonrandomness of Chromosome Breaks

The nonrandomness of chromosome breaks may be observed in different cells or in various chromosome segments within a cell. As previously mentioned, a nonrandom distribution between cells applies to spontaneous breaks, as well as to breaks induced by chemical compounds and those occurring in chromosome-breakage syndromes.

Banding techniques reveal that breaks in human chromosomes, whatever their cause, practically always take place in the Q-dark (G-light) chromosome regions. However, it is not clear whether breaks occur preferentially in these segments or whether the nonrandomness is the result of differential repair. Breaks are very unevenly distributed even among the Q-dark segments, with certain of them emerging as clear hot spots. But the hot spots are not the same when chromosome breakage caused by different agents is compared (von Koskull and Aula, 1977).

The possible role played by fragile sites in the nonrandomness of chromosome breaks is not clear (Chapter 9).

The large chromosomes of *Vicia faba* ($2n = 12$) are especially suitable for mutagenesis studies (Ma, 1982). Detailed analyses of breakage in these chromosomes have been done by Rieger and his colleagues (Rieger and Michaelis, 1972; Rieger et al. 1973, 1982; Schubert et al., 1986). For instance, maleic hydrazide breaks certain C-bands in particular (Schubert et al., 1981), and the nucleolus organizing region is also sensitive to various mutagens (Schubert and Rieger, 1980). In human chromosomes, mitomycin C induces breaks largely in the heterochromatin of chromosomes 1, 9, 16, and the acrocentrics (Shaw and Cohen, 1965).

Methods in Chromosome-Breakage Studies

In plants and animals, chromosome breakage has been analyzed both in vivo and in vitro. In vivo studies are naturally preferable for many investigations, since they permit us to observe the effects of a mutagen in an intact organism. Effects in vivo often differ drastically from the mutagen's effects on cells in culture.

A promising technique in chromosome aberration studies is cell fusion and the resulting formation of prematurely condensed chromosomes (Chapter 13; Hittelman, 1990). With this method, the induction of breaks and their healing can be followed through interphase.

Another technique that allows the determination of chromosome abnormalities in both metaphase and interphase is chromosomal in situ suppression (CISS) hybridization with biotinylated DNA library probes (Chapter 5; Cremer et al., 1988, 1990).

In man, in vivo experiments are usually impractical, unethical, or both. Nevertheless, it is possible to analyze chromosome damage in persons who have been exposed to ionizing radiation for medical reasons, through occupational exposure, or by accident. The most extensively studied persons are the atomic bomb survivors of Hiroshima and Nagasaki; results of chromosome studies on them are reviewed by Awa (1974). The victims show a significantly higher incidence of chromosome abnormalities in their lymphocytes than do nonexposed controls. One of the most interesting phenomena is that those who received heavy doses of radiation still exhibit, more than 40 years later, abnormal chromosomes, such as dicentrics, acentrics, reciprocal translocations, inversions, rings, and deleted chromosomes. Often clones of cells with the same abnormal chromosome constitution have been found. The same is true of persons who have been exposed to large amounts of radiation for medical reasons.

However, most of the information we have about the induction of chromosome aberrations has been obtained from studies on cultured lymphocytes and fibroblasts. Cultured human cancer cells, especially various strains of HeLa cells (long-term human cell lines originating from a cervical carcinoma), have also been used in mutagenesis experiments. Numerous studies on the effects of chromosome-breaking agents have been performed on transplantable ascites tumors of the mouse, which are grown in suspension in the abdominal cavity of the animal (Adler, 1970).

This method makes it easy to obtain beautiful chromosome preparations.

Various methods have been employed to determine chromosome damage (Schoeller and Wolf, 1970; Nichols, 1973). One of the older techniques consists of scoring dicentric bridges and acentric fragments in anaphase. Another method involves counting the micronuclei formed by damaged or lagging chromosomes in mitoses following the treatment (Nichols, 1973; Prosser et al., 1988). However, an increase in the frequency of micronuclei tells us only *something* has happened, not *what*. Determination of micronuclei is thus a suitable first step in a mutation study, but it should be followed up by a chromosomal analysis.

Naturally, the most accurate results are achieved by analyzing whole metaphase plates, especially by the various banding techniques. However, even when this is done, the results of comparable studies conducted by different groups often yield discordant results. Apart from variation in the biological material and in culture techniques, the discrepancies result mainly from different criteria being used in scoring chromosome and chromatid aberrations. For example, one frequent source of confusion is the scoring of so-called gaps. These are mostly despiralized chromosome regions that appear as thinner and less well-stained regions in the chromatids. Since even a broken chromatid fragment tends to stick to its sister chromatid, it is often impossible to decide whether or not a true break has taken place. The dislocation of a fragment has commonly been used as a criterion to distinguish breaks from gaps (Schoeller and Wolf, 1970). Nevertheless, many scored breaks in reality may represent gaps. In addition, in most studies no definition or illustration is furnished to show the criteria used for classifying the various aberrations.

Two-break aberrations, such as quadriradials, dicentrics, and ring chromosomes, are naturally easier to distinguish than are one-break aberrations. However, their use does not guarantee consistency, as demonstrated by a study in which identical photomicrographs, depicting various chromosome aberrations, were sent to several different laboratories for analysis (Brøgger et al., 1984). The resulting diagnoses were disturbingly inconsistent. Clearly, general agreement on the definitions of the various anomalies is sorely needed. (However, nothing helps if the investigator cannot distinguish, for instance, a chromatid overlap from a second centromeric constriction). Furthermore, since two-break aberrations are much rarer than those resulting from one break, the collection of an adequate number of the former often requires that a prohibitively large number of cells be checked, or that the concentration of a drug or the amount of radiation used be so high as to interfere with cell division or to cause cell death. Consequently, many recent studies on chromosome-breaking mutagens take advantage of the more sensitive system of sister chromatid exchanges, which is free from many of the difficulties just discussed. However, it should be kept in mind that the correlation of chromosome breaks and sister chromatid exchanges is far from perfect.

Rules for Chromosome-Breakage Studies

Increasing awareness of the dangers of radiation and of environmental poisons has given new impetus to studies on chromosome breakage. However, the results have often been controversial. Surprisingly, the results of studies on sister chromatid exchanges (Chapter 12) have been equally inconsistent, although these exchanges should be easier to score than chromatid and chromosome breaks. At least some of the controversies might be resolved if certain rules were followed:

1. If the analysis is done on cultured cells, the control cells should be from the same individual, cultured at the same time. If this is not possible (for instance, when whole-body irradiation is studied), the control person should be of the same age and sex, and have the same habits of smoking and alcohol consumption (Natarajan, 1984). In animal studies,the controls should belong to the same inbred strain.
2. An illustration should show what is scored as a gap or a break, and the other scored abnormalities should also be illustrated.
3. The chromosome slides of the treated and control cells, made and stained at the same time, ought to be randomly coded to avoid the bias of the investigator.
4. Clear rules should be established as to which metaphases are included in the study (how many chromosomes may be missing or extra). Furthermore, it should be stated whether the whole chromosome complement has been analyzed in all cells, or only in those with obvious abnormalities.
5. The analysis should be done by a competent cytogeneticist (and not by part-time, inexperienced laboratory helpers).

References

Adler I-D (1970) Cytogenetic analysis of ascites tumour cells of mice in mutation research. In: Vogel F, Röhrborn G (eds) Chemical mutagenesis in mammals and man. Springer, New York, pp 251–259

Auerbach C (1976) Mutation research. Problems, results and perspectives. Chapman and Hall, London

Awa AA (1974) Cytogenetic and oncogenic effects of the ionizing radiations of the atomic bombs. In: German J (ed) Chromosomes and cancer. Wiley, New York, pp 637–674

Awa AA, Neel JV (1986) Cytogenetic "rogue" cells: what is their frequency, origin, and evolutionary significance? Proc Natl Acad Sci USA 83:1021–1025

Bijlsma JB, deFrance HF, Bleeker-Wagenmakers LM, et al. (1978) Double translocation t(7;12), t(2;6) heterozygosity in one family. A contribution to the trisomy 12p syndrome. Hum Genet 40:135–137

Bochkov NP, Kuleshov NP (1972) Age sensitivity of human chromosomes to alkylating agents. Mutat Res 14:345–353

Brøgger A, Norum R, Hansteen I-L, et al. (1984) Comparison between five Nordic laboratories on scoring of human lymphocyte chromosome aberrations. Hereditas 100:209–218

Bryant PE (1988) Use of restriction endonucleases to study relationships between DNA double-strand breaks, chromosomal aberrations and other end-points in mammalian cells. Int J Radiat Biol 54:869–890

Coleman LC (1947) Chromosome abnormalities in an individual of *Chorthippus longicornis* (Acrididae). Genetics 32:435–447

Cremer T, Lichter P, Borden J, et al. (1988) Detection of chromosome aberrations in metaphase and interphase tumor cells by in situ hybridization using chromosome-specific library probes. Hum Genet 80:235–246

Cremer T, Popp S, Emmerich P, et al. (1990) Rapid metaphase and interphase detection of radiation-induced chromosome aberrations in human lymphocytes by chromosomal suppression in situ hybridization. Cytometry 11:110–118

Evans HJ (1974) Effects of ionizing radiation on mammalian chromosomes. In: German J (ed) Chromosomes and cancer. Wiley, New York, pp 191–237

Harnden DG (1974) Viruses, chromosomes, and tumors: the interaction between viruses and chromosomes. In: German J (ed) Chromosomes and cancer. Wiley, New York, pp 151–190

Hayflick L, Moorhead PS (1961) The serial cultivation of human diploid cell strains. Exp Cell Res 25:585–621

Hittelman WN (1990) Direct measurement of chromosome repair by premature chromosome condensation. In: Mendelsohn ML, Albertini RJ (eds) Mutation and the environment, part B. Wiley-Liss, New York, pp 337–346

Kihlman BA (1966) Actions of chemicals on dividing cells. Prentice-Hall, Englewood Cliffs, New Jersey

Koskull H von, Aula P (1977) Distribution of chromosome breaks in measles, Fanconi's anemia and controls. Hereditas 87:1–10

Kuhn EM, Therman E (1979) No increased chromosome breakage in three Bloom's syndrome heterozygotes. J Med Genet 16:219–222

Ma T-H (1982) Vicia cytogenetic tests for environmental mutagens. A report of the U.S. Environmental Protection Agency Gene–Tox Program. Mutat Res 99:257–271

Mendelsohn ML, Albertini RJ (eds) (1990) Mutation and the environment, part B. Wiley-Liss, New York

Natarajan AT (1984) Origin and significance of chromosomal alterations. In: Obe G (ed) Mutations in man. Springer, Berlin–Heidelberg

Nichols WW (1970) Virus-induced chromosome abnormalities. Annu Rev Microbiol 24:479–500

Nichols WW (1973) Cytogenetic techniques in mutagenicity testing. Agents Actions 3:86–92

Nichols WW (1975) Somatic mutation in biologic research. Hereditas 81:225–236

Nichols WW (1983) Viral interactions with the mammalian genome relevant to neoplasia. In: German J (ed) Chromosome mutation and neoplasia. Liss, New York, pp 317–332

Pai GS, Thomas GH, Mahoney W, et al. (1980) Complex chromosome rearrangements. Report of a new case and literature review. Clin Genet 18:436–444

Prosser JS, Moquet JE, Lloyd DC, et al. (1988) Radiation induction of micronuclei in human lymphocytes. Mutat Res 199:37–45

Rapp M, Therman E (1977) The effect of procarbazine on the chromosomes of normal and malignant mouse cells. Ann Génét 20:249–254

Rieger R, Michaelis A (1967) Die Chromosomenmutationen. Gustav Fischer, Jena

Rieger R, Michaelis A (1972) Effects of chromosome repatterning in *Vicia faba* L. I. Aberration distribution, aberration spectrum, and karyotype sensitivity after treatment with ethanol of differently reconstructed chromosome complements. Biol Zbl 91:151–169

Rieger R, Nicoloff H, Michaelis A (1973) Intrachromosomal clustering of chromatid aberrations induced by N-methyl-N-nitrosourethan in *Vicia faba* and barley. Biol Zbl 92:681–689

Rieger R, Michaelis A, Nicoloff H (1982) Inducible repair processes in plant root tip meristems? "Below-additivity effects" of unequally fractionated clastogen concentrations. Biol Zbl 101:125–138

Savage JRK (1990) Mechanisms of chromosome aberrations. In: Mendelsohn ML, Albertini RJ (eds) Mutation and the environment, part B. Wiley-Liss, New York, pp 385–396

Schoeller L, Wolf U (1970) Possibilities and limitations of chromosome treatment in vitro for the problem of chemical mutagenesis. In: Vogel F, Röhrborn G (eds) Chemical mutagenesis in mammals and man. Springer, New York, pp 232–240

Schroeder TM, German J (1974) Bloom's syndrome and Fanconi's anemia: demonstration of two distinctive patterns of chromosome disruption and rearrangement. Humangenetik 25:299–306

Schubert I, Rieger R (1980) Cytochemical and cytogenetic features of the nucleolus organizing region (NOR) of *Vicia faba*. Biol Zbl 99:65–72

Schubert I, Michaelis A, Rieger R (1981) Effects of chromosome repatterning in *Vicia faba* L. V. Influence of segment transpositions on maleic hydrazide-specific aberration clustering on a heterochromatin containing chromosome region. Biol Zbl 100:167–179

Schubert I, Rieger R, Michaelis A (1986) Effects of 'G2-repair' inhibitors on 'clastogenic adaptation' in *Vicia faba*. Mol Gen Genet 204:174–179

Seabright M, Gregson N, Pacifico E, et al. (1978) Rearrangements involving four chromosomes in a child with congenital abnormalities. Cytogenet Cell Genet 20:150–154

Shaw DD, Wilkinson P, Coates DJ (1983) Increased chromosomal mutation rate after hybridization between two subspecies of grasshoppers. Science 220:1165–1167

Shaw MW, Cohen MM (1965) Chromosome exchanges in human leukocytes induced by mitomycin C. Genetics 51:181–190

Therman E (1972) Chromosome breakage by 1-methyl-2-benzylhydrazine in mouse cancer cells. Cancer Res 32:1133–1136

Therman E, Kuhn EM (1976) Cytological demonstration of mitotic crossing-over in man. Cytogenet Cell Genet 17:254–267

White MJD (1963) Cytogenetics of the grasshopper *Moraba scurra* VIII. A complex spontaneous translocation. Chromosoma 14:140–145

11
Chromosome Instability Syndromes

Genotypic Chromosome Breakage

In humans, chromosome aberrations, including nondisjunction and structural changes, increase with age. Another factor determining the frequency of chromosome aberrations is the genotype of the individual, some persons showing considerably higher rates than others.

Several genes are known that greatly increase the incidence of chromosome aberrations. The most extensively studied of such conditions, each caused by a different recessive autosomal gene, are Bloom syndrome (BS), Fanconi anemia (FA), and ataxia telangiectasia (AT), which has also been called Louis-Bar syndrome. In addition, in a few other diseases, claims of increased chromosome aberrations have been raised. The three main chromosome instability syndromes, as well as xeroderma pigmentosum, have been reviewed extensively by Cohen and Levy (1989). The book, *Fanconi Anemia* (Schroeder-Kurth et al., 1989a), surveys various aspects of that condition.

The great interest in BS, FA, and AT is out of proportion to their rare occurrence. The studies have been inspired by the hope that they would throw light on chromosome structure and behavior. Furthermore, the risk of cancer is enhanced in such individuals: one-fourth of BS patients and one-eighth of AT patients develop cancer at an early age, and it is estimated that 10–15 percent of FA patients do also (German, 1983).

Bloom Syndrome

The most typical features in BS are low birth weight and stunted growth. Patients often seek medical help because they develop sun-sensitive

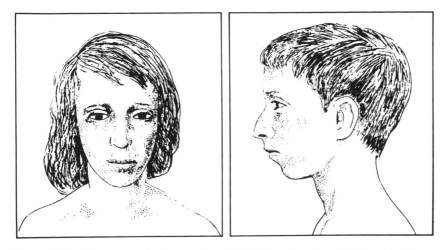

Figure 11.1. Characteristic faces of a girl (left) and a boy (right) with Bloom syndrome. (Reproduced with permission from German J, 1973, Oncogenic implications of chromosomal instability. Hospital Practice 8,2: p. 99.)

telangiectatic erythema (dilation of blood vessels) (Fig. 11.1) (Passarge, 1983). The Bloom's Syndrome Registry lists 103 patients, among whom 25 have developed 28 cancers (German et al., 1984). The patients suffer from immunodeficiency, which often leads to respiratory tract infections. About half of the BS patients are of Ashkenazic Jewish origin, and in two-thirds of the non-Jewish families, the parents are consanguineous.

German et al. (1965) described a high frequency of chromosome aberrations in BS patients. The chromosome aberrations are of two types. In the first, random breaks lead to fragments or to reciprocal translocations between non-homologous chromosomes. The second feature is exclusive to BS and consists of a greatly enhanced tendency to homologous exchanges. All the breakage probably takes place in S–G$_2$ (Therman and Kuhn, 1985). The increased tendency to homologous exchanges expresses itself in a 12-fold increase of sister chromatid exchanges (SCE) (Chaganti et al., 1974; Fig. 11.2) and in a 50- to 100-times increased incidence of mitotic crossing-over (Therman and Kuhn, 1981; Kuhn and Therman 1986). A further interesting feature is that BS cells fuse spontaneously (Fig. 13.3); apart from bone, muscle, and trophoblast tissues, this has been observed only when one cell type is malignant (Otto and Therman, 1982). As reviewed by Cohen and Levy (1989), a great amount of work has been done to find out whether chromosome aberrations, especially SCE, are decreased in BS or increased in normal cells, when the two types of cells are grown together or fused. However, the results have been so controversial that no conclusion is possible at present.

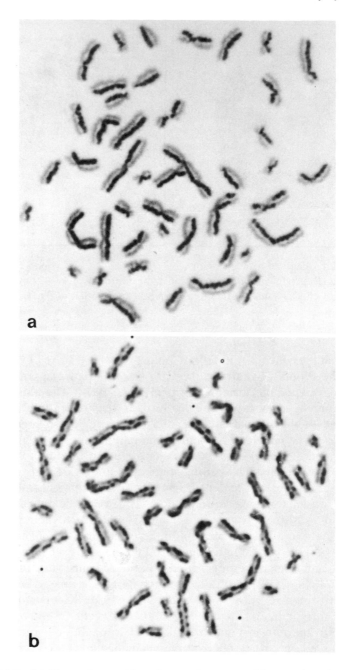

Figure 11.2. (a) Sister chromatid exchanges in a normal human lymphocyte; (b) Highly increased rate of sister chromatid exchanges in a lymphocyte from a Bloom syndrome patient (courtesy of RSK Chaganti). (See Chapter 12 for staining procedures.)

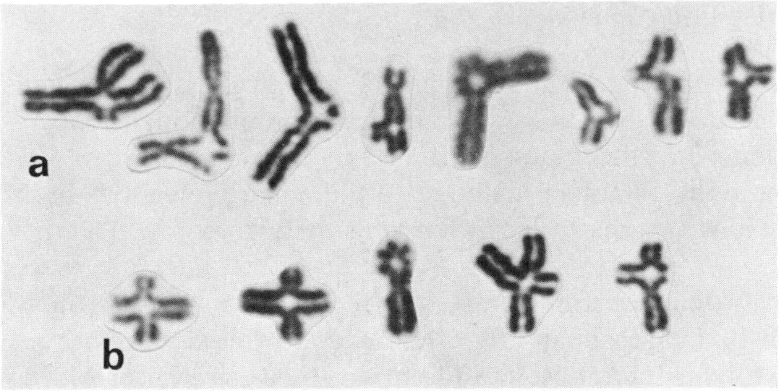

Figure 11.3. Characteristic chromosome aberrations in lymphocytes of a Fanconi anemia patient. (a) Adjacent quadriradials; (b) alternate quadriradials (courtesy of EM Kuhn).

The BS gene(s) has not been localized to a chromosome. However, ligase I activity is lower in BS than in normal cells (Chan et al., 1987; Willis and Lindahl, 1987).

Fanconi Anemia

Known FA patients number over 300. They show a variety of symptoms, such as skeletal anomalies (often the thumbs are affected), hyperpigmentation of the skin, strabismus, and hypogonadism (Alter and Potter, 1983). The patients develop lethal pancytopenia (lack of all blood elements) at the mean age of 5 years in boys and 6 years in girls. In a few cases, bone marrow transplants seem to have cured the anemia.

The most characteristic chromosome anomalies in FA are translocations between non-homologous chromosomes (Fig. 11.3), which were first described by Schroeder et al. (1964). Although the proportion of lymphocytes with aberrations may be as high as 30 percent, no increase in SCE has been observed (Chaganti et al., 1974).

The somatic anomalies displayed by FA patients vary greatly even within families. The same is true of spontaneous chromosome aberrations. Independent diagnostic tests have been based on the hypersensitivity of homozygous FA cells to polyfunctional alkylating agents (Schroeder-Kurth et al., 1989b). In particular, the greatly increased chromosome breakage induced by DEB (diepoxybutane) has facilitated both prenatal and postnatal diagnosis (Auerbach et al., 1989).

The FA gene has not been identified, nor are its biochemical or molecular effects known.

Ataxia Telangiectasia

The most important symptoms in AT are progressive cerebellar ataxia, telangiectasia of eyes and skin, and severe immunodeficiency. Some 300 AT patients have been described. Ataxia develops between 3 and 6 years of age, and the patients usually die of pulmonary infections or cancer. AT patients have a greatly increased sensitivity to x-rays (Gatti and Hall, 1983).

Chromosome aberrations are less frequent in AT than in BS or FA. Random breakage apparently often leads to cell clones with a transloca- tion, involving chromosome 14 in most cases (Kaiser-McCaw et al., 1975). A characteristic translocation is t(14;14)(q12;q32) (Kaiser-McCaw and Hecht, 1983). SCE are not increased.

The risk for solid tumors is greatly increased, and so is the tendency to develop lymphatic leukemia and non-Hodgkin's lymphoma (Hecht and Hecht, 1990). Many patients have more than one primary cancer. The most important cause of death in AT is pulmonary disease, and the second is cancer.

The AT gene has been localized to 11q22–q23 (Gatti et al., 1988).

Xeroderma Pigmentosum

In xeroderma pigmentosum (XP), the chromosomes do not break spon- taneously, so the disease is not dealt with here. The excision repair of chromosome lesions caused by UV light is defective in XP (Pawsey et al., 1979; Cohen and Levy, 1989). Exposure to light causes multiple skin lesions, which can develop into malignant neoplasms.

Other Conditions with Increased Chromosome Aberrations

Apart from BS, FA, and AT, increased chromosome aberrations have been described in some other diseases, in individual families or in isolated individuals. However, adequate illustrations are often lacking, and many of these claims should be reinvestigated in more detail.

Werner syndrome, which is caused by a rare recessive autosomal gene, involves short stature, premature aging, and early death. Both chromo- some structural aberrations and risk for cancer are increased (Brown, 1983; Salk et al., 1981).

Other conditions in which increased chromosome breakage has been reported include the Sézary syndrome (Bosman and van Vloten, 1976; Johnson et al., 1985), psoriasis (Bruun Petersen et al., 1979), multiple endocrine adenomatosis (Gustavson et al., 1983), and familial polyposis coli (Delhanty et al., 1983).

Table 11.1. Chromosome aberrations in BS that may cause/promote cancer.

Chromosome change	Result	Possible effect on oncogenes
Deletion	Hemizygosity of genes	Expression of recessive genes
Duplication	Trisomy for a segment	Amplification of genes
Reciprocal translocation	Position effect	Activation of an oncogene
Segregation of mitotic chiasma	Homozygosity of segment distal to chiasma	Expression of recessive genes
Unequal crossing-over	Amplification/deletion	Promotion of oncogene effect
Unequal SCE	Amplification/deletion	Promotion of oncogene effect

In Alzheimer's disease, which is characterized by premature senility, the incidence of X chromosomes with an inactivated centromere is increased (Fig. 22.2a; Moorhead and Heyman, 1983). In Roberts syndrome the centromeres divide prematurely (German, 1979; Tomkins et al., 1979).

Chromosome Instability Syndromes and Cancer

The three main chromosome instability syndromes (BS, FA, and AT) have in common a tendency to spontaneous chromosome breaks in the homozygotes—in each disease the aberrations are of a different type—and a greatly increased risk of developing malignant disease. Severe immunodeficiency in AT and a milder one in BS are probably also cancer-promoting factors. The various chromosome aberrations in BS that may increase the incidence of cancer are collected in Table 11.1 (also see Chapter 12).

The combined frequency of heterozygotes for the chromosome instability syndromes has been estimated to be around 1 percent. Only in AT heterozygotes is there significant evidence for an increased incidence of cancer (Swift et al., 1990).

A great deal of work has been done in the hope of developing a reliable test for determining heterozygotes. Although in some individual cases chromosome aberrations seem to be increased, no valid test has yet been developed to diagnose heterozygotes for any of these diseases (Cohen and Levy, 1989).

References

Alter BP, Potter NU (1983) Long-term outcome in Fanconi's anemia: description of 26 cases and review of the literature. In: German J (ed) Chromosome mutation and neoplasia. Liss, New York, pp 43–62

Auerbach AD, Ghosh R, Pollio PC, et al. (1989) Diepoxybutane test for prenatal and postnatal diagnosis. In: Schroeder-Kurth TM, Auerbach AD, Obe G (eds)

Fanconi anemia: clinical, cytogenetic and experimental aspects. Springer, Berlin, pp 71–82

Bosman FT, van Vloten WA (1976) Sézary's syndrome: A cytogenetic, cytophotometric and autoradiographic study. J Pathol 118:49–57

Brown WT (1983) Werner's syndrome. In: German J (ed) Chromosome mutation and neoplasia. Liss, New York, pp 85–93

Bruun Petersen G, Christiansen JV, Voetmann E, et al. (1979) Chromosome aberrations in affected and unaffected skin of patients with psoriasis. Acta Dermatovener (Stockholm) 54:147–151

Chaganti RSK, Schonberg S, German J (1974) A manyfold increase in sister chromatid exchanges in Bloom's syndrome lymphocytes. Proc Natl Acad Sci USA 71:4508–4512

Chan JYH, Becker FF, German J, et al. (1987) Altered DNA ligase I activity in Bloom's syndrome cells. Nature 325:357–359

Cohen MM, Levy HP (1989) Chromosome instability syndromes. Adv Hum Genet 18:43–149

Delhanty JDA, Davis MB, Wood J (1983) Chromosome instability in lymphocytes, fibroblasts, and colon epithelial-like cells from patients with familial polyposis coli. Cancer Genet Cytogenet 8:27–50

Gatti RA, Hall K (1983) Ataxia-telangiectasia: search for a central hypothesis. In: German J (ed) Chromosome mutation and neoplasia. Liss, New York, pp 23–41

Gatti RA, Berkel I, Boder E, et al. (1988) Localization of an ataxia-telangiectasia gene to chromosome 11q22–23. Nature 336:577–580

German J (1979) Roberts' syndrome. I. Cytological evidence for a disturbance in chromatid pairing. Clin Genet 16:441–447

German J (1983) Patterns of neoplasia associated with the chromosome-breakage syndromes. In: German J (ed) Chromosome mutation and neoplasia. Liss, New York, pp 97–134

German J, Archibald R, Bloom D (1965) Chromosomal breakage in a rare and probably genetically determined syndrome of man. Science 148:506–507

German J, Bloom D, Passarge E (1984) Bloom's syndrome. XI. Progress report for 1983. Clin Genet 25:166–174

Gustavson K-H, Jansson R, Oberg K (1983) Chromosomal breakage in multiple endocrine adenomatosis (types I and II). Clin Genet 23:143–149

Hecht F, Hecht BK (1990) Cancer in ataxia-telangiectasia patients. Cancer Genet Cytogenet 46:9–19

Johnson GA, Dewald GW, Strand WR, et al. (1985) Chromosome studies in 17 patients with the Sézary syndrome. Cancer 55:2426–2433

Kaiser-McCaw B, Hecht F (1983) The interrelationships in ataxia-telangiectasia of immune deficiency, chromosome instability, and cancer. In: German J (ed) Chromosome mutation and neoplasia. Liss, New York, pp 193–202

Kaiser-McCaw B, Hecht F, Harnden DG, et al. (1975) Somatic rearrangement of chromosome 14 in human lymphocytes. Proc Natl Acad Sci USA 72:2071–2075

Kuhn EM, Therman E (1986) Cytogenetics of Bloom's syndrome. Cancer Genet Cytogenet 22:1–18

Moorhead PS, Heyman A (1983) Chromosome studies of patients with Alzheimer disease. Am J Med Genet 14:545–556

Otto PG, Therman E (1982) Spontaneous cell fusion and PCC formation in Bloom's syndrome. Chromosoma 85:143–148

Passarge E (1983) Bloom's syndrome. In: German J (ed) Chromosome mutation and neoplasia. Liss, New York, pp 11–21

Pawsey SA, Magnus IA, Ramsay CA, et al. (1979) Clinical, genetic and DNA repair studies on a consecutive series of patients with xeroderma pigmentosum. Q J Med New Series 48, 190:179–210

Salk D, Au K, Hoehn H, et al. (1981) Cytogenetics of Werner's syndrome cultured skin fibroblasts: variegated translocation mosaicism. Cytogenet Cell Genet 30:92–107

Schroeder TM, Anschütz F, Knopp A (1964) Spontane Chromosomenaberrationen bei familiarer Panmyelopathie. Humangenetik 1:194–196

Schroeder-Kurth TM, Auerbach AD, Obe G (eds) (1989a) Fanconi anemia: clinical, cytogenetic and experimental aspects. Springer, Berlin

Schroeder-Kurth TM, Zhu TH, Hong Y, et al. (1989b) Variation in cellular sensitivities among Fanconi anemia patients, non-Fanconi anemia patients, their parents and siblings, and control probands. In: Schroeder-Kurth TM, Auerbach AD, Obe G (eds) Fanconi anemia: clinical, cytogenetic and experimental aspects. Springer, Berlin, pp 105–136

Swift M, Chase CL, Morrell D (1990) Cancer predisposition of ataxia-telangiectasia heterozygotes. Cancer Genet Cytogenet 46:21–27

Therman E, Kuhn EM (1981) Mitotic crossing-over and segregation in man. Hum Genet 59:93–100

Therman E, Kuhn EM (1985) Incidence and origin of symmetric and asymmetric dicentrics in Bloom's syndrome. Cancer Genet Cytogenet 15:293–301

Tomkins D, Hunter A, Roberts M (1979) Cytogenetic findings in Roberts–SC phocomelia syndrome(s). Am J Med Genet 4:17–26

Willis AE, Lindahl T (1987) DNA ligase deficiency in Bloom's syndrome. Nature 325:355–357

12
Sister Chromatid Exchanges and Mitotic Crossing-Over

Detection of Sister Chromatid Exchanges

Sister chromatid exchanges (SCEs) were discovered in the late 1950s with the same type of experiment as demonstrated the semiconservative replication of chromosomes (Chapter 3). When cells are grown for one cycle in medium containing [^{3}H]thymidine and for another without it, autoradiography shows that one chromatid is labeled and the other is not (Figs. 3.2 and 3); this makes exchanges between them visible (Taylor, 1958).

A more accurate technique is based on the observation that chromosomes in which thymidine is replaced by bromodeoxyuridine (BrdU) can be stained differentially (Fig. 12.1; Zakharov and Egolina, 1972). Three types of chromatids can be distinguished on the basis of whether both DNA strands, one, or none contains BrdU (Latt, 1974). Differential staining after various pretreatments can be done with Giemsa or with the fluorescent dyes Hoechst 33825, acridine orange, or coriphosphine O (Korenberg and Freedlender, 1974).

Occurrence of SCE

Since both [^{3}H]thymidine and BrdU not only make SCEs visible, but also induce them, determination of the spontaneous exchange rate is not simple. That SCEs do occur spontaneously is demonstrated by the behavior of ring chromosomes. Single rings often change into double dicentric rings through an uneven number of SCEs (Wolff, 1977).

In other types of cells, the spontaneous SCE rate can only be estimated. In Chinese hamster cells, the estimates range from 2.5 to 5/cell per two

126

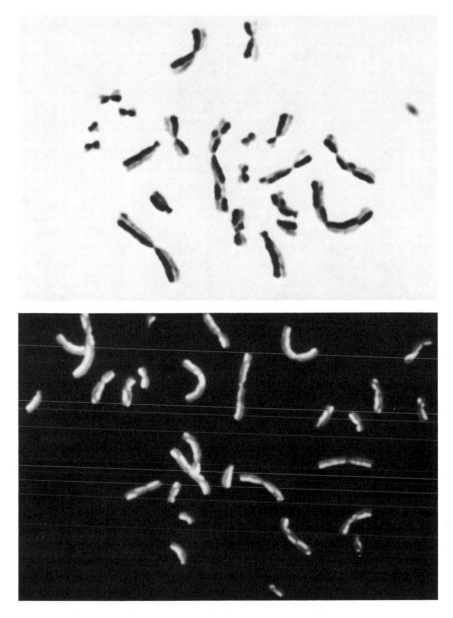

Figure 12.1. Sister chromatid exchanges demonstrated with BrdU. Top: Giemsa-stained Chinese hamster cell (courtesy of JR Korenberg). Bottom: human lymphocyte stained with coriphosphine O.

cell cycles (Wolff, 1977), and in mouse bone marrow, from 1.5 to 2/cell per two cell generations (Kanda, 1982).

SCEs have been found in all organisms in which they have been sought: in a variety of mammals, including humans, in birds, in fishes, in insects, and in plants (Schubert and Rieger, 1981). Most SCE analyses have been performed on cultured cells, but in vivo studies have been done on mammalian bone marrow, spleen, regenerating liver, and spermatogonia (Kanda, 1982).

Since SCEs are more numerous and easier to analyze accurately than chromosome breaks, it is surprising that many of the basic questions about SCE remain unsolved. Thus, we do not know whether SCEs are randomly distributed among different chromosomes and chromosome regions. Although the same agent often causes both SCE and chromosome breakage, the relationship of these phenomena is still unclear.

The results of the attempts to localize SCE within chromosomes have been highly contradictory. To quote Schubert and Rieger (1981, page 122): "Conformity is more or less confined to the observation of SCE clustering in weakly fluorescent or Giemsa-stained bands and their borders." It is almost impossible to summarize such results. The breakpoints of the SCEs thus cannot be compared with those of chromosome breaks or of mitotic chiasmata.

Two factors seem to be responsible for the controversial results obtained in studies of SCE, as well as chromosome breakage. The quality of slides and photomicrographs tends to be poor, making accurate analysis difficult. Generally, too few cells have been analyzed, and the statistical analysis of the data has been inadequate (Schubert and Rieger, 1981).

SCE in Mutagenesis Research

A wide variety of agents that, as a rule, also cause chromosome breaks have been found to induce SCE (Latt, 1981; Schubert and Rieger, 1981; Sandberg, 1982). SCEs have, therefore, become a major tool in mutagenesis research, as shown by the veritable flood of articles in this field. SCEs are more sensitive indicators of mutagenic activity than chromosome breaks. However, the two effects, chromosome breakage and SCE induction, do not always agree (Schubert and Rieger, 1981). Furthermore, as in many other aspects of SCE research, the results of mutagenesis studies have often been contradictory.

The highest incidence of SCEs has been achieved with bifunctional alkylating agents. The most effective SCE inducers include methylmethanesulfonate, mitomycin C, dimethylsulfate, ethylmethanesulfonate, and the mustards (Latt, 1981). Ultraviolet light is also a powerful inducer of SCE. Of the chromosome breakage syndromes, only in BS are the SCEs also increased (Fig. 11.2). Although AT and, even more, FA show a high incidence of chromosome aberrations (Chapter 11), no increase in SCE rates has been observed in them. Similarly, ionizing radiation breaks chromosomes effectively, but increases SCE only slightly. A dose of x-rays that increases chromosome breaks 20-fold only doubles the SCE rate (Kato, 1977).

An increase in SCE rate is certainly an indication of the mutagenic and carcinogenic potential of an agent. However, in view of the discrepancies between the induction of SCEs and chromosome breaks, as well as of the many controversies in SCE research in general, a discovery of an increased SCE rate should be followed up by chromosome studies.

The biological significance of SCE is unclear, since the genetic makeup of a cell is not changed if the exchanges take place at identical points. However, *unequal* SCEs lead to the amplification of genes on one chromatid and their deletion on the other. For instance, the variation of the heterochromatic segment on the Y chromosome obviously has come about through unequal SCE. The importance of gene duplication is discussed at the end of this chapter.

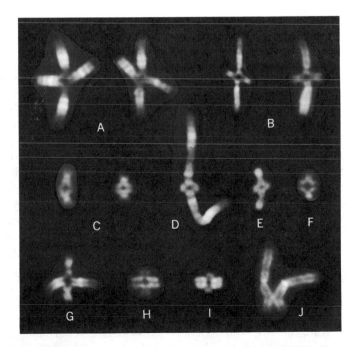

Figure 12.2. Examples of mitotic chiasmata in Bloom syndrome. (A) Two chiasmata in 1q; (B) two chiasmata in 6p; (C) two chiasmata in 19; (D) chiasma in 1q; (E) chiasma in 20q; (F) chiasma in 22q; (G) chiasma in 12q; (H) chiasma in 18q; (I) chiasma in centric region of 18; (J) chiasma in 3p (Kuhn, 1976).

Mitotic Crossing-Over

Although there is little genetic evidence of mitotic crossing-over in mammals, including humans (for instance, blood group mosaicisms, twin color spots in fur or skin), a variety of cytological observations demonstrate that it takes place in human cells, especially in BS patients (German, 1964).

A mitotic chiasma in metaphase corresponds to a one-chiasma bivalent in meiotic metaphase (Fig. 12.2A–I) or sometimes to a diplotene bivalent (Fig. 12.2J). As in meiosis, the two homologues can also be joined by a terminal chiasma (Therman and Kuhn, 1976; Kuhn and Therman, 1986). That a mitotic chiasma represents true recombination is shown by heteromorphic "bivalents" in which the sister chromatids are attached to different centromeres (Patau and Therman, 1969; Therman and Kuhn, 1976; Kuhn and Therman, 1986). This is especially striking in a mitotic chiasma between satellite stalks when the satellites are distinct, for instance, brightly fluorescent in one of the cross-over chromosomes (Therman et al., 1981). Recombination at a mitotic chiasma has also been demonstrated by the pattern of SCE (Chaganti et al., 1974) and recently confirmed with molecular analysis (Groden et al., 1990).

BS as a Model for Chromosome Instability Syndrome

BS is a suitable model for a chromosome breakage condition caused by a recessive mutant gene. It displays a wide range of chromosome aberrations, which have been analyzed extensively (Chapter 11; Kuhn and Therman, 1986). The same aberrations seem to take place in normal cells, although at a much lower rate (Therman and Kuhn, 1976).

The chromosome aberrations in BS fall into three groups. Chromosome breaks (Kuhn and Therman, 1979) and translocations between nonhomologous chromosomes (Kuhn and Therman, 1986) occur nonrandomly, but at different points. The breakpoints of these also differ from those of the mitotic chiasmata (Kuhn, 1976). The second feature, which seems to be exclusive to BS, is the greatly increased tendency to homologous exchanges, expressed in the high rates of SCE and mitotic chiasmata. All of these aberrations take place in S–G2. The anomalies of the third group, such as acentrics and dicentrics, seem to be the secondary results of primary changes in previous mitoses (Therman and Kuhn, 1985).

The highly nonrandom distribution of mitotic chiasmata was demonstrated by Kuhn (1976), who analyzed 481 Q-banded chiasmata from BS. Most of them were situated in short Q-dark regions (or at their borders), special hot spots being 3p21, 6p21, 11q13, 12q13, 17q12, and 19p or q. A high chiasma frequency was found also in the distal segments of 1p and 22q. About 17 percent of the chiasmata were situated in centric heterochromatin.

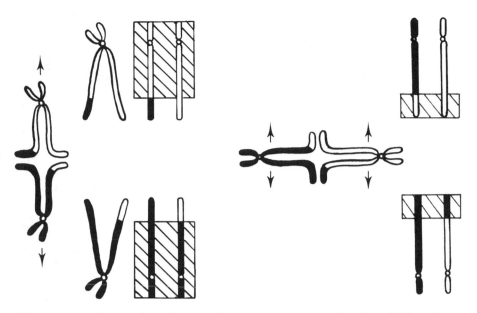

Figure 12.3. Segregation after crossing-over in a meiotic bivalent (left) and a mitotic chiasma (right). In meiotic segregation the chromatids distal to the chiasma are non-sister, in mitotic segregation, sister (Therman and Kuhn, 1981).

Segregation after Mitotic Recombination

The difference in segregation after meiotic and mitotic recombination is shown in Fig. 12.3. In meiotic segregation the chromatids distal to the chiasma are non-homologous (left), whereas after mitotic segregation they are sister chromatids (right), because human chromosomes show almost no relational coiling (i.e., coiling of sister chromatids around one another).

Visible demonstration of segregation after mitotic recombination is provided by distinct satellites. Exchanges between the repeated ribosomal RNA genes on the satellite stalks are especially frequent in BS (6/1000 cells). Thus, in a BS patient with Q-bright satellites, 31 different combinations were found in 58 cells, 12 cells being homozygous for the Q-bright satellites (Therman et al., 1981).

Obviously many other chromosome segments in BS have also become homozygous. This would allow presumed recessive cancer genes to express themselves and would explain, in part, the high incidence of cancer in BS (1 in 4 patients) (Therman and Kuhn, 1981).

Origin of Mitotic Chiasmata

Kuhn et al. (1985; 1987) have shown that significantly more genes are localized to the chiasma-rich chromosomes than to similar-sized control

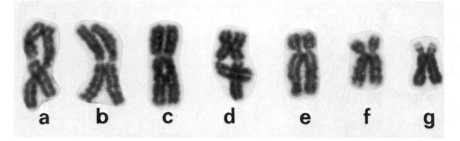

Figure 12.4. Chiasmata in diplochromosomes from BS fibroblasts. Chromosome arm involved: (a) 1p; (b) 1q; (c) two chiasmata in 2q; (d) 3p; (e) Bq; (f) Cq; (g) Dq (Kuhn, 1981).

chromosomes. Chiasma-rich chromosomes are also significantly rarer as trisomics in spontaneous abortions and in live-born children. The conclusion is that the chiasma-rich regions have a high density of active genes and are therefore extended in interphase (Korenberg et al., 1978). They would in consequence be more likely to pair and to cross over than other segments.

The genotype of the individual and the closeness of homologous chromatids play a decisive role in the rate of homologous exchanges (Therman and Kuhn, 1981). In normal human meiosis, in which pairing is most intimate, chiasma frequencies range from one to five per bivalent (meiosis in BS has not been studied). The rate for SCE is estimated as 1.5–5/cell per two generations (in BS, this rate is increased 12–15 times). Diplochromosomes show 100 chiasmata per 1000 cells (in BS, 2500/1000 cells; Fig. 12.4). Normal diploid cells, in which chromosomes apparently pair only by chance, have a mitotic chiasmata number of 0.1–1/1000 cells (in corresponding BS cells the rate is 5–150 mitotic chiasmata/1000 cells).

Gene Amplification

Table 11.1 summarizes the chromosome aberrations in BS that promote cancer incidence. One of the most important mechanisms is probably unequal crossing-over (Fig. 12.5). This may take place during meiosis, mitosis, or SCE. The prerequisite for unequal crossing-over is first mispairing, for which repeated sequences have a special tendency, followed by an exchange between non-homologous points.

The variation in heterochromatin within individuals or species probably is the result of unequal crossing-over. The variation in the length of the satellite stalks is another result of unequal exchanges between repeated genes. A further example is provided by homogeneously stained regions and double minutes (Chapter 28).

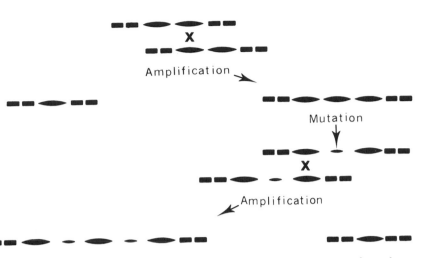

Figure 12.5. Amplification and reduction of chromosome segments through un-equal crossing-over.

The importance of unequal crossing-over in the evolution of proteins was predicted by Smithies (1964). This idea has been amply confirmed (for instance, Maeda et al., 1984). Gene amplification has been found in a variety of organisms ranging from bacteria to humans (Schimke, 1982), and it is now clear that this process has played a major role in evolution.

References

Chaganti RSK, Schonberg S, German J (1974) A manyfold increase in sister chromatid exchanges in Bloom's syndrome lymphocytes. Proc Natl Acad Sci USA 71:4508–4512

German J (1964) Cytological evidence for crossing-over in vitro in human lymphoid cells. Science 144:298–301

Groden J, Nakamura Y, German J (1990) Molecular evidence that homologous recombination occurs in proliferating human somatic cells. Proc Natl Acad Sci USA 87:4315–4319

Kanda N (1982) Spontaneous sister chromatid exchange in vivo. In: Sandberg AA (ed) Sister chromatid exchange. Liss, New York, pp 279–296

Kato H (1977) Spontaneous and induced sister chromatid exchanges as revealed by the BUdR-labeling method. Int Rev Cytol 49:55–97

Korenberg JR, Freedlender EF (1974) Giemsa technique for the detection of sister chromatid exchanges. Chromosoma 48:355–360

Korenberg JR, Therman E, Denniston C (1978) Hot spots and functional organization of human chromosomes. Hum Genet 43:13–22

Kuhn EM (1976) Localization by Q-banding of mitotic chiasmata in cases of Bloom's syndrome. Chromosoma 57:1–11

Kuhn EM (1981) A high incidence of mitotic chiasmata in endoreduplicated Bloom's syndrome cells. Hum Genet 58:417–421

Kuhn EM, Therman E (1979) Chromosome breakage and rejoining of sister chromatids in Bloom's syndrome. Chromosoma 73:275–286

Kuhn EM, Therman E (1986) Cytogenetics of Bloom's syndrome. Cancer Genet Cytogenet 22:1–18

Kuhn EM, Therman E, Denniston C (1985) Mitotic chiasmata, gene density and oncogenes. Hum Genet 70:1–5

Kuhn EM, Sarto GE, Bates B-J G, et al. (1987) Gene-rich chromosome regions and autosomal trisomy. A case of chromosome 3 trisomy mosaicism. Hum Genet 77:214–220

Latt SA (1974) Localization of sister chromatid exchanges in human chromosomes. Science 185:74–76

Latt SA (1981) Sister chromatid exchange formation. Annu Rev Genet 15:11–55

Maeda N, Yang F, Barnett DR, et al. (1984) Duplication within the haptoglobin Hp^2 gene. Nature 309:131–135

Patau K, Therman E (1969) Mitotic crossing-over in man. Genetics 61:Suppl 45–46

Sandberg AA (1982) Sister chromatid exchange in human states. In: Sandberg AA (ed) Sister chromatid exchange. Liss, New York, pp 619–651

Schimke RT (1982) Summary. In: Schimke RT (ed) Gene amplification. Cold Spring Harbor Laboratory Press, Cold Spring Harbor, New York, pp 317–333

Schubert I, Rieger R (1981) Sister chromatid exchanges and heterochromatin. Hum Genet 57:119–130

Smithies O (1964) Chromosomal rearrangements and protein structure. Cold Spring Harbor Symp Quant Biol 29:309–319

Taylor JH (1958) Sister chromatid exchanges in tritium labeled chromosomes. Genetics 43:515–529

Therman E, Kuhn EM (1976) Cytological demonstration of mitotic crossing-over in man. Cytogenet Cell Genet 17:254–267

Therman E, Kuhn EM (1981) Mitotic crossing-over and segregation in man. Hum Genet 59:93–100

Therman E, Kuhn EM (1985) Incidence and origin of symmetric and asymmetric dicentrics in Bloom's syndrome. Cancer Genet Cytogenet 15:293–301

Therman E, Otto PG, Shahidi NT (1981) Mitotic recombination and segregation of satellites in Bloom's syndrome. Chromosoma 82:627–636

Wolff S (1977) Sister chromatid exchange. Annu Rev Genet 11:183–201

Zakharov AF, Egolina NA (1972) Differential spiralization along mammalian mitotic chromosomes. I. BUdR-revealed differentiation in Chinese hamster chromosomes. Chromosoma 38:341–365

13
Cell Fusion, Prematurely Condensed Chromosomes, and the Origin of Allocyclic Chromosomes

Fusion of normal, untreated mammalian cells has been described only in the development of bone, muscle, and trophoblast tissues. Otherwise, at least one of the fusing cells has been malignant. Early studies on cell fusion have been reviewed, for example by Otto and Therman (1982). Cell fusion was originally detected in vitro, but has been found in an increasing number of malignant diseases in vivo (for instance, Kovacs, 1985; Sandberg, 1987). It is not clear whether fusion, malignant–malignant or malignant–host cell, plays any significant role in the creation of aneuploid–polyploid chromosome constitutions in cancer (Sreekantaiah et al., 1987). Spontaneous fusion of nonmalignant lymphocytes and fibroblasts has so far been observed only in Bloom syndrome (Otto and Therman, 1982).

The observation that infection by a variety of viruses caused cell fusion has led to the technique of cell fusion by treatment with inactivated Sendai virus (Creagan and Ruddle, 1977). Nowadays, cell fusion is accomplished mainly with polyethylene glycol (PEG). Recently, electrofusion has also been used successfully for this purpose (Cervenka and Camargo, 1987). Cell fusion is a widely used tool in gene mapping (Chapter 31) and in the creation of hybridomas.

Prematurely Condensed Chromosomes (PCC)

The phenomenon that has attracted attention to cell fusion is premature chromosome condensation. This can be used to determine that cell fusion, and not some other polyploidization mechanism, has given rise to a polyploid cell. When a cell whose chromosomes are in metaphase is fused

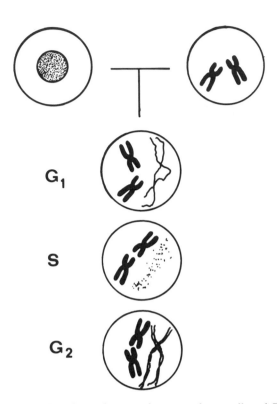

Figure 13.1. Fusion of an interphase and a metaphase cell and PCC formation. In G_1, the PCC are single and thin; in S they appear "pulverized"; in G_2 they resemble prophase chromosomes.

with a cell in interphase, the nuclear membrane of the interphase nucleus dissolves and the chromosomes condense. The condensation becomes visible some 15–20 min after the fusion and reaches its peak in 1 h (Rao, 1982; Sperling, 1982). The appearance of PCC depends on the nuclear stage—G_1, S, or G_2—at the time of the fusion (Fig. 13.1). PCC in early G_1 are short, but become longer and thinner as G_1 progresses (Fig. 13.1). The chromosomes in G_0 (interphase of cells that do not undergo mitosis) are similar to those in G_1.

Chromosomes condensed in the S phase have been called "pulverized", or "fragmented", because of their appearance. However, even at this stage, the chromosomes are continuous, the gaps in them representing the segments that at the moment are in the process of replication. That the S type PCC, indeed, are synthesizing DNA can be demonstrated with [3H]thymidine and autoradiography (Fig. 13.2). The G_2 type PCC resem-

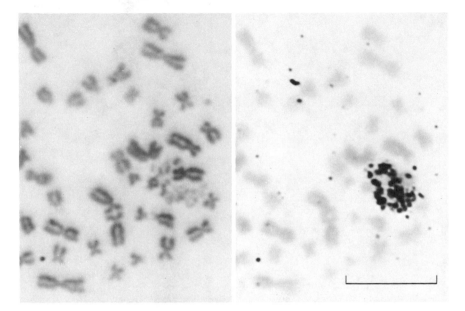

Figure 13.2. Part of a tetraploid lymphocyte metaphase from Bloom syndrome with an allocyclic chromosome, before (left) and after (right) autoradiography. [³H]thymidine was added to the cell culture 4 hours before fixation (the plate also contains a mitotic chiasma) (Otto et al., 1981).

ble long, thin prophase chromosomes, which gradually shorten (Fig. 13.3). They can be banded with the usual techniques, but sometimes appear spontaneously banded (Fig. 13.3, bottom). The spontaneous banding resembles that of chromosomes that have been fed BrdU in the late S period (Otto and Therman, 1982). Obviously, the late-replicating segments have not had enough time to coil and have remained stretched.

The term "premature condensation" does not describe S-PCC very well; these are seen as a group of dots. Sandberg and his co-workers (Sandberg, 1987) have, therefore, recommended the usage "prophasing" for this phenomenon.

An interesting aspect of cell fusion and PCC formation is that cells from very different organisms can be induced to undergo these processes, the extremes being combinations like *Drosophila*–soybean and human–carrot cells (Dudits et al., 1982). These experiments show that the same or similar factors are involved in chromosome condensation and mitosis in the widest variety of organisms. That this applies even to meiosis has been shown by experiments combining amphibian oocytes and human cells (Sunkara et al., 1982). The substances involved in all these processes are under intensive study (Hittelman, 1986).

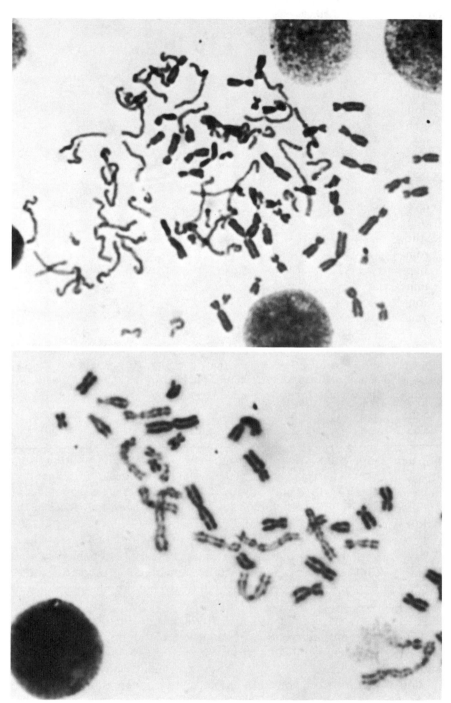

Figure 13.3. Spontaneous fusion of two Bloom syndrome lymphocytes and PCC formation. Top: PCC in G_1; bottom: naturally banded PCC in G_2 (Otto and Therman, 1982).

Uses of PCC Formation

Cell fusion combined with PCC is an important technique in a variety of fields. PCC provide an opportunity to study interphase chromosomes and to follow the changes that they undergo from G_1 through S and G_2. Since the chromosomes in late G_1 and early G_2 are longer than at any mitotic stage, their fine structure can be analyzed in greater detail. This also makes the determination of DNA and RNA synthesis more accurate (Sperling, 1982).

PCC have been used to study the chromosomes of differentiated cells, such as spermatids (Drwinga et al., 1979) and sperm cells, which do not divide spontaneously. These techniques might also be useful in the study of the cytogenetics of somatic cells. Furthermore, the arrangement of chromosomes in interphase nuclei can be followed by means of PCC (Chapter 14). Such studies have confirmed that in different types of mammalian cells the chromosomes retain their polarized anaphase orientation (Rabl orientation) throughout interphase, but are otherwise situated at random (Sperling and Lüdtke, 1981; Cremer et al., 1982).

A further field in which PCC have been and probably will be increasingly useful is the study of chromosome breakage. With ordinary cytological techniques, chromosome breakage can be studied, at the earliest, several hours after its induction, whereas with PCC, breaks can be analyzed in 20–30 min. This gives a good idea of the original breakage rate, before the majority of breaks have had time to be repaired. Indeed, analysis of the PCC at different times after treatment demonstrates a gradual decrease of visible chromosome aberrations (Hittelman et al., 1980). The course of leukemias and the effects of treatments can also be followed by means of PCC (Hittelman, 1986).

Origin of Allocyclic Chromosomes

An otherwise normal metaphase plate may, although extremely rarely, contain one or a few chromosomes that resemble PCC chromosomes in G_1, S, or G_2. The "pulverized" S-type chromosomes are in the process of synthesizing DNA, while the rest of the chromosomes are in metaphase (Fig. 13.2). The rarity of such allocyclic chromosomes in normal, untreated cells is shown by the observation that in 2324 cells from 171 persons under 40 years of age who did not have a chromosome-breakage syndrome, only one cell with an allocyclic chromosome was found (C Trunca, unpublished). However, ring chromosomes often appear as allocyclics. The shape of the S-type allocyclic chromosomes probably reflects fairly accurately their structure in intact interphase nuclei (Kuhn et al., 1987).

Agents that break chromosomes also increase the incidence of allocyclic chromosomes (Rao, 1977). In Bloom syndrome, in which other chromosome abnormalities are common, the frequency of allocyclic chromosomes is greatly increased (Otto et al., 1981).

A commonly accepted hypothesis—in fact, no other explanation is usually considered—is that allocyclic chromosomes are derived from micronuclei in which the chromosomes condense prematurely under the influence of the main nucleus in metaphase (Kato and Sandberg, 1968; Obe and Beek, 1982). An alternative hypothesis has been proposed by Otto et al. (1981). According to them, an allocyclic chromosome has undergone a mutation (possibly in a hypothetical coiling center) that renders it unable to keep up with the rest of the chromosomes. Such chromosomes have been left behind in their coiling cycle and will form micronuclei in the *next* mitosis.

The main argument for the micronucleus hypothesis is that the frequencies of allocyclic chromosomes and of micronuclei are similar. This would agree equally well with the idea that allocyclic chromosomes end up as micronuclei. However, further evidence for the micronucleus hypothesis is that the allocyclic chromosomes appear only at the second division after the induction of chromosome breakage (Obe and Beek, 1982). On the other hand, several other observations, made mainly on Bloom syndrome patients, are easily explained by the hypothesis of Otto et al. (1981), but fit less well, or not at all, the micronuclear origin of allocyclic chromosomes: (1) In only 11/115 cells was the allocyclic chromosome lying at the rim of the metaphase plate. (2) In 24/115 metaphases, only a part of a chromosome was "pulverized." (3) A "pulverized" acrocentric was often found to be in satellite association with another acrocentric. (4) When a ring chromosome is replaced by an allocyclic chromosome, as often happens, it is practically always a member of a 46-chromosome complement and not an extra chromosome, as it should be equally frequently if it arose from a micronucleus. (5) Allocyclic chromosomes occur five times more frequently in cells with other chromosome abnormalities. (6) Allocyclic chromosomes are found in 16% of the tetraploid, but in only 2% of the diploid cells. (7) When human micronuclei are fused with human or rodent cells, the chromosomes in them are metaphasic and do not appear as PCC (Viaggi et al., 1987).

On the basis of present evidence, it seems probable that allocyclic chromosomes represent both those chromosomes that have been left behind in their cycle and micronuclei that have undergone PCC. Both hypotheses should be considered in analyses of future observations.

References

Cervenka J, Camargo M (1987) Premature chromosome condensation induced by electrofusion. Cytogenet Cell Genet 45:169–173

Creagan RP, Ruddle FH (1977) New approaches to human gene mapping by somatic cell genetics. In: Yunis JJ (ed) Molecular structure of human chromosomes. Academic, New York, pp 89–142

Cremer T, Cremer C, Baumann H, et al. (1982) Rabl's model of the interphase chromosome arrangement tested in Chinese hamster cells by premature chromosome condensation and laser-UV-microbeam experiments. Hum Genet 60: 46–56

Drwinga HL, Hsu TC, Pathak S (1979) Induction of prematurely condensed chromosomes from testicular cells of the mouse. Chromosoma 75:45–50

Dudits D, Szabados L, Hadlaczky G (1982) Premature chromosome condensation in plant cells and its potential use in genetic manipulation. In: Rao PN, Johnson RT, Sperling K (eds) Premature chromosome condensation. Academic, New York, pp 359–369

Hittelman WN (1986) The technique of premature chromosome condensation to study the leukemic process: review and speculations. CRC Crit Rev Oncol/ Hematol 6:147–221

Hittelman WN, Sognier MA, Cole A (1980) Direct measurement of chromosome damage and its repair by premature chromosome condensation. In: Meyn RE, Withers HR (eds) Radiation biology in cancer research. Raven, New York, pp 103–123

Kato H, Sandberg AA (1968) Chromosome pulverization in human cells with micronuclei. J Natl Cancer Inst 40:165–179

Kovacs G (1985) Premature chromosome condensation: evidence for *in vivo* cell fusion in human malignant tumours. Int J Cancer 36:637–641

Kuhn EM, Therman E, Buchler DA (1987) Do individual allocyclic chromosomes in metaphase reflect their interphase domains? Hum Genet 77:210–213

Obe G, Beek B (1982) Premature chromosome condensation in micronuclei. In: Rao PN, Johnson RT, Sperling K (eds) Premature chromosome condensation. Academic, New York, pp 113–130

Otto PG, Therman E (1982) Spontaneous cell fusion and PCC formation in Bloom's syndrome. Chromosoma 85:143–148

Otto PG, Otto PA, Therman E (1981) The behavior of allocyclic chromosomes in Bloom's syndrome. Chromosoma 84:337–344

Rao PN (1977) Premature chromosome condensation and the fine structure of chromosomes. In: Yunis JJ (ed) Molecular structure of human chromosomes. Academic, New York, pp 205–231

Rao PN (1982) The phenomenon of premature chromosome condensation. In: Rao PN, Johnson RT, Sperling K (eds) Premature chromosome condensation. Academic, New York, pp 1–41

Sandberg AA (1987) Prophasing: What's in a name? Cancer Genet Cytogenet 27:181–183

Sperling K (1982) Cell cycle and chromosome cycle: morphological and functional aspects. In: Rao PN, Johnson RT, Sperling K (eds) Premature chromosome condensation. Academic, New York, pp 43–78

Sperling K, Lüdtke E-K (1981) Arrangement of prematurely condensed chromosomes in cultured cells and lymphocytes of the Indian muntjac. Chromosoma 83:541–553

Sreekantaiah C, Bhargava MK, Shetty NJ (1987) Premature chromosome condensation in human cervical carcinoma. Cancer Genet Cytogenet 24:263–269

Sunkara PS, Wright DA, Adlakha RC, et al. (1982) Characterization of chromo-
    some condensation factors of mammalian cells. In: Rao PN, Johnson RT,
    Sperling K (eds) Premature chromosome condensation. Academic, New York,
    pp 234–251
Viaggi S, Bonatti S, Abbondandolo A (1987) New evidence for the presence of
    chromosomes in micronuclei of human and Chinese hamster cells. Mutagenesis
    2:367–370

14
Chromosome Arrangement in Interphase and in Differentiated Nuclei

Chromosome Arrangement

Until some 10 years ago our knowledge of the structure of interphase nuclei was limited to a few aspects of chromosome arrangement. As early as 1885, Carl Rabl showed that chromosomes remain in the same polarized orientation through interphase that they had assumed in anaphase. This Rabl orientation, as it has been called, is often still visible in the following prophase (Fig. 14.1a, b; Heitz, 1933). Rabl also found that chromosomes in interphase do not form a tangle of threads, but that each of them occupies a defined territory, a domain. Recent studies done by creating prematurely condensed chromosomes (Sperling and Lüdtke, 1981; Cremer et al., 1982) and by hybridizing specific DNA probes to nuclei (Manuelidis, 1985; Schardin et al., 1985) have shed new light on the nuclear structure. The latter technique, especially, has made visible the domains of individual chromosomes and has enabled the determination of numerical and structural chromosome abnormalities in interphase nuclei (Cremer et al., 1988).

Since the 1940s it has been known that both constitutive and facultative heterochromatin, in most cases, are attached to the nuclear membrane (Vanderlyn, 1949; Geitler, 1953; Tschermak-Woess, 1971; Nagl, 1985). It is possible that the telomeres also lie at the nuclear membrane.

However, the scarcity of solid evidence concerning chromosome arrangement has provided fertile ground for hypotheses.

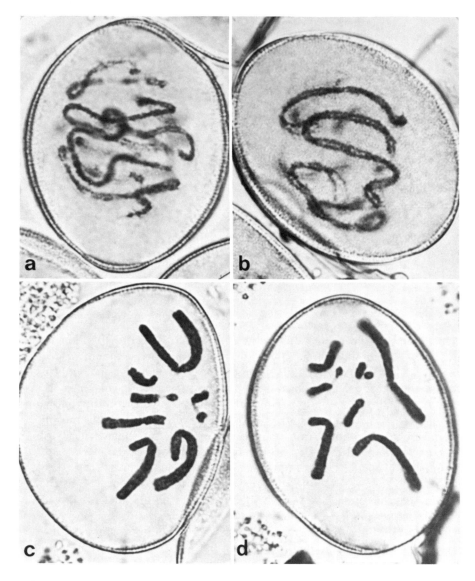

Figure 14.1. Haploid mitotic stages in pollen grains of *Uvularia* (*n* = 7). (a, b) Prophases showing Rabl orientation; (c, d) metaphases with random orientation of chromosomes (untreated, Feulgen-smear) (Therman and Denniston, 1984).

Hypotheses Proposing a Nonrandom Chromosome Arrangement

Three hypotheses have presumed a nonrandom chromosome arrangement in interphase. A singularly long-lived idea has been that homologous chromosomes are paired in all interphases (Avivi and Feldman, 1980;

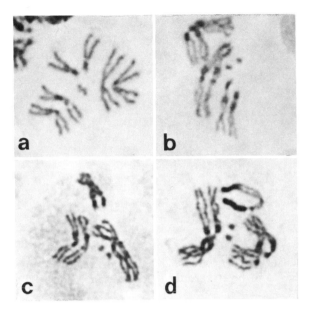

Figure 14.2. Four metaphases with paired homologues from larval brain cells of *Drosophila melanogaster* (*2n* = 8). (a–c) Female cells; (d) male cell in which the short and long arms of the· Y chromosome are attached to the X (colcemid, hypotonic, orcein).

Comings, 1980). However, this is true only in Diptera, whose homologues are clearly paired even in metaphases treated with colcemid and hypotonic solutions (Fig. 14.2). Indeed, a comparison of Dipteran and human metaphases, for instance, provides the most convincing argument against a general pairing of homologous chromosomes. Another hypothesis claims that each chromosome is attached at a specific predetermined point on the nuclear membrane (Comings, 1968). This would lead to a more or less constant chromosome order in metaphase. The most surprising of the three hypotheses assumes that chromosome arms of similar size have a tendency to lie side-by-side, independent of homology (Bennett, 1982; Heslop-Harrison and Bennett, 1983a and b).

In spite of these hypotheses, a random chromosome arrangement in metaphase has been confirmed repeatedly. In locusts and grasshoppers, the metaphase plates are ring-shaped, which allows an accurate determination of the neighbors of each chromosome. A random chromosome organization in these organisms has been described, for instance, by Nur (1973), Fox et al. (1975), and John et al. (1985). The same phenomenon has been found in the gonial cells of several organisms (Fig. 17.1; Therman and Sarto, 1977). In muntjac cells, a random arrangement has been reported by Cohen et al. (1972) and by Korf and Diacumakos (1977).

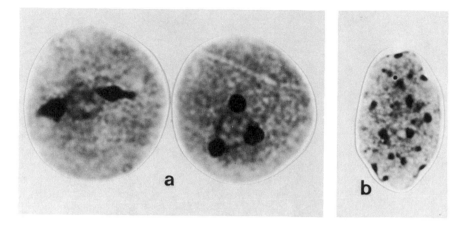

Figure 14.3. (a) Two mouse Sertoli cells in which the heterochromatin has fused at the nucleoli into two and three clumps, respectively; (b) a mouse spermatogonium in which the heterochromatic segments are attached to the nuclear membrane.

Therman and Denniston (1984) determined the chromosome order in the haploid pollen grain mitosis of the liliaceous plant *Uvularia* ($n = 7$; two of the smallest chromosomes have secondary constrictions; Fig. 14.1c, d). Again, the order was found to be completely random. This provides further evidence against the hypotheses of Comings (1968) and of the Bennett group. Moreover, Callow (1985) has pointed out weaknesses in the observations, statistics, and conclusions of the Bennett group.

Apparently, chromosome arrangement is basically random in most organisms. Possibly in some cell types, or as a result of a treatment (prefixation exposure to cold?), nonrandomness may occur. Moreover, slight deviations from a random metaphase distribution may be caused by stickiness of heterochromatin, satellite associations, and the tendency of small chromosomes to lie in the middle of metaphase plates.

Chromosome Arrangement and Differentiation

Differentiated cells represent an enormous variety of types, whose nuclei differ in size, shape, and amount of facultative and constitutive heterochromatin (Kuhn and Therman, 1988). Differences in chromosome arrangement also add to this variation. Although a correlation obviously exists between differentiation and chromosome arrangement, the causal relationship between them is unclear.

In mouse (and human) Sertoli cells, heterochromatin has fused into two to three clumps which lie at the nucleoli (Fig. 14.3a). In spermatogonia, on the other hand, the chromocenters are separately attached to the nuclear membrane (Fig. 14.3b; Hsu et al., 1971).

Manuelidis (1984) has shown that the centromeres in different types of mouse cerebellar cells occupy characteristic sites. In the Purkinje cells, most centromeres are clustered around the nucleolus, whereas in the granule neurons centromere clusters are attached to the nuclear membrane.

Conclusions

Chromosomes occupy definite domains in interphase and, as a rule, move very little relative to one another. Therefore, metaphase plates reflect interphase organization. Generally, chromosomes retain their polarized Rabl orientation through interphase and into prophase.

In general, the chromosomes are arranged at random relative to each other. An exception is found in the Diptera, in which the homologous chromosomes are paired throughout the mitotic cycle.

In many differentiated nuclei, the centromeres adhere to the nuclear membrane or to the nucleoli or to both.

Although it seems clear that chromosome arrangement and differentiation are in some way correlated, the actual relationship between these two phenomena remains unknown.

References

Avivi L, Feldman M (1980) Arrangement of chromosomes in the interphase nucleus of plants. Hum Genet 55:281–295

Bennett MD (1982) Nucleotypic basis of the spatial ordering of chromosomes in eukaryotes and the implications of the order for genome evolution and phenotypic variation. In: Dover GA, Flavell RB (eds) Genome evolution. Academic, New York, pp 239–261

Callow RS (1985) Comments on Bennett's model of somatic chromosome disposition. Heredity 54:171–177

Cohen MM, Enis P, Pfeifer CG (1972) An investigation of somatic pairing in the muntjak (*Muntiacus muntjak*). Cytogenetics 11:145–152

Comings DE (1968) The rationale for an ordered arrangement of chromatin in the interphase nucleus. Am J Hum Genet 20:440–460

Comings DE (1980) Arrangement of chromatin in the nucleus. Hum Genet 53:131–143

Cremer T, Cremer C, Baumann H, et al. (1982) Rabl's model of the interphase chromosome arrangement tested in Chinese hamster cells by premature chromosome condensation and laser–UV–microbeam experiments. Hum Genet 60:46–56

Cremer T, Lichter P, Borden J, et al. (1988) Detection of chromosome aberrations in metaphase and interphase tumor cells by in situ hybridization using chromosome-specific library probes. Hum Genet 80:235–246

Fox DP, Mello-Sampayo T, Carter KC (1975) Chromosome distribution in neuroblast metaphase cells of *Locusta migratoria* L. Chromosoma 53:321–333

Geitler L (1953) Endomitose und endomitotische Polyploidisierung. In: Protoplasmatologia, Handbuch der Protoplasmaforschung, Vol VI, C. Springer, Vienna

Heitz E (1933) Die Herkunft der Chromocentren. Planta 18:571–635

Heslop-Harrison JS, Bennett MD (1983a) Prediction and analysis of spatial order in haploid chromosome complements. Proc R Soc Lond B 218:211–223

Heslop-Harrison JS, Bennett MD (1983b) The spatial order of chromosomes in root-tip metaphases of *Aegilops umbellulata*. Proc R Soc Lond B 218:225–239

Hsu TC, Cooper JEK, Mace ML Jr, et al. (1971) Arrangement of centromeres in mouse cells. Chromosoma 34:73–87

John B, King M, Schweizer D, et al. (1985) Equilocality of heterochromatin distribution and heterochromatin heterogeneity in acridid grasshoppers. Chromosoma 91:185–200

Korf BR, Diacumakos EG (1977) Random arrangements of mitotic chromosomes in radial metaphases of the Indian muntjac. Cytogenet Cell Genet 19:335–343

Kuhn EM, Therman E (1988) The behavior of heterochromatin in mouse and human nuclei. Cancer Genet Cytogenet 34:143–151

Manuelidis L (1984) Different central nervous system cell types display distinct and nonrandom arrangements of satellite DNA sequences. Proc Natl Acad Sci USA 81:3123–3127

Manuelidis L (1985) Individual interphase chromosome domains revealed by in situ hybridization. Hum Genet 71:288–293

Nagl W (1985) Chromatin organization and the control of gene activity. Int Rev Cytol 94:21–56

Nur U (1973) Random arrangement of chromosomes in a radial metaphase configuration. Chromosoma 40:263–267

Rabl C (1885) Über Zelltheilung. Morphol Jahrb 10:214–330

Schardin M, Cremer T, Hager HD, et al. (1985) Specific staining of human chromosomes in Chinese hamster × man hybrid cell lines demonstrates interphase chromosome territories. Hum Genet 71:281–287

Sperling K, Lüdtke E-K (1981) Arrangement of prematurely condensed chromosomes in cultured cells and lymphocytes of the Indian muntjac. Chromosoma 83:541–553

Therman E, Denniston C (1984) Random arrangement of chromosomes in *Uvularia* (*Liliaceae*). Pl Syst Evol 147:289–297

Therman E, Sarto GE (1977) Premeiotic and early meiotic stages in the pollen mother cells of *Eremurus* and in human embryonic oocytes. Hum Genet 35:137–151

Tschermak-Woess E (1971) Endomitose. Handb Allg Pathol 2:569–625

Vanderlyn L (1949) The heterochromatin problem in cyto-genetics as related to other branches of investigation. Bot Rev 15:507–582

15
Modifications of Mitosis

Although normal mitosis is characterized by the regular alternation of chromosome reproduction and segregation of daughter chromosomes, the two processes are not necessarily correlated, and their relationship can be changed in different ways (Oksala, 1954). As a rule, such modifications lead to a chromosome constitution differing from the basic complement of the individual (Fig. 15.1). Apart from multipolar mitoses, all other mitotic modifications are characterized by an absent or defective spindle, and in most cases these result in the duplication of the chromosome number (Fig. 15.2). Nagl (1978) has united the most important of these mechanisms, endoreduplication and endomitosis, under the term endocycles. The terminology referring to mitotic modifications has been the subject of considerable dispute. We shall use that proposed by Levan and Hauschka (1953a), since it is established in the literature.

Restitution and mitosis without cell division, as well as cell fusion, lead to polyploidy or the formation of multinucleate cells. D'Amato (1989) has recently reviewed all these processes.

Endoreduplication

The most common modification of mitosis is endoreduplication, in which the chromosomes replicate two or more times between mitoses instead of once as in normal mitosis (Levan and Hauschka, 1953a). If two replications have occurred, the chromosomes in a subsequent mitosis consist of four chromatids instead of the usual two. As mentioned in Chapter 3, such structures are called diplochromosomes (Fig. 25.4). After three or four endoreduplications, bundles consisting of 8 or 16 chromatids, respectively, can be observed (Fig. 15.3c).

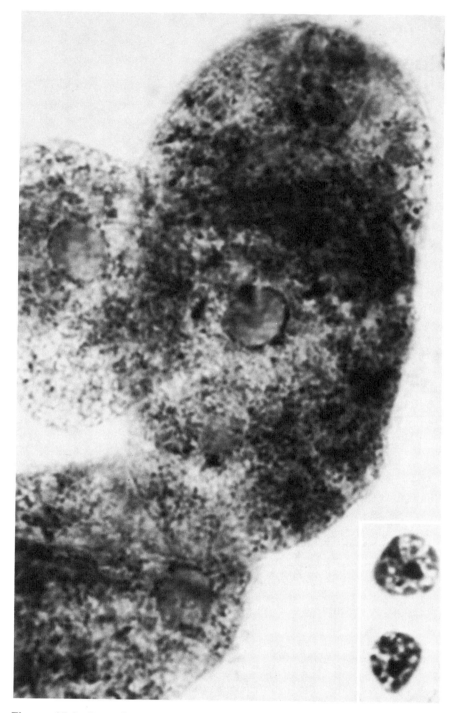

Figure 15.1. Part of a giant lobed nucleus from human cervical cancer. Inset: normal stroma nuclei with most of the chromatin condensed as chromocenters (Therman and Kuhn, 1989, reprinted with permission of CRC Press, Inc.).

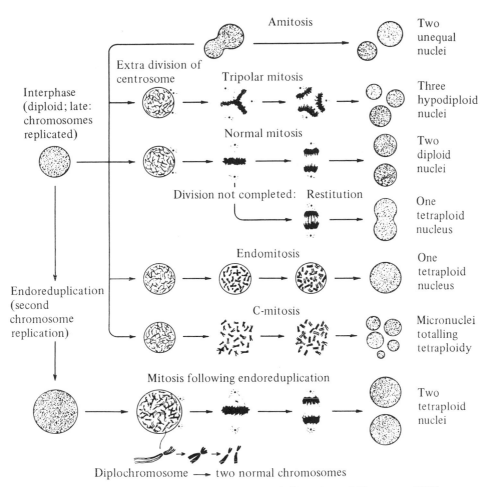

Figure 15.2. Modifications of mitosis (see text) (Oksala and Therman, 1974).

In differentiated cells one endoreduplication after another may take place, so that the nucleus increases stepwise in both size and degree of polyploidy. Enormous nuclei, which obviously have come about through repeated endoreduplications, are characteristic especially of secretory cells and of tumor cells in both plants and animals (Fig. 15.1).

Endoreduplication probably occurs occasionally in all tissues. For instance, in human fibroblast cultures 3–5 percent of the dividing cells show a tetraploid chromosome number (a few are even octoploid), whereas such divisions are rare in cultured lymphocytes. Diplochromosomes are found in only a fraction of the tetraploid divisions, however, since they occur only in the first division after endoreduplication. In differentiated tissues, endoreduplication is the most common mode of polyploidization.

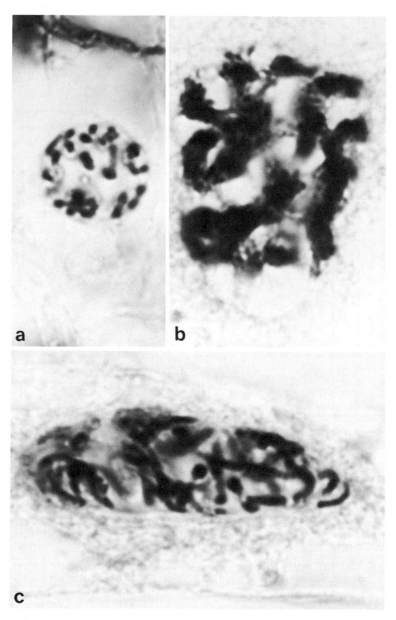

Figure 15.3. Nuclei from cultured pea roots. (a) Diploid prophase; (b) polytene chromosomes without banding; (c) nucleus with multiple chromatid bundles (Therman and Murashige, 1984).

Polyteny

Polytenization is a modification of endoreduplication in which the re-plicated homologous chromatids remain paired. The best known polytene chromosomes are the giant chromosomes of Dipteran salivary glands (Fig. 15.4c).

Variants of these typically giant chromosomes are found in many other insect tissues (Beerman, 1962). A polytene chromosome is composed of partially uncoiled chromosome strands paired side-by-side. At certain points, called chromomeres, the strand is folded. The chromomeres are aligned and form the visible bands in the polytene chromosome. In the *Diptera*, each polytene chromosome consists of the two homologues. The stretched-out parts of the chromosome strands are the interband regions, whereas each band is thought to contain one gene. The chromosomes replicate time and again, and a Dipteran salivary chromosome may finally consist of as many as 16,000 units (Beerman, 1962).

During the development of a tissue, certain bands specific for the tissue form so-called puffs. Puffing involves the unraveling of the coiled DNA of a particular chromomere; RNA is being synthesized at the puffs, and this demonstrates that the puffed genes are active in specific tissues during specific periods in development.

Polytene chromosomes are not limited to insects but are also found in certain specialized plant cells, such as the synergids and antipods in the embryo sac as well as in suspensor and endosperm cells (Tschermak-Woess, 1956; Nagl, 1981). Polytene chromosomes induced by culture conditions in pea roots (ordinarily pea roots consist of 2C and 4C cells) are illustrated in Fig. 15.3b (Therman and Murashige, 1984).

Interestingly, polytene chromosomes have also been described in the giant trophoblast cells of the rabbit, mouse, and rat (Zybina et al. 1975). (Whether polytene chromosomes also occur in giant human cells is still uncertain.) The banded structure is usually much less clear in non-Dipteran polytene chromosomes, since mitotic chromosomes tend to pair only in Diptera. However, good banding has been obtained in the bean *Phaseolus* by growing the plants at low temperatures (Nagl, 1976).

Endomitosis

In endomitosis, prophase is normal. However, the nuclear membrane never dissolves, and the chromosomes continue to contract within it (Fig. 15.2). After they have reached their maximum contraction in endometa-phase, the sister chromatids separate in endoanaphase but do not move far apart. The chromosomes then undergo telophasic changes and the nucleus reverts to interphase, having doubled its chromosome number.

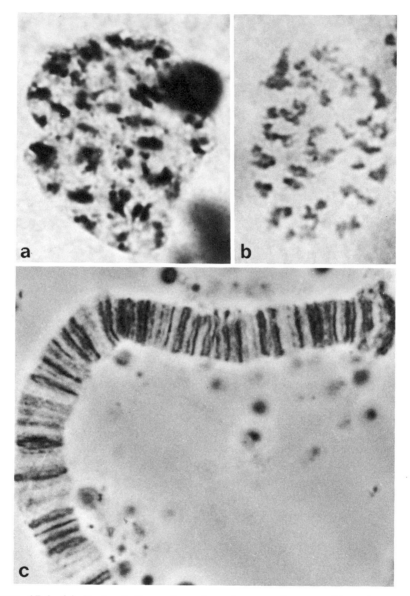

Figure 15.4. (a) Endomitotic nucleus from human placenta; (b) endomitotic nucleus from a septal cell of a testicular follicle in a grasshopper; (c) polytene chromosome from *Drosophila melanogaster* (c, courtesy of R Kreber).

This was the classic description of endomitosis by Geitler (1939) in various tissues of the Heteropteran insect *Gerris*. However, it is now clear that other types of endomitosis exist. In the septal cells of the testicular follicles of grasshoppers, no DNA synthesis but intensive RNA synthesis takes place in the endomitotic cells (Fig. 15.4b; Kiknadze and Istomina, 1980; Therman et al., 1983b). Such cells have obviously reached the final stage in their differentiation and are specialized for manufacturing some gene products.

In endomitotic cells of human hydatidiform moles, the chromosomes replicate nonsynchronously, part of them remaining condensed at all times. Thus a typical prophase and interphase are absent (Therman et al., 1986). Clearly, endomitosis in various organisms should be restudied with modern techniques.

In the salivary gland of the insect *Gerris*, the cells become 1024-ploid to 2048-ploid as a result of successive endomitoses. Endomitosis is also found in the tissues of many other insects as well as of other animal groups (Geitler, 1953; Heitz, 1953; Nagl, 1978). The tapetum cells of anther lobes in many plants undergo endomitosis (D'Amato, 1952, 1989; Oksala and Therman, 1977). It has also been repeatedly described in cancer cells of both mouse and humans (Levan and Hauschka, 1953a; Oksala and Therman, 1974; Therman et al., 1983a), but the only *normal* human tissue in which it has so far been observed is the placenta (Fig. 15.4a; Sarto et al., 1982).

C-Mitosis

In C-mitosis (named after the drug colchicine) the chromosomes behave normally throughout prophase and up until metaphase. However, the spindle is defective or absent so that the chromosomes do not collect into a metaphase plate. Scattered around the cell, they divide and thereafter either unite into one tetraploid restitution nucleus or form a number of micronuclei of variable sizes (Fig. 15.2). Such micronuclei are usually unable to divide further. C-mitosis is extremely rare in normal cells, but it has been described often in mammalian cancer cells, where it probably reflects anoxia and tissue degeneration.

Restitution

Still another mitotic abnormality that leads to the doubling of the chromosome number is restitution. If the two groups of daughter chromosomes fail to separate in anaphase, for example, they may form one dumbbell-shaped nucleus (Fig. 15.2). Restitution may also take place in prophase or metaphase; or, if a cell has two nuclei that divide simultaneously (a common phenomenon in plant tapetum and mammalian liver cells), two metaphase or anaphase plates may fuse. Restitution may occur very occasionally in normal human cells, but it is relatively common in malignant tumors.

Processes Giving Rise to Multinucleate Cells

Mitosis without a subsequent cell division results in the formation of binucleate or multinucleate cells. This is a common phenomenon in plant tapetum and in mammalian liver (D'Amato, 1989). It occurs occasionally also in cancer, especially when the mitotic configuration is multipolar. Cell fusion, which is a rarer phenomenon, occurs regularly in the formation of the mammalian cytotrophoblast as well as in muscle cells.

Amitosis

Amitosis is the direct constriction of a nucleus into two parts without chromosome condensation (Fig. 15.2). Although the macronuclei of ciliates generally divide through amitosis (Blackburn and Karrer, 1986), the mechanism has been widely believed to be absent in higher organisms.

However, in early cultured mouse trophoblast a proportion of cells showed two nuclei or stages that were interpreted as amitosis (Kuhn et al., 1991). Such nuclei differ from those resulting from normal mitosis without cell division in that they are asymmetric both in regard to size and structure. Furthermore, the nuclei lie side by side, which is not characteristic of other binucleate or multinucleate cells. In addition, Cotte et al. (1980) have followed a live human trophoblast cell through amitosis. Amitotic stages have also been described in mammalian decidua (Ansell et al., 1974).

Whether nuclear fragmentation, which has been observed in mouse lymphosarcoma cells and in giant trophoblast cells of the mouse, rat, and rabbit (Levan and Hauschka, 1953b; Zybina et al., 1975; Zybina and Rumyantsev, 1980), represents a form of amitosis is not clear.

Multipolar Mitoses

A mitotic aberration that can be regarded as the reverse of an absent or defective spindle is the formation of multipolar spindles. The most common are spindles with three poles (Fig. 15.2). The next in frequency are quadripolar mitoses; spindles with larger numbers of poles are correspondingly rarer. Most tripolar and quadripolar spindles come about when one or both centrosomes divide twice during a mitotic cycle (Therman and Timonen, 1950) and not as a result of cell and nuclear fusions, as assumed earlier. Like so many other mitotic abnormalities, multipolar divisions are frequent in malignant tumors but practically nonexistent in untreated normal cells (Oksala and Therman, 1974; Therman and Kuhn, 1989). Multipolar anaphases often end in nuclear restitution. However, if a multipolar anaphase is followed by cell division, the resulting three or more daughter cells have abnormal chromosome constitutions and often will not divide again.

Other Mitotic Abnormalities

Mitotic abnormalities other than those described above, in most cases, depend on faulty alignment of chromosomes in the metaphase or anaphase spindle. This results in loss, nondisjunction, or misdivision of chromosomes. Such abnormal alignment is rare in untreated normal cells, but common in cancer.

References

Ansell JD, Barlow PW, McLaren A (1974) Binucleate and polyploid cells in the decidua of the mouse. J Embryol Exp Morphol 31:223–227

Beerman W (1962) Riesenchromosomen. In: Protoplasmatologia, Handbuch der Protoplasmaforschung, Vol VI, D. Springer, Vienna

Blackburn EH, Karrer KM (1986) Genomic reorganization in ciliated protozoans. Annu Rev Genet 20:501–521

Cotte C, Easty GC, Neville AM, et al. (1980) Preparation of highly purified cytotrophoblast from human placenta with subsequent modulation to form syncytiotrophoblast in monolayer cultures. In Vitro 16:639–646

D'Amato F (1952) Polyploidy in the differentiation and function of tissues and cells in plants. Caryologia 4:311–358

D'Amato F (1989) Polyploidy in cell differentiation. Caryologia 42:183–211

Geitler L (1939) Die Entstehung der polyploiden Somakerne der Heteropteren durch Chromosomenteilung ohne Kernteilung. Chromosoma 1:1–22

Geitler L (1953) Endomitose und endomitotische Polyploidisierung. In: Protoplasmatologia, Handbuch der Protoplasmaforschung, Vol VI, C. Springer, Vienna

Heitz E (1953) Über intraindividuale Polyploidie. Arch Julius Klaus-Stiftung 28:260–271

Kiknadze II, Istomina AG (1980) Endomitosis in grasshoppers. I. Nuclear morphology and synthesis of DNA and RNA in the endopolyploid cells of the inner layer of the testicular follicle. Eur J Cell Biol 21:122–133

Kuhn EM, Therman E, Susman B (1991) Amitosis and endocycles in early cultured mouse trophoblast. Placenta 12:251–261

Levan A, Hauschka TS (1953a) Endomitotic reduplication mechanism in ascites tumors of the mouse. J Natl Cancer Inst 14:1–46

Levan A, Hauschka TS (1953b) Nuclear fragmentation—a normal feature of the mitotic cycle of lymphosarcoma cells. Hereditas 39:137–148

Nagl W (1976) Nuclear organization. Annu Rev Plant Physiol 27:39–69

Nagl W (1978) Endopolyploidy and polyteny in differentiation and evolution. Elsevier/North-Holland, Amsterdam

Nagl W (1981) Polytene chromosomes of plants. Int Rev Cytol 73:21–53

Oksala T (1954) Timing relationships in mitosis and meiosis. Caryologia (Suppl) 6:272–281

Oksala T, Therman E (1974) Mitotic abnormalities and cancer. In: German J (ed) Chromosomes and cancer. Wiley & Sons, New York, pp 239–263

Oksala T, Therman E (1977) Endomitosis in tapetal cells of *Eremurus* (*Liliaceae*). Am J Bot 64:866–872

Sarto GE, Stubblefield PA, Therman E (1982) Endomitosis in human trophoblast. Hum Genet 62:228–232

Therman E, Kuhn EM (1989) Mitotic modifications and aberrations in cancer. CRC Crit Rev Oncogenesis 1:293–305

Therman E, Murashige T (1984) Polytene chromosomes in cultured pea roots (*Pisum, Fabaceae*). Pl Syst Evol 148:25–33

Therman E, Timonen S (1950) Multipolar spindles in human cancer cells. Hereditas 36:393–405

Therman E, Sarto GE, Buchler DA (1983a) The structure and origin of giant nuclei in human cancer cells. Cancer Genet Cytogenet 9:9–18

Therman E, Sarto GE, Stubblefield PA (1983b) Endomitosis: a reappraisal. Hum Genet 63:13–18

Therman E, Sarto GE, Kuhn EM (1986) The course of endomitosis in human cells. Cancer Genet Cytogenet 19:301–310

Tschermak-Woess E (1956) Karyologische Pflanzenanatomie. Protoplasma 46: 798–834

Zybina EV., Rumyantsev PP (1980) Formation of a complex plasmatic membrane and microfilament bundles during the completion of nuclear fragmentation in the trophoblast giant polykaryocytes. Tsitologiya 22:890–897

Zybina EV, Kudryavtseva MV, Kudryavtsev BN (1975) Polyploidization and endomitosis in giant cells of rabbit trophoblast. Cell Tiss Res 160:525–537

16
Chromosomal Differentiation of Cells

Methods

The chromosomes of differentiated cells have been much less studied than those of meristematic or germline cells, probably because such cells do not usually divide spontaneously. However, in many cases they can be induced to undergo mitosis. Plant cells renew their mitotic activity around a wound, or after application of plant growth substances (Therman, 1951; D'Amato, 1952; Tschermak-Woess, 1956). Similarly, a portion of the mouse liver can be removed to stimulate tissue regeneration. Mouse liver cells can also be induced to divide by injecting the animal with carbon tetrachloride (CCl_4). However, as a rule, highly polyploid cells cannot be induced to undergo mitosis, although sometimes in cancer they do so spontaneously (Figs. 30.2d and 30.4d).

Nuclear measurements, by and large, are done by spectrophotometric DNA determinations, which measure the total DNA content of the nucleus (Patau and Srinivasachar, 1960). Flow cytometry yields a profile of the nuclear DNA content of a cell population. The creation of prematurely condensed chromosomes and the hybridization of specific DNA probes to nuclei (Chapters 13 and 14) may also have important roles in future studies of differentiated nuclei.

Somatic Polyploidy

Although a number of convincing examples of somatic polyploidy had appeared before the 1930s, they were usually regarded as cytological oddities (Heitz, 1953). Real interest in the cytology of somatic cells was kindled by the realization that the intriguing structures in the Dipteran salivary gland cells were, indeed, chromosomes (Heitz and Bauer, 1933; Painter, 1933). Since then, somatic polyploidy has been extensively analyzed, especially in plants and insects. Major credit for this work goes to the Viennese school under the direction of Geitler (for instance, 1953) and Tschermak-Woess (for instance, 1971). Important studies have been performed by the D'Amato group in Pisa (D'Amato, 1977, 1984, 1989) and by Nagl (1978) and his co-workers in Kaiserslautern. Other studies have been done in many laboratories around the world.

The most common cytological difference between the germline and soma is that in most organisms somatic tissues are mosaics of diploid and of different types of polyploid cells, and some tissues may consist entirely of polyploid cells. Species or larger taxa that lack endopolyploidy (for example, conifers and compositous plants) are exceptions (Nagl, 1978).

Differentiated plant tissues are usually mosaics of diploid, tetraploid, and more highly polyploid cells. Consider an onion root. In the growing point, which occupies a few millimeters of the tip, the cells are diploid and divide normally. Above this meristematic region is a zone where cell divisions have stopped and the cells can be seen in the process of differentiation. They grow in size, and the nuclei attain various degrees of ploidy through endoreduplication. Higher still, one finds only differentiated cells, which do not change further. These form a mosaic of diploid, tetraploid, octoploid, and even more highly polyploid cells (Therman, 1951). In certain plants, the best studied of which is spinach, cells still divide in the zone of differentiation, and the metaphases exhibit $2n$, $4n$, and $8n$ diplochromosomes, in addition to diploid chromosome constitutions (D'Amato, 1989).

Many mammalian tissues are similar mosaics. Examples of such tissues in humans are myocardium, megakaryocytes, glial cells, liver, pancreas, and the trophoblast (D'Amato, 1989). The nuclear DNA content in normal human tissues can range between 2C and 128C (see Chapter 3). In insects, on the other hand, most cells in a tissue represent, more or less, the same ploidy level (Nagl, 1978).

When a tissue to some extent escapes the forces of developmental controls, as is the case with ephemeral organs such as the anther tapetum in plants, the placenta in mammals, or abnormal tissues such as hydatidiform moles, the variety of cells and the mechanisms giving rise to them show a considerably wider range than is the case in normal tissues. This is even more true of malignant tumors, which seem to have escaped controlling mechanisms completely (Oksala and Therman, 1974; Therman et al., 1983, 1986). Indeed, malignant tumors manifest all possible mitotic aberrations and the resulting variable cell types.

Human hydatidiform moles (Chapter 24) provide a good example of abnormal, but not malignant growth; the mechanisms include cell division, endomitosis, and endoreduplication (Fig. 16.1; Sarto et al., 1984; Therman

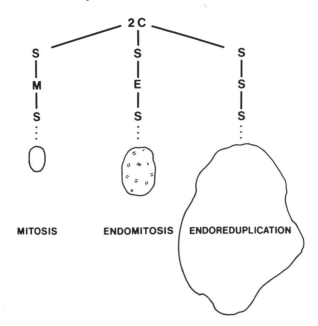

Figure 16.1. Modes of growth in hydatidiform moles (S = DNA synthesis; M = mitosis; E = endomitosis) (Therman et al., 1986).

et al., 1986). The same modes of growth are found in malignant tumors (Therman and Kuhn, 1989) and probably in many normal tissues.

Amplification and Underreplication

Amplification and underreplication are especially characteristic of cells undergoing endoreduplication. These terms refer to situations in which whole chromosomes or segments of chromosomes replicate a greater or lesser number of times than do the rest of the chromosomes. The more abundant segments are said to be amplified, the less abundant to be underreplicated. As early as 1933, Heitz (see 1953) realized that the heterochromatin in Dipteran polytene chromosomes is underreplicated. Many examples of amplification-underreplication have since been described in Diptera and in other organisms (D'Amato, 1977; Nagl, 1978). In the ovarian follicle cells of Drosophila, the amplified genes can be demonstrated directly in the electron microscope (Osheim and Miller, 1983). In mouse and human cells, heterochromatin has shown underreplication, especially in giant cells (Kuhn and Therman, 1988). Or, less probably, the heterochromatin is not condensed in them (John, 1988).

Genes coding for rRNA have a tendency to be amplified in the diplotene stages of amphibian oocytes (and in the oocytes of other organisms;

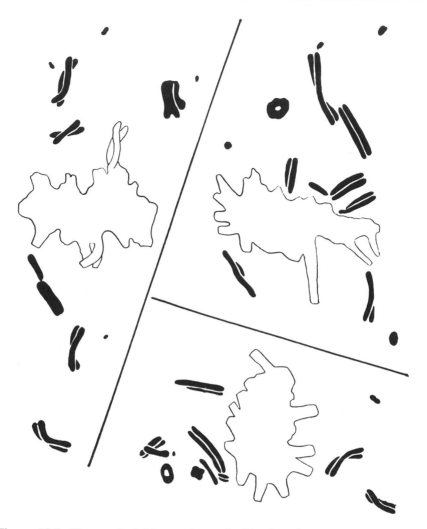

Figure 16.2. Three polyploid metaphases, in side view, from differentiated onion root cells containing numerous broken chromosomes, acentric fragments, and ring chromosomes (Therman, 1951).

D'Amato, 1977; Nagl, 1978). In mouse trophoblast cells, NOR silver staining has revealed a great increase in size and number of nucleoli (Kuhn et al., 1991).

The first example of underreplication of presumed euchromatic segments was described by Therman (1951). When the differentiated cells in onion roots are induced to divide with indole-3-acetic acid, the diploid mitoses show normal chromosomes, whereas in tetraploid and more highly polyploid cells the chromosomes have undergone extensive breakage and rejoining (Fig. 16.2). This was interpreted by Therman (1951) to mean that only those genes that are expressed replicate, while the others remain at the diploid level. When such chromosomes are compelled to divide, they naturally break at the underreplicated regions.

Chromosomes and Cell Differentiation

It is clear that endopolyploidy, as such, is not the cause of differentiation (D'Amato, 1989). However, obviously these two phenomena are in some way related. Barlow (1978) has pointed out that the advantage of endopolyploidy needs only to be marginal for such a system to be established. The advantages of somatic polyploidy become clear if we compare a tissue consisting of thousands of diploid cells to one made up of a few polyploid ones. Beerman (1962) suggested that it was more economical for the organism to increase the number of genes through polyploidization than through the process of chromosome replication, mitosis, and cell division. The synchronization of gene activity is also probably easier in a polyploid cell than in thousands of diploid cells. Furthermore, RNA synthesis can continue uninterrupted by mitosis (Nagl, 1981).

The movement of substances within one cell is easier than between many small cells (Barlow, 1978). Endopolyploidy is also advantageous in that amplification and underreplication are more easily realized during endoreduplication than in diploid interphases.

These ideas are in agreement with the observation that glandular and other active cells show especially high levels of polyploidy. The high multiplicity of Dipteran salivary gland chromosomes was mentioned in Chapter 8. The trophoblast cells of many mammals are also highly polyploid. In the rat, such cells reach a DNA content of 4096C. Suspensor cells in plant embryos vary between 1000C and 8000C. The record for ploidy seems to be held by the silk gland cells of *Bombyx mori*, at 524,288C, corresponding to 19 duplications (Nagl, 1982).

Presumably, endomitosis and endoreduplication, amplification and underreplication, the behavior of facultative heterochromatin, and the arrangement of chromosomes in the nucleus all play roles in cell differentiation. However, the causal relationships of the phenomena to one another and to the differentiation process are at present largely unknown.

References

Barlow PW (1978) Endopolyploidy: towards an understanding of its biological significance. Acta Biotheor (Leiden) 27:1–18

Beerman W (1962) Riesenchromosomen. In: Protoplasmatologia, Handbuch der Protoplasmaforschung, Vol VI, D. Springer, Vienna

D'Amato F (1952) Polyploidy in the differentiation and function of tissues and cells in plants. Caryologia 4:311–358

D'Amato F (1977) Nuclear cytology in relation to development. University Press, Cambridge, England

D'Amato F (1984) Role of polyploidy in reproductive organs and tissues. In: Johri BM (ed) Embryology of angiosperms. Springer, Heidelberg, pp 519–566

D'Amato F (1989) Polyploidy in cell differentiation. Caryologia 42:183–211

Geitler L (1953) Endomitose und endomitotische Polyploidisierung. In: Protoplasmatologia, Handbuch der Protoplasmaforschung, Vol VI, C. Springer, Vienna

Heitz E (1953) Über intraindividuale Polyploidie. Arch Julius Klaus-Stiftung 28: 260–271

Heitz E, Bauer H (1933) Beweise für die Chromosomennatur der Kernschleifen in den Knäuelkernen von *Bibio hortulanus* L. Z Zellforsch 17:67–82

John B (1988) The biology of heterochromatin. In: Verma RS (ed) Heterochromatin: molecular and structural aspects. Cambridge University, Cambridge, pp 1–147

Kuhn EM, Therman E (1988) The behavior of heterochromatin in mouse and human nuclei. Cancer Genet Cytogenet 34:143–151

Kuhn EM, Therman E, Susman B (1991) Amitosis and endocycles in early cultured mouse trophoblast. Placenta 12:251–261

Nagl W (1978) Endopolyploidy and polyteny in differentiation and evolution. Elsevier/North-Holland, Amsterdam

Nagl W (1981) Polytene chromosomes of plants. Int Rev Cytol 73:21–53

Nagl W (1982) Cell growth and nuclear DNA increase by endoreduplication and differential DNA replication. In: Nicolini C (ed) Cell growth. Plenum, New York, pp 619–651

Oksala T, Therman E (1974) Mitotic abnormalities and cancer. In: German J (ed) Chromosomes and cancer. Wiley & Sons, New York, pp 239–263

Osheim YN, Miller OL Jr (1983) Novel amplification and transcriptional activity of chorion genes in *Drosophila melanogaster* follicle cells. Cell 33:543–553

Painter TS (1933) A new method for the study of chromosome rearrangements and the plotting of chromosome maps. Science 78:585–586

Patau K, Srinivasachar D (1960) A microspectrophotometer for measuring the DNA-content of nuclei by the two wave length method. Cytologia 25:145–151

Sarto GE, Stubblefield PA, Lurain J, et al. (1984) Mechanisms of growth in hydatidiform moles. Am J Obstet Gynecol 148:1014–1023

Therman E (1951) The effect of indole-3-acetic acid on resting plant nuclei. I. *Allium cepa*. Ann Acad Sci Fenn A IV 16:1–40

Therman E, Kuhn EM (1989) Mitotic modifications and aberrations in cancer. CRC Crit Rev Oncogen 1:293–305

Therman E, Sarto GE, Stubblefield PA (1983) Endomitosis: a reappraisal. Hum Genet 63:13–18

Therman E, Sarto GE, Kuhn EM (1986) The course of endomitosis in human cells. Cancer Genet Cytogenet 19:301–310

Tschermak-Woess E (1956) Karyologische Pflanzenanatomie. Protoplasma 46: 798–834

Tschermak-Woess E (1971) Endomitose. Handb Allg Pathol 2:569–625

17
Main Features of Meiosis

Significance of Meiosis

The most important modification of mitosis is meiosis, which is the reduction division that gives rise to the haploid generation in the life cycle. In mammals, the haploid generation is restricted to one cell type, the gamete, whereas the other cells in the animal are diploid. However, in many other organisms, especially lower plants, the haploid generation is more important than the diploid; or the two generations may be more or less equal, as in the mosses. In those organisms in which the haploid phase dominates, the diploid generation may be represented by only one cell, the zygote. Under those circumstances, meiosis takes place immediately after fertilization.

In the alternation of the haploid and diploid generations, the main events are fertilization, which doubles the chromosome number, and meiosis, which halves it. The reduction of the chromosome number during meiosis occurs because the nucleus divides twice, while the chromosomes replicate only once. Another essential characteristic of meiosis is the pairing of homologous chromosomes, which makes their orderly segregation possible.

A further phenomenon, typical of meiosis in most organisms, is the crossing-over or exchange of homologous segments between two of the four chromatids of the paired chromosomes. Crossing-over, as such, is not an absolute prerequisite for orderly meiotic segregation. For instance, in the *Drosophila* male, normal meiosis occurs, but crossing-over is absent. Another indication of the mutual independence of crossing-over and segregation is provided by *mitotic* crossing-over, which does not result in the segregation of homologous chromosomes.

If crossing-over is absent in one sex, it is usually present in the other. Thus, in the *Drosophila* female, crossing-over takes place regularly; its failure leads to the dissociation of paired chromosomes and resultant abnormalities in segregation.

The almost ubiquitous presence of crossing-over in at least one sex per species carries possible evolutionary benefits. In the offspring, it greatly increases genetic recombination beyond the variability already derived from the independent segregation of maternal and paternal chromosomes in the first meiotic anaphase.

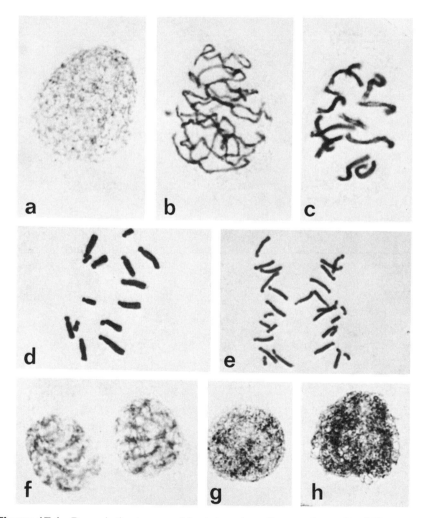

Figure 17.1. Premeiotic stages and leptotene in pollen mother cells of *Eremurus*. (a) Interphase; (b–c) prophase; (d) metaphase; (e) anaphase; (f) telophase; (g) interphase; (h) leptotene (Feulgen squash).

The main features of meiosis—one DNA synthesis, two cell divisions, chromosome pairing, crossing-over, and segregation—are strikingly similar throughout the plant and animal kingdoms. As Darlington puts it, "The lily can tell us what happens in the mouse. The fly can tell us what happens in man." (Darlington and La Cour, 1975, p. 20). In spite of this, many mistaken identifications of premeiotic and meiotic stages can be found in the literature. The main reason is probably the lack of independent criteria for the seriation of stages. However, a few exceptions exist: in the compositous plant *Gazania*, the pollen mother cells form one-cell rows in which each cell, as one moves along the row, is in a slightly more advanced stage of meiosis than the previous cells (Lima-de-Faria, 1964). In the liliaceous genus *Eremurus*, the buds form a spiral in which each bud represents a slightly later stage than its neighbor (Figs. 17.1, 3 and 6). A detailed series of meiotic stages in salamanders has been presented by Kezer (1970). Electron microscopic studies have greatly advanced both the seriation and subclassification of meiotic stages (von Wettstein et al., 1984).

Meiosis in various organisms has been described in numerous studies since the beginning of the century, and the results have been reviewed in many books and articles (for instance, Wilson, 1925; Darlington, 1937; White, 1973; von Wettstein et al., 1984; Moens, 1987).

Meiotic Stages

Figure 17.4 illustrates the stages of meiosis in diagrammatic form and gives the names of the stages. We will follow the premeiotic and meiotic stages in the pollen mother cells of a liliaceous plant, *Eremurus*, which has 14 relatively large chromosomes (Oksala and Therman, 1958; Therman and Sarto, 1977). Before meiosis, the pollen mother cells, which are located in the anther lobes, undergo a number of mitoses. The last of these is shown in Fig. 17.1. Despite a number of claims that the homologous chromosomes show a tendency toward mitotic pairing during the premeiotic stages, no sign of homologous chromosomes lying side by side is observed. Little, if any, solid evidence exists for chromosome pairing before meiosis (Walters, 1970; John, 1976; von Wettstein et al., 1984).

Premeiotic Interphase

Premeiotic contraction has been described in a number of organisms, especially plants (Walters, 1970). Toward the end of the last premeiotic interphase, the chromosomes contract and come to resemble mitotic prophase chromosomes. Later in interphase, these contracted chromosomes unravel to form the leptotene threads. No sign of such premeiotic contraction is seen in *Eremurus* (Fig. 17.1). Indeed, this phenomenon

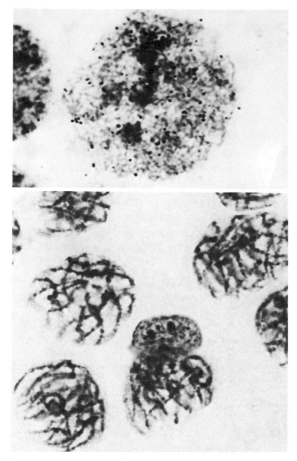

Figure 17.2. Top: leptotene stage from a human embryonic oocyte undergoing DNA synthesis. Bottom: pachytene bouquet stages in newt (*Triturus vulgaris*) spermatocytes.

varies greatly between closely related species and even between cells in the same plant. Possibly, these contracted chromosomes correspond to the so-called prochromosomes observed in the meiocytes of many animals (Wilson, 1925), including human oocytes.

In some organisms, premeiotic DNA synthesis takes place in the interphase preceding leptotene (Stern and Hotta, 1974). In the liliaceous plant *Trillium*, the period between DNA synthesis and the beginning of meiosis is a couple of weeks; in *Lilium*, a few days. However, in *Eremurus* and in human oocytes (Fig. 17.2), this synthesis occurs in early leptotene (Therman and Sarto, 1977).

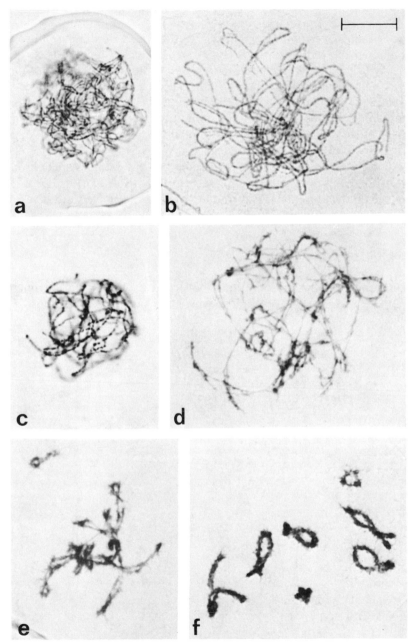

Figure 17.3. Early meiotic stage in pollen mother cells of *Eremurus*. (a) "Distance pairing" stage; (b) zygotene; (c) pachytene; (d) early diplotene; (e) second contraction in diplotene; (f) late diplotene (Feulgen squash; bar = 15 μm; Therman and Sarto, 1977).

Leptotene (or Leptonema)

The beginning of meiotic prophase is characterized by the chromosomes becoming visible as thin threads (Fig. 17.1h). Thicker points, or chromomeres, which are coiled segments in the stretched-out chromosomal strand, appear and become clearer as the chromosomes gradually contract. At this stage in *Eremurus*, DNA synthesis can be demonstrated by autoradiography. An ephemeral stage that has been called the "distance pairing" stage follows after typical leptotene (Therman and Sarto, 1977). During this phase, the homologues lie side by side for long stretches, apparently without touching. It is possible that the homologous chromosomes sort themselves out in some way during this stage (Fig. 17.3a); or this stage may represent early zygotene; synapsis may have started at some points, although it is not visible.

Zygotene (or Zygonema)

In zygotene, the chromosome ends collect at a spot inside the nuclear membrane close to the centrioles, which are outside the nucleus. This

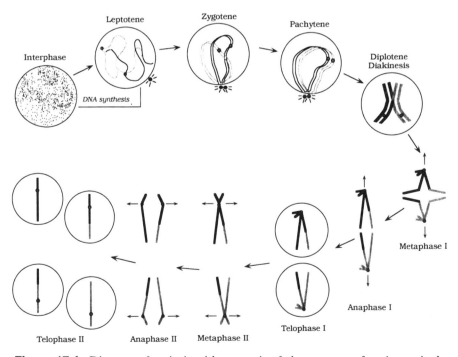

Figure 17.4. Diagram of meiosis with one pair of chromosomes forming a single chiasma. Note: a pachytene bivalent consists of four chromatids.

movement causes the so-called *bouquet* formation (Figs. 17.2, 4). Although the bouquet configuration varies, it seems to be ubiquitous in both plants and animals (Oksala and Therman, 1958), but the centriole is not.

The homologous chromosomes pair during zygotene. Parts of the chromosomes are thin leptotene threads, whereas the rest have synapsed to form thicker pachytene-like chromosomes. The points where the pairing has started can be clearly seen (Fig. 17.5). Now the chromomeres are visible as different-sized "beads" in the chromosome thread.

That paired and unpaired regions are visible in the same chromosome pair indicates that the pairing of homologues starts at several points. Synapsis takes place not only between two homologous chromosomes but between strictly homologous segments. This is convincingly demonstrated by the pairing configuration of two homologues, if one of them has an inversion. To achieve point-by-point pairing in the inverted segment, one of the chromosomes has to form a loop, and such loops are seen regularly. Similarly, if a translocation has taken place between two chromosomes, the corresponding segments of translocated and nontranslocated chromosomes synapse, leading to a characteristic X-shaped figure.

Figure 17.5. Zygotene in three pollen mother cells of *Eremurus*; paired and unpaired segments are clearly visible (Feulgen squash; bar = 10 μm; Therman and Sarto, 1977).

Pachytene (or Pachynema)

In pachytene, synapsis is complete, and the paired chromosomes appear as thicker threads with clearly visible chromomeres (Fig. 17.3c). The two paired homologues form a *bivalent*. The length of a bivalent at pachytene is estimated to be about one-fifth the length of the same chromosome in leptotene. The chromomere pattern corresponds to the G-dark bands in the same chromosomes during mitosis. In many organisms, for instance the newt (Fig. 17.2), the bouquet organization is still visible, whereas in others (most plants) it has disintegrated. Naturally the bouquet is much easier to detect if it persists into pachytene. Crossing-over, which consists of an exchange of homologous segments between two of the four chromatids, takes place in pachytene, although the results of this process cannot be seen until the next meiotic stage, diplotene.

Diplotene (or Diplonema)

The shortening and thickening of chromosomes, which take place between leptotene and pachytene, continue in diplotene. The two homologous chromosomes forming a bivalent begin to repel each other until they are held together only at the points of crossing-over or, as these are called in cytological terms, *chiasmata* (singular: *chiasma*) (Fig. 17.3d–f).

A special type of diplotene chromosome, the lampbrush chromosome, has been studied extensively, especially in the giant oocytes of amphibians, as described in Chapter 8. It is probable that a stage corresponding to the lampbrush diplotene occurs in the meiocytes of many—possibly all—organisms. Indications of this phenomenon are seen in the "hairy" appearance of diplotene chromosomes in both plants and animals. This is especially clear in many grasshoppers.

At some point in mid-diplotene, most of the bivalents collect into one group in the middle of the nucleus (Fig. 17.3e). The significance of this phenomenon (the second contraction) is not known. Another substage of diplotene is the diffuse stage. Apart from heterochromatic bodies, the nuclei appear evenly stained. This stage has been described in insects and salamanders, but not in plants.

Diakinesis

Chromosome condensation reaches its final stage in diakinesis. The hairy appearance characteristic of diplotene disappears, and the bivalents are smooth and compact. They seem to be attached to the nuclear membrane, whereas until this stage they appeared free inside the nucleus.

Metaphase I

The nuclear membrane vanishes, and during a short prometaphase stage the bivalents collect into a metaphase plate at the midpoint of the spindle, which has now been formed between the two centrioles (Figs. 17.6a and 2.2b). The two centromeres of each bivalent orient themselves toward different poles. The maternal and paternal centromeres are oriented at random, forming the material basis for the independent Mendelian segregation of genes.

The shortening and thickening of chromosomes between leptotene and metaphase I are caused largely by the spiralization of the chromosome strand. Compared with mitotic chromosomes, there is an additional supercoil that is beautifully visible in large plant chromosomes, such as those found in *Scilla* or *Tradescantia*.

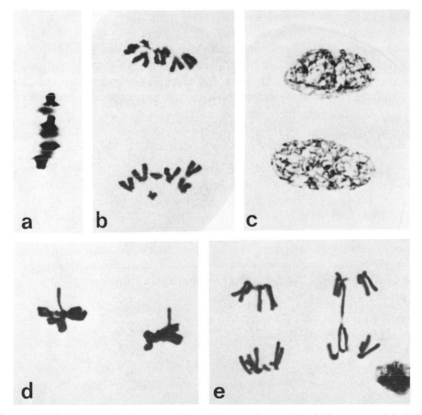

Figure 17.6. Late meiotic stages in pollen mother cells of *Eremurus*. (a) Side view of metaphase I; (b) anaphase I; (c) interkinesis; (d) side view of metaphase II; (e) anaphase II (Feulgen squash).

Anaphase I

In the first meiotic anaphase, the undivided centromeres, with two chromatids attached to each, move to opposite poles.

Telophase I

In the first meiotic telophase, each of the two chromosome groups contains the haploid number of centromeres. If crossing-over has occurred, the two chromatids of a chromosome are not identical. Therefore, these chromosomes are different from their mitotic counterparts.

Interkinesis

In many organisms including *Eremurus*, the first meiotic telophase is followed by a short interphase stage, the *interkinesis* (Fig. 17.6c), during which the chromosomes decondense. However, during this stage the chromosomes do not replicate and thus have the same basic structure in prophase as they had in the preceding telophase. In those organisms that have no interkinesis (grasshoppers, for example), the chromosome groups of anaphase I become the metaphase plates for the second meiotic division.

Meiotic Division II

In organisms both with and without interkinesis, the second meiotic division is indistinguishable from an ordinary, although haploid, mitosis (Fig. 17.6d and e). However, the chromosomes in metaphase II often differ from the mitotic chromosomes in the same organism by being shorter and by having widely separated chromatids held together only at the centromere. In anaphase II, the centromeres divide and move to the poles, with one chromatid attached to each daughter centromere. The end result is four nuclei, each with the haploid chromosome complement, of which no two are identical in gene content.

Some Meiotic Features

In some organisms, "terminalization" of chiasmata occurs between diplotene and metaphase I. Chiasmata move toward the chromosome ends and apparently decrease in number by slipping off the ends. This is a different phenomenon from the sliding of chiasmata toward the chromosome ends that takes place regularly in anaphase I. Because true terminalization of chiasmata between diplotene and metaphase I is probably a much rarer phenomenon than has been assumed (Hultén et al., 1978), many of the older claims should be reinvestigated. As far as we know, terminalization does not have any biological meaning.

After the premeiotic DNA synthesis, the amount of DNA in the nucleus is the same as in the mitotic prophase, 4C. In anaphase I it is reduced to 2C. Since a DNA synthesis never takes place in interkinesis, the DNA amount in each of the four nuclei resulting from meiosis is 1C, which is characteristic of the gametes.

Extensive biochemical studies of meiosis have been made, especially by the group of H. Stern (Stern and Hotta, 1974, 1980, 1987). One of the many features distinguishing meiosis from mitosis is that 99.7 percent of the DNA is synthesized in premeiotic interphase or early leptotene. The remaining 0.3 percent of the DNA synthesis occurs during zygotene and seems to play an important role in chromosome pairing. A small amount of repair DNA synthesis occurs in pachytene in connection with crossing-over (Hotta et al., 1977).

The durations of the meiotic stages differ markedly from the mitotic ones in the same organism. Thus, the premeiotic DNA synthesis lasts about twice as long as the mitotic S period. Pachytene lasts 8 days in the male mouse and 16 days in human males, whereas the duration of the mitotic prophase can be measured in hours. Diplotene in the oocytes is a special case; in amphibians, the lampbrush stage lasts about six months; in human oocytes, it may last as long as 45 years (to be described later).

References

Darlington CD (1937) Recent advances in cytology, 2nd edn. Churchill, London

Darlington CD, La Cour LF (1975) The handling of chromosomes, 6th edn. Wiley, New York

Hotta Y, Chandley AC, Stern H (1977) Meiotic crossing-over in lily and mouse. Nature 269:240–242

Hultén M, Luciani JM, Kirton V, et al. (1978) The use and limitations of chiasma scoring with reference to human genetic mapping. Cytogenet Cell Genet 22:37–58

John B (1976) Myths and mechanisms of meiosis. Chromosoma 54:295–325

Kezer J (1970) Observations on salamander spermatocyte chromosomes during the first meiotic division. DIS 45:194–200

Lima-de-Faria A (1964) Seriation of meiotic stages and spindle orientation in *Gazania*. Portugal Acta Biol 8:147–152

Moens PB (1987) Introduction to meiosis. In: Moens PB (ed) Meiosis. Academic, Orlando, Florida, pp 1–17

Oksala T, Therman E (1958) The polarized stages in the meiosis of liliaceous plants. Chromosoma 9:505–513

Stern H, Hotta Y (1974) Biochemical controls of meiosis. Annu Rev Genet 7:37–66

Stern H, Hotta Y (1980) The organization of DNA metabolism during the recombinational phase of meiosis with special reference to humans. Mol Cell Biochem 29:145–158

Stern H, Hotta Y (1987) The biochemistry of meiosis. In: Moens PB (ed) Meiosis. Academic, Orlando, Florida, pp 303–331

Therman E, Sarto GE (1977) Premeiotic and early meiotic stages in the pollen mother cells of *Eremurus* and in human embryonic oocytes. Hum Genet 35: 137–151

Walters MS (1970) Evidence on the time of chromosome pairing from prelepto-tene spiral stage in *Lilium longiflorum* "Croft". Chromosoma 29:375–418

Wettstein D von, Rasmussen SW, Holm PB (1984) The synaptonemal complex in genetic segregation. Annu Rev Genet 18:331–431

White MJD (1973) Animal cytology and evolution, 3rd edn. University Press, Cambridge, England

Wilson EB (1925) The cell in development and heredity, 3rd edn. MacMillan, New York

18
Details of Meiosis

Structure of Chiasmata

The structure of a diplotene bivalent with one chiasma, as seen in the microscope, can be interpreted according to either the *chiasma-type theory* or the *two-plane theory* (Fig. 18.1; Darlington, 1937; Jones, 1987). The latter assumes that the paired chromatids on the distal side of a chiasma belong to different chromosomes, one paternal and one maternal. According to the chiasma-type theory, two maternal chromatids and two paternal chromatids remain paired on both sides of the chiasma: in other words, a chiasma is the result of crossing-over. Observations of normal bivalents do not allow one to distinguish between these two possibilities.

Heteromorphic bivalents provide one of the means of distinguishing between the two theories. If one of the homologues had an added heterochromatic segment resulting from translocation, such a heteromorphic bivalent would have the configuration shown in Fig. 18.1 (left), if the two-plane theory were correct. However, such a configuration has never been observed. Instead, heteromorphic bivalents always have the configuration shown in Fig. 18.1 (right), which would be expected on the basis of the chiasma-type theory.

Figure 18.2 illustrates the structure of three bivalents according to the chiasma-type theory. In Fig. 18.2a, a diplotene bivalent with one chiasma is shown; in Fig. 18.2b, a bivalent with three chiasmata and one chromatid overlap; and in Fig. 18.2c, a metaphase bivalent with one chiasma is shown (note that the solid chromatid always pairs with another solid one, and the interrupted chromatid with an interrupted one).

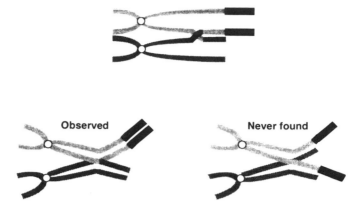

Figure 18.1. Two-plane versus chiasma-type theory as an explanation for the relationship of chiasma and crossing-over. A heteromorphic bivalent with one of its chromosomes having an added heterochromatic segment is shown. Such a bivalent always behaves according to the chiasma-type theory, resulting in the configuration on the left, whereas the configuration (right) that agrees with the two-plane theory is never found.

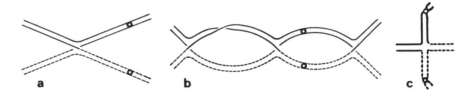

Figure 18.2. Diagram of three bivalents. (a) Diplotene bivalent with one chiasma; (b) bivalent with three chiasmata and one chromatid overlap; (c) metaphase bivalent with one chiasma.

Number of Chiasmata

The typical bivalent has at least one chiasma. If an organism has chromosomes of different sizes, the larger ones usually show a higher number of chiasmata, sometimes as many as six or eight. At metaphase I, a bivalent with one chiasma may appear cross-shaped, or the homologues may be connected end to end by a more-or-less terminal chiasma. Two chiasmata often result in a ring-shaped bivalent. In a bivalent with several chiasmata, the loops between them are at right angles to each other, so that such a configuration resembles a chain.

Since pairing starts at several points and often several chiasmata are formed between the homologues, one might expect that bivalents, and even more multivalents, would interlock. Actually, interlocking is an exceedingly rare phenomenon in diplotene or metaphase. A number of hypotheses have been put forward to explain this. It has been assumed that the "distance pairing" stage, or the bouquet formation, or both, represent some type of homologue-sorting process before synapsis takes place: this might prevent interlocking when the homologues pair (Oksala and Therman, 1958). Electron microscopic studies also indicate that the homologous chromosomes align themselves in some way before pairing actually takes place (Westergaard and von Wettstein, 1972). However, the most important clue to the lack of interlocking has been provided by electron microscopic observations (Bojko, 1983; Holm and Rasmussen, 1983; von Wettstein et al., 1984). In zygotene of both male and female meiosis, in which interlocking is frequent, the interlocked chromosomes break, and afterwards the breaks heal. In other words, the chromosomes are able to "walk through" each other, and therefore no interlocking is visible at later stages.

Statistical studies show that chiasmata do not form independently of one another. After one chiasma has formed, a second cannot arise in the immediate vicinity but has to be a certain distance from the first. This phenomenon is called *chiasma interference*. That crossing-over, which is detected by genetic means, shows a similar interference supplies one of the proofs that chiasmata are the cytological consequence of crossing-over. The correspondence of chiasmata and cross-overs has been demonstrated with autoradiography in the grasshopper (Jones, 1971; 1987), and with BrdU in mice (Polani and Crolla, 1982). Furthermore, in corn, the total frequency of cross-overs (as measured by genetic means) was one-half the frequency of chiasmata, just as expected if each chiasma corresponds to a cross-over between two of the four chromatids in the bivalent (Whitehouse, 1969).

Chiasmata may also be more-or-less strictly localized in a certain chromosome region. Thus, in some species of the liliaceous genera, *Paris*, *Allium*, and *Fritillaria*, as well as in certain grasshoppers, each bivalent has only one chiasma, which is localized near the centromere. In other plants, as well as in some newts, the chiasmata are formed at the ends of chromosomes (Darlington, 1937; John and Lewis, 1965; White, 1973).

Although chiasmata in most organisms are not localized to this extent, they are not randomly distributed either. Each pair of chromosomes forms at least one chiasma, and in human meiosis each chromosome arm, apart from the short arms of the acrocentrics, shows at least one chiasma. No crossing-over seems to take place in the heterochromatin (John, 1988). In both male and female human meiosis, the greatest density of chiasmata is next to the telomeres, and a smaller peak is found in the middle of the longest chromosome arms (Hultén, 1974; Bojko, 1985; Laurie and Hultén, 1985).

In exceptional cases, crossing-over can "go wrong," leading to a dicentric and an acentric chromatid. Such configurations are called U-type exchanges, because they resemble the letter U (Rees and Jones, 1977).

Synaptonemal Complex

The similarity of the meiotic process in different organisms is based on the universality of the *synaptonemal complex*, which has remained remarkably stable throughout eukaryotic evolution. Synaptonemal complexes play a decisive role in pairing, four-strand crossing-over, and disjunction of chromosomes.

Synaptonemal complexes have been analyzed successfully in sections prepared for electron microscopy, which allows a three-dimensional reconstruction of the nuclei. This technique has been used especially by the Carlsberg Laboratory group, as reviewed by von Wettstein et al. (1984). On the other hand, slides on which the chromosomes have been surface-spread and silver-stained can be analyzed in either a light or an electron microscope (Fig. 18.3; Pathak and Hsu, 1979).

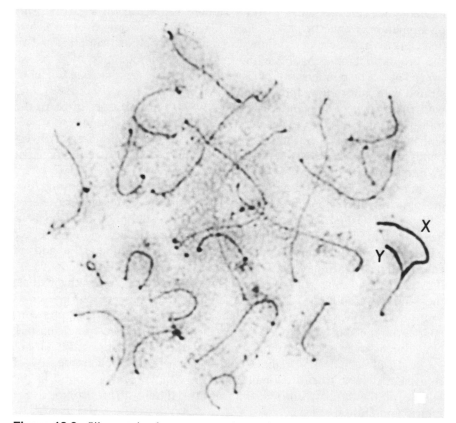

Figure 18.3. Silver-stained synaptonemal complexes in a spermatocyte of Syrian hamster; the sex chromosomes have a synaptonemal complex between them and more heavily stained unpaired differential segments (Pathak, 1983).

A synaptonemal complex consists of two lateral elements (Fig. 18.4). These contain protein and RNA and begin to form in leptotene. When chromosome pairing starts in zygotene, one or both ends of each homologue become attached to the nuclear membrane, and the two homologues become roughly aligned; a lateral element attaches to each of them. The lateral elements pair to form the synaptonemal complex, which includes a central element that completes the synapsis (Fig. 18.4). The formation of a synaptonemal complex between a pair of homologues is initiated at several points. During diplotene, the synaptonemal complexes separate from the bivalents and either collect into so-called polycomplexes or disintegrate (von Wettstein et al., 1984). Fragments of synaptonemal complexes may temporarily mark the positions of chiasmata in diplotene.

Synaptonemal complexes have been found in all organisms in which chromosome pairing and crossing-over occur (Westergaard and von Wettstein, 1972; von Wettstein et al., 1984). They obviously play an important role in the effective chromosome pairing that is a prerequisite

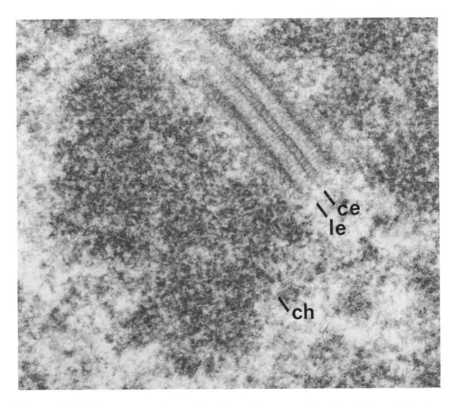

Figure 18.4. Synaptonemal complex from the spermatocyte of the spittle bug *Philaemus* (le = lateral element, ce = central element, ch = chromatin) (courtesy of H Ris).

for crossing-over. For example, they are absent in the meiocytes of the *Drosophila* male (an organism in which crossing-over does not take place), but they are present in the female of the same species (in which chiasmata are formed). Although synaptonemal complexes are apparently needed for crossing-over, their presence does not guarantee the occurrence of this process. For instance, they have been found in the meiocytes of haploid plants where no chiasmata are formed (Gillies, 1975).

New light has been thrown on the mechanics of crossing-over by the electron microscopic discovery of *recombination nodules*. These are electron-dense structures that are associated with the central element of the synaptonemal complex. They arise in zygotene and transform during pachytene into bridge-like structures, called *bars*. Crossing-over takes place during this transformation, which has been inferred from the agreement between crossing-over and the number, distribution, and structure of the nodules and bars. Recombination nodules are thought to be a prerequisite for crossing-over, as first suggested by Carpenter (1975; see also Holm and Rasmussen, 1981, 1983; von Wettstein et al., 1984).

The synaptonemal complex is a $0.2\,\mu$m wide ribbon, and its length, as a proportion of total haploid DNA length, varies from 0.3% in yeast to 0.006% in the lily (von Wettstein et al., 1984). The mechanics of the exact pairing of the long DNA molecule and the short lateral element are not understood. Moreover, it is not known how a chromosome recognizes "its" lateral element or how the two elements belonging to the same bivalent find each other. Presumably, the precise pairing of homologues is based on the complementarity of the chromosomal DNA molecules, but the molecular details of pairing are not understood. The molecular structure of the synaptonemal complex, not to mention that of the recombination nodules and bars, is all but unknown. How the homologous DNA sequences find each other and pair within the synaptonemal complex, a prerequisite for crossing-over, is a further riddle. However, it has been assumed that segments of DNA are trapped in the central region of the synaptonemal complex and that the chiasmata are formed between them.

Meiotic Behavior of More Than Two Homologous Chromosomes

Meiosis in polyploids has been analyzed extensively, especially in plants. It is of little significance in human cytogenetics, since the only polyploids known—triploids and tetraploids—as a rule die prenatally and survive birth only exceptionally. However, the early meiotic stages in oocytes of a triploid human fetus have been analyzed by Luciani et al. (1978).

Women with Down syndrome (21 trisomy) are the only individuals with autosomal trisomy known to have reproduced; their offspring consist of children with Down syndrome and normal children, in a ratio that does not differ significantly from the expected 1:1 (Hamerton, 1971, p. 214).

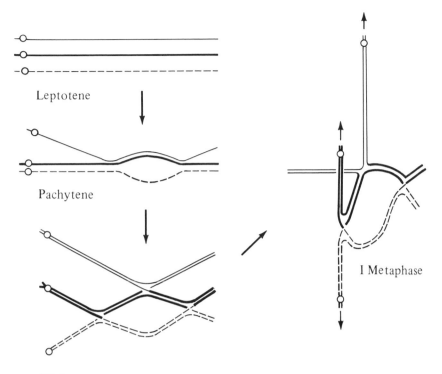

Leptotene

Pachytene

Diplotene

I Metaphase

Figure 18.5. Pairing of three homologous chromosomes. Note: the chromosomes are *double* in pachytene although they are drawn single.

Three homologous chromosomes usually pair to form a *trivalent* in meiosis (Fig. 18.5). However, at any one point only two of them synapse (Darlington, 1937). As shown in Fig. 18.5, two chromosomes (the thick and the interrupted line) start to pair, then there is an exchange of partners (the thick pairs with the thin), and at the second exchange, the first two chromosomes (the thick and the interrupted lines) resume pairing. If chiasmata are formed in the three paired segments, the diplotene configuration shown in Fig. 18.5 results. An alternate centromere orientation gives rise to the metaphase I trivalent in Fig. 18.5. Depending on the number and length of the paired segments and the number and location of chiasmata, trivalents come in a variety of shapes. Three homologues may also form a bivalent and a univalent. Of the three homologues, usually two go to one pole and one to the other in anaphase I. This type of segregation is called *secondary nondisjunction*.

Four homologous chromosomes may form a *quadrivalent*, or two bivalents, or a trivalent and a univalent. Even more possibilities exist in higher polyploids, such as hexaploids, in which chains or rings of six chromosomes are observed. Because meiotic segregation in polyploids is often irregular, the gametes may have inviable chromosome constitutions, resulting in partial sterility.

Human Meiosis

In the human male, as in the males of most plants and animals, the four meiotic products (spermatids) form four functional gametes. Meiosis in the oocyte results in one functional egg cell containing one of the four meiotic products. In animals, the other three nuclei segregate into very small cells called polar bodies, which degenerate. In plants, the other three nuclei are included in the structure of the embryo sac.

From a cytologist's point of view, meiosis in human oocytes complements that in spermatocytes, in that the meiotic prophase stages have been studied—and are much clearer—in the female, whereas our information on stages from diplotene onward comes mainly from the male.

Premeiotic and Early Meiotic Stages in the Human

The early meiotic stages in the human female are seen in 12- to 16-week-old embryos. The last premeiotic mitosis, in which the metaphase chromosomes appear short and thick, is followed by an interphase, in which

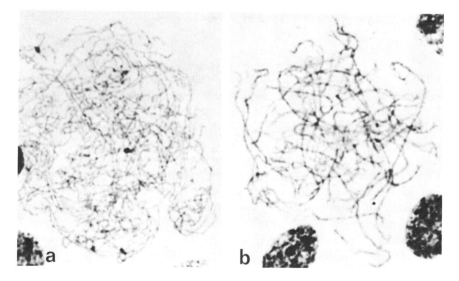

Figure 18.6. Meiotic stages in human oocytes. (a) "Distance pairing"stage; (b) zygotene (Therman and Sarto, 1977). (Note that the X chromosomes are not distinguishable from the autosomes).

most or all of each chromosome remains condensed as a chromocenter. These chromocenters unravel to form the leptotene threads. The meiotic DNA synthesis occurs in early leptotene (Fig. 17.2), as in *Eremurus* pollen mother cells. Between leptotene and zygotene, there is a short "distance pairing" stage (Therman and Sarto, 1977)—again as in *Eremurus*—during which the homologues appear to lie side-by-side, but at a distance (Fig. 18.6).

The diplotene stage in human oocytes is a very long phase, lasting from the embryonic stage until the egg cell is released in the adult female. This type of diplotene, called the *dictyotene*, represents a period of enormous growth of the cell. The chromosomes are greatly extended and invisible with most cytological techniques. Dictyotene corresponds to the lampbrush stage in amphibian eggs. In addition to the normal nucleoli, 15–20 extra nucleoli are formed. These seem to be attached to the heterochromatic centric regions of the chromosomes, especially of chromosome 9 (Stahl et al., 1975). An apparently similar diffuse diplotene stage is also described in the spermatocytes of insects and many other organisms.

The bivalent consisting of the two X chromosomes behaves, in the oocytes, like the autosomal bivalents (Fig. 18.6); that is, it shows no heteropycnotic condensation. In this respect, the X chromosomes behave differently in the oocytes than in the female somatic cells, where one of them acts heterochromatically. In the spermatocytes of the male, both the X and the Y chromosomes are heteropycnotically condensed in the meiotic prophase, from zygotene to diplotene. The condensed X and Y chromosomes join to form an *XY body*.

Meiosis in Human Spermatocytes

Figure 18.7 (top) illustrates a spermatogonial metaphase in which the spiral structure of the chromosomes is clearly visible. In Fig. 18.7 (bottom), a pachytene stage with an XY body is shown; the bouquet structure has been destroyed by squashing. The mean chiasma frequency in human spermatocytes, as determined from diakinesis and metaphase I stages, is 51 (SD 3.9) (Hultén, 1974). The number of chiasmata in individual cells varies from 43 to 60. In more recent studies, similar chiasma counts have been obtained (Laurie and Hultén, 1985). These have been confirmed with analyses of recombination nodules and bars (Holm and Rasmussen, 1983; von Wettstein et al., 1984; Bojko, 1985). As seen in Fig. 18.8 (top), the largest human bivalents usually have four chiasmata; the medium-sized, two or three; and the smallest ones, one each. In many organisms, the chiasma frequency in the oocytes and the spermatocytes is significantly different. Whether this applies to the human also is not known, since so little information exists about the later meiotic stages in the female. However, it is known that frequencies of recombination differ significantly between human males and females.

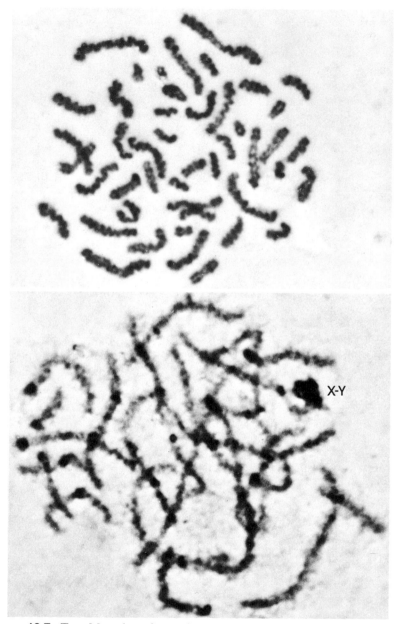

Figure 18.7. Top: Metaphase from a human spermatogonial cell. Bottom: Pachytene from a human spermatocyte with an XY body (the bouquet arrangement has been destroyed by squashing; courtesy of M Hultén).

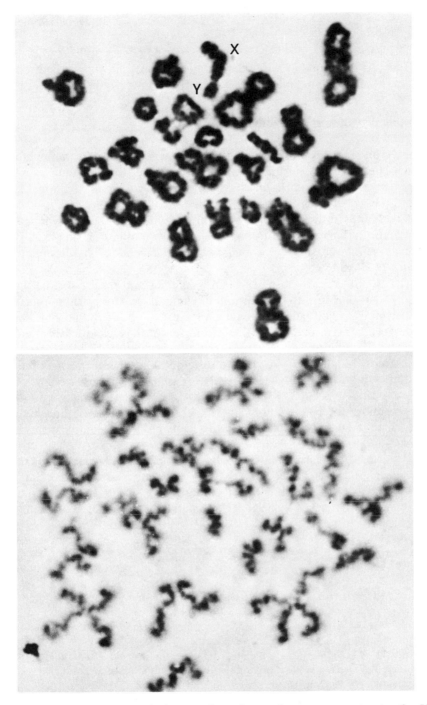

Figure 18.8. Top: First meiotic metaphase from a human spermatocyte; the X and the Y are attached, short arm to short arm. Bottom: Second meiotic metaphase from a human spermatocyte (courtesy of M Hultén).

The second meiotic division in the spermatocytes follows the usual scheme, as described in the pollen mother cells of *Eremurus*. Figure 18.8 (bottom) shows a metaphase in the second meiotic division.

Behavior of X and Y Chromosomes

The X and Y chromosomes in the human, as in most other animals, appear heteropycnotic from zygotene to diplotene. In pachytene, in which a clear bouquet organization is visible, they form a paired clump called the XY body or (less appropriately) the "sex vesicle" (Fig. 18.7, bottom; Solari, 1974). In diplotene, the sex chromosomes cease to show a heterochromatic behavior, and during diplotene–metaphase I, the XY body appears similar to the autosomal bivalents, except for its asymmetrical structure (Fig. 18.8, top).

The X and Y chromosomes of both human and mouse are paired at their ends; short arm to short arm in the human, and long arm to long arm in the mouse. The pairing behavior of the two sex chromosomes shows wide variations in mammals: the X and the Y may have a considerable segment in common where pairing and crossing-over take place, as in the autosomes. In addition, they have a differential segment, in which the sex determinants are situated (Fig. 18.3). A real chiasma between the sex chromosomes has been observed, for instance, in several hamster species representing different genera (Solari, 1974). In both mouse and human, the pairing segment is small, and a short synaptonemal complex is formed (Solari, 1980).

However, no chiasma has been observed between the human sex chromosomes. It is not clear how this is to be reconciled with the claim of Holm and Rasmussen (1983) that crossing-over occurs between them in 75 percent of cases, as concluded from the presence of recombination nodules.

References

Bojko M (1983) Human meiosis VIII. Chromosome pairing and formation of the synaptonemal complex in oocytes. Carlsberg Res Commun 48:457–483

Bojko M (1985) Human meiosis IX. Crossing over and chiasma formation in oocytes. Carlsberg Res Commun 50:43–72

Carpenter ATC (1975) Electron microscopy of meiosis in *Drosophila melanogaster*. II. The recombination nodule—a recombination-associated structure at pachytene? Proc Natl Acad Sci USA 72:3186–3189

Darlington CD (1937) Recent advances in cytology, 2nd edn. Churchill, London

Gillies CB (1975) Synaptonemal complex and chromosome structure. Annu Rev Genet 9:91–109

Hamerton JL (1971) Human cytogenetics II. Academic, New York

Holm PB, Rasmussen SW (1981) Chromosome pairing, crossing over, chiasma formation and disjunction as revealed by three dimensional reconstructions. In:

Schweiger HG (ed) International cell biology 1980–1981. Springer, Berlin, pp 195–204

Holm PB, Rasmussen SW (1983) Human meiosis. VI. Crossing over in human spermatocytes. Carlsberg Res Commun 48:385–413

Hultén M (1974) Chiasma distribution at diakinesis in the normal human male. Hereditas 76:55–78

John B (1988) The biology of heterochromatin. In: Verma RS (ed) Heterochromatin: molecular and structural aspects. Cambridge University, Cambridge, pp 1–147

John B, Lewis KR (1965) The meiotic system. In: Protoplasmatologia, Vol VI, F1. Springer, New York

Jones GH (1971) The analysis of exchanges in tritium-labelled meiotic chromosomes. Chromosoma 34:367–382

Jones GH (1987) Chiasmata. In: Moens PB (ed) Meiosis. Academic, Orlando, Florida, pp 213–244

Laurie DA, Hultén MA (1985) Further studies on bivalent chiasma frequency in human males with normal karyotypes. Ann Hum Genet 49:189–201

Luciani JM, Devictor M, Boué J, et al. (1978) The meiotic behavior of triploidy in a human 69,XXX fetus. Cytogenet Cell Genet 20:226–231

Oksala T, Therman E (1958) The polarized stages in the meiosis of liliaceous plants. Chromosoma 9:505–513

Pathak S (1983) The behavior of X chromosomes during mitosis and meiosis. In: Sandberg AA (ed) Cytogenetics of the mammalian X chromosome. Part A: Basic mechanisms of X chromosome behavior. Liss, New York, pp 67–106

Pathak S, Hsu TC (1979) Silver-stained structures in mammalian meiotic prophase. Chromosoma 70:195–203

Polani PE, Crolla JA (1982) Experiments on female mammalian meiosis. In: Crosignani PG, Rubin BL (eds) Genetic control of gamete production and function. Academic, London, pp 171–186

Rees H, Jones RN (1977) Chromosome genetics. University Park Press, Baltimore

Solari AJ (1974) The behavior of the XY pair in mammals. Int Rev Cytol 38:273–317

Solari AJ (1980) Synaptonemal complexes and associated structures in microspread human spermatocytes. Chromosoma 81:315–337

Stahl A, Luciani JM, Devictor M, et al. (1975) Constitutive heterochromatin and micronucleoli in the human oocyte at the diplotene stage. Humangenetik 26: 315–327

Therman E, Sarto GE (1977) Premeiotic and early meiotic stages in the pollen mother cells of *Eremurus* and in human embryonic oocytes. Hum Genet 35: 137–151

Westergaard M, Wettstein D von (1972) The synaptonemal complex. Annu Rev Genet 6:71–110

Wettstein D von, Rasmussen SW, Holm PB (1984) The synaptonemal complex in genetic segregation. Annu Rev Genet 18:331–431

White MJD (1973) Animal cytology and evolution, 3rd edn. University Press, Cambridge, England

Whitehouse HLK (1969) Towards an understanding of the mechanism of heredity. Arnold, London

19
Meiotic Abnormalities

The main events of meiosis are collected in Table 19.1 (Chapters 17 and 18). Since meiosis is a much more complicated series of events than mitosis, it is also more apt to go wrong at some point (Chandley, 1988). The main results of meiotic abnormalities are infertility or partial sterility, the latter often being combined with an increased frequency of chromosomal abnormalities in abortuses or liveborn offspring.

One important cause of infertility is the degeneration of germ cells at some developmental stage (Table 19.1). Numerous studies (for instance, Speed, 1988; Speed and Chandley, 1990) indicate that if two homologues, or parts of homologues, remain unpaired, the meiotic process does not continue. However, severe germ cell failure may also occur in individuals before chromosome pairing in embryos with the following chromosome constitutions: XO, autosomal trisomy, triploidy, XXY, and XYY (Coerdt et al., 1985; Speed and Chandley, 1990). Mutant genes and environmental factors may also bring about germ cell degeneration.

Nondisjunction of Autosomes

Next to degeneration of germ cells, nondisjunction of chromosomes is the most important cause of chromosomal infertility. Nondisjunction refers to any process that causes two chromosomes to go to the same pole when they ought to segregate to opposite poles. Some meiotic aberrations leading to nondisjunction are illustrated in Fig. 19.1. The two homologues are distinguished by alleles A and a. These alleles are far enough from the centromere to be genetically independent of it. Thus, allele A is

Table 19.1. Principal meiotic events and outcomes of their failures

Stage	Meiotic Events	Results of Unsuccessful Completion of Meiotic Events
Leptotene	Chromosomes become visible; lateral elements begin to form	Germ cell degeneration; sometimes nondisjunction
Zygotene	Chromosomes form bouquet; each chromosome pairs with its lateral element; homologous lateral elements unite into a synaptonemal complex which completes the pairing	Germ cell degeneration; sometimes nondisjunction
Pachytene, early	Recombination nodules attach to the central elements	No crossing-over; chromosomes remain univalent
Pachytene, late	During crossing-over, recombination nodules change into bars	Because of lack of chiasmata, bivalents fall into univalents
Diplotene	Homologues repel each other until they are held together only at the chiasmata	More univalents visible than in earlier stages
Metaphase I, Anaphase I, Metaphase II, Anaphase II	Orderly segregation of chromosomes is prerequisite for regular gametogenesis	Univalents may undergo nondisjunction, loss, or misdivision; spindle abnormalities interfere with chromosome segregation

equally likely to segregate with its own centromere or with the centromere of the homologous chromosome.

The products of the first meiotic division are shown in the column labeled Telophase I. The products of a normal meiosis are shown in the top pair of nuclei. The next pair shows the results of a failure to disjoin, in which both chromosomes in a bivalent migrate to the same pole at cell division. One nucleus contains all four chromatids and the other contains none. When these nuclei undergo the second meiotic division, the result is the daughter nuclei shown in the column labeled Telophase II. The nullosomic nucleus produces nullosomic daughter nuclei, of course. The other nucleus undergoes a division in which the centromeres split normally and migrate to opposite poles, producing diploid daughter nuclei. Because A and a are so far from the centromere, the products of the second meiotic division are equally likely to be AA/aa or Aa/Aa, as shown in the figure.

The lower half of Figure 19.1 shows the results of aberrant divisions, in which homologues either fail to pair or fail to form chiasmata. The results in both cases are the same. The homologues fall apart and appear as univalents in diplotene. Univalents may behave in different ways, as shown in the Telophase I column. They may drift at random to the two poles in the first division and divide regularly in the second, as shown in

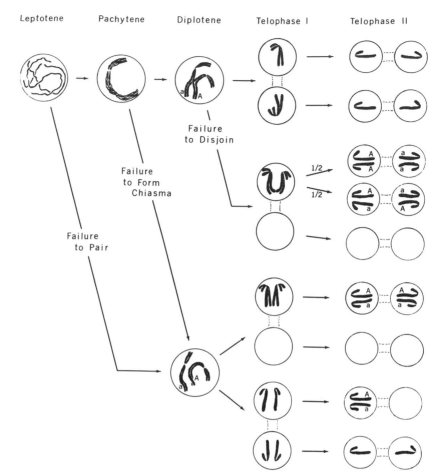

Figure 19.1. Diagram of the processes resulting in meiotic nondisjunction (see text) (Patau, 1963).

the upper pair of nuclei. Alternatively, they may divide mitotically in anaphase I, and then appear as single chromatids in the second division. Being unable to divide further at the second division, these single chromatids drift at random to the poles, or misdivide at the centromere. Another possibility is that the drifting univalents do not reach the poles but remain as laggards and are lost. Univalents also often undergo centromeric misdivision.

Nondisjunction of Sex Chromosomes

Since the XX bivalent in mammalian oocytes behaves like the autosomes, the two X chromosomes, in the female, exhibit the same irregularities in pairing and segregation as the rest of the chromosomes.

Although in humans the X and the Y chromosomes have short homologous pairing segments and form a synaptonemal complex in which crossing-over takes place, their behavior differs from that of the autosomes; they remain as univalents much more often than the smallest autosomes. In a study of meiosis in 53 normal men, the mean fraction of spermatocytes in which the X and the Y were unpaired was 3.2 percent (McDermott, 1971). Much higher frequencies of separation of the sex chromosomes have also been reported (Solari, 1974, page 304; Laurie and Hultén, 1985). Frequencies of univalents appear to vary among different individuals. The mean frequency of unpaired sex chromosomes in the human male lies around 10 percent (Laurie and Hultén, 1985). Similarly, in normal mice, 8–10 percent of the spermatocytes show separate X and Y chromosomes, whereas, in a study in the hybrid strain BDF$_1$, the corresponding figures were 35–40 percent (Rapp et al., 1977). The autosomes were normally paired in these BDF$_1$ mice. The structure and behavior of the human Y chromosome will be discussed in greater detail in Chapter 20.

Misdivision of the Centromere

Misdivision or *fission* of the centromere may happen during mitosis or meiosis. Since it probably occurs much more often during meiosis, it is discussed at this point. In misdivision or fission, the centromere divides crosswise, separating the two chromosome arms, instead of the two sister chromatids, as in normal division (Fig. 19.2).

If misdivision takes place during the stages from S to anaphase, when the chromosomes are double, the result is two isochromosomes. If a single chromatid misdivides during the stages from anaphase to S, two telocentric chromosomes arise. In six humans, chromosome 4 (two cases), chromosome 7 (three cases), and chromosome 10 (one case) have undergone fission, resulting in two telocentrics in each cell of each person (Therman et al., 1981; Rivera and Cantú, 1986).

An abnormal child with symptoms of 13 trisomy was found to have two cell lines, one with a telocentric chromosome 13, and another with i(13q) (Therman et al., 1963). Other similar cases, involving chromosomes 13, 21, and the X, have since been described (Therman et al., 1981). In these cases, either the telocentric or the isochromosome has arisen through misdivision of a normal chromosome, and the other, through further

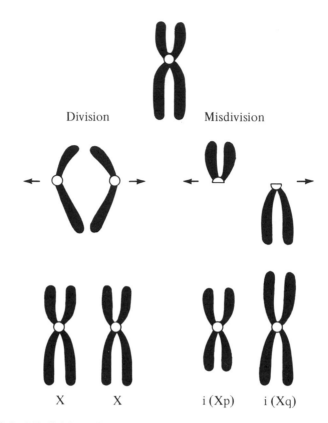

Figure 19.2. Misdivision of the human X chromosome resulting in the formation of a long-arm isochromosome i(Xq) and a short-arm isochromosome i(Xp) (presumably inviable).

misdivision of the first abnormal chromosome (once a centromere misdivides, it often continues to be unstable).

However, misdivision most often affects univalents during the first meiotic division. In humans, the most frequent result of misdivision is a monocentric i(Xq), whereas i(Xp) does not seem to be viable (Therman and Patau, 1974; Therman and Sarto, 1983).

Misdivision and its consequences have been studied especially in plants (Darlington, 1939; Sears, 1952). In addition to the centromere dividing crosswise, it can separate into four parts, which will give rise to two long-arm telocentric chromosomes and two short-arm telocentrics. Misdivision of centromeres may also take place in the second meiotic division, or in mitosis, although this is much rarer than its occurrence in the first meiotic division.

Chromosomally Abnormal Human Sperm

The technique for analyzing the chromosome content of the pronuclei of male mammals involves the fertilization of golden hamster eggs that have been freed from the zona pellucida (Rudak et al., 1978). This method has opened up new fields of research, as reviewed by Martin (1988a). While revealing the chromosome constitution of sperm cells, it also allows conclusions on the course of meiosis. Segregation, in normal males as well as in balanced carriers of abnormal chromosomes, has been analyzed with this technique (Martin, 1988a, 1988b; Martin et al., 1990).

More than 30 years ago, spectrophotometric DNA determination showed that the sperm of normal fertile men contains a surprisingly high proportion of abnormal chromosome constitutions. However, what these chromosome constitutions actually are has only recently become clear. In a study of 1582 sperm cells, from 30 normal males of proven fertility (Martin et al., 1987), the mean frequency of chromosomally abnormal cells was 10.4% ($\pm$5.0%), with a range of 0–24%. For aneuploidy, the mean was 4.7% ($\pm$2.9%), with a range of 0–10%, whereas for structural aberrations the mean was 6.2% ($\pm$6.0%), and the range, 0–23.1%. All chromosome groups were involved in the aneuploidy, and the proportions of X-bearing and Y-bearing sperm did not differ significantly.

Male Infertility

Male infertility in mammals is usually correlated with a low number of sperm cells in the semen (oligospermia) or with their total lack (azoospermia). (Female infertility is discussed in Chapters 22 and 23.)

These conditions may be caused by meiotic abnormalities, which interrupt the development of spermatocytes at some stage, usually during the first meiotic division. For instance, Koulischer et al. (1982) reported meiotic abnormalities in 13.2 percent of infertile men.

A great variety of chromosomal anomalies cause male sterility. Thus, depending on patient selection, from 5 to 15 percent of the males sampled in infertility clinics have abnormal chromosome constitutions. For instance, the incidence of balanced translocations, including Robertsonian translocations, is 8.9 per thousand in infertile men, as compared with 1.4 per thousand in the newborn (Zuffardi and Tiepolo, 1982). Translocations between two autosomes, between the X or the Y and an autosome, or between an X and a Y cause sterility in both mouse (Searle, 1982) and human males (Chandley, 1982). It has been assumed that a translocation involving either (or both) of the sex chromosomes would interfere with the inactivation of the XY bivalent and thereby disturb spermatogenesis (Chandley, 1988).

Practically all abnormal sex chromosome constitutions lead to male sterility (Chandley, 1982). For instance, in males with Klinefelter syndrome (47,XXY), the atrophied seminiferous tubules contain only Sertoli cells; such males are always sterile. On the other hand, males with 47,XYY range from fully fertile to sterile. In many of the fertile representatives of this group, one of the Y chromosomes is lost from the germline. How the mode of pairing of the one X and the two Y chromosomes affects the fertility of the male is so far unclear.

Interestingly, in mouse and human spermatocytes with normal sex chromosomes, the pairing of the X and the Y chromosomes seems to be a prerequisite for the completion of meiosis and thus for the formation of spermatozoa (Rapp et al., 1977). As noted above, the X and Y fail to pair in about 10% of spermatocytes in both species.

Mutant genes that affect male meiosis are known in many organisms, both plants and animals. Several lines of evidence indicate that similar genes, which prevent chromosome pairing or recombination, also exist in humans (Chandley, 1982).

Environmental Causes of Meiotic Nondisjunction

The causes of nondisjunction may be environmental or genetic. Experiments conducted on plants and animals reveal that a variety of environmental agents, both physical and chemical, affect meiosis. For example, in many organisms heat shocks prevent chromosome pairing and lead to a totally irregular meiosis. Cold treatment causes the same phenomenon in mouse embryos (Karp and Smith, 1975). Similarly, ionizing radiation increases nondisjunction in *Drosophila* (Uchida, 1977) and in mice (Tease, 1988).

Many substances known to break chromosomes probably also give rise to occasional nondisjunction (Pacchierotti, 1988). Another class of substances, of which the most widely used is the alkaloid colchicine, specifically destroys the spindle structure. Instead of collecting into a metaphase plate, the chromosomes are scattered around the cell. In milder cases, this leads to nondisjunction and, in extreme cases, to restitution, giving rise to a tetraploid cell. As early as 1939, Levan showed that colchicine interfered with chromosome pairing in the meiosis of the onion. Shepard et al. (1974) found that colchicine largely destroys the lateral elements of the synaptonemal complex. As a result, only limited stretches of the chromosomes pair effectively and form chiasmata. Interestingly, the decrease in chiasma formation preferentially affects the bivalents that normally have a single chiasma, these chromosomes thus remaining univalents, whereas the chiasma frequency is not decreased in bivalents with four chiasmata (Bennett et al., 1979). The cytological effects of colchicine should be taken into consideration when this alkaloid is used as a gout treatment for patients of reproductive age.

Parental Age

A well-established cause of nondisjunction in humans is increased maternal age, which, as far as the gametes are concerned, can be classified as an environmental influence. At the maternal age of 20 years, the incidence of 21-trisomic children is 0.4 per 1000 newborns; for women age 45 years and over, the risk increases to 17 per 1000 newborns (Hassold and Jacobs, 1984). A similar maternal age effect is found for 18- and 13-trisomic children, as well as for offspring with XXX and XXY sex chromosome constitutions. However, this rule does not apply to Turner syndrome children, with the 45,X chromosome constitution. Spontaneous abortions with aneuploid chromosome numbers also occur more frequently in older women (Carr, 1971; Hassold et al., 1980). It is estimated that if women over 35 years of age refrained from having offspring, the incidence of children with abnormal chromosome numbers would decrease by one-third to one-half.

It was once believed that the father's age played no role in the birth of aneuploid children. However, chromosome banding techniques and more refined statistical methods have shown that this is not true. Identification of parental chromosomes 21 with banding techniques shows that nondisjunction for this chromosome also occurs in the father; possibly one-third of 21-trisomic children owe this effect to paternal nondisjunction (Wagenbichler et al., 1976; Uchida, 1977; Mattei et al., 1979), and their frequency increases with paternal age from age 55 onward (Stene et al., 1977). Juberg and Mowrey (1983), using the pooled data from relevant studies through 1982, have shown that maternal origin accounts for 80 percent of 21 trisomy cases, and paternal origin for 20 percent. Nondisjunction in the mother takes place during the first meiotic division in 80 percent of the cases, and during the second meiotic division in 20 percent; the corresponding percentages in the father are 60 and 40.

It has also been claimed that the frequency of chromosomally abnormal embryos increases more with advancing paternal age when the mother is also older than when she is young (Stene et al., 1981).

In mouse oocytes, the frequency of chiasmata is decreased and the incidence of univalents increased with increasing age of the female (Henderson and Edwards, 1968). These results were confirmed by Luthardt et al. (1973), who also observed that the univalent formation was nonrandom, involving mainly the smaller chromosomes. This finding agrees with observations on many organisms that the smallest chromosomes of the complement, with at most one chiasma, are the most likely to remain univalents. The mechanism by which the age of the female acts on meiosis is not known. Preconception exposure to ionizing radiation has been assumed to increase nondisjunction (Uchida, 1977). However, studies in human populations have not borne out this view (Tease, 1988). No increase in nondisjunction has been found in the Hiroshima and

Nagasaki victims (Awa et al., 1987). On the other hand, experiments have clearly shown that radiation occurring prior to conception increases nondisjunction in the mouse (Tease, 1988).

Genetic Causes of Nondisjunction

In many organisms, for instance in *Drosophila* and maize, genes are known that upset the normal course of meiosis by affecting either synapsis or chiasma formation. In the human, a number of abnormal individuals have been described who show aneuploidy for more than one chromosome. This fact naturally reflects a more serious disturbance of meiosis than simple nondisjunction. For example, both an extra 21 and an extra 18 were found in an infant who died 8 hours after birth (Gagnon et al., 1961). Other combinations are trisomy 21 and an XXX or XXY sex chromosome constitution, or an extra 21 combined with a missing X chromosome (Mikkelsen, 1971; Villaverde and DaSilva, 1975). Other types of double aneuploidy are occasionally found (Tuck et al., 1984); even a child with 49,XXYY,+18 has been described (Webb et al., 1984).

The occurrence of more than one child with an aneuploid chromosome constitution in the same sibship has led to the conclusion that such families may have an inherent tendency to nondisjunction. Thus, the second D-trisomic child ever described had a sister with a 45,X chromosome constitution (Therman et al., 1961). However, the most convincing evidence that some families have a genetic predisposition to nondisjunction is from Hecht et al. (1964). The study started with 60 families with either an 18-trisomic or a D-trisomic offspring. Three of the 18-trisomic children had siblings with 21 trisomy, as compared with an expectation of 0.15 Down syndrome children for the same group—a highly significant statistical difference. In addition, one of the children with D-trisomy had an uncle with 21 trisomy. The record for different trisomic conceptuses in one family would seem to have been achieved by a woman who, between the ages of 40 and 43 years, had three consecutive pregnancies, prenatally diagnosed as 21, 18, and 13 trisomic, respectively (FitzPatrick and Boyd, 1989). In this case, both parents were phenotypically and karyotypically normal.

Genetic factors are probably also responsible for the observation that, if a couple has one trisomic child, the risk of having another increases some ten times compared with the general population. This probably is dependent on some families having a much higher risk, whereas in others the risk is not increased. An example of a high-risk family was studied in our laboratory (unpublished data). The couple had three children with Down syndrome, and the father's brother also had a Down syndrome child. The two fathers had normal chromosomes, and the affected children had "normal" 47,+21 chromosome constitutions.

Origin of Diploid Gametes

Tetraploid and triploid abortuses, and even a few liveborn children, demonstrate that unreduced gametes are formed and occasionally are able to function. Further, spectrophotometric measurements show that some sperm contain double the usual amount of DNA. (Interestingly, these do not show up in the studies done on male pronuclei in hamster eggs). Such gametes owe their origin mainly to two processes. First, the same agents causing nondisjunction may disturb meiosis to the extent that a restitution nucleus, which contains the unreduced diploid complement, is formed in the first meiotic division. Then too, endoreduplication in a gonial cell may lead to one or more tetraploid meiocytes. If such a cell subsequently undergoes normal meiosis, it may give rise to diploid gametes.

By using banding techniques to extract informative data on 10 triploid abortuses, Kajii and Niikawa (1977) found that one originated in the maternal first meiotic division; five apparently resulted from two sperm fertilizing the same egg; two owed their origin to an aberration in either the second paternal division or the first mitotic division; and the last two were of undefined paternal origin. One tetraploid abortion obviously came about by the suppression of the first cleavage division. Similar results were obtained by Jacobs et al. (1978) in a study on 26 triploid abortions. To quote their paper (page 56): "The best fit for the data using a maximum-likelihood method was that 66.4% of the triploids were the result of dispermy, 23.6% the result of fertilization of a haploid ovum by a diploid sperm formed by failure of the first meiotic division in the male, and 10% the result of a diploid egg formed by failure of the first maternal meiotic division." These observations have been confirmed by Uchida and Freeman (1985).

A recent technique that will accurately reveal the parental origin of any chromosome, or set of chromosomes, is the determination of their restriction fragment length polymorphisms (RFLPs) (Jacobs et al., 1988) (Chapter 5). The origin of the extra X chromosomes in several individuals with XXXXY (and one with XXXXX) sex chromosome constitutions has been determined with similar methods (Deng et al., 1991; Huang et al., 1991). In all cases, the X chromosomes came from the mother, presumably through nondisjunction in meiosis I combined with double nondisjunction in meiosis II.

References

Awa AA, Honda T, Neriishi S, et al. (1987) Cytogenetic study of the offspring of atomic bomb survivors, Hiroshima and Nagasaki. In: Obe G, Basler A (eds) Cytogenetics. Springer, Berlin/Heidelberg, pp 166–183

Bennett MD, Toledo LA, Stern H (1979) The effect of colchicine on meiosis in *Lilium speciosum* cv. "Rosemede". Chromosoma 72:175–189

Carr DH (1971) Chromosomes and abortion. In: Harris H, Hirschhorn K (eds) Advances in human genetics. Plenum, New York

Chandley AC (1982) Normal and abnormal meiosis in man and other mammals. In: Crosignani PG, Rubin BL (eds) Genetic control of gamete production and function. Academic, London, pp 229–237

Chandley AC (1988) Meiosis in man. Trends Genet 4:79–84

Coerdt W, Rehder H, Gausmann I, et al. (1985) Quantitative histology of human fetal testes in chromosomal disease. Pediatr Pathol 3:245–259

Darlington CD (1939) Misdivision and the genetics of the centromere. J Genet 37:341–364

Deng H-X, Abe K, Kondo I, et al. (1991) Parental origin and mechanism of formation of polysomy X: an XXXXX case and four XXXXY cases determined with RFLPs. Hum Genet 86:541–544

FitzPatrick DR, Boyd E (1989) Recurrences of trisomy 18 and trisomy 13 after trisomy 21. Hum Genet 82:301

Gagnon J, Katyk-Longtin N, de Groot JA, et al. (1961) Double trisomie autosomique a 48 chromosomes (21+18). L'Union Med Canada 90:1–7

Hassold TJ, Jacobs PA (1984) Trisomy in man. Annu Rev Genet 18:69–97

Hassold TJ, Jacobs P, Kline J, et al. (1980) Effect of maternal age on autosomal trisomies. Ann Hum Genet 44:29–36

Hecht F, Bryant JS, Gruber D, et al. (1964) The nonrandomness of chromosomal abnormalities. N Eng J Med 271:1081–1086

Henderson SA, Edwards RG (1968) Chiasma frequency and maternal age in mammals. Nature 218:22–28

Huang T H-M, Greenberg F, Ledbetter DH (1991) Determination of the origin of nondisjunction in a 49,XXXXY male using hypervariable dinucleotide repeat sequences. Hum Genet 86:619–620

Jacobs PA, Angell RR, Buchanan IM, et al. (1978) The origin of human triploids. Ann Hum Genet 42:49–57

Jacobs PA, Hassold TJ, Whittington E, et al., (1988) Klinefelter's syndrome: an analysis of the origin of the additional sex chromosome using molecular probes. Ann Hum Genet 52:93–109

Juberg RC, Mowrey PN (1983) Origin of nondisjunction in trisomy 21 syndrome: all studies compiled, parental age analysis, and international comparisons. Am J Med Genet 16:111–116

Kajii T, Niikawa N (1977) Origin of triploidy and tetraploidy in man: 11 cases with chromosome markers. Cytogenet Cell Genet 18:109–125

Karp LE, Smith WD (1975) Experimental production of aneuploidy in mouse oocytes. Gynecol Invest 6:337–341

Koulischer L, Schoysman R, Gillerot Y, et al. (1982) Meiotic chromosome studies in human male infertility. In: Crosignani PG, Rubin BL (eds) Genetic control of gamete production and function. Academic, London, pp 239–260

Laurie DA, Hultén MA (1985) Further studies on bivalent chiasma frequency in human males with normal karyotypes. Ann Hum Genet 49:189–201

Levan A (1939) The effect of colchicine on meiosis in *Allium*. Hereditas 25:9–26

Luthardt FW, Palmer CG, Yu P-L (1973) Chiasma and univalent frequencies in aging female mice. Cytogenet Cell Genet 12:68–79

Martin RH (1988a) Human sperm karyotyping: a tool for the study of aneuploidy. In: Vig BK, Sandberg AA (eds) Aneuploidy, Part B: induction and test systems. Liss, New York, pp 297–316

Martin RH (1988b) Meiotic segregation of human sperm chromosomes in translocation heterozygotes: report of a t(9;10) (q34;q11) and a review of the literature. Cytogenet Cell Genet 47:48–51

Martin RH, Rademaker AW, Hildebrand K, et al. (1987) Variation in the frequency and type of sperm chromosomal abnormalities among normal men. Hum Genet 77:108–114

Martin RH, Barclay L, Hildebrand, et al. (1990) Cytogenetic analysis of 400 sperm from three translocation heterozygotes. Hum Genet 86:33–39

Mattei JF, Mattei MG, Aymé S, et al. (1979) Origin of the extra chromosome in trisomy 21. Hum Genet 46:107–110

McDermott A (1971) Human male meiosis. Can J Genet Cytol 13:536–549

Mikkelsen M (1971) Down's syndrome. Current stage of cytogenetic research. Humangenetik 12:1–28

Pacchierotti F (1988) Chemically induced aneuploidy in germ cells of mouse. In: Vig BK, Sandberg AA (eds) Aneuploidy, Part B: induction and test systems. Liss, New York, pp 123–139

Patau K (1963) The origin of chromosomal abnormalities. Pathol Biol 11:1163–1170

Rapp M, Therman E, Denniston C (1977) Nonpairing of the X and Y chromosomes in the spermatocytes of BDF$_1$ mice. Cytogenet Cell Genet 19:85–93

Rivera H, Cantú JM (1986) Centric fission consequences in man. Ann Génét 29:223–225

Rudak E, Jacobs PA, Yanagimachi R (1978) Direct analysis of the chromosome constitution of human spermatozoa. Nature 274:911–913

Searle AG (1982) The genetics of sterility in the mouse. In: Crosignani PG, Rubin BL (eds) Genetic control of gamete production and function. Academic, London, pp 93–114

Sears ER (1952) Misdivision of univalents in common wheat. Chromosoma 4:535–550

Shepard J, Boothroyd ER, Stern H (1974) The effect of colchicine on synapsis and chiasma formation in microsporocytes of Lilium. Chromosoma 44:423–437

Solari AJ (1974) The behavior of the XY pair in mammals. Int Rev Cytol 38:273–317

Speed RM (1988) The possible role of meiotic pairing anomalies in the atresia of human fetal oocytes. Hum Genet 78:260–266

Speed RM, Chandley AC (1990) Prophase of meiosis in human spermatocytes analysed by EM microspreading in infertile men and their controls and comparisons with human oocytes. Hum Genet 84:547–554

Stene J, Fischer G, Stene E (1977) Paternal age effect in Down's syndrome. Ann Hum Genet 40:299–306

Stene J, Stene E, Stengel-Rutkowski S, et al. (1981) Paternal age and Down's syndrome. Data from prenatal diagnoses (DFG). Hum Genet 59:119–124

Tease C (1988) Radiation-induced aneuploidy in germ cells of female mammals. In: Vig BK, Sandberg AA (eds) Aneuploidy, Part B: Induction and test systems. Liss, New York, pp 141–157

Therman E, Patau K (1974) Abnormal X chromosomes in man: Origin, behavior and effects. Humangenetik 25:1–16

Therman E, Sarto GE (1983) Inactivation center on the human X chromosome. In: Sandberg AA (ed) Cytogenetics of the mammalian X chromosome, Part A. Basic mechanisms of X chromosome behavior. Liss, New York, pp 315–325

Therman E, Patau K, Smith DW, et al. (1961) The D trisomy syndrome and XO gonadal dysgenesis in two sisters. Am J Hum Genet 13:193–204

Therman E, Patau K, DeMars RI, et al. (1963) Iso/telo–D_1 mosaicism in a child with an incomplete D_1 trisomy syndrome. Portugal Acta Biol 7:211–224

Therman E, Sarto GE, DeMars RI (1981) The origin of telocentric chromosomes in man: A girl with tel(Xq). Hum Genet 57:104–107

Tuck CM, Bennett JW, Varela M (1984) Down's syndrome and familial aneuploidy. In: Berg, JM (ed) Perspectives and progress in mental retardation II. University Park Press, Baltimore, pp 167–180

Uchida IA (1977) Maternal radiation and trisomy 21. In: Hook EB, Porter IH (eds) Population cytogenetics. Academic, New York, pp 285–299

Uchida IA, Freeman VCP (1985) Triploidy and chromosomes. Am J Obstet Gynecol 151:65–69

Villaverde MM, DaSilva JA (1975) Turner–Mongolism polysyndrome. Review of the first eight known cases. J Am Med Assoc 234:844–847

Wagenbichler P, Killian W, Rett A, et al. (1976) Origin of the extra chromosome no. 21 in Down's syndrome. Hum Genet 32:13–16

Webb GC, Krumins EJ, Leversha MA, et al. (1984) 49,XXYY,+18 in a liveborn male. J Med Genet 21:232

Zuffardi O, Tiepolo L (1982) Frequencies and types of chromosome abnormalities associated with human male infertility. In: Crosignani PG, Rubin BL (eds) Genetic control of gamete production and function. Academic, London, pp 261–273

20
Human Sex Determination and the Y Chromosome

Y Chromosome

The human male has two sex chromosomes, one X and one Y. The Y chromosome is in the same size range as the two smallest pairs (the G group) of autosomes. However, even with ordinary staining techniques, the following features enable one to distinguish the Y from the G chromosomes: the short arm of the Y does not have satellites, a constriction is sometimes visible in the middle of the long arm, the chromatids of the long arm stick together, and the distal end of the long arm often looks fuzzy. During the mitotic cycle, the Y replicates later than do the G chromosomes.

The Q-banding pattern of the Y chromosome is much more spectacular than that of the G-group chromosomes, thanks to the very bright distal segment of the long arm (Fig. 20.1b). Without causing any apparent phenotypic effects, the length of this segment may range from practically zero, which is exceedingly rare, to two or three times its length in the average Y chromosome. The Japanese (Cohen et al., 1966), Chinese, and Kirghis (Ibraimov and Mirrakhimov, 1985) have much higher percentages of long Y chromosomes than Caucasians. (It is not known whether the length of the Y has any phenotypic effect.) The length of the brightly fluorescent distal segment is reflected in the size of a bright Y-body that can be seen in interphase nuclei. A sperm cell with a Y chromosome is distinguishable from an X-carrying sperm by its bright fluorescent spot. In cells with two Y chromosomes, two Y-bodies can be seen (Fig. 20.1c).

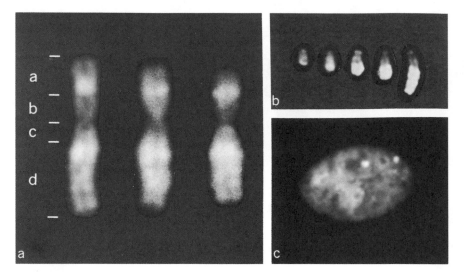

Figure 20.1. (a) Q-banded human X chromosomes (Therman et al., 1974); (b) variation in the size of the human Y chromosome (Dutrillaux, 1977); (c) two Y bodies in a buccal cell from a 47,XYY male.

Sex Determination in Humans

The mechanisms of sex determination may differ greatly, even among closely related groups (Bull, 1983). A sex chromosome mechanism is only one possibility, and even among such mechanisms considerable variation occurs. In the plant *Melandrium*, in which abnormal sex chromosome constitutions have been studied extensively, it is the presence of the Y chromosome that primarily determines male development. In *Drosophila*, sex is determined by the *ratio* of X chromosomes to the haploid sets of autosomes. Sex determination in man and in other mammals resembles the plant *Melandrium* rather than *Drosophila*. The finding that individuals with the chromosome complement 45,X are females and those with 47,XXY males showed that the Y chromosome determines male sex in humans. The basic plan of human sex differentiation is female; the Y chromosome turns an individual into a male. A Y chromosome guarantees a male phenotype (albeit an abnormal one), even if four X chromosomes are present.

That the male-determining factor(s) is situated on the short arm of the Y chromosome was demonstrated by the observation that individuals having an isochromosome for Yq, in addition to an X, are females. Phenotypically, they often appear to have Turner syndrome. In other words, they resemble females with a 45,X chromosome constitution (for example, Robinson and Buckton, 1971; Magnelli et al., 1974). A girl with several of the symptoms characteristic of Turner syndrome and a deletion of Yp (she had one X chromosome) was described by Rosenfeld et al. (1979).

Fine Structure of the Y Chromosome

In most mammals the X and Y chromosomes have a nonhomologous differential segment and a homologous pairing region (Fig. 20.2). The distal ends of the X and Y chromosome short arms constitute the pairing regions of the human sex chromosomes. In the short, distal-most parts of these regions crossing-over occurs, and therefore these were called pseudo-autosomal regions (PAR) by Burgoyne (1982). The occurrence of crossing-over has been confirmed by molecular (Ellis and Goodfellow, 1989) and electron microscopic studies which have demonstrated the presence of recombination nodules and bars (Holm and Rasmussen, 1983).

The much longer pairing segments form synaptonemal complexes (Chandley, 1988). The sex bivalent is heterochromatic and inactive in zygotene and pachytene. In diplotene–metaphase I, the attachment appears to be end-to-end, a typical terminal chiasma (Fig. 18.8). The pairing regions on the X and Y replicate synchronously, a further indication of their homology (Schempp, 1985). The pairing segment stays active in the inactive X of female cells.

As mentioned above, the putative testis-determining factor (TDF), first ascertained on the Y chromosome and then on Yp, is now known to lie

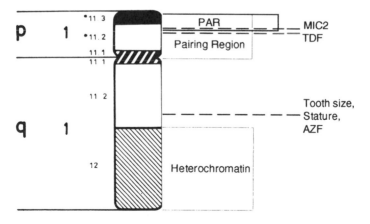

Figure 20.2. Cytogenetic diagram of the human Y chromosome showing the approximate positions of PAR (pseudoautosomal region), pairing region, MIC2 (antigen factor mapped to Xp22.32 and Yp11.3), TDF (testis-determining factor), factors affecting height and tooth size, AZF (factor preventing azoospermia), and heterochromatic region.

proximally of the border of the pseudoautosomal region, in which the last
known factor is MIC2 (Ellis and Goodfellow, 1989; McLaren, 1990).

For some 10 years, a regulator of the H–Y antigen was thought to be
the TDF (Wolf, 1981, 1983; Wachtel, 1983). However, this factor was
replaced as a TDF candidate by a gene coding for zinc finger protein
(Page et al., 1987). Recently, this ZFY, in turn, has given place to a gene
called SRY (sex-determining region Y). It is Y-specific in a wide range of
mammals and encodes a testis-specific transcript (Sinclair et al., 1990). It
seems unlikely that this latest TDF candidate will be relegated to the
same "has-been" status as its predecessors, since Koopman et al. (1991)
have demonstrated with transgenic mice that the *Sry* gene alone (the
mouse homologue of the human *SRY*) is able to confer maleness on a
mouse that is chromosomally XX.

Especially useful in studies of this sort have been males with 46,XX,
and females with 46,XY chromosome constitutions. More than 200 males
with a 46,XX (or rarely, a 45,X) constitution have been described. They
have male levels of the H–Y antigen and are sterile (de la Chapelle,
1972). They somewhat resemble males with Klinefelter syndrome
(47,XXY), but are shorter. Their tooth size is in the female range, which
is to be expected, since they lack the part of Yq in which the determinants for height and tooth size are believed to be situated (Fig. 20.2).
In the majority of the XX males, a part of Yp is attached to Xp. The
translocated segment can be seen in the light microscope, in many cases
(Evans et al., 1979). In others, its presence on Xp has been determined
with hybridization of DNA probes (for instance, Andersson et al., 1986;
Magenis et al., 1987; Schempp et al., 1989). In 45,X males, it is attached
to an autosome (for instance, Abbas et al., 1990). Corresponding studies
have shown that in XY women, TDF is missing from the Y (for instance,
Disteche et al., 1986). The most probable mechanism for creating such
abnormal X and Y chromosomes is an exceptional unequal exchange, in
which one break is proximal to TDF (Fig. 20.2).

Genes on the Y Chromosome

Apart from the male-determining factor(s) on the Yp, the human Y
chromosome seems to be peculiarly "empty," even considering that the
Q-bright distal segment consists of constitutive heterochromatin. However, it has been shown that the Y chromosome contains factor(s) that
influence tooth crown size. Both enamel and dentin growth are promoted,
possibly in a regulative way. It is suggested that in the presence of the Y
chromosome the mitotic potential is increased; this may explain larger
tooth crown sizes in males than in females, sex predilection for males in
the number of supernumerary and ordinary teeth, and possibly sex ratio
at birth. Also, statural growth might be influenced by this factor (for
example, Alvesalo, 1971, 1985). The growth-promoting factor is situated

near the border of the heterochromatic region (Fig. 20.2; Alvesalo, 1978; Alvesalo and de la Chapelle, 1981). Between these factors and the heterochromatin lies a gene whose presence prevents azoospermia (AZF) (Chandley et al., 1989). Homologues for the X-linked factors STS (steroid sulfatase) and Xg are situated in the pairing region. The status of the gene causing hairy ears in some Indian males is still unclear (Daiger and Chakraborty, 1985).

Abnormal Y Chromosomes

Y chromosome abnormalities have been reviewed in many articles in *The Y Chromosome, Parts A and B* (Sandberg, 1985). Apart from the polymorphism of the heterochromatin on Yq, human Y chromosomes show two other types of aberrations that do not affect the phenotype, including fertility. The more common of these is an inversion, which, in most cases, moves the centromere next to the border of the heterochromatin. It is estimated that one in 200 males has such an aberration, and Y chromosomes of this type have been found in large family clans (Friedrich and Nielsen, 1974). In a Muslim Indian Gujerati community in South Africa, some 30 per cent of the males had such a chromosome (Bernstein et al., 1986). A much rarer abnormality than a Y inversion is the presence of satellites on Yq. This comes about through a translocation between Yq and a short arm of an acrocentric. In Canada, a satellited Y chromosome has been inherited in twelve generations, spanning more than 300 years (Genest, 1973).

Deletions of the Y chromosome and i(Yq) chromosomes have been mentioned above. Isochromosomes for Yp also exist. Ring chromosomes involve deletions in both arms. Y isodicentrics, with one or both centromeres active, have been described.

The phenotypes of the carriers of deleted Y chromosomes form a series—Turner-like girls, intersexes, sterile males, normal males—depending on which part of the Y is missing. However, correlations between sex chromosome aberrations and the resulting phenotypes are often difficult to interpret, since most carriers are mosaics with an XO, XX, or XY cell line, and/or the mosaicism involves more than one aberrant sex chromosome constitution. In any case, a cytological and molecular analysis of such persons is especially important, since the presence of TDF induces testicular tissue, which in a female environment often becomes malignant.

Males with 45,X chromosome constitutions, and those with the satellited Y chromosomes mentioned above, result from translocations between the Y chromosome and the autosomes. The most common autosomal regions taking part in these translocations are the short arms of the acrocentrics, especially of chromosome 15 (Narahara et al., 1978; Fryns et al., 1985). Such translocations may be balanced or unbalanced, familial or occurring de novo. They may appear in males or females and may result in normal or abnormal phenotypes.

Translocations between the two sex chromosomes are discussed in Chapter 23.

References

Abbas N, Novelli G, Stella NC, et al., (1990) A 45,X male with molecular evidence of a translocation of Y euchromatin onto chromosome 1. Hum Genet 86:94–98

Alvesalo L (1971) The influence of sex-chromosome genes on tooth size in man. Proc Finn Dent Soc 67:3–54

Alvesalo L (1978) Tooth sizes in a male with 46,X del(Y)(q11) chromosome constitution. IADR Abstr A 57

Alvesalo L (1985) Dental growth in 47,XYY males and in conditions with other sex-chromosome anomalies. In: Sandberg AA (ed) The Y chromosome, Part B: Clinical aspects of Y chromosome abnormalities. Liss, New York, pp 277–300

Alvesalo L, Chapelle A de la (1981) Tooth sizes in two males with deletions of the long arm of the Y-chromosome. Ann Hum Genet 45:49–54

Andersson M, Page DC, Chapelle A de la (1986) Chromosome Y-specific DNA is transferred to the short arm of X chromosome in human XX males. Science 233:786–788

Bernstein R, Wadee A, Rosendorff J, et al. (1986) Inverted Y chromosome polymorphism in the Gujerati Muslim Indian population of South Africa. Hum Genet 74:223–229

Bull JJ (1983) Evolution of sex determining mechanisms. Benjamin/Cummings, Menlo Park, California

Burgoyne PS (1982) Genetic homology and crossing over in the X and Y chromosomes of mammals. Hum Genet 61:85–90

Chandley AC (1988) Meiosis in man. Trends Genet 4:79–84

Chandley AC, Gosden JR, Hargreave TB, et al. (1989) Deleted Yq in the sterile son of a man with a satellited Y chromosome (Yqs). J Med Genet 26:145–153

Chapelle A de la (1972) Analytic review: nature and origin of males with XX sex chromosomes. Am J Hum Genet 24:71–105

Cohen MM, Shaw MW, MacCluer JW (1966) Racial differences in the length of the human Y chromosome. Cytogenetics 5:34–52

Daiger SP, Chakraborty R (1985) Mapping the human Y chromosome. In: Sandberg AA (ed) The human Y chromosome, Part A: Basic characteristics of the Y chromosome. Liss, New York, pp 93–124

Disteche CM, Casanova M, Saal H, et al. (1986) Small deletions of the short arm of the Y chromosome in 46,XY females. Proc Natl Acad Sci USA 83:7841–7844

Dutrillaux B (1977) New chromosome techniques. In: Yunis JJ (ed) Molecular structure of human chromosomes. Academic, New York, pp 233–265

Ellis N, Goodfellow PN (1989) The mammalian pseudoautosomal region. Trends Genet 5:406–410

Evans HJ, Buckton KE, Spowart G, et al. (1979) Heteromorphic X chromosomes in 46,XX males: Evidence for the involvement of X-Y interchange. Hum Genet 49:11–31

Friedrich U, Nielsen J (1974) Pericentric inversion Y in a population of newborn boys. Hereditas 76:147–152

Fryns JP, Kleczkowska A, Van den Berghe H (1985) Clinical manifestations of Y/autosome translocations in man. In: Sandberg AA (ed) The Y chromosome, Part B: Clinical aspects of Y chromosome abnormalities. Liss, New York, pp 213–243

Genest P (1973) Transmission héréditaire, depuis 300 ans, d'un chromosome Y à satellites dans une lignée familiale. Ann Génét 16:35–38

Holm PB, Rasmussen SW (1983) Human meiosis V. Substages of pachytene in human spermatogenesis. Carlsberg Res Commun 48:351–383

Ibraimov AI, Mirrakhimov MM (1985) Q-band polymorphism in the autosomes and the Y chromosome in human populations. In: Sandberg AA (ed) The Y chromosome, Part A: Basic characteristics of the Y chromosome. Liss, New York, pp 213–287

Koopman P, Gubbay J, Vivian N, et al. (1991) Male development of chromosomally female mice transgenic for *Sry*. Nature 351:117–121

Magenis RE, Casanova M, Fellous M, et al. (1987) Further cytological evidence for Xp–Yp translocation in XX males using in situ hybridization with Y-derived probe. Hum Genet 75:228–233

Magnelli NC, Vianna-Morgante AM, Frota-Pessoa O, et al. (1974) Turner's syndrome and 46,X,i(Yq) karyotype. J Med Genet 11:403–406

McLaren A (1990) What makes a man a man? Nature 346:216–217

Narahara K, Yabuuchi H, Kimura S, et al. (1978) A case of a reciprocal translocation between the Y and no. 1 chromosomes. Jpn J Hum Genet 23:225–231

Page DC, Mosher R, Simpson EM, et al., (1987) The sex-determining region of the human Y chromosome encodes a finger protein. Cell 51:1091–1104

Robinson JA, Buckton KE (1971) Quinacrine fluorescence of variant and abnormal human Y chromosomes. Chromosoma 35:342–352

Rosenfeld RG, Luzzatti L, Hintz RL, et al. (1979) Sexual and somatic determinants of the human Y chromosome: studies in a 46,XYp– phenotypic female. Am J Hum Genet 31:458–468

Sandberg AA (ed) (1985) The Y chromosome, Parts A and B. Liss, New York

Schempp W (1985) High-resolution replication of the human Y chromosome. In: Sandberg AA (ed) The Y chromosome, Part A: Basic characteristics of the Y chromosome. Liss, New York, pp 357–371

Schempp W, Müller G, Scherer G, et al. (1989) Localization of Y chromosome sequences and X chromosomal replication studies in XX males. Hum Genet 81:144–148

Sinclair AH, Berta P, Palmer MS, et al. (1990) A gene from the human sex-determining region encodes a protein with homology to a conserved DNA-binding motif. Nature 346:240–244

Therman E, Sarto GE, Patau K (1974) Center for Barr body condensation on the proximal part of the human Xq: a hypothesis. Chromosoma 44:361–366

Wachtel SS (1983) HY antigen and the biology of sex determination. Grune and Stratton, New York

Wolf U (1981) Genetic aspects of H–Y antigen. Hum Genet 58:25–28

Wolf U (1983) X-linked genes and gonadal differentiation. Differentiation 23, Suppl:104–106

21
Human X Chromosome

Structure of the X Chromosome

The normal female chromosome complement contains, in addition to 44 autosomes, two X chromosomes that are members of the medium-sized C group. The X chromosome constitutes 5.3 percent of the length of the haploid karyotype, and its centromere index is 0.38. The fluorescent pattern of the X chromosome is shown in Fig. 20.1a. In the short arm, two main regions can be seen: a brighter distal segment (a), and a less Q-bright region (b), next to the centromere. On the other side of the centromere is another Q-dark segment (c), which is shorter than the corresponding region on the Xp (b). The rest of the Xq is Q-bright (d) and is divided into two almost equal parts by a narrow darker band.

X Chromatin or Barr Body Formation

In 1949, Barr and Bertram discovered that the nuclei of the nerve cells of the female cat had a condensed, deeply stained body that was absent in the cells of the males. This X chromatin (also called sex chromatin or the Barr body) was later found to represent one X chromosome that is condensed and inactive in the female. The same behavior has been

Figure 21.1. Behavior of the inactive X chromosome(s). (a) A drumstick in a polymorphonuclear blood cell; (b) two Barr bodies in the buccal nucleus of a 47,XXX woman; (c) one Barr body in a normal woman; (d) inactive X chromosome in early prophase; (e) Barr body in a fibroblast; (f) inactive X chromosome in late prophase (Feulgen staining; bar = $5\,\mu$m).

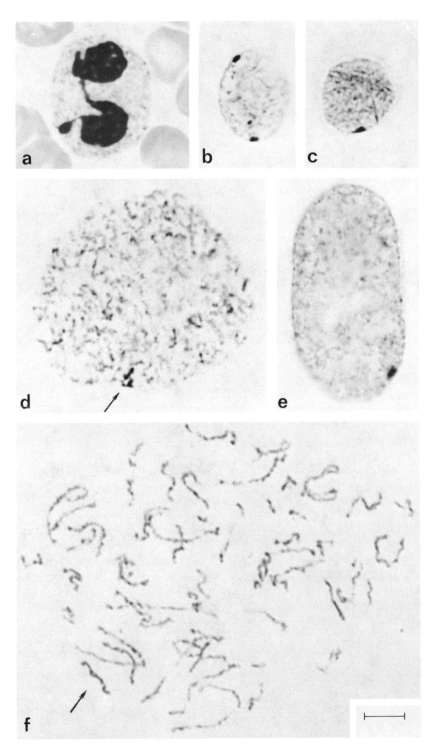

established for one X chromosome in practically all mammalian females. If an individual, female or male, has an abnormal number of X chromosomes, all but one of them form Barr bodies. The Barr body consists of a loop-shaped X chromosome in which the two telomeres lie close together at the nuclear membrane (Walker et al., 1991).

Fig. 21.1d–f illustrates the behavior of the Barr body-forming X chromosome in interphase and through prophase, in human fibroblast cells. Even in prophase, it continues to be more condensed than the other chromosomes. Apart from cultured fibroblasts, Barr bodies in the human are most often studied in buccal smears (Fig. 21.1b–c), but also in vaginal

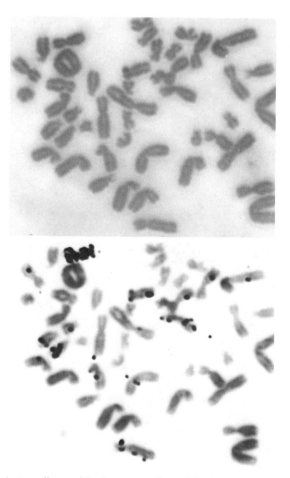

Figure 21.2. Autoradiographic demonstration of the late-replicating X in a human lymphocyte with a double r(9). Top: Before autoradiography. Bottom: After autoradiography; one X is heavily labeled.

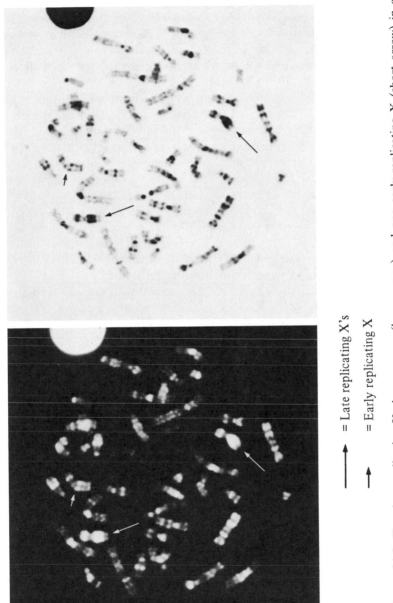

Giemsa

Fluorescence

⟶ = Late replicating X's

⟶ = Early replicating X

Figure 21.3. Two late-replicating X chromosomes (long arrows) and one early-replicating X (short arrow) in a woman with 47,XXX (BrdU, left stained with Hoechst 33258, right with Giemsa) (Latt et al., 1976).

smears, and sometimes in hair-root follicles. In normal females, 30 to 50 percent of the buccal cells show a Barr body, but the counts from different laboratories vary greatly. This relatively low frequency probably results from the fact that many of the cells are dead (the deeper one digs in the buccal mucosa, the higher the incidence of Barr bodies). In fibroblasts, the incidence of cells with Barr bodies is more than 90 percent when most of the cells are in the G_2 phase. In polymorphonuclear white blood cells, the inactive X appears as a drumstick-shaped extrusion, with a frequency of 1 to 10 percent (Fig. 21.1a).

The allocycly or being out of step with the other chromosomes, shown by the inactive X chromosome, also expresses itself in other ways. The inactive X replicates late during the S period, as demonstrated by autoradiography. When tritiated thymidine is fed to a cell late in the S phase, the inactive X may be the only labeled chromosome in the next metaphase (Fig. 21.2). In most cells, the inactive X is the "latest labeling" (last to be labeled) of the C-group chromosomes.

A more refined technique to distinguish the Barr body-forming X in metaphase was invented by Latt (1973). It involves growing the cells for 40 to 44 hours in a medium containing BrdU, and then substituting thymidine during the last 6 to 7 hours before fixation. The inactive X appears very bright when stained with the fluorescent stains, Hoechst 33258 or coriphosphine O (Fig. 21.3). Stained with Giemsa techniques, it is darker than the other X. This technique can also be used in reverse by first feeding the cells thymidine and then, at the end, BrdU. In this case, the inactive X is the least fluorescent chromosome when stained with a fluorochrome, and the faintest when stained with Giemsa.

The inactive X is often shorter in metaphase than the active one, and it may show differential staining even with ordinary cell culture methods (Takagi and Oshimura, 1973; Sarto et al., 1974).

Inactivation of the X Chromosome

Unlike the Y chromosome, the human X seems to contain genes in proportion to its length. Actually, more genes have been localized on the X chromosome than on any of the autosomes. Despite the fact that males have one and females two X chromosomes, the sexes do not differ from each other very much, apart from sexual development and secondary sex characteristics. In many other animal groups, gender differences are considerable. This relative similarity of the male and female in mammals is achieved by a mechanism of dosage compensation that allows all but one X chromosome in each cell to be turned off.

Lyon (1961) proposed the single-active X hypothesis to explain the observation, in the mouse, that females heterozygous for X-linked fur color genes are patchy mosaics of two colors. To quote Lyon (1961, p.

372): "... the evidence of mouse genetics indicates: (1) that the hetero-pycnotic X-chromosome can be either paternal or maternal in origin in different cells of the same animal; (2) that it is genetically inactivated." This hypothesis has inspired an enormous amount of research, and the following principles have been established with respect to X-inactivation. The inactivation of one X chromosome in the normal female, or of all but one X in individuals with several X chromosomes, takes place early in embryonic development, at an estimated 1000- to 2000-cell stage of the blastocyst, or possibly even earlier (Lyon, 1974). The inactivation involves the paternal or maternal X chromosome at random, and once an X chromosome is turned off, the event seems to be irreversible. In all the descendents of the cell in which the inactivation took place, the same X is turned off and forms the Barr body. The inactive X is not transcribed; it is facultatively heterochromatic. The occurrence of "always active" regions on the inactive X chromosome will be discussed in Chapter 23.

The single-active X hypothesis implies that a female heterozygous for a gene on the X chromosome should have two different cell populations, each with a different allele being expressed. Studies of patchy fur colors, which have yielded so much information in the mouse, are not possible in human populations. However, in a few human conditions, a patchy appearance resulting from X-inactivation seems to be expressed, for instance, in ocular albinism and in choroideremia (Gartler and Andina, 1976).

On the cellular level, this phenomenon has been studied for a limited number of X-linked genes (Davies, 1991). The first demonstration of the expression of a single X was done by Davidson et al. (1963). They cloned fibroblasts from a woman heterozygous for two allozymes of the enzyme glucose-6-phosphate dehydrogenase (G6PD). On starch-gel electrophoresis, the uncloned cells showed the double pattern, whereas clones of cells revealed only one or the other allozyme.

In a mouse with patchy fur color and with a normal and an abnormal X chromosome (the so-called Cattanach translocation), one X formed the Barr body in one type of patch, and the other X formed the Barr body in other patches. This observation was in accord with the known fur-color genes on the two X chromosomes (Cattanach, 1975). Another advance in the evidence that the late-replicating X chromosome is also the inactive one was provided by observations on mules and hinnies (reviewed by Gartler and Andina, 1976). In these hybrids, the donkey-X and the horse-X can be distinguished morphologically. Each species has its own type of G6PD, and the predominant G6PD isozyme in both fibroblasts and erythrocytes of the two hybrids has turned out to be the one that is characteristic of the horse. In agreement with this observation, in both hybrids, the donkey-X was late-replicating in about 90 percent of the cells, and the horse-X in 10 percent. Whether this inequality of expression of the two X chromosomes depends on original nonrandomness of the inactivation or originally random inactivation, followed by selection for the cell line in which the horse-X is active, is not known.

Reactivation of the X Chromosome

As already pointed out, once X inactivation has taken place, it seems to be irreversible. All experimental attempts, whether by treatment with chemicals or by hybridization with cells of other mammals, as a rule have failed to reactivate the inactive X chromosome. However, a few genes have been found to be derepressed spontaneously (Kahan and DeMars, 1975). Furthermore, treatment with the demethylating agent, 5-azacytidine, has been observed to derepress some genes (Mohandas et al., 1981; Lester et al., 1982). This led to the hypothesis that X inactivation on the molecular level involves the methylation of cytosine-guanine (CpG) dinucleotide clusters (Gartler and Riggs, 1983; Mohandas and Shapiro, 1983). However, recent results indicate that methylation locks in X inactivation, but does not cause it (Kaslow and Migeon, 1987).

The inactive X is reactivated in the oocytes at some time before meiosis, the exact timing being still under dispute (Gartler and Andina, 1976). Both X chromosomes are transcribed, and neither shows heteropycnotic behavior. In meiosis, the two X chromosomes pair normally, and the bivalent formed by them does not differ from autosomal bivalents (Fig. 18.6). Whether the inactive X is spontaneously derepressed under abnormal conditions, as in malignant tumors, is still unclear (Sandberg, 1983; Takagi et al., 1983; Therman et al., 1985).

In marsupial females, the inactivated X chromosome is always of paternal origin. Furthermore, in some tissues, a few normally inactive genes are partly active: they leak (Migeon et al., 1985). In mammalian trophoblast, some genes on the inactive X chromosome have shown a similar leakage. Moreover, the whole trophoblastic inactive X may become reactivated in human–mouse hybrid cells (Migeon et al., 1986).

X;Y Translocations

In humans, apart from XX males and XY females who originate from a translocation between the sex chromosomes (Chapter 20), 38 other individuals with t(X;Y) have been described (Bernstein, 1985). Twenty-five females and four males showed the chromosome constitution, 46,X,t(X;Y). Thirteen males had the constitution, 46,Y,t(X;Y). The phenotypic sex of these translocation carriers depended on their chromosome constitutions, the breakpoints on the X and Y chromosomes, and the patterns of X inactivation The X;Y translocations have been useful in localizing various factors on the sex chromosomes. For instance, short stature is caused by monosomy of the distal Xp in females, while nullosomy has the same effect in males (Bernstein, 1985). Such effects will be discussed in Chapter 23.

Sex Reversal

Apart from the testis determining factor (TDF), which is decisive in primary sex determination, other genes, both X-linked and autosomal, play a role in sex development. A mutation in any of them may lead to abnormal sexual development or to sex reversal. Sex reversal genes have been found in many animal species, such as *Drosophila*, mouse, rat, and goat.

The various types of XY women have been reviewed by Wolman et al. (1985). One of the best known of these conditions in which an individual with the XY sex chromosome constitution develops into a female is the *testicular feminization syndrome*. The locus determining testicular feminization and other androgen insensitivity syndromes is now known to lie at Xq11–q12 (Migeon et al., 1981; Brown et al., 1989). Families in which the testicular feminization gene is inherited are characterized by a preponderance of female births. The affected individuals usually have a fully feminine appearance and often come to the attention of a physician only because of primary amenorrhea (lack of menstruation) and/or sterility. They have testes in the abdominal cavity or in the inguinal canal, but the mutant gene renders the target organs insensitive to androgens produced by the testes (Wachtel, 1983).

Individuals with *XY gonadal dysgenesis* (*Swyer syndrome*) are females of greater than average height. They have streak (mainly connective tissue without oogonia) gonads, and do not develop any secondary sex characteristics. One possible explanation for this syndrome is a defective gonadal receptor (Damiani et al., 1990).

A further rare sex reversal syndrome, in which individuals with 46,XY chromosome constitutions are females, is *campomelic dysplasia*, with an autosomal recessive inheritance (Wolf, 1981).

Phenotypic females who have a Y chromosome or the portion of the Y that contains the TDF are especially susceptible to malignant disease. The testicular tissue in patients with an androgen insensitivity syndrome has a 10% probability of becoming malignant, and in XY gonadal dysgenesis the streak gonads have been reported to undergo malignant transformation in 30% of the cases (Wolman et al., 1985). An early cytological or molecular diagnosis of the presence of Y chromosome material would allow the prophylactic removal of the susceptible tissues.

218   21. Human X Chromosome

References

Barr ML, Bertram EG (1949) A morphological distinction between neurones of the male and female, and the behaviour of the nucleolar satellite during accelerated nucleoprotein synthesis. Nature 163:676–677

Bernstein R (1985) X;Y chromosome translocations and their manifestations. In: Sandberg AA (ed) The Y chromosome, Part B: Clinical aspects of Y chromosome abnormalities. Liss, New York, pp 171–206

Brown CJ, Goss SJ, Lubahn DB, et al. (1989) Androgen receptor locus on the human X chromosome: regional localization to Xq11–12 and description of a DNA polymorphism. Am J Hum Genet 44:264–269

Cattanach BM (1975) Control of chromosome inactivation. Annu Rev Genet 9:1–18

Damiani D, Billerbeck AEC, Goldberg ACK, et al. (1990) Investigation of the ZFY gene in XX true hermaphroditism and Swyer syndrome. Hum Genet 85:85–88

Davidson RG, Nitowsky HM, Childs B (1963) Demonstration of two populations of cells in the human female heterozygous for glucose-6-phosphate dehydrogenase variants. Proc Natl Acad Sci USA 50:481–485

Davies K (1991) The essence of inactivity. Nature 349:15–16

Gartler SM, Andina RJ (1976) Mammalian X-chromosome inactivation. In: Harris H, Hirschhorn K (eds) Advances in human genetics, Vol 7. Plenum, New York

Gartler SM, Riggs AD (1983) Mammalian X-chromosome inactivation. Annu Rev Genet 17:155–190

Kahan B, DeMars RI (1975) Localized derepression on the human inactive X chromosome in mouse–human cell hybrids. Proc Natl Acad Sci USA 72:1510–1514

Kaslow DC, Migeon BR (1987) DNA methylation stabilizes X chromosome inactivation in eutherians but not in marsupials: evidence for multistep maintenance of mammalian X dosage compensation. Proc Natl Acad Sci USA 84:6210–6214

Latt SA (1973) Microfluorometric detection of deoxyribonucleic acid replication in human metaphase chromosomes. Proc Natl Acad Sci USA 70:3395–3399

Latt SA, Willard HF, Gerald PS (1976) BrdU-33258 Hoechst analysis of DNA replication in human lymphocytes with supernumerary or structurally abnormal X chromosomes. Chromosoma 57:135–153

Lester SC, Korn NJ, DeMars R (1982) Derepression of genes on the human inactive X chromosome: evidence for differences in locus-specific rates of derepression and rates of transfer of active and inactive genes after DNA-mediated transformation. Somatic Cell Genet 8:265–284

Lyon MF (1961) Gene action in the X-chromosome of the mouse (*Mus musculus* L.). Nature 190:372–373

Lyon MF (1974) Mechanisms and evolutionary origins of variable X-chromosome activity in mammals. Proc R Soc Lond B 187:243–268

Migeon BR, Brown TR, Axelman J, et al. (1981) Studies of the locus for androgen receptor: Localization on the human X chromosome and evidence for homology with the *Tfm* locus in the mouse. Proc Natl Acad Sci USA 78:6339–6343

Migeon BR, Wolf SF, Axelman J, et al. (1985) Incomplete X chromosome dosage compensation in chorionic villi of human placenta. Proc Natl Acad Sci USA 82:3390–3394

Migeon BR, Schmidt M, Axelman J, et al. (1986) Complete reactivation of X chromosomes from human chorionic villi with a switch to early DNA replication. Proc Natl Acad Sci USA 83:2182–2186

Mohandas T, Shapiro LJ (1983) Factors involved in X-chromosome inactivation. In: Sandberg AA (ed) Cytogenetics of the mammalian X chromosome, Part A: Basic mechanisms of X chromosome behavior. Liss, New York, pp 271–297

Mohandas T, Sparkes RS, Shapiro LJ (1981) Reactivation of an inactive human X-chromosome: evidence for X inactivation by DNA methylation. Science 211:393–396

Sandberg AA (1983) The X chromosome in human neoplasia, including sex chromatin and congenital conditions with X-chromosome anomalies. In: Sandberg AA (ed) Cytogenetics of the mammalian X chromosome, Part B: X chromosome anomalies and their clinical manifestations. Liss, New York, pp 459–498

Sarto GE, Therman E, Patau K (1974) Increased Q fluorescence of an inactive Xq– chromosome in man. Clin Genet 6:289–293

Takagi N, Oshimura M (1973) Fluorescence and Giemsa banding studies in the allocyclic X chromosome in embryonic and adult mouse cells. Exp Cell Res 78:127–135

Takagi N, Yoshida MA, Sugawara O, et al. (1983) Reversal of X-inactivation in female mouse somatic cells hybridized with murine teratocarcinoma stem cells in vitro. Cell 34:1053–1062

Therman E, Denniston C, Nieminen U, et al. (1985) X chromatin, endomitoses, and mitotic abnormalities in human cervical cancer. Cancer Genet Cytogenet 16:1–11

Wachtel SS (1983) H–Y antigen and the biology of sex determination. Grune and Stratton, New York

Walker CL, Cargile CB, Floy KM, et al. (1991) The Barr body is a looped X chromosome formed by telomere association. Proc Natl Acad Sci USA 88: 6191–6195

Wolf U (1981) Genetic aspects of H–Y antigen. Hum Genet 58:25–28

Wolman SR, David R, Koo GC (1985) The "Y" chromosome in the female phenotype. In: Sandberg AA (ed) The Y chromosome, Part A: Basic characteristics of the Y chromosome. Liss, New York, pp 477–505

22
Abnormal Human Sex Chromosome Constitutions

Aneuploidy of X Chromosomes in Individuals with a Female Phenotype

The sex chromosomes show a much wider range of viable aneuploidy than do the autosomes, presumably for the following reasons. On the one hand, the Y chromosome seems to contain very few genes apart from those determining the male sex; on the other, all but one X chromosome in a cell are inactivated, forming X chromatin bodies in the interphase. This rule can be stated another way: there is one active X chromosome for each diploid complement of autosomes.

Fig. 22.1 summarizes the nonmosaic numerical sex chromosome abnormalities found so far, their incidence in newborn infants of the same sex, and the number of Barr bodies formed by them. In addition to the examples in this figure, the chromosome constitution XYYYY has been found in a few highly abnormal individuals (listed in Noël et al., 1988).

Mosaicism is also much more common for sex chromosomal than for autosomal aneuploidies and, in addition, often involves structurally abnormal X and Y chromosomes.

Aneuploidy results from nondisjunction in either the meiotic division of the parents or the early cleavage divisions of the affected individuals. Aneuploidy for more than one chromosome is the result of nondisjunction in both meiotic divisions, nondisjunction in the meiosis of both parents (which must be a rare coincidence), multiple nondisjunction in the same mitosis or meiosis, or abnormalities in more than one mitosis. A study of eight cases having four or five sex chromosomes, performed with restriction fragment length polymorphisms (RFLPs), showed that in every

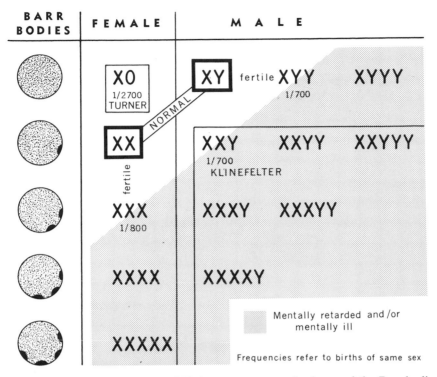

Figure 22.1. The human X and Y chromosome constitutions and the Barr bodies formed by the X chromosomes. (The male with 49,XYYYY is missing from the diagram.)

case successive nondisjunction had happened in one parent (Hassold et al., 1990).

The incidence of 47,XXX and 47,XXY children increases with maternal age, as does that of autosomal trisomies. In these cases, nondisjunction apparently occurs mainly in maternal meiosis. The incidence of 45,X children, on the other hand, seems to be independent of maternal age. Indeed, studies of the Xg blood group gene, which is located on the X chromosome, show that in 78 percent of the XO cases studied, the gamete without a sex chromosome came from the father (Sanger et al., 1971). Similar results have been obtained with molecular methods by Jacobs et al. (1990) and Mathur et al. (1991).

The syndromes caused by various sex chromosome aneuploidies have been reviewed by de Grouchy (1974) and de la Chapelle (1990).

One of the prerequisites for production of normal gametes is a complete pairing of chromosomes in meiotic prophase. It is, therefore, surprising that some 30% of normal human oocytes show pairing abnormalities (Speed, 1985). This is probably the chief cause of oocyte degeneration. In early embryos, the oocytes number some 7 million; at birth the number has decreased to 2 million. In Turner syndrome, the pairing anomalies are even more frequent, since the whole X, or a portion of it, is lacking a homologous partner. The gonads, which lack oocytes, become streaks, resulting in primary or secondary amenorrhea (Speed, 1988; Speed and Chandley, 1990). A large number of phenotypic abnormalities have been described in Turner syndrome, the most common one being short stature (under 5 ft or 150 cm). Other anomalies (Table 22.1), such as webbed neck, low hairline, shield chest, cubitus valgus (changed carrying angle of the elbow), and pigmented nevi are somewhat less frequent. Often the cardiovascular and urinary systems are also affected. Patients with Turner syndrome do not seem to be mentally retarded any more often than do females with two X chromosomes (Table 24.2).

An interesting, although so far unexplained, phenomenon is that over 99 percent of zygotes with a 45,X chromosome constitution end up as spontaneous abortions (Jacobs et al., 1990).

Table 22.1. Symptoms of nonmosaic adult carriers of XO, Xp−, and Xq− chromosomes. All ascertainment types pooled. Revised from Therman and Susman (1990).

Symptom	% XO (n = 332)	% Xp− (n = 52)	% Xq− (n = 67)
Short stature	100	88	43
Low hairline	72	19	9
Shield chest	74	35	13
Pigmented nevi	64	27	19
Cubitus valgus	77	25	16
Short metacarpal	55	29	12
Arched palate		6	9
Nail anomaly	57	8	7
Lymphedema		8	3
Hearing anomaly			4
Auricle anomaly		12	1
Cardiovascular anomaly	23	2	
Webbed neck	42	2	1
Epicanthic folds		2	3
Micrognathia		6	1
Short neck	77	38	21
Eye anomaly		8	1
Urinary tract anomaly	44	8	6
Hypertension	37	8	7
Mental retardation	19	13	7
Retarded bone age	64	17	10
Thyroid disease	18	6	3
Diabetes		2	6
Color blindness	11		3
Gonadal dysgenesis	91	65	93

Individuals with three X chromosomes do not seem to form a well-defined syndrome. They are often mentally retarded or psychotic. Their mental status, as well as that of persons with other types of sex chromosome anomalies, is reviewed by Polani (1977). Triple-X women have normal fertility and they overwhelmingly produce children with normal chromosome constitutions, instead of having one-half of the daughters with 47,XXX and one-half of the sons with 47,XXY constitutions, as might be expected. One possible explanation is that in the first meiotic division of the oocyte, the extra chromosome always ends up in the polar body. Other examples in which aberrant chromosomes are relegated to the polar bodies are found in *Drosophila* and in moths. Mosaicism is another possibility.

Patients with more than three X chromosomes suffer from severe mental retardation and have several somatic anomalies. However, their sex development is usually normal. Nielsen et al. (1977) reviewed the 26 cases of 48,XXXX found up to that time. They showed a wide range of abnormalities and varied considerably from case to case.

As Fig. 22.1 demonstrates, more than one X chromosome can be found in individuals with a male phenotype. These are discussed in the following paragraphs.

Sex chromosome aneuploidies—mainly XO, XXY, and XXX—are also described in a number of other mammals (Lyon, 1974; Wurster-Hill et al., 1983).

Sex Chromosome Aneuploidy with a Male Phenotype

In the group of sex chromosome aneuploidies with a male phenotype, the XXY and XYY conditions are about equally frequent at birth. Individuals with 47,XXY chromosome constitutions form a fairly well-defined, so-called Klinefelter syndrome. They are characterized by a eunuchoid habitus, their small testes are devoid of sperm cells, and they are sterile. They also show a tendency to breast development (gynecomastia). The XXY sex chromosome constitution seems to lower the IQ to some extent, and as a result the affected individuals are often mildly retarded mentally (Murken, 1973). They also show psychotic tendencies and may eventually end up in mental institutions (Polani, 1977).

Patients with one Y chromosome and more than two X chromosomes are mentally retarded and display various other symptoms. To take one example, males with the 49,XXXXY chromosome constitution have an IQ in the range of 20 to 50, extensive skeletal anomalies, severe hypogenitalism, strabismus, wide-set eyes, and other anomalies. Over 100 such males have been described in the literature.

The 47,XYY syndrome has unfortunately been sensationalized by the news media, which have often depicted these individuals as a group of murderers and other violent criminals. This is not true. What *is* true is that persons with this chromosome complement have a higher probability of coming into conflict with the law than normal males, but their crimes are usually nonviolent (reviews by Hook, 1973; Polani, 1977; Witkin et al., 1976; Welch, 1985). Most males with an XYY sex chromosome constitution lead normal lives and are not distinguishable from normal males except that they usually are considerably taller than their male relatives, often being 6 feet tall and more (>180 cm) (Murken, 1973).

The highest incidence of XYY males is found when prisoners who are 6 ft tall, or taller, are chosen for chromosome studies. Apart from their above-average height, XYY males do not represent a defined syndrome, although some neurological symptoms and specific features of body build have been described in them (Daly, 1969). With the exception of some individuals, their fertility does not seem to be impaired to any great extent. The XYY condition is often accompanied by mental retardation (Murken, 1973).

Males with the chromosome constitution 48,XXYY are also found in increased numbers in prisons. They show features in common with Klinefelter syndrome, are tall, and are more or less mentally retarded.

Higher aneuploidies like XXXYY and XYYY are rare, and individuals with XYYYY have also been described. Patients with such sex chromosome constitutions are retarded and display numerous anomalies (Noël et al., 1988).

Various Abnormalities in X Chromosome Behavior

Examples of abnormal behavior characteristic of, but not exclusive to, the X chromosome are collected in Fig. 22.2. Cells with the 45,X chromosome constitution are often significantly increased in older women. At the same time, cells that display what, at first sight, simulates acentric fragments make their appearance. Banding studies have shown these to be X chromosomes in which the centromere is inactivated but shows a C-band. Their appearance and behavior are more in agreement with the idea that the centromere is not functioning than with the claim that it has undergone premature division, as the phenomenon has also been interpreted (Fitzgerald, 1983) (chromosomes with a prematurely divided centromere do not resemble acentric fragments). Chromosomes with an inactivated centromere replicate and divide, but their segregation is random and results in some cells lacking these chromosomes, while other cells may accumulate several of them (Drets and Therman, 1983).

A similar inactivation of the centromere often takes place in dicentric chromosomes, but it seems to be especially common in dicentrics consisting of two X chromosomes, possibly because trisomy for the X is much better tolerated than imbalance for the autosomes. The two X chromo-

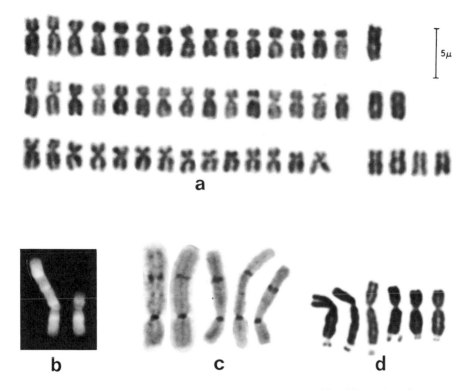

Figure 22.2. (a) The C-group and the X chromosome(s) with an inactive centromere from three cells; (b) idic(Xp−) with telomeric attachment and the normal X chromosome; (c) C-banded idic(Xp−) chromosome showing one active and one inactive centromere from five cells; (d) X chromosome expressing the fragile region from six cells (d, courtesy of S Roberts).

somes are attached, either by their short, idic(Xp−), or by their long arms, idic(Xq−). The site of the inactivated centromere is marked by a C-band, but no Cd band, and the primary constriction is lacking (Fig. 22.2b,c; Sarto and Therman, 1980).

Lists of t(X;X) chromosomes are found in Mattei et al. (1981b), Zakharov and Baranovskaya (1983), and Therman and Susman (1990).

Figure 22.2d illustrates six X chromosomes in which the so-called fragile region is expressed; this usually occurs only in a small proportion of cells. It appears as a gap at Xq27, and the chromosome is apt to break or form a triradial at this point. As discussed in Chapter 9, fragile regions are found in several autosomes also. However, the fra(X) is different from the autosomes in that, in the hemizygous state, it has severe phenotypic effects. Most male carriers are mentally retarded (one reason for the higher incidence of mental retardation in men than women). They also display the following somatic anomalies: macro-orchidism (large testes), high forehead, prominent nose, and large protruding ears (Carpenter, 1983). The fra(X) is inherited in Mendelian fashion, and most heterozygous women are normal, whereas the overwhelming majority of male carriers are affected. However, some female carriers are slightly retarded, and even severely retarded female carriers have been described (for example Mattei et al., 1981a).

These exceptions and other complications require a more sophisticated explanation than simple X-linked inheritance (Nussbaum and Ledbetter, 1986). One of the most interesting hypotheses has been put forward by Laird (1987). According to this, two main steps are needed for the creation of the fra(X) syndrome. The first event is a mutation of the normal into a fra(X) locus, and subsequently the mutated locus on the inactive X must remain inactive when the rest of the chromosome is reactivated in oogenesis. This event in the fra(X) locus has been assumed to be correlated with late replication and DNA methylation, which are under intensive study (Khalifa et al., 1990; Yu et al., 1990).

References

Carpenter NJ (1983) The fragile X chromosome and its clinical manifestations. In: Sandberg AA (ed) Cytogenetics of the mammalian X chromosome, Part B: X chromosome anomalies and their clinical manifestations. Liss, New York, pp 399–414

Chapelle A de la (1990) Sex chromosome abnormalities. In: Emery AEH, Rimoin DL (eds) Principles and practice of medical genetics, Vol 1. Churchill Livingstone, Edinburgh, pp 273–299

Daly RF (1969) Neurological abnormalities in XYY males. Nature 221:472–473

Drets ME, Therman E (1983) Human telomeric 6;19 translocation chromosome with a tendency to break at the fusion point. Chromosoma 88:139–144

Fitzgerald PH (1983) Premature centromere division of the X chromosome. In: Sandberg AA (ed) Cytogenetics of the mammalian X chromosome, Part A. Basic mechanisms of X chromosome behavior. Liss, New York, pp 171–184

Grouchy J de (1974) Sex chromosome disorders. In: Busch H (ed) The cell nucleus, Vol II. Academic, New York, pp 415–436

Hassold T, Pettay D, May K, et al. (1990) Analysis of non-disjunction in sex chromosome tetrasomy and pentasomy. Hum Genet 85:648–650

Hook EB (1973) Behavioral implications of the human XYY genotype. Science 179:139–150

Jacobs PA, Betts PR, Cockwell AE, et al. (1990) A cytogenetic and molecular reappraisal of a series of patients with Turner's syndrome. Ann Hum Genet 54:209–223

Khalifa MM, Reiss AL, Migeon BR (1990) Methylation status of genes flanking the fragile site in males with the fragile-X syndrome: a test of the imprinting hypothesis. Am J Hum Genet 46:744–753

Laird CD (1987) Proposed mechanism of inheritance and expression of the human fragile-X syndrome of mental retardation. Genetics 117:587–599

Lyon MF (1974) Mechanisms and evolutionary origins of variable X-chromosome activity in mammals. Proc R Soc Lond B 187:243–268

Mathur A, Stekol L, Schatz D, et al. (1991) The parental origin of the single X chromosome in Turner syndrome: lack of correlation with parental age or clinical phenotype. Am J Hum Genet 48:682–686

Mattei JF, Mattei MG, Aumeras C, et al. (1981a) X-linked mental retardation with the fragile X. A study of 15 families. Hum Genet 59:281–289

Mattei MG, Mattei JF, Vidal I, et al. (1981b) Structural anomalies of the X chromosome and inactivation center. Hum Genet 56:401–408

Murken J-D (1973) The XYY-syndrome and Klinefelter's syndrome. George Thieme, Stuttgart

Nielsen J, Homma A, Christiansen F, et al. (1977) Women with tetra-X (48,XXXX). Hereditas 85:151–156

Noël B, Bénézech M, Bouzon MT, et al. (1988) Un garçon de sept ans 49,XYYYY. Ann Génét 31:111–116

Nussbaum RL, Ledbetter DH (1986) Fragile X syndrome: a unique mutation in man. Annu Rev Genet 20:109–145

Polani PE (1977) Abnormal sex chromosomes, behavior and mental disorder. In: Tanner JM (ed) Developments in psychiatric research. Hodder and Stoughton, London, pp 89–128

Sanger R, Tippett P, Gavin J (1971) Xg groups and sex abnormalities in people of northern European ancestry. J Med Genet 8:417–426

Sarto GE, Therman E (1980) Replication and inactivation of a dicentric X formed by telomeric fusion. Am J Obstet Gynecol 136:904–911

Speed RM (1985) The prophase stages in human foetal oocytes studied by light and electron microscopy. Hum Genet 69:69–75

Speed RM (1988) The possible role of meiotic pairing anomalies in the atresia of human fetal oocytes. Hum Genet 78:260–266

Speed RM, Chandley AC (1990) Prophase of meiosis in human spermatocytes analysed by EM microspreading in infertile men and their controls and comparisons with human oocytes. Hum Genet 84:547–554

Therman E, Susman B (1990) The similarity of phenotypic effects caused by Xp and Xq deletions in the human female: a hypothesis. Hum Genet 85:175–183

Welch JP (1985) Clinical aspects of the XYY syndrome. In: Sandberg AA (ed) The Y chromosome, Part B. Liss, New York, pp 323–343

Witkin HA, Mednick SA, Schulsinger F, et al. (1976) Criminality in XYY and XXY men. Science 193:547–555

Wurster-Hill DH, Benirschke K, Chapman DI (1983) Abnormalities of the X chromosome in mammals. In: Sandberg AA (ed) Cytogenetics of the mammalian X chromosome, Part B: X chromosome anomalies and their clinical manifestations. Liss, New York, pp 283–300

Yu W-D, Wenger SL, Steele MW (1990) X chromosome imprinting in fragile X syndrome. Hum Genet 85:590–594

Zakharov AF, Baranovskaya LJ (1983) X–X chromosome translocations and their karyotype-phenotype correlations. In: Sandberg AA (ed) Cytogenetics of the mammalian X chromosome, Part B: X chromosome anomalies and their clinical manifestations. Liss, New York, pp 261–279

23
Functional Structure of the Human X Chromosome

Functional Map of the Human X Chromosome

Superimposed on the gene map and the banding pattern, the human X chromosome can be divided into functional regions, which mostly reflect inactivation–activation phenomena. These are presented in Fig. 23.1. Some of the evidence on which these interpretations are based will be discussed in this chapter.

Most of the borders of the functional regions are hypothetical and are not as well defined as might be imagined on the basis of Fig. 23.1. Advances in this field will require more accurate breakpoint determinations in structurally abnormal chromosomes and the finding of more genes that can be studied on the cellular level (Davies, 1991).

The tip of the Xp (Fig. 23.1) forms the meiotic pairing region, and crossing-over takes place at its distal end in the pseudoautosomal region (PAR) (Burgoyne, 1982). The pairing regions always stay active and replicate synchronously in the X and Y chromosomes (Schempp, 1985). There are indications that a tooth enamel-producing gene always stays active and is situated on Xp, possibly at its distal end (Alvesalo and Tammisalo, 1981; Alvesalo et al., 1987, 1991).

The Xcen—p11 (b) region was assumed to stay always-active on cytological grounds (Therman et al., 1976), and now an always-active gene, *A1S9T*, has been localized to it (Brown and Willard, 1991). This region is also early-replicating (Schempp and Meer, 1983).

The Q-dark region Xcen—q13, which also is among the early-replicating bands, is never missing from an abnormal X chromosome (Therman et al., 1974b, 1976; Mattei et al., 1981). Interestingly, a gene, *XIST*,

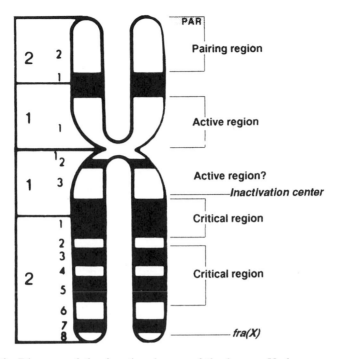

Figure 23.1. Diagram of the functional map of the human X chromosome (see text).

situated in this region is always *active*, but only on the *inactive* X (Brown et al., 1991a and b).

The so-called critical region starts at the distal end of Xq13. It consists of two parts, separated by a short intercalary band at Xq22 (Madan et al., 1981; Therman et al., 1990). Chromosome breaks in the critical region cause gonadal dysgenesis in carriers of balanced translocations and inversions. Carriers of translocations with breaks outside the region or in the intercalary band rarely display gonadal dysgenesis. Therman et al. (1990) have proposed that both parts of the critical region act as "super-genes," which must be intact on the two X chromosomes to allow normal sex development.

All deletions involving the tip of Xp cause short stature. Thus, a very short deletion of the Xp (Ross et al., 1985) led to short stature in monosomic females, and in nullosomic males to shortness, mental retardation, and other anomalies. On the other hand, the loss of the tip of Xq lets a woman develop normally, as a rule (Trunca et al., 1984).

A survey of the various X chromosome deletions (Table 22.1) shows surprisingly that, apart from the symptoms just mentioned, on the average Xp and Xq deletions cause the same symptoms. Moreover, no specific abnormalities are induced by Xq deletions. Therman and Susman (1990) explained this by assuming that a deleted X chromosome has a surplus of the factor needed for the inactivation. This surplus would inactivate those regions (the tip of Xp, b, and c) that usually remain active. Thus, the symptoms correlated with X deletions would reflect inactivation phenomena and not be caused directly by the lack of specific chromosome regions (Therman and Susman, 1990).

Inactivation Center

The human X chromosome shows a variety of unbalanced structural abnormalities, such as deletions, telocentrics, isochromosomes, and isodicentrics (Wyss et al., 1982; Carpenter, 1983; Zakharov and Baranovskaya, 1983; Therman and Susman, 1990). Although i(Xp) and tel(Xp) should occur as frequently as i(Xq) and tel(Xq), respectively, they have never been found (Therman et al., 1974b; Therman and Sarto, 1983).

In the existing chromosome types (Fig. 23.2), the region Xcen—q13 (c) is present, whereas it is not in i(Xp) and tel(Xp) (Therman et al., 1974b Therman and Patau, 1974). In persons with i(Xq) chromosomes and in those with X;X translocation chromosomes with this region in duplicate, a certain proportion of the Barr bodies is bipartite. From these observations, the conclusion was drawn that the c region (Figs. 23.3 and 4) contains the *X inactivation center*, without which the chromosome cannot form a Barr body and thus remains active. Two active X chromosomes in the same cell would presumably be a nonviable condition. If two inactivation centers are located on the same abnormal X chromosome, each acts as a center for X chromatin condensation, which leads to the formation of bipartite bodies (Therman et al., 1974a; Therman and Sarto, 1983).

Also arguing for the existence and location of the inactivation center is the fact that those women who are carriers of an unbalanced X;autosome translocation have been found always to have the c region included in the translocation chromosome (Mattei et al., 1981).

In a comparison of an X chromosome having the longest possible deletion with a translocation chromosome containing the shortest possible segment of Xq, both being capable of inactivation, the position of the inactivation center was estimated to be at the distal end of Xq13 (Therman et al., 1979). This location has been verified with molecular means (Brown et al., 1991b).

Always-Active Regions

Observations on the behavior of bipartite Barr bodies have also yielded information concerning the always-active regions. An X chromosome that resembled i(Xq), but had a b region inserted between the two inactivation centers, formed an especially high proportion of bipartite bodies

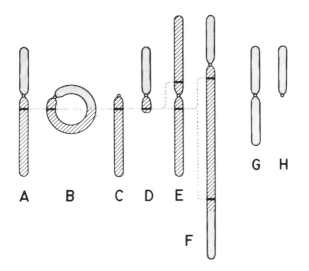

Figure 23.2. Six structurally different X chromosomes found in humans (A–F), and two never observed (G–H). Crossline marks presumed inactivation center. A, normal X; B, ring X; C, telocentric Xq; D, Xq−; E, isochromosome Xq; F, X;X translocation chromosome, attachment long arm to long arm; G, isochromosome Xp; H, telocentric Xp (Therman et al., 1974a).

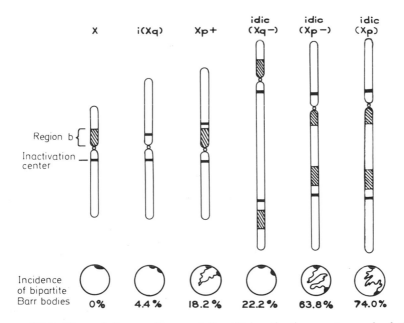

Figure 23.3. The relative positions of the X inactivation center and of the presumably always-active region on Xp in six structurally different human X chromosomes, and the incidence and hypothetical structure of bipartite Barr bodies formed by them (in idic(Xp) the attachment is telomeric; Therman et al., 1976).

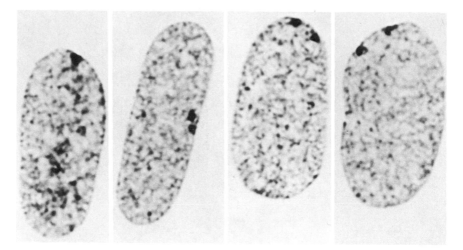

Figure 23.4. Four fibroblast nuclei from a woman with an X;X translocation in which the X chromosomes are attached telomere to telomere of their short arms. Left to right: nucleus with one large Barr body; nucleus with an almost bipartite body; two nuclei with bipartite bodies.

(Fig. 23.3; Daly et al., 1977). When two b regions were situated between the inactivation centers, in idic(Xp−) chromosomes, the frequency of bipartite Barr bodies and the distances between the two parts increased still further (Figs. 23.3 and 4; Therman et al., 1976). The conclusion was that the b region remains always-active and is unravelled in interphase, allowing the two inactivation centers (and the two parts of the Barr body) to move further from each other.The c region on the inactive X chromosome is also believed to stay active. Probably the inactivation center (XIC) must remain active to exert its effect.

Early replication is an indication of activity for a chromosome or for a part of one (Schmidt and Migeon, 1990). This applies to the pairing segment on the tip of Xp (and of Yp), on which at least four genes have been shown to stay active (Davies, 1991). The early-replication criterion for activity also applies to the b and c regions (Fig. 4.3; Schempp and Meer, 1983).

Critical Region

The number of known female carriers of balanced X;autosomal translocations has increased steadily (Sarto et al., 1973; Madan et al., 1981; Therman et al., 1990). Therman et al. (1990) have listed 120 such adult carriers. In the overwhelming majority of balanced carriers, the normal X is inactivated, but a few mosaics for two or more inactivation patterns have also been described.

In carriers of unbalanced translocations, who often are offspring of balanced carriers, the abnormal chromosome is almost always inactivated. The inactivation may or may not spread to the autosomal part of the translocation chromosome, whether it is attached to Xp or to Xq. All autosomes have been involved, but in a third of the translocations the autosome is either 21 or 22.

As mentioned above, in practically all women with a balanced X;autosome translocation, the normal X is inactivated in the lymphocytes, or in any case the predominant cell line consists of such cells. However, the use of the BrdU technique and the study of other tissues besides lymphocytes have shown that, in many cases, a minority cell line exists with one of the translocation chromosomes inactivated (Zuffardi, 1983). An interesting example has been presented by Hellkuhl et al. (1982). The normal X was inactivated in all lymphocytes of a woman with 46,X,t(X;3)(q28;q21). However, in 117 fibroblasts, the normal X was late-replicating, whereas in 61 cells the Xq+ chromosome was inactivated; the inactivation in the latter type of cell had not spread to the chromosome 3 portion.

The balanced carriers fall into two groups in regard to sexual development: normal women, often of proven fertility, and another group characterized by various degrees of gonadal dysgenesis, which in most cases results in primary amenorrhea.

On the basis of the six cases of balanced X;autosome translocations then available, Sarto et al. (1973) proposed the hypothesis of the "critical region" on the Xq: if a translocation or inversion break is within this region, the carriers suffer from gonadal dysgenesis, whereas a break outside this region, including a break in band Xq22, does not affect sexual development.

The critical region represented the first case of position effect found in humans. It differs from other known position effects in that neither the location of the breakpoint within the region, nor the chromosome band to which the broken end is attached, matters. The two parts of the critical region act like "super-genes," which must be intact to allow normal sex development. Since the replication of the bands is strictly ordered, as a rule (Fig. 4.3; Schempp and Meer, 1983; Reddy et al., 1988), a break in the critical region may affect this order and thus interfere with the function of these regions (Therman et al., 1990).

Summary of X Inactivation

Different aspects of X inactivation have been discussed at various points in this book. A summary of this scattered information is attempted here. It should also throw some light on the origin of symptoms caused by abnormal X chromosome constitutions (Therman et al., 1980; Therman, 1983).

1. Each diploid cell, as a rule, has one active X chromosome; the other(s) is inactivated. Inactivation takes place at the blastocyst stage and is random for the maternal and paternal X chromosomes. The same X remains inactive in the descendants of the original cell, which thus form a clone.
2. The inactivated X chromosomes are reactivated during oogenesis and may thereafter affect the phenotype. Abnormal X chromosome constitutions may interfere with meiotic pairing, which would induce oocyte degeneration. This, in turn, would give rise to streak gonads.
3. An unbalanced abnormal X chromosome forms a Barr body in a cell. In carriers of balanced X;autosomal translocations, as a rule, the normal X is inactivated. The behavior of the normal and abnormal X chromosomes supports the hypothesis that the X chromosomes originally are inactivated at random, but during development the genetically better-balanced cell line will take over (Therman and Patau, 1974). In an individual with several X chromosomes, one remains active and the others form Barr bodies. However, in males with four, and in females with four or five X chromosomes, the late-replication is not synchronized. This means that more than one X chromosome may remain active, or that they may not be coordinated in their activity (Sarto et al., 1987). Either disturbance may result in phenotypic abnormalities.
4. The always-active regions probably play an important role in the causation of abnormal phenotypes in individuals with abnormal X chromosome numbers. It is known that the tip of Xp stays always-active, and it is assumed that the same is true of the Q-dark regions on both sides of the centromere (b, c).
5. In carriers of balanced X chromosome aberrations, the critical region on Xq must be intact for normal female sex development. A position effect expresses itself as gonadal dysgenesis in those carriers in whom the break is within the critical region. When the break is outside this segment, or in the short, intercalary region at Xq22, as a rule carriers show normal sex development.

References

Alvesalo L, Tammisalo E (1981) Enamel thickness in 45,X females' permanent teeth. Am J Hum Genet 33:464–469

Alvesalo L, Tammisalo E, Therman E (1987) 47,XXX females, sex chromosomes and tooth crown structure. Hum Genet 77:345–348

Alvesalo L, Tammisalo E, Townsend G (1991) Upper central incisor and canine tooth crown size in 47,XXY males. J Dent Res 70:1057–1060

Brown CJ, Willard HF (1990) Localization of a gene that escapes inactivation to the X chromosome proximal short arm: implications for X inactivation. Am J Hum Genet 46:273–279

Brown CJ, Ballabio A, Rupert JL, et al. (1991a) A gene from the region of the human X inactivation centre is expressed exclusively from the inactive X chromosome. Nature 349:38–44

Brown CJ, Lafreniere RG, Powers VE, et al. (1991b) Localization of the X inactivation centre on the human X chromosome in Xq13. Nature 349:82–84

Burgoyne PS (1982) Genetic homology and crossing over in the X and Y chromosomes of mammals. Hum Genet 61:85–90

Carpenter NJ (1983) Balanced X;autosome translocations and gonadal dysfunction in females and males. In: Sandberg AA (ed) Cytogenetics of the mammalian X chromosome, Part B: X chromosome anomalies and their clinical manifestations. Liss, New York, pp 211–224

Daly RF, Patau K, Therman E, et al. (1977) Structure and Barr body formation of an Xp+ chromosome with two inactivation centers. Am J Hum Genet 29:83–93

Davies K (1991) The essence of inactivity. Nature 349:15–16

Hellkuhl B, Chapelle A de la, Grzeschik K-H (1982) Different patterns of X chromosome inactivity in lymphocytes and fibroblasts of a human balanced X;autosome translocation. Hum Genet 60:126–129

Madan K, Hompes PGA, Schoemaker J, et al. (1981) X–autosome translocation with a breakpoint in Xq22 in a fertile woman and her 47,XXX infertile daughter. Hum Genet 59:290–296

Mattei MG, Mattei JF, Vidal I, et al. (1981) Structural anomalies of the X chromosome and inactivation center. Hum Genet 56:401–408

Reddy KS, Savage JRK, Papworth DG (1988) Replication kinetics of X chromosomes in fibroblasts and lymphocytes. Hum Genet 79:44–48

Ross JB, Allderdice PW, Shapiro LJ, et al. (1985) Familial X-linked ichthyosis, steroid sulfatase deficiency, mental retardation, and nullisomy for Xp223—pter. Arch Dermatol 121:1524–1528

Sarto GE, Therman E, Patau K (1973) X inactivation in man: A woman with t(Xq−; 12q+). Am J Hum Genet 25:262–270

Sarto GE, Otto PG, Kuhn EM, et al. (1987) What causes the abnormal phenotype in a 49,XXXXY male? Hum Genet 76:1–4

Schempp W (1985) High-resolution replication of the human Y chromosome. In: Sandberg AA (ed) The Y chromosome, Part A: Basic characteristics of the Y chromosome. Liss, New York, pp 357–371

Schempp W, Meer B (1983) Cytologic evidence for three human X-chromosomal segments escaping inactivation. Hum Genet 63:171–174

Schmidt M, Migeon BR (1990) Asynchronous replication of homologous loci on human active and inactive X chromosomes. Proc Natl Acad Sci USA 87:3685–3689

Therman E (1983) Mechanisms through which abnormal X-chromosome constitutions affect the phenotype. In: Sandberg AA (ed) Cytogenetics of the mammalian X chromosome, Part B: X chromosome anomalies and their clinical manifestations. Liss, New York, pp 159–173

Therman E, Patau K (1974) Abnormal X chromosomes in man: origin, behavior and effects. Humangenetik 25:1–16

Therman E, Sarto GE (1983) Inactivation center on the human X chromosome. In: Sandberg AA (ed) Cytogenetics of the mammalian X chromosome, Part A: Basic mechanisms of X chromosome behavior. Liss, New York, pp 315–325

Therman E, Susman B (1990) The similarity of phenotypic effects caused by Xp and Xq deletions in the human female: a hypothesis. Hum Genet 85: 175–183

Therman E, Sarto GE, Patau K (1974a) Apparently isodicentric but functionally monocentric X chromosome in man. Am J Hum Genet 26:83–92

Therman E, Sarto GE, Patau K (1974b) Center for Barr body condensation on the proximal part of the human Xq: a hypothesis. Chromosoma 44:361–366

Therman E, Sarto GE, Distèche C, et al. (1976) A possible active segment on the inactive human X chromosome. Chromosoma 59:137–145

Therman E, Sarto GE, Palmer CG, et al. (1979) Position of the human X inactivation center on Xq. Hum Genet 50:59–64

Therman E, Denniston C, Sarto GE, et al. (1980) X chromosome constitution and the human female phenotype. Hum Genet 54:133–143

Therman E, Laxova R, Susman B (1990) The critical region on the human Xq. Hum Genet 85:455–461

Trunca C, Therman E, Rosenwaks Z (1984) The phenotypic effects of small, distal Xq deletions. Hum Genet 68:87–89

Wyss D, DeLozier CD, Daniell J, et al. (1982) Structural anomalies of the X chromosome: personal observation and review of non-mosaic cases. Clin Genet 21:145–159

Zakharov AF, Baranovskaya LJ (1983) X–X chromosome translocations and their karyotype-phenotype correlations. In: Sandberg AA (ed) Cytogenetics of the mammalian X chromosome, Part B: X chromosome anomalies and their clinical manifestations. Liss, New York, pp 261–279

Zuffardi O (1983) Cytogenetics of human X/autosome translocations. In: Sandberg AA (ed) Cytogenetics of the mammalian X chromosome, Part B: X chromosome anomalies and their clinical manifestations. Liss, New York, pp 193–209

24
Numerically Abnormal Chromosome Constitutions in Humans

Abnormalities of Human Chromosome Number

As described in Chapter 2, the chromosome number may change in two different ways. Either the number of *sets* of chromosomes increases, resulting in polyploidy (a decrease, leading to haploidy, does not occur in humans), or the number of *individual* normal chromosomes changes, giving rise to aneuploidy.

The only types of polyploidy found in humans are triploidy and tetraploidy, and the overwhelming majority of these cases end as spontaneous abortions. The only known autosomal monosomy is the extremely rare 21 monosomy, and of the autosomal trisomies only three—those for chromosomes 13, 18, and 21—occur with any appreciable frequency in liveborn children (Hecht and Hecht, 1987). However, trisomies for most autosomes have been found in spontaneous abortions (Boué et al., 1976, 1985; Carr and Gedeon, 1977).

Human Triploids

A triploid zygote may occur as the result of various processes (Niebuhr, 1974). Either the egg cell or the sperm cell may have an unreduced chromosome number as a result of restitution in either the first or second meiotic division; or the second polar body may reunite with the egg nucleus; or two sperms may penetrate and fertilize the same egg cell.

Triploids form one of the largest groups of *heteroploid* (abnormal chromosome number) spontaneous abortions (Table 24.1), representing about 17 percent (Carr and Gedeon, 1977). Only about 1/10,000 triploid

Table 24.1. Relative frequencies of different types of chromosome anomalies in 1863 chromosomally abnormal spontaneous abortions.[a]

Chromosome Anomaly	%
Trisomy	52
45,X	18
Triploidy	17
Tetraploidy	6
Other (mainly translocations)	7

[a] Modified from Carr and Gedeon, 1977.

zygotes results in a live birth, and of these most die within a day (Niebuhr, 1974). Four triploid infants have survived 2 to 7 months (Schröcksnadel et al., 1982). In such rare cases, one always suspects hidden mosaicism, and indeed, most polyploid infants have turned out to have a diploid cell line.

Imprinting and Uniparental Disomy

In recent years, the phenomena, imprinting and disomy, have been under extensive study. Imprinting refers to the differential effect of a gene, a chromosome, or a chromosome set, depending on the parent from whom it is inherited (Warburton, 1988; Reik, 1989; Hall, 1990; Moore and Haig, 1991).

In uniparental disomy, the two members of a chromosome pair come from the same parent, instead of one being maternal and the other paternal. Thus, for example, two unrelated children with cystic fibrosis were reported. The gene for this autosomal recessive disease is known to be on chromosome arm 7q, and it was possible in both these cases to determine that each child had received both maternal chromosomes 7 (Spence et al., 1988; Voss et al., 1989). It is not clear how common uniparental disomy actually is, although many apparent deviations from Mendelian inheritance *could* be explained on this basis (Reik, 1989; Hall, 1990; Schinzel, 1991).

The simplest explanation for the creation of uniparental disomy is a trisomic cell. Since this is often a lethal condition, a cell line from which the third chromosome is lost has an advantage.

Human Tetraploids

Tetraploid zygotes are rarer than triploids among spontaneous abortions. Five infants with apparently nonmosaic tetraploidy were reported by Scarbrough et al. (1984), and Lafer and Neu (1988) described a girl who was alive at 22 months. The few other liveborn children have been diploid/tetraploid mosaics. It is not surprising that tetraploid zygotes are rarer than triploids, since nonmosaic tetraploidy is also incompatible with life and, more importantly, there are fewer mechanisms that result in it. The most probable origin of tetraploidy is chromosome duplication in a somatic cell at a very early stage of development. Other possible origins —for example, the chance fertilization by a rare, unreduced sperm of an equally rare diploid ovum—are highly unlikely. The fertilization of one egg cell by three sperm cells is also a possibility, but that would usually result in the development of a hydatidiform mole.

Hydatidiform Moles

Hydatidiform moles represent abnormal trophoblastic growth. Imprinting and uniparental disomy also play important roles in their development. Rarely, they develop after a normal pregnancy: usually the zygote is abnormal. In Western countries, 1/2,000 pregnancies results in the development of a mole, whereas in the Orient, Taiwan for instance, the frequency is 1/200. Hydatidiform moles fall morphologically, histologically, and genetically into two main groups: partial and complete moles (Vassilakos et al., 1977; Boué et al., 1985).

In partial moles, an abnormal, usually triploid, embryo is present. As a rule, the triploidy has arisen through the fertilization of an egg cell by two sperms (Jacobs et al., 1982).

In complete moles, no embryo is found. In most cases they arise through fertilization of an "empty" egg (without nucleus) by an X-bearing sperm, and a subsequent doubling of the paternal chromosome set. (The origin of the empty egg cells is not known.) In other words, the chromosome complement of complete moles is 46,XX, the two chromosome sets being identical. This was first shown by an analysis of chromosome polymorphisms (Kajii and Ohama, 1977) and confirmed by the determination of enzyme polymorphisms and human leukocyte antigen (HLA) specificities (Jacobs et al., 1980). Cytologically, complete moles resemble malignant tumors more than normal placenta, being characterized by giant nuclei arising through endomitosis and endoreduplication (Fig 16.1) (Sarto et al., 1984).

A few tetraploid moles, resulting from fertilization of a haploid oocyte by three sperm cells, have also been described (Surti et al., 1986; Vejerslev et al., 1987). There are additional ways in which abnormal chromosome constitutions may affect trophoblast growth. Usually the embryo and the trophoblast have the same chromosome constitution, but sometimes the abnormality is limited to one or the other of these tissues (Ledbetter et al., 1990). This is important when genetic counseling and information is provided to the patient and family.

Moles have attracted special interest because more than 50 percent of choriocarcinomas arise from them. Thus, 2.1 percent of partial, and 10 percent of complete moles become malignant. Fortunately, chemotherapy cures some 80 percent of these highly malignant tumors (Dodson, 1983).

Anomalies Caused by Chromosomal Imbalance

In this book, only a few chromosome syndromes will be described, because there is a great deal of literature dealing with the phenotypes of such conditions (Smith, 1976; de Grouchy and Turleau, 1984; Borgaonkar, 1984; Schinzel, 1984; Hamerton, 1971; de Grouchy, 1974; Makino, 1975; Yunis, 1977).

It is well known that no single phenotypic abnormality is exclusive to any chromosome syndrome, but rather that each of them is characterized by a combination of characteristics that make the phenotypes of some syndromes recognizable, e.g., Down syndrome, trisomy 13, 18, 18p−, and others (Table 24.2). In the main this is true, although there are anomalies that occur so much more frequently in patients with certain specific chromosomal abnormalities that these symptoms can be regarded as characteristic of the syndromes. The cat cry syndrome is characterized by prematurely gray hair; trisomy 13 by persistence of fetal hemoglobin (HbF) and by abnormal projections in the neutrophils.

In contrast to such specific chromosomal symptoms, many patients with chromosome abnormalities have multiple characteristics in common. Thus, for example, imbalance for even a small autosomal segment causes mental retardation. This is not surprising, since the central nervous system is the most complicated of all organ systems, and therefore even a slight genetic imbalance has a deleterious effect on it. Furthermore, a high proportion of chromosomal syndromes is characterized by seizures of various kinds, as well as growth retardation, which seems to be almost ubiquitous in chromosomal syndromes. In many chromosomal syndromes, failure to grow, which is also reflected in intrauterine growth retardation, is so extreme that it is essentially a lethal condition; for instance, few infants with trisomy 18 gain weight after birth.

Table 24.2 shows common signs and symptoms that may occur in most individuals with autosomal or sex chromosome abnormalities and characteristics that usually are not correlated with chromosome abnormalities. Heteroploidy seems to affect organ systems according to their complexity. Thus, abnormalities of the cardiovascular system are characteristic of a great variety of chromosomal syndromes. Ventricular septal defect is found in 47 percent of infants with trisomy 13, in 34 percent of 18-trisomic patients, and in 20 percent of 21-trisomic children (Lewandowski and Yunis, 1977). A whole spectrum of other heart defects is also present in chromosomal syndromes.

Table 24.2. Comparison of autosomal, sex chromosomal, and non-chromosomal syndromes.

Characteristics of Syndromes Induced By:		
Autosomal Anomalies[a]	Sex Chromosomal Anomalies[a]	Other Causes
Mental retardation almost always present.	Mental retardation rare; instead, emotional and behavioral problems. 45,X: not retarded. XXX, XXY, & XYY: mildly retarded. Persons with more than three sex chromosomes are severely retarded.	Mental retardation without other abnormalities.
Multiple *unrelated* anomalies in different developmental systems.	Birth defects rarer and milder. Motor coordination impaired, speech delayed, spatial perception deficient.	Physical malformations without mental retardation. Single or several malformations in the same developmental field.
Low birth weight, failure to thrive.	Low birth weight in females with abnormal X chromosome constitutions.	—
Short stature.	Short stature in females with X chromosome anomalies. Increased height in persons with XXX, XXY, XYY, & XXYY chromosome constitutions.	—
Patient looks odd, may not resemble other family members.	Certain sex chromosome anomalies cause characteristic appearances.	Abnormal appearance varies among different syndromes.
Often affected: heart, head (small), eyes, genito-urinary system, hands and feet.	Anomalies affect many systems, but especially sex development.	—

[a] These two columns show the sorts of patients for whom chromosome analysis should be done.

One prerequisite for normal sex development is an XX or XY sex chromosome constitution. However, many autosomal syndromes exhibit a range of malformations of the reproductive system. For instance, infants with trisomy 13 often show cryptorchidism or a bicornuate uterus, those with trisomy 18 have abnormally developed genitalia, and individuals with trisomy 21 are rarely fertile. The incidence of such effects is probably underestimated, since many infants with chromosomal syndromes die early, and their mature phenotypes remain unknown.

13 Trisomy (D₁ Trisomy, Patau Syndrome)

The chromosomes of an infant with 13 trisomy (Fig. 24.1 and 24.2) were first studied in this laboratory (Patau et al., 1960), and therefore this syndrome is described in detail as an example of trisomic syndromes. The extra D chromosome, which is the cause of the syndrome, was called D_1 by Patau et al. (1960) because it was thought that trisomy of the other two D chromosomes might be discovered later. Most 13-trisomic zygotes end as spontaneous abortions (Table 24.3), their frequency being 100 times greater in abortuses than in liveborns.

The incidence of trisomy 13 (47,+13) in liveborns is between 1/7,000 and 1/21,000 with 95 percent confidence, the most likely frequency being about 1/12,000 (Hook, 1980). Increased maternal age is a factor in trisomy 13, as it is in other full trisomies. Even those infants with trisomy 13 who survive birth have a limited life expectancy; about 45 percent die within

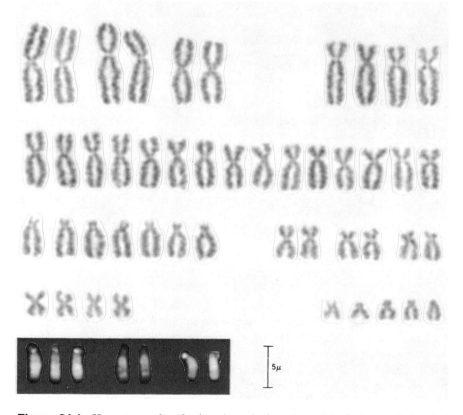

Figure 24.1. Karyotype of a 13-trisomic male (orcein staining). Insert: Q-banded D-group with three chromosomes 13.

Figure 24.2. First D-trisomic child described, with anophthalmia, harelip, six toes, retroflexed thumbs, and hemangiomata (Patau et al., 1960).

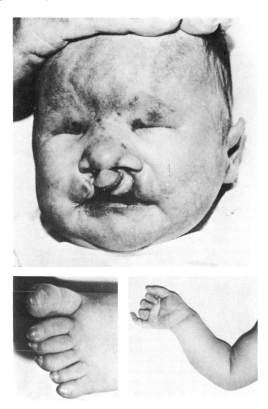

the first month, 90 percent are dead before 6 months, and fewer than 5 percent reach the age of 3 years (Gorlin, 1977; Niebuhr, 1977). Two exceptional 13-trisomic patients have been reported who lived much longer—11 and 19 years, respectively (Redheendran et al., 1981).

Infants with trisomy 13 are severely mentally retarded and are often deaf. Various degrees of forebrain defects (holoprosencephaly) are common (Table 24.4). Eye anomalies range from anophthalmia (absence of eyes) to microphthalmia (Fig. 24.2), often combined with coloboma of the iris (fissure of the iris). Cleft lip, cleft palate, or both are also characteristic of this syndrome (Fig. 24.2). Capillary hemangiomata and scalp defects have often been described. Postaxial polydactyly (Fig. 24.2) is frequently seen. The heel is often prominent, and the feet are severely deformed, mostly in calcaneovalgous position (rocker bottom). The thumb may be retroflexed (Fig. 24.2). Different types of complex heart anomalies are common.

Table 24.4 gives the frequencies of the most common clinical anomalies in trisomy 13 (Niebuhr, 1977; see also de Grouchy, 1974; Hodes et al., 1978; Moerman et al., 1988). The incidence of various symptoms shows a

Table 24.3. Numbers of liveborn trisomics, trisomic abortions, localized genes, average Q-brightness, and length for different autosomes.[a]

Chromosome	No. live trisomics	No. trisomic abortions	No. genes localized	Average Q-brightness	Length (% of autosomal genome)
1	**0**	**0**	**69**	**0.56**	**9.25**
2	0	53	37	0.65	8.63
3	**2**	**8**	**20**	**0.60**	**7.12**
4	0	26	32	0.79	6.69
5	0	1	22	0.57	6.41
6	**0**	**3**	**62**	**0.66**	**6.23**
7	6	46	38	0.61	5.58
8	98	37	19	0.59	5.08
11	**0**	**2**	**53**	**0.55**	**4.78**
9	26	33	26	0.50	4.95
12	**2**	**9**	**38**	**0.49**	**4.70**
10	7	22	21	0.52	4.76
13	1/12,000	63	16	0.78	3.29
14	9	51	31	0.59	3.12
15	1	75	19	0.46	2.89
16	0	326	28	0.41	3.27
17	**0**	**7**	**32**	**0.35**	**3.03**
18	1/6,000	51	13	0.43	2.80
19	**1**	**1**	**32**	**0.20**	**2.43**
20	2	28	9	0.33	2.35
22	**0**	**107**	**18**	**0.19**	**1.38**
21	1/700	89	14	0.41	1.26

Data for chromosomes containing mitotic cross-over hot spots in Bloom syndrome are in bold-face and are paired with data for their similarly sized control chromosomes.
[a] Modified from Kuhn et al., 1987.

Table 24.4. Frequency of main symptoms in 13 trisomy.[a]

Symptom	% of cases	Symptom	% of cases
Severe retardation	100	Simian crease	64
Hypertelorism	93	Microcephaly	59
Malformed ears	81	Harelip	55
Microphthalmia or anophthalmia	78	Deafness	53
Polydactyly	78	Renal anomaly	53
Distal triradius	77	Epicanthic folds	52
Heart disease	76	Abnormal projections of neutrophils	>50
Hemangiomata	73	Elevated fetal hemoglobin (HbF)	>50
Arhinencephaly (absent olfactory bulbs)	71	Bicornuate uterus	43
Cleft palate	65	Coloboma	35
		Low-set ears	11

[a] Data from Niebuhr, 1977; other authors give somewhat different frequencies.

wide range of variation, from severe mental retardation, which is always present, to low-set ears, which have been reported in 11 percent of the cases. The considerable phenotypic variation displayed by infants with trisomy 13, as well as by other patients with well-defined chromosomal abnormalities, probably reflects the differences in the allelic content of the three homologous chromosomes, or could depend on a uniparental disomy effect. The variation in described symptoms may also be caused by differing ages of the patients, some symptoms becoming more apparent with increasing age.

A normal cell line, if present, dilutes the effect of the trisomic cells, and as a result mosaic individuals tend to have fewer and less severe anomalies than do those with full trisomy. In most individuals with mosaic trisomy 13, for example, the abnormal cell line simply has an extra chromosome 13. However, a child with an unusual karyotype was described by Therman et al. (1963). In about 45 percent of her cells with a 46,XX chromosome constitution, one D_1 chromosome was telocentric, whereas in the remaining cells this chromosome was replaced by an isochromosome. It was subsequently shown by autoradiography and by banding that this interpretation was correct. The then 4-year-old girl was less retarded and had fewer anomalies than fully trisomic individuals.

21 Trisomy Syndrome (Down Syndrome)

This condition, which is the least severe of the autosomal trisomy syndromes, is described in detail in the books and reviews referred to previously (see also *Trisomy 21*, American Journal of Medical Genetics, Suppl 7, 1990). The chromosomal cause of Down syndrome was discovered by Lejeune et al. (1959). It is by far the most frequent of the autosomal trisomy syndromes, the estimates of its incidence ranging from 1/500 to 1/1,000 newborns, the usual estimate being 1/700. In roughly 95 percent of the cases the chromosome constitution is 47,+21. An additional 2 percent of patients are mosaic for a normal and a trisomic cell line. However, low-grade trisomy 21 mosaicism, which does not affect the phenotype, may sometimes be found, particularly in parents of children with trisomy 21; in fact, gonadal mosaicism may, in such individuals, account for the occurrence as well as recurrence in some families of a child with Down syndrome. In the remaining 3 percent of the patients, the extra chromosome is attached to another chromosome, usually as a result of centric fusion to another acrocentric. Such Robertsonian translocations and their inheritance are discussed in Chapter 27. The gene and trisomy mapping of chromosome 21 are discussed in Chapter 31.

In individuals with trisomy 21, the probability of developing leukemia is increased 20-fold, and the disease is estimated to occur in about one in 1000 children with Down syndrome. Other causes of mortality are severe congenital heart disease, intestinal obstruction, and low resistance to infections.

Interestingly, conditions corresponding to trisomy 21, in both symptoms and chromosomal cause, are found in the chimpanzee (McClure et al., 1969; Benirschke et al., 1974), the gorilla (Turleau et al., 1972), the orangutan (Andrle et al., 1979), and the trisomy 16 mouse.

18 Trisomy Syndrome (Edwards Syndrome)

In the article in which 13 trisomy was described (Patau et al., 1960), the authors mentioned that they had also found a child with 18 trisomy. In the same issue of *Lancet*, Edwards et al. (1960) reported on a child with what they thought was 17 trisomy. This, however, turned out to be 18 trisomy (Smith et al., 1960).

Because they rarely have facial clefting malformations, 18-trisomic infants often appear less severely affected at birth than those with trisomy 13. In general, however, their condition is no less life-threatening. The many anomalies characteristic of this syndrome have been described by de Grouchy (1974), Gorlin (1977), and Hodes et al. (1978). The reported incidence of trisomy 18 varies from 1/3,500 to 1/7,000, or about 1/6,000 in the newborn. Of those born alive, 30 percent die within one month, and only 10 percent survive one year (Gorlin, 1977). About 80 percent of the patients have straight trisomy, another 10 percent are mosaics, whereas the rest are either trisomic for another chromosome also, or have a translocation (de Grouchy, 1974).

Other Autosomal Aneuploidy Syndromes

It is not yet clear whether the presumed 22 trisomy actually exists—although new claims appear yearly (for instance, Kukolich et al., 1989; McPherson and Stetka, 1990; Sundareshan et al., 1990)—or whether the extra chromosome, in apparently trisomic individuals, represents t(11:22) (q23;q11) (Hsu and Hirschhorn, 1977; Kuhn et al., 1987). Apparently, chromosome arms 11q and 22q have a homologous segment in which exchanges take place preferentially. Of some 100 translocations involving 11q, only 13 cases had a second chromosome that was not a 22 (Schinzel et al., 1981; Pihko et al., 1981; Zackai and Emanuel, 1980). One would also expect the symptoms caused by trisomy 22 and by the translocation chromosome to be similar. The fact that no carrier of a Robertsonian translocation involving chromosome 22 (Chapter 27) has had offspring with trisomy 22 also speaks against the existence of 22 trisomy. It is to be hoped that molecular techniques will solve the 22 trisomy riddle.

Of the other autosomes (Table 24.3), mosaicism for trisomy 3 has been found twice. One of the patients was studied in our laboratory (Kuhn et al., 1987). She was a 30-year-old, severely retarded woman with multiple anomalies. It is possible that a higher percentage of trisomic cells had been present when she was younger, but during development normal cells were preferentially selected at the time of evaluation they represented 95 percent of her lymphocytes. Another instance of trisomy 3 mosaicism was described in an infant (Metaxotou et al., 1981).

Full trisomy for chromosome 7 was reported in a newborn who died at 2 days of age (Yunis et al., 1980). Chromosome 7 has also been involved in trisomy mosaicism, and an interesting family in which mother and daughter, both mentally ill, were such mosaics was found by De Bault and Halmi (1975). The most probable explanation for this family was that the zygote from which the daughter developed was trisomic, but later a normal cell line arose through loss of one chromosome 7, resulting in disomy.

Trisomy for chromosome 8 has been found repeatedly, but almost always in a mosaic state (Fig. 24.3). Of the 61 patients reviewed by Riccardi (1977), only one was apparently nonmosaic.

Full trisomy for chromosome 9 has been reported in 20 cases and twice in a mosaic state (Schinzel, 1984).

One patient with trisomy mosaicism for chromosome 10 has been described (Nakagome et al., 1972), and one with trisomy mosaicism for chromosome 12 (Patil et al., 1983).

Both mosaic and full trisomy 14 are virtually lethal conditions, and only a few such cases have been born alive (Johnson et al., 1979; Kaplan et al., 1986; Lipson, 1987). One severely affected infant with full trisomy 15 has also been reported (Coldwell et al., 1981).

Trisomy 16 is the most common trisomy found in spontaneous abortions; it has never been observed in liveborn infants (Schinzel, 1984).

Of the F group chromosomes, a couple of mosaics for trisomy 19 have been found; claims of trisomy 20 have not been supported by sufficient evidence (Schinzel, 1984).

Monosomy in liveborn infants has been established for only one autosome, chromosome 21, and even that is extremely rare: six cases have been reported (Wisniewski et al., 1983). It is also infrequent in spontaneous abortions. Monosomy 21 has never arisen as a result of a Robertsonian translocation involving this chromosome.

Spontaneous Abortions

Table 24.1 gives an estimate of the incidence of spontaneous abortions caused by different kinds of chromosome abnormalities. Carr and Gedeon (1977) estimated that 38 percent of spontaneous abortions are heteroploid. Many factors affect such estimates, which vary greatly in different studies (Boué et al., 1985). A number of abortions undoubtedly occur so early

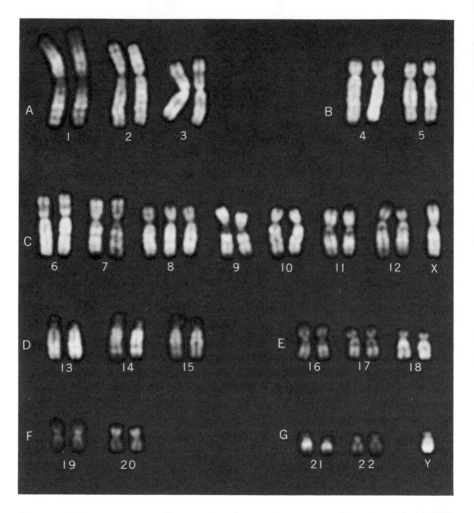

Figure 24.3. Karyotype of an 8-trisomic cell from a mosaic male with 46,XY/ 47,XY,+8 (Q-banding).

that they are unrecognizable, and even of the recognized ones not all are amenable to chromosome analysis. Early abortions show more chromosome abnormalities than later ones. The incidence of trisomic abortions increases with maternal age. The frequencies of polyploid as well as of 45,X abortions, on the other hand, are independent of maternal age (Carr and Gedeon, 1977).

Apart from trisomic abortions (which, in pooled data, have been found for all autosomes except chromosome 1), polyploidy—mainly triploidy—is the leading chromosomal cause of fetal loss. Among other causes, the lack of one sex chromosome (the chromosome constitution 45,X) is the most frequent. It is estimated that fewer than 1 percent of XO zygotes are born alive. Obviously, 45,X zygotes fall into separate classes, one of which is lethal, whereas those who are born alive can lead almost normal lives.

Since monosomy arises through both chromosome loss and nondisjunction (whereas trisomy results only from the latter process), monosomic conceptions should be more frequent among spontaneous abortions than trisomic ones. In reality, autosomal monosomy is almost as rare in recognizable abortions as it is in liveborn children. Obviously, monosomy for a chromosome—or for a chromosome segment—has a much more deleterious effect than the corresponding trisomy. Apparently, monosomic zygotes, as a rule, die so early that they are not recognized as abortions.

A factor that may bias the observed numbers is the time at which the trisomic condition is lethal. For instance, the times of death caused by trisomy 13 range from early embryonic development to (rarely) several years postnatally, whereas the lethal effect of chromosome 16 apparently occurs within a very limited period of gestation; the reported times vary from 22 to 31 days, at which stage chromosome studies are feasible (Boué et al., 1976). This may be the most important reason for the preponderance of 16-trisomic abortions in the various studies.

Nonrandom Participation of Chromosomes in Trisomy

The highly nonrandom participation of individual chromosomes in trisomy of the newborn and of spontaneous abortions is apparent at a glance (Table 24.3). It depends on the positive and negative correlations of trisomy with various chromosome parameters (Kuhn et al., 1987), as discussed in Chapter 7. The occurrence of trisomy is positively correlated with the Q-brightness of the chromosome, which in turn is negatively correlated with the number of localized genes on it. The so-called hot spots (short Q-dark regions with a high density of mitotic chiasmata in Bloom syndrome) act as effective trisomy lethals (Patau, 1964) (Table 24.3). The chromosomes with hot spots (1, 3, 6, 11, 12, 17, 19, and 22) have a higher gene frequency than the similar-sized controls (2, 4, 7, 9, 10, 18, 20, and 21) The test chromosomes show significantly fewer newborn or abortion trisomics than do the control chromosomes (Kuhn et al., 1987). This suggests that trisomies for the test chromosomes result in abortions at such early stages that they are unrecognized or that chromosome studies on them are impracticable.

References

Andrle M, Fiedler W, Rett A, et al. (1979) A case of trisomy 22 in *Pongo pygmaeus*. Cytogenet Cell Genet 24:1–6

Bault E De, Halmi KA (1975) Familial trisomy 7 mosaicism. J Med Genet 12:200–203

Benirschke K, Bogart MH, McClure HM, et al. (1974) Fluorescence of the trisomic chimpanzee chromosomes. J Med Primatol 3:311–314

Borgaonkar DS (1984) Chromosomal variation in man: a catalog of chromosomal variants and anomalies, 4th edn. Liss, New York

Boué J, Daketsé M-J, Deluchat C, et al. (1976) Identification par les bandes Q et G des anomalies chromosomiques dans les avortements spontanés. Ann Genet (Paris) 19:233–239

Boué A, Boué J, Gropp A (1985) Cytogenetics of pregnancy wastage. In: Harris H, Hirschhorn K (eds) Advances in human genetics, Vol 14. Plenum, New York, pp 1–57

Carr DH, Gedeon M (1977) Population cytogenetics of human abortuses. In: Hook EB, Porter IH (eds) Population cytogenetics. Academic, New York, pp 1–9

Coldwell S, Fitzgerald B, Semmens JM, et al. (1981) A case of trisomy of chromosome 15. J Med Genet 18:146–148

Dodson MG (1983) New concepts and questions in gestational trophoblastic disease. J Reprod Med 28:741–749

Edwards JH, Harnden DG, Cameron AH, et al. (1960) A new trisomic syndrome. Lancet i:787–790

Gorlin RJ (1977) Classical chromosome disorders. In: Yunis JJ (ed) New chromosomal syndromes. Academic, New York, pp 59–117

Grouchy J de (1974) Clinical cytogenetics: autosomal disorders. In: Busch H (ed) The cell nucleus. Academic, New York, pp 371–414

Grouchy J de, Turleau C (1984) Clinical atlas of human chromosomes, 2nd edn. Wiley, New York

Hall JG (1990) Genomic imprinting: Review and relevance to human diseases. Am J Hum Genet 46:857–873

Hamerton JL (1971) Human cytogenetics I & II. Academic, New York

Hecht F, Hecht BK (1987) Aneuploidy in humans: dimensions, demography, dangers of abnormal numbers of chromosomes. In: Vig BK, Sandberg AA (eds) Aneuploidy, Part A: Incidence and etiology. Liss, New York, pp 9–49

Hodes ME, Cole J, Palmer CG, et al. (1978) Clinical experience with trisomies 18 and 13. J Med Genet 15:48–60

Hook EB (1980) Rates of 47,+13 and 46 translocation D/13 Patau syndrome in live births and comparison with rates in fetal deaths and at amniocentesis. Am J Hum Genet 32:849–858

Hsu LYF, Hirschhorn K (1977) The trisomy 22 syndrome and the cat eye syndrome. In: Yunis JJ (ed) New chromosomal syndromes. Academic, New York, pp 339–368

Jacobs PA, Wilson CM, Sprenkle JA, et al. (1980) Mechanism of origin of complete hydatidiform moles. Nature 286:714–716

Jacobs PA, Szulman AE, Funkhouser J, et al. (1982) Human triploidy: relationship between parental origin of the additional haploid complement and development of partial hydatidiform mole. Ann Hum Genet 46:223–231

Johnson VP, Aceto T Jr, Likness C (1979) Trisomy 14 mosaicism: case report and review. Am J Med Genet 3:331–339

Kajii T, Ohama K (1977) Androgenetic origin of hydatidiform mole. Nature 268:633–634

Kaplan LC, Wayne A, Crowell S, et al. (1986) Trisomy 14 mosaicism in a liveborn male: clinical report and review of the literature. Am J Med Genet 23:925–930

Kuhn EM, Sarto GE, Bates B-J G, et al. (1987) Gene-rich chromosome regions and autosomal trisomy. A case of chromosome 3 trisomy mosaicism. Hum Genet 77:214–220

Kukolich MK, Kulharya A, Jalal SM, et al. (1989) Trisomy 22: no longer an enigma. Am J Med Genet 34:541–544

Lafer CZ, Neu RL (1988) A liveborn infant with tetraploidy. Am J Med Genet 31:375–378

Ledbetter DH, Martin AO, Verlinsky Y, et al. (1990) Cytogenetic results of chorionic villus sampling: High success rate and diagnostic accuracy in the United States collaborative study. Am J Obstet Gynecol 162:495–501

Lejeune J, Turpin R, Gautier M (1959) Le mongolisme, premier example d'aberration autosomique humaine. Ann Genet (Paris) 1:41–49

Lewandowski RC, Yunis JJ (1977) Phenotypic mapping in man. In: Yunis JJ (ed) New chromosomal syndromes. Academic, New York, pp 369–394

Lipson MH (1987) Brief clinical report: Trisomy 14 mosaicism syndrome. Am J Med Genet 26:541–544

Makino S (1975) Human chromosomes. Igaku Shoin, Tokyo

McClure HM, Belden KH, Pieper WA, et al. (1969) Autosomal trisomy in chimpanzee: resemblance to Down's syndrome. Science 165:1010–1012

McPherson E, Stetka DG (1990) Trisomy 22 in a liveborn infant with multiple congenital anomalies. Am J Med Genet 36:11–14

Metaxotou C, Tsenghi I, Bitzos M, et al. (1981) Trisomy 3 mosaicism in a liveborn infant. Clin Genet 19:37–40

Moerman P, Fryns J-P, van der Steen K (1988) The pathology of trisomy 13 syndrome: a study of 12 cases. Hum Genet 80:349–356

Moore T, Haig D (1991) Genomic imprinting in mammalian development: a parental tug-of-war. Trends Genet 7:45–49

Nakagome Y, Iinuma K, Matsui I (1972) Trisomy 10 with mosaicism: a clinical and cytogenetic entity. Jpn J Hum Genet 18:216–219

Niebuhr E (1974) Triploidy in man: cytogenetical and clinical aspects. Humangenetik 21:103–125

Niebuhr E (1977) Partial trisomies and deletions of chromosome 13. In: Yunis JJ (ed) New chromosomal syndromes. Academic, New York, pp 273–299

Patau K (1964) Partial trisomy. In: Fishbein M (ed) Second international conference of congenital malformations. International Medical Congress, New York, pp 52–59

Patau K, Smith DW, Therman E, et al. (1960) Multiple congenital anomaly caused by an extra autosome. Lancet i:790–793

Patil SR, Bosch EP, Hanson JW (1983) First report of mosaic trisomy 12 in a liveborn individual. Am J Med Genet 14:453–460

Pihko H, Therman E, Uchida IA (1981) Partial 11q trisomy syndrome. Hum Genet 58:129–134

Redheendran R, Neu RL, Bannerman RM (1981) Long survival in trisomy-13-syndrome: 21 cases including prolonged survival in two patients 11 and 19 years old. Am J Med Genet 8:167–172

Reik W (1989) Genomic imprinting and genetic disorders in man. Trends Genet 5:331–336

Riccardi VM (1977) Trisomy 8: an international study of 70 patients. In: Birth defects: original article series, XIII, 3C. The National Foundation, New York, pp 171–184

Sarto GE, Stubblefield PA, Lurain J, et al. (1984) Mechanisms of growth in hydatidiform moles. Am J Obstet Gynecol 148:1014–1023

Scarbrough PR, Hersh J, Kukolich MK, et al. (1984) Tetraploidy: a report of three live-born infants. Am J Med Genet 19:29–37

Schinzel A (1984) Catalogue of unbalanced chromosome aberrations in man. De Gruyter, Berlin

Schinzel AA (1991) Uniparental disomy and gene localization. Am J Hum Genet 48:424–425

Schinzel A, Schmid W, Fraccaro M, et al. (1981) The "cat eye syndrome": dicentric small marker chromosome probably derived from a no. 22 (tetrasomy 22pter→q11) associated with a characteristic phenotype. Hum Genet 57:148–158

Schröcksnadel H, Guggenbichler P, Rhomberg K, et al. (1982) Komplette Triploidie (69,XXX) mit einer Überlebensdauer von 7 Monaten. Wien Klin Wochenschr 94:309–315

Smith DW (1976) Recognizable patterns of human malformation, 2nd edn. Saunders, Philadelphia

Smith DW, Patau K, Therman E, et al. (1960) A new autosomal trisomy syndrome: multiple congenital anomalies caused by an extra chromosome. J Pediatr 57:338–345

Spence JE, Perciaccante RG, Greig GM, et al. (1988) Uniparental disomy as a mechanism for human genetic disease. Am J Hum Genet 42:217–226

Sundareshan TS, Naguib KK, Al-Awadi SA, et al. (1990) Apparently nonmosaic trisomy 22: clinical report and review. Am J Med Genet 36:7–10

Surti U, Szulman AE, Wagner K, et al. (1986) Tetraploid partial hydatidiform moles: two cases with a triple paternal contribution and a 92,XXXY karyotype. Hum Genet 72:15–21

Therman E, Patau K, DeMars RI, et al. (1963) Iso/telo–D₁ mosaicism in a child with an incomplete D₁ trisomy syndrome. Portugal Acta Biol 7:211–224

Trisomy 21 (1990) American Journal of Medical Genetics, Suppl 7

Turleau C, Grouchy J de, Klein M (1972) Phylogénie chromosomique de l'homme et des primates hominiens (Pan troglodytes, Gorilla gorilla, et Pongo pygmaeus): essai de reconstitution du caryotype de l'ancetre commun. Ann Genet (Paris) 15:225–240

Vassilakos P, Riotton G, Kajii T (1977) Hydatidiform mole: two entities. Am J Obstet Gynecol 127:167–170

Vejerslev LO, Dissing J, Hansen HE, et al. (1987) Hydatidiform mole: genetic origin in polyploid conceptuses. Hum Genet 76:11–19

Voss R, Ben-Simon E, Avital A, et al. (1989) Isodisomy of chromosome 7 in a patient with cystic fibrosis: Could uniparental disomy be common in humans? Am J Hum Genet 45:373–380

Warburton D (1988) Editorial: Uniparental disomy: a rare consequence of the high rate of aneuploidy in human gametes. Am J Hum Genet 42:215–216

Wisniewski K, Dambska M, Jenkins EC, et al. (1983) Monosomy 21 syndrome: Further delineation including clinical, neuropathological, cytogenetic and biochemical studies. Clin Genet 23:102–110

Yunis E, Ramirez E, Uribe JG (1980) Full trisomy 7 and Potter syndrome. Hum
    Genet 54:13–18
Yunis JJ (ed) (1977) New chromosomal syndromes. Academic, New York
Zackai EH, Emanuel BS (1980) Site-specific reciprocal translocation, t(11;22)
    (q23;q11), in several unrelated families with 3:1 meiotic disjunction. Am J Med
    Genet 7:507–521

25
Structurally Abnormal Human Autosomes

Structurally Abnormal Chromosomes

In contrast to full trisomy and monosomy, which in liveborn infants are limited to a few autosomes, the variety of structurally abnormal chromosomes is virtually infinite. This is to be expected, since chromosomes may break at almost any point, and the broken ends may join randomly to form new combinations. Chromosome breaks occur in meiocytes as well as in somatic cells. The only limitation to the variety of structurally abnormal chromosomes is their possible lethal effect on the individuals or cells carrying them. Deletions, duplications, ring chromosomes, inversions, and translocations cause partial trisomy and/or monosomy syndromes which have been described for all chromosome arms (de Grouchy and Turleau, 1984; Schinzel, 1984). It would be impossible to review the entire field of structural chromosome abnormalities even in a much more comprehensive book than this one; therefore, only the main classes of abnormal chromosomes are described herein, illustrated by a few examples of the resulting syndromes. Reciprocal and Robertsonian translocations and their segregation are discussed in Chapters 26 and 27, respectively.

Chromosomal Polymorphisms

Chromosomal polymorphisms, or *heteromorphisms*, are structural variants of chromosomes that are widespread in human populations and have no effect on the phenotype, even in their most extreme forms. The apparent harmlessness of chromosomal polymorphisms led to the conclusion that segments displaying such variants must be heterochromatic. With banding techniques we now know that these polymorphisms represent constitutive heterochromatin, often at the centric regions of the chromosomes. In a comparison of the incidence of such chromosome variants in 200 mentally retarded patients and in the same number of normal controls, no difference was found between the two groups (Tharapel and Summitt, 1978). However, different results have been obtained in other studies.

Polymorphic segments vary in size, position (through inversion), and staining properties. This has been shown with C-banding, Q-banding, R-banding with acridine orange, and with various combinations of fluorescent dyes such as DAPI and DIPI (Verma and Dosik, 1980; Schnedl et al., 1981). The following chromosome segments are frequently polymorphic: (1) The Q-bright distal end of the Y chromosome, which varies from zero to three or four times its average length (Fig. 20.1b), extreme variants being very rare. (2) The short arms and satellites of acrocentric chromosomes, which vary both in size and in fluorescent characteristics. The lengths of the satellite stalks, where the ribosomal RNA genes are situated, also vary, or the stalks may be absent on certain chromosomes (Mikelsaar et al., 1977). (3) A Q-bright centric region may or may not be present in chromosomes 3, 4, 13, and 22. (4) Centric heterochromatin, as revealed by C-banding, shows a wide range of variation, especially in chromosomes 1 (Fig. 6.1f), 9, and 16, but some variation is seen in many other chromosomes, such as 12, 17, 21 (Mayer et al., 1978) and 19 (Trunca Doyle, 1976). It is likely that all the C-bands vary to some extent (Craig-Holmes, 1977).

In addition to variation in size, heterochromatic regions are prone to other structural changes, all of which are also phenotypically insignificant. Numerous inversions that involve the centric heterochromatin of chromosomes 1 and 9 (Fig. 27.1) and the Q-bright centric band on chromosome 3 have been described.

Quantitative Comparisons

Quantitative comparisons of the sizes of C-bands are difficult, even within one study (Verma and Dosik, 1980). This is also true of determining inversions in these regions. It is, therefore, not surprising that the estimates of the incidence of heterochromatic size variants in chromosome 9 range from 0.1 percent to 12.5 percent (Sanchez and Yunis, 1977), and the frequency of inversions involving the same region ranges from 0.7 percent to 11.3 percent (Sanchez and Yunis, 1977). Although populations may indeed vary with respect to the incidence of heterochromatic variants, clearly the strikingly different results are caused mainly by the non-uniform criteria used, combined with technical difficulties. However, recent improvements in staining techniques have made observations on heterochromatin much more accurate (Verma, 1988; Verma and Babu, 1989). Restriction endonucleases have also been used to treat chromosomes before staining, which further refines the analysis of polymorphisms (Babu, 1988). Chromosomal polymorphisms have been used as markers in gene mapping and cell hybridization studies. They can be helpful in determining zygosity in twins and in settling disputes about paternity (Fig. 25.1). They also can show which parent provided an extra chromosome in a trisomic infant, or an extra chromosome set in triploids. In addition, polymorphisms have played an important role in cytogenetic studies of hydatidiform moles. Finally, the origins of the different cell lines in mosaics and chimeras, including persons with bone marrow transplants, can be determined with the help of polymorphisms. However, many of these phenomena are now being studied with more accurate molecular methods.

Pericentric Inversions

Inversions fall into two groups: *pericentric* inversions involve breaks in opposite arms, *paracentric* ones in the same arm. Pericentric inversions

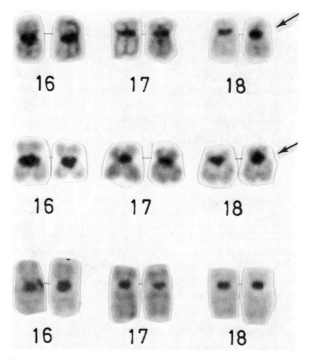

Figure 25.1. E group from father, daughter, and mother. The exceptionally large C-band in chromosome 18 in father and daughter was used for determination of paternity (courtesy of HD Hager and TM Schroeder).

are often discovered because they change the position of the centromere. Pericentric inversions have been observed in all chromosomes except chromosome 20 (Kaiser, 1984, 1988; Kleczkowska et al., 1987). However, different chromosomes are involved nonrandomly; for instance, inv(9) comprises some 40 percent of all pericentric inversions. Breakpoints are also nonrandom: for example, bands 2p13, 2q21, 5q31, 6q21, 10q22, and 12q13 are involved repeatedly (Kleczkowska et al., 1987).

The estimated incidence of all inversions in human populations varies greatly in different studies: a number often mentioned is 1 percent. Variations in estimates may, in part, be caused by the difficulty in drawing lines between harmless polymorphisms and "real" inversions, those that may result in the birth of abnormal offspring.

In meiosis, short heterozygous inversions remain unpaired. A large inverted segment usually forms a loop to pair with its homologue, or it may pair straight, leaving the now nonhomologous ends unpaired. Crossing-over in a pericentric inversion leads to a deletion and a duplication (Fig. 25.2). Crossing-over in a paracentric inversion may produce a dicentric and an acentric chromosome. The complicated relationships of various types of crossing-over in inversions and the chromosome configurations arising from them are reviewed in many cytogenetics textbooks, for instance, in Burnham (1962).

It is surprising how few of the inversions in man seem to result in reproductive trouble—either the birth of recombinant offspring, or partial sterility (Moorhead, 1976). This is understandable for small inversions, since they rarely undergo legitimate pairing. However, even larger inversions are often genetically benign.

Trunca and Opitz (1977), in a study of a woman with inv(14) and her

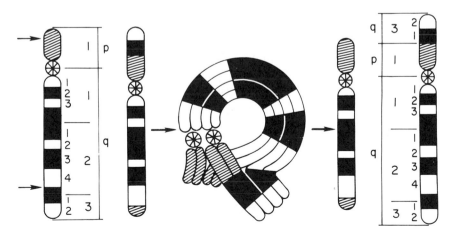

Figure 25.2. Breakpoints in a pericentric inversion of chromosome 14 and two types of abnormal chromosomes (one with duplication, the other with deletion) resulting from crossing-over in an inversion (Trunca and Opitz, 1977).

abnormal child who had a duplication in the same chromosome (Fig. 25.2), reviewed the factors promoting the incidence of abnormal offspring. The risk for an inversion carrier was determined by the probability of either type of recombinant offspring surviving birth. The above authors divided pericentric inversions into those involving less than one-third of the chromosome and those involving more. All families in the latter group had at least one abnormal child; those in the former had none. The obvious explanation was that the longer the inversion, relative to the chromosome, the greater the probability that crossing-over would occur. At the same time, the duplicated and deleted segments became smaller, as less of the chromosome remained outside the inverted segment. Both factors promote the birth of abnormal but viable offspring.

Of recombinant offspring, the type with the larger duplication and smaller deletion is usually more viable. However, in some unfortunate families both types of abnormal children have been born alive (for example, in the family described by Vianna-Morgante et al., 1976).

Paracentric Inversions

Although far fewer paracentric than pericentric inversions have been observed, they have involved many of the autosomes, including 1, 2, 3, 4, 5, 7, 8, 9, 10, 11, 12, 13, 14, 15, 16, 21, and the X (Madan, 1988). Nonrandomness is also reflected in the frequent involvement of chromosome arms, 7q, 11q, 3p and 3q. Of the 65 inversions cited by Madan (1988), ten were within 7q, and five of these had their breakpoints in bands q11 and q22.

The relative rarity of observed paracentric inversions is probably caused by several factors. First, it is less probable that two breaks will occur on the same arm than on different arms. Paracentric inversions are also more difficult to detect, since they do not change the arm ratio. Furthermore, crossing-over in a paracentric inversion results in a dicentric and acentric chromosome, and thus in fewer viable offspring, through whom chromosomal abnormalities are usually ascertained.

Deletions or Partial Monosomies

Chromosome deletions or partial monosomies may be divided into two groups, pure deletions and deletions combined with a duplication, both of which usually occur as the result of reciprocal translocations. Deletions affecting all chromosome ends, as well as many interstitial segments, have been found in liveborn children (de Grouchy and Turleau, 1984; Schinzel, 1984). Some deletions are relatively frequent, for instance, 4p−, 5p−, 9p−, 11p−, 11q−, 13q−, 18p−, and 18q−; others have been found only a few times. As with sex chromosome anomalies, monosomy for an entire autosome or segment thereof has much more serious phenotypic consequences than the corresponding trisomy.

Short deletions, those with a break presumably through a gene, and other structural changes involving a limited region of a chromosome have been used successfully in gene mapping, especially when combined with molecular techniques (Chapter 31). The analysis of the X-linked Duchenne muscular dystrophy locus provides a classic example of such studies.

Cri du Chat (Cat Cry) Syndrome

By far the most common of the deletion syndromes, and the one most extensively studied, is the so-called *cri du chat syndrome*, caused by a partial deletion of 5p. The incidence of this condition in infants is estimated as 1/45,000, and its frequency among the mentally retarded as 1.5/1000 (Niebuhr, 1978b).

Niebuhr (1978b) reviewed 331 patients with cri du chat syndrome. One of the most consistent symptoms is the cat-like infant cry, which, however, is modified with age. The cry seems to be caused mainly by defects of the central nervous system (Schroeder et al., 1967). Niebuhr (1978b) lists 50 symptoms characteristic of this syndrome, many of which are probably interdependent. In addition to the characteristic cry, the most common abnormalities according to Smith (1976) are: mental retardation in most patients; hypotonia (100 percent), which in adults becomes hypertonia; microcephaly (100 percent); round face in children (68 percent); hypertelorism (94 percent); epicanthic folds (85 percent); downward slanting of palpebral fissures (81 percent); strabismus (61 percent); low-set or poorly developed ears (58 percent); heart disease of various types (30 percent); and characteristic dermatoglyphics (about 80 percent).

In Fig. 25.3 three cri du chat patients representing different age groups are portrayed. The differences in the severity of corresponding monosomy and trisomy syndromes are well demonstrated by cases in which segregation in translocation families has produced both cri du chat and its "countertype" offspring, who have partial trisomy for 5p. As a rule, the latter are less severely affected (Yunis et al., 1978).

In a family described by Opitz and Patau (1975), two carriers had a translocation, t(5p−;12q+). Six infants with numerous anomalies and partial trisomy for 5p had been born in two generations. It is possible that the severity of the syndrome and the lack of any cri du chat offspring were associated with the deletion of most of 5p, which could be lethal. The diplochromosome karyotype of a carrier is shown in Fig. 25.4.

The size of the deletion of 5p causing cri du chat syndrome varies from very small to about 60 percent of the length of the chromosome arm. It was observed years ago that the length of the deletion showed little correlation with the severity of the syndrome. This became understand-

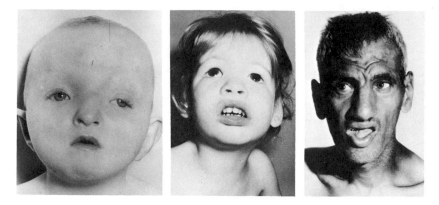

Figure 25.3. Three cri du chat patients (infant, 4 years, 40 years), showing moon face, hypertelorism, antimongoloid slant of the eyes, downward slant of the mouth, and low-set ears (courtesy of R Laxova).

able when Niebuhr (1978a), in a detailed cytological study of 35 patients, showed that the critical segment (whose absence caused most of the symptoms) was a very small region around the middle of 5p15 (Fig. 25.5). Twenty-seven of the 35 patients apparently had a terminal deletion, whereas four were the results of translocations, two of which were familial. Similar results have been obtained in larger populations (Niebuhr, 1978b): in 80 percent of the patients the syndrome was caused by a deletion, in 10 percent one of the parents had a translocation, and another 10 percent of the patients showed other chromosome abnormalities, such as rings, de novo translocations, and mosaicism. All in all, 12 percent of the cases were familial.

Ring Chromosomes

Ring chromosomes have been found for all human chromosomes (Wyandt, 1988). Since a ring involves a deletion at each end of the chromosome, the resulting phenotypes overlap with deletion syndromes for the same chromosome. However, it has been observed repeatedly that the phenotypes of carriers of ring chromosomes vary greatly, from mentally retarded with multiple anomalies to apparently normal, fertile persons (Hecht and Vlietinck, 1973). Sometimes even persons with apparently identical ring chromosomes have nothing in common phenotypically (for example, Zackai and Breg, 1973; Dallapiccola et al., 1977).

Causes of the phenotypic variation in carriers of rings involving the same chromosome include: (1) the size of the original deletion, (2) the rate of sister chromatid exchanges in the ring, and (3) the viability of the cell lines with aberrant ring chromosomes. Figure 25.6 illustrates a ring 9

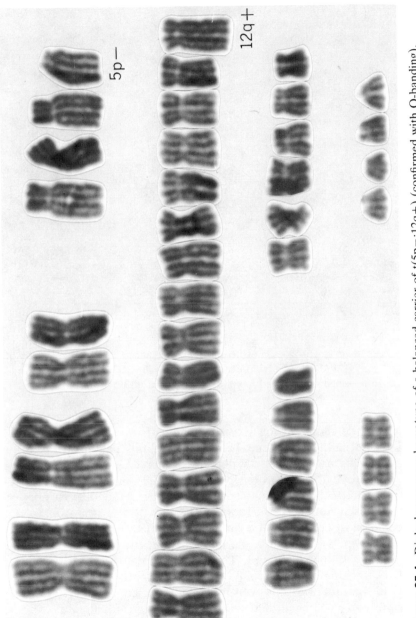

Figure 25.4. Diplochromosome karyotype of a balanced carrier of t(5p−;12q+) (confirmed with Q-banding).

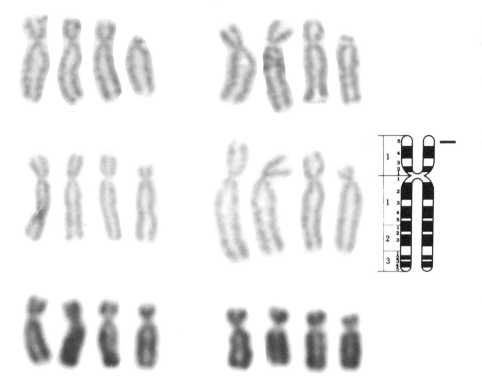

Figure 25.5. The B chromosomes from two cells each, of three cri du chat patients; length of the deletion is different in each patient. The lack of the middle part of 5p15 (marked in diagram) is believed to cause all the symptoms.

in which the deletions obviously were minute. However, the severe retardation and multiple congenital anomalies in this patient are easy to understand, because roughly 25 percent of her cells had a double or otherwise abnormal ring chromosome (Fig. 25.7). Her phenotype falls into the—admittedly variable—range of conditions found in carriers of an r(9) (Nakajima et al., 1976; Inouye et al., 1979).

Although most persons with a ring chromosome are both mentally and physically severely affected, a number of apparently normal and even fertile carriers have been found. This obviously depends on the minute size of the deletion and the relative stability of the ring. Thus, a 5-year-old girl with an r(4) was not even mentally retarded. However, she had short stature, a small head, and retarded bone age (Surana et al., 1971). More puzzling was the case of a non-retarded 9-year-old girl, described by Lansky et al. (1977), who had very few other anomalies. One-half of her lymphocytes showed a ring 10, whereas the other half were monosomic for chromosome 10. Since only lymphocytes were studied, she may

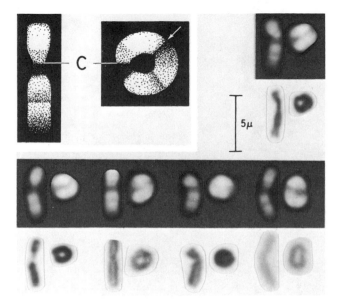

Figure 25.6. Ring chromosome 9 with very small deletions and the normal 9 and r(9) from 5 cells (courtesy of ML Motl).

have been a mosaic with a normal cell line, which is also the most probable explanation for other cases that deviate from expectation.

At least five apparently normal women with 46,XX,r(21) have been described (Matsubara et al., 1982; Schmid et al., 1983; Kleczkowska and Fryns, 1984; Rhomberg, 1984). One of them had a normal son with the same ring, and two others had Down syndrome children with an extra r(21), one of them a mosaic. A further woman with 46,XX,r(14) and low normal intelligence had two retarded children and a therapeutically aborted fetus with the same ring (Riley et al., 1981). Finally, a retarded and psychotic woman with r(18) gave birth to a daughter bearing the same chromosome, who was more severely retarded and psychotic. It should be noted, however, that the child's father suffered from schizophrenia (Christensen et al., 1970). A less affected mother and son with r(18) were described by Donlan and Dolan (1986), and a mother with r(15) had two affected sons with the same anomaly (Fujimaki et al., 1987).

Apart from the two children with Down syndrome, the ring chromosome replaced a member of the normal chromosome complement in all the other cases discussed in the preceding paragraph. In addition, numerous patients have been described who had a small extra ring chromosome. Such small rings may disappear, and lead to mosaicism, or they may open up. The origin of an extra ring chromosome is usually impossible to determine.

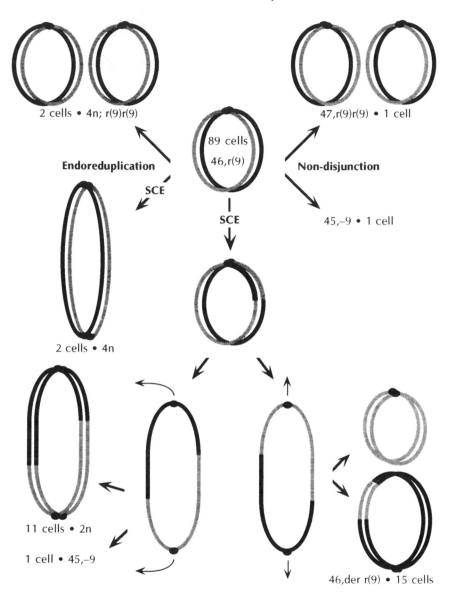

Figure 25.7. Behavior of r(9) (Fig. 25.6) in 122 lymphocytes; the ring is normal in 89 cells, abnormal or missing in 33. Endoreduplication: tetraploid cells with two rings (two cells); with SCE, tetraploid cells with double rings (two cells). Nondisjunction: two rings (one cell) or no ring (one cell). SCE: double ring in which the centromeres go to the same pole (11 cells), or to different poles, which results in different-sized monocentric rings (15 cells) (Therman and Susman, unpublished).

Insertions

While deletions require only one or two breaks, and inversions two, *insertions* are necessarily the result of three breaks. Consequently, they are considerably rarer than abnormalities involving one or two breaks. An insertion may occur either between two chromosomes or within one chromosome, and the segment may be inserted straight or in an inverted position.

As an example, let us take the interesting family described by Therkelsen et al. (1973). In the carrier father, a segment from 2p had been inserted into 2q. Two abnormal infants were born, representing different types of recombination products.

In another family in which a segment from chromosome 13 had been inserted in an inverted position into 3q, segregation could be followed in three generations (Toomey et al., 1978). Both the monosomic and the trisomic types of recombinant individuals, as well as carriers and normals, were observed.

Duplication or Pure Partial Trisomy

Partial trisomy that is not combined with a deletion, either for the same chromosome or for a nonhomologous one, is relatively rare. In a couple of cases, an abnormal individual has been found to have a de novo duplication (Vogel et al., 1978). Either of two mechanisms would give rise to such a tandem duplication: an insertion from the homologous chromosome, or unequal sister chromatid exchange or crossing-over in meiosis or mitosis.

As a rule, crossing-over in an inversion leads to abnormal chromosomes that have both a duplication and a deletion. Only when the inversion involves an acrocentric chromosome and one break has taken place in the short arm will the recombinant chromosome have a pure duplication (Fig. 25.2; Trunca and Opitz, 1977).

One of the clearest examples of pure partial trisomy is provided by isochromosomes. However, such chromosomes are very rarely members of a 46-chromosome complement, since this would involve monosomy for the other chromosome arm. In consequence, apart from Xq and Yq, isochromosomes have been found only for 9p and 18q (Rodiere et al., 1977) and for the acrocentrics, in which the lack of the short arm is not deleterious.

Isochromosomes or isodicentrics, in addition to a normal chromosome complement, have been described for very short arms, such as 18p (Nielsen et al., 1978; Fryns et al., 1985) and 17p (Mascarello et al., 1983). In such cases, the individual is naturally tetrasomic for the arm concerned. A chromosomally interesting child was described by Leschot and Lim

(1979). She had a translocation t(2q;5q), while 5p formed an isochromosome, which resulted in pure trisomy for this arm. A similar combination of translocation and isochromosome formation for 4p has also been found (André et al., 1976).

Trisomy for 9p is caused by either an isochromosome for this arm or an extra free 9p chromosome (Biederman, 1979). Even tetrasomy for major parts of chromosome 9 seems to be compatible with at least a limited life span. The largest partial tetrasomy has been described in a patient with an extra isodicentric, consisting of two chromosomes 9 attached long arm to long arm (breakpoint in both q22), with the second centromere inactivated (Wisniewski et al., 1978). The infant was highly abnormal and lived for only a couple of hours. Four other cases of partial tetrasomy for the same chromosome are reviewed by Wisniewski et al. (1978). Ten cases of a variant of i(9p) in which the breaks were in the centric heterochromatin have also been described (Jalal et al., 1991).

Tetrasomy for 12p, caused by an extra i(12p), has been observed in some 20 mosaic individuals (Kawashima, 1987; Pauli et al., 1987; Reynolds et al., 1987; Warburton et al., 1987).

Mosaicism

In all populations selected for study because of a presumed abnormal chromosome constitution, mosaicism has turned out to play an important role. This holds true for the sex chromosomes, where it is especially frequent, and the autosomes, for simple monosomy and trisomy, as well as for structurally abnormal chromosomes. Mosaicism could, therefore, be discussed with equal justification at many different points in this book.

In humans, and in mammals in general, two types of mosaicism constitute the building blocks of normal development. In the female, one X in each cell is inactivated, usually at random (Chapter 21). The other type of mosaicism is correlated with normal differentiation in many tissues (Chapter 16). It includes endopolyploidy (Chapter 16), created through different mechanisms, as well as amplification and underreplication of various chromosome segments.

Apart from occasional events affecting individual cells, mosaicism involves at least two cell lines. The simplest type of mosaicism consists of a normal and a trisomic cell line. Of the patients selected because of 21, 18, or 13 trisomy symptoms, between 2 and 10 percent have turned out to be mosaics. The proportion of hidden mosaicism is probably considerably higher. Parental mosaicism plays an important role in the origin of trisomic individuals (2.7 percent of the parents of 21 trisomic children are mosaics; Uchida and Freeman, 1985).

Nondisjunction or chromosome loss are the simplest mechanisms creating mosaicism. However, a sequence of events has to be assumed to explain the development of an individual having 13 trisomic, 18 trisomic, and normal cell lines. Wilson et al. (1983), who described such a mosaic, have reviewed other similar cases.

Phenotypically normal mosaics create difficulties for genetic counseling. Moreover, cultured amniotic cells, in many cases, have shown chromosome constitutions, often mosaic, different from those of the fetal cells. A common situation is that the amniotic culture has a trisomic cell line, especially for chromosome 20 (Miny and Pawlowitzki, 1984), whereas the fetal cells are normal. Discrepancies have been found even more often between direct analyses of chorionic villi and of fetal tissue cultures (Kalousek et al., 1987). To avoid misdiagnoses, cultures of fetal cells should be compared with results obtained from chorionic villi (Sachs et al., 1990).

A mechanism that gives rise in one step to different cell lines is segregation of a chromatid translocation (quadriradial) (Daly et al., 1977). This has rarely been considered in the literature when mechanisms creating mosaicism are discussed.

Ring chromosomes have a built-in mechanism for continuously creating new chromosomes. Figure 25.7 summarizes the behavior of the r(9) chromosome (Fig. 25.6) mentioned above. Following the occurrence of one sister chromatid exchange, a continuous double ring with one centromere is found in the next metaphase. When the centromere divides in anaphase, the daughter centromeres may go to the same pole, leading to a double, dicentric ring in one daughter cell and no ring in the other; or, if the centromeres go to opposite poles, the daughter cells may obtain unequal rings. If the chromosome is twisted when the chromatids join, a new dicentric will be formed. It is easy to see how such mechanisms can give rise to an almost infinite variety of derivatives of the original ring. The main variants are: rings with different numbers of centromeres (even an octocentric ring in a polyploid cell has been described by Niss and Passarge, 1975), interlocking rings, rings consisting of variable combinations of chromosome segments, rings that have opened up, interphase-like chromosomes in metaphase, and several rings in one cell (Hoo et al., 1974).

It is interesting that in many ring chromosome carriers, cells or cell lines in which the ring is missing have been observed. However, what is unexpected is that cell lines that are monosomic for certain chromosomes, for instance 6 (van den Berghe et al., 1974) or 10 (Lansky et al., 1977), are viable, although they are not observed in persons without a ring chromosome. One cannot help wondering whether the cells with double rings might somehow compensate for the monosomic cells.

So far, the type of mosaicism in which a normal chromosome is replaced by a ring in the abnormal cell line, in two or three successive generations, is incomprehensible (Stoll and Roth, 1983; Back et al., 1989). Could one specific chromosome be affected by an "instability syndrome"?

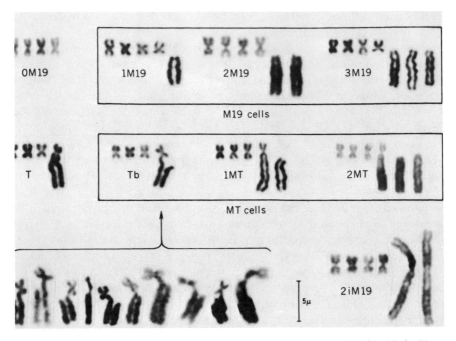

Figure 25.8. Partial karyotypes of cells of a woman with 46,XX,t(6p;19p), illustrating the behavior of the translocation chromosome. Nomenclature: 0M19, cell without marker; 1M19, cell with one large marker fragment; 2M19, cell with two markers; 3M19, cell with three markers; T, 6;19, translocation chromosome; Tb, translocation chromosome showing a chromatid break at the fusion point; 1MT, cell carrying the translocation chromosome plus a marker fragment; 2MT, translocation plus two markers. Chromosomes in brackets are examples of Tb from 10 cells; 2iM19, cell with two isofragments, each consisting of two chromosomes 6 (Drets and Therman, 1983).

Complex mosaicism also has been created by a dicentric t(6p;19p), in which the centromere of chromosome 6 is inactivated (Drets and Therman, 1983). This chromosome behaves exceptionally in that it has a tendency to break at the fusion point of the two chromosomes (1/733 cells). Since the centromere of the broken-off chromosome 6 is not reactivated, this chromosome behaves like an acentric fragment. These processes have led to complicated mosaicism. Figure 25.8 illustrates partial karyotypes of 12 different cell types found among the 8800 lymphocyte metaphases analyzed (other abnormalities were also present). As in the ring chromosome cases, surprisingly unbalanced cells seem to be able to divide, as demonstrated by the cell with two isofragments of chromosome 6, which thus in effect has five chromosomes 6.

Malignant tissues are often complicated mosaics exhibiting all possible mitotic and chromosome abnormalities (Table 30.1).

References

André M-J, Aurias A, Berranger P de, et al. (1976) Trisomie 4p de novo par isochromosome 4p. Ann Genet (Paris) 19:127–131

Babu A (1988) Heterogeneity of heterochromatin of human chromosomes as demonstrated by restriction endonuclease treatment. In: Verma RS (ed) Heterochromatin: molecular and structural aspects. Cambridge University Press, Cambridge, pp 250–275

Back E, Voiculescu I, Brünger M, et al. (1989) Familial ring (20) chromosomal mosaicism. Hum Genet 83:148–154

Berghe H van den, Fryns J-P, Cassiman J-J, et al. (1974) Chromosome 6 en anneau. Caryotype 46,XY,r(6)/45,XY,−6. Ann Genet (Paris) 17:29–35

Biederman B (1979) Trisomy 9p with an isochromosome of 9p. Hum Genet 46:125–126

Burnham CR (1962) Discussions in cytogenetics. Burgess, Minneapolis

Christensen KR, Friedrich U, Jacobsen P, et al. (1970) Ring chromosome 18 in mother and daughter. J Ment Defic Res 14:49–67

Craig-Holmes AP (1977) C-band polymorphism in human populations. In: Hook EB, Porter IH (eds) Population cytogenetics. Academic, New York, pp 161–177

Dallapiccola B, Brinchi V, Curatolo P (1977) Variability of r(22) chromosome phenotypical expression. Acta Genet Med Gemellol 26:287–290

Daly RF, Patau K, Therman E, et al. (1977) Structure and Barr body formation of an Xp+ chromosome with two inactivation centers. Am J Hum Genet 29:83–93

Donlan MA, Dolan CR (1986) Ring chromosome 18 in a mother and son. Am J Med Genet 24:171–174

Drets ME, Therman E (1983) Human telomeric 6;19 translocation chromosome with a tendency to break at the fusion point. Chromosoma 88:139–144

Fryns JP, Kleczkowska A, Marien P, et al. (1985) 18p tetrasomy. Further evidence for a distinctive clinical syndrome. Ann Genet (Paris) 28:111–112

Fujimaki W, Baba K, Tatara K, et al. (1987) Ring chromosome 15 in a mother and her children. Hum Genet 76:302

Grouchy J de, Turleau C (1984) Clinical atlas of human chromosomes, 2nd edn. Wiley, New York

Hecht F, Vlietinck RF (1973) Autosomal rings and variable phenotypes. Humangenetik 18:99–100

Hoo JJ, Obermann U, Cramer H (1974) The behavior of ring chromosome 13. Humangenetik 24:161–171

Inouye T, Matsuda H, Shimura K (1979) A ring chromosome 9 in an infant with malformations. Hum Genet 50:231–235

Jalal SM, Kukolich MK, Garcia M, et al. (1991) Tetrasomy 9p: an emerging syndrome. Clin Genet 39:60–64

Kaiser P (1984) Pericentric inversions: problems and significance for clinical genetics. Hum Genet 68:1–47

Kaiser P (1988) Pericentric inversions: their problems and clinical significance. In: Daniel A (ed) The cytogenetics of mammalian autosomal rearrangements. Liss, New York, pp 163–247

Kalousek DK, Dill FJ, Pantzar T, et al. (1987) Confined chorionic mosaicism in prenatal diagnosis. Hum Genet 77:163–167

Kawashima H (1987) Brief clinical report: Skeletal anomalies in a patient with the Pallister/Teschler-Nicola/Killian syndrome. Am J Med Genet 27:285–289

Kleczkowska A, Fryns JP (1984) Ring chromosome 21 in a normal female. Ann Genet (Paris) 27:126–127

Kleczkowska A, Fryns JP, Van den Berghe H (1987) Pericentric inversions in man: personal experience and review of the literature. Hum Genet 75:333–338

Lansky S, Daniel W, Fleiszar K (1977) Physical retardation associated with ring chromosome mosaicism: 46,XX,r(10)/45,XX,10−. J Med Genet 14:61–63

Leschot NJ, Lim KS (1979) "Complete" trisomy 5p: de novo translocation t(2;5) (q36;p11) with isochromosome 5p. Hum Genet 46:271–278

Madan K (1988) Paracentric inversions and their clinical implications. In: Daniel A (ed) The cytogenetics of mammalian autosomal rearrangements. Liss, New York, pp 249–266

Mascarello JT, Jones, MC, Hoyme HE, et al. (1983) Duplication (17p) in a child with an isodicentric (17p) chromosome. Am J Med Genet 14:67–72

Matsubara T, Nakagome Y, Ogasawara N, et al. (1982) Maternally transmitted extra ring(21) chromosome in a boy with Down's syndrome. Hum Genet 60:78–79

Mayer M, Matsuura J, Jacobs P (1978) Inversions and other unusual heteromorphisms detected by C-banding. Hum Genet 45:43–50

Mikelsaar A-V, Schmid M, Krone W, et al. (1977) Frequency of Ag-stained nucleolus organizer regions in the acrocentric chromosomes of man. Hum Genet 37:73–77

Miny P, Pawlowitzki I-H (1984) Trisomy 20 mosaicism. Prenat Diag 4:411–419

Moorhead PS (1976) A closer look at chromosomal inversions. Am J Hum Genet 28:294–296

Nakajima S, Yanagisawa M, Kamoshita S, et al. (1976) Mental retardation and congenital malformations associated with a ring chromosome 9. Hum Genet 32:289–293

Niebuhr E (1978a) Cytologic observations in 35 individuals with a 5p− karyotype. Hum Genet 42:143–156

Niebuhr E (1978b) The cri du chat syndrome. Hum Genet 44:227–275

Nielsen KB, Dyggve H, Friedrich U, et al. (1978) Small metacentric nonsatellited extra chromosome. Hum Genet 44:59–69

Niss R, Passarge E (1975) Derivative chromosomal structures from a ring chromosome 4. Humangenetik 28:9–23

Opitz JM, Patau K (1975) A partial trisomy 5p syndrome. In: New chromosomal and malformation syndromes. Birth defects: original article series, II. New York: The National Foundation, pp 191–200

Pauli RM, Zeier RA, Sekhon GS (1987) Letter to the editor: Mosaic isochromosome 12p. Am J Med Genet 27:291–294

Reynolds JF, Daniel A, Kelly TE, et al. (1987) Isochromosome 12p mosaicism (Pallister mosaic aneuploidy or Pallister-Killian syndrome): report of 11 cases. Am J Med Genet 27:257–274

Rhomberg K (1984) Ring chromosome 21 in a healthy woman with three spontaneous abortions. Hum Genet 67:120

Riley SB, Buckton KE, Ratcliffe SG, et al. (1981) Inheritance of a ring 14 chromosome. J Med Genet 18:209–213

Rodiere M, Donadio D, Emberger J-M, et al. (1977) Isochromosomie 18:46,XX, i(18q). Ann Pediat 24:611–616

Sachs ES, Jahoda MGJ, Los FJ, et al. (1990) Interpretation of chromosome mosaicism and discrepancies in chorionic villi studies. Am J Med Genet 37: 268–271

Sanchez O, Yunis JJ (1977) New chromosome techniques and their medical applications. In: Yunis JJ (ed) New chromosomal syndromes. Academic, New York, pp 1–54

Schinzel A (1984) Catalogue of unbalanced chromosome aberrations in man. De Gruyter, Berlin

Schmid W, Tenconi R, Baccichetti C, et al. (1983) Ring chromosome 21 in phenotypically apparently normal persons: report of two families from Switzerland and Italy. Am J Med Genet 16:323–329

Schnedl W, Abraham R, Dann O, et al. (1981) Preferential fluorescent staining of heterochromatic regions in human chromosomes 9, 15, and the Y by D287/170. Hum Genet 59:10–13

Schroeder H-J, Schleiermacher E, Schroeder TM, et al. (1967) Zur klinischen Differentialdiagnose des Cri du Chat-Syndroms. Humangenetik 4:294–304

Smith DW (1976) Recognizable patterns of human malformation, 2nd edn. Saunders, Philadelphia

Stoll C, Roth M-P (1983) Segregation of a 22 ring chromosome in three generations. Hum Genet 63:294–296

Surana RB, Bailey JD, Conen PE (1971) A ring-4 chromosome in a patient with normal intelligence and short stature. J Med Genet 8:517–521

Tharapel AT, Summitt RL (1978) Minor chromosome variations and selected heteromorphisms in 200 unclassifiable mentally retarded patients and 200 normal controls. Hum Genet 41:121–130

Therkelsen AJ, Hultén M, Jonasson J, et al. (1973) Presumptive direct insertion within chromosome 2 in man. Ann Hum Genet 36:367–373

Toomey KE, Mohandas T, Sparkes RS, et al. (1978) Segregation of an insertional chromosome rearrangement in 3 generations. J Med Genet 15:382–387

Trunca C, Opitz JM (1977) Pericentric inversion of chromosome 14 and the risk of partial duplication of 14q (14q31→14qter). Am J Med Genet 1:217–228

Trunca Doyle C (1976) The cytogenetics of 90 patients with idiopathic mental retardation/malformation syndromes and of 90 normal subjects. Hum Genet 33:131–146

Uchida IA, Freeman VCP (1985) Trisomy 21 Down syndrome: parental mosaicism. Hum Genet 70:246–248

Verma RS (1988) Heteromorphisms of heterochromatin. In: Verma RS (ed) Heterochromatin: molecular and structural aspects. Cambridge University Press, Cambridge, pp 276–292

Verma RS, Babu A (eds) (1989) Human chromosomes: manual of basic techniques. Pergamon, New York

Verma RS, Dosik H (1980) Human chromosomal heteromorphisms: nature and clinical significance. Int Rev Cytol 62:361–383

Vianna-Morgante AM, Nozaki MJ, Ortega CC, et al. (1976) Partial monosomy and partial trisomy 18 in two offspring of carrier of pericentric inversion of chromosome 18. J Med Genet 13:366–370

Vogel W, Back E, Imm W (1978) Serial duplication of 10(q11→q22) in a patient with minor congenital malformations. Clin Genet 13:159–163

Warburton D, Anyane-Yeboa K, Francke U (1987) Mosaic tetrasomy 12p: four new cases, and confirmation of the chromosomal origin of the supernumerary chromosome in one of the original Pallister-mosaic syndrome cases. Am J Med Genet 27:275–283

Wilson WG, Shires MA, Wilson KA, et al. (1983) Trisomy 18/trisomy 13 mosaicism in an adult with profound mental retardation and multiple malformations. Am J Med Genet 16:131–136

Wisniewski L, Politis GD, Higgins JV (1978) Partial tetrasomy 9 in a liveborn infant. Clin Genet 14:147–153

Wyandt HE (1988) Ring autosomes: identification, familial transmission, causes of phenotypic effects and in vitro mosaicism. In: Daniel A (ed) The cytogenetics of mammalian autosomal rearrangements. Liss, New York, pp 667–695

Yunis E, Silva R, Egel H, et al. (1978) Partial trisomy-5p. Hum Genet 43:231–237

Zackai EH, Breg WR (1973) Ring chromosome 7 with variable phenotypic expression. Cytogenet Cell Genet 12:40–48

26
Reciprocal Translocations

Occurrence

Reciprocal translocations, or interchanges, have been observed in most organisms, plants as well as animals, that have been studied cytogenetically (Burnham, 1962; White, 1978). They may occur as floating or stable polymorphisms, or in single individuals. Like other chromosome structural changes, such as Robertsonian translocations or inversions, translocations that are originally heterozygous may become homozygous, and this sometimes provides a mechanism for isolating two populations. The spontaneous rate of interchanges is estimated to lie between 10^{-1} and 10^{-3} per gamete per generation, in such different organisms as *Drosophila*, grasshopper, mouse, and humans (Lande, 1979).

In plants, balanced carriers of heterozygous translocations are usually discovered because a proportion of the pollen grains are abnormal in shape and size. In animals, balanced carriers are often detected because they are semi-sterile, and their litter sizes are smaller than normal. In humans, the ascertainment is either through a phenotypically abnormal offspring, infertility, or by chance in cytogenetic surveys of variously chosen populations.

By now translocations involving all human chromosome arms have been observed (Borgaonkar, 1984; de Grouchy and Turleau, 1984; Schinzel, 1984). A reciprocal translocation gives rise either to two abnormal but monocentric chromosomes, or to a dicentric and an acentric chromosome. Dicentrics have been discussed in Chapter 9. Whole-arm transfers, or Robertsonian translocations, are dealt with in Chapter 27. A variety of highly complicated translocations between several chromosomes have also been published, as described later in this chapter.

Breakpoints in Reciprocal Translocations

Human chromosomes do not break at random but mainly in the Q-dark regions. Breaks are also distributed differently with particular chromosome-breaking agents. The location of hot spots depends on the chromosome-breaking agent. Nonrandomness also applies to so-called spontaneous breaks—the ones whose causes we do not know.

The number of breaks that can be analyzed when the material consists of individual cells is naturally of an order of magnitude different from the number of translocation carriers whose chromosomes can be studied. Consequently, the fact that the various studies deal with limited material has led to contradictory claims. The confusion is compounded by the pooling of translocations ascertained in different ways. A group ascertained through an unbalanced individual is different from that detected by chance, since the former is affected by powerful selection, resulting from the differential viability of individuals partially trisomic or monosomic for various chromosome regions.

An extensive analysis has been done by Trunca (Trunca et al., 1981; Trunca and Mendel, unpublished) on 828 translocations. When the translocation was ascertained by chance, the breaks occurred at random points. When the ascertainment was through an unbalanced individual, the breakpoints were nonrandom, with an excess of breaks at the telomeres. Chromosomes 9, 11, 13, 18, 21, and 22 were significantly overrepresented, whereas chromosomes 1, 2, 3, 6, 7, and 19 were significantly underrepresented.

A related question is whether chromosomes exchange segments at random or whether specific combinations are preferred. Apart from a couple of exceptions, the exchanges seem to be at random (Trunca and Mendel, unpublished). The most glaring exception is the affinity of the segments 11q23 and 22q11. Of some 100 translocations involving 11q, in only 13 cases was the other chromosome not 22 (Fraccaro et al., 1980; Zackai and Emanuel, 1980; Pihko et al., 1981). This suggests that the two bands involved in 11q and 22q have a homologous sequence that has a tendency to pair and cross over. This hypothesis is further borne out by the similarity of symptoms caused by partial trisomy for the distal segment of 11q and for 22q. Other combinations that occur significantly more frequently than expected are t(9;22) and t(9;15) (Trunca and Mendel, unpublished).

Multiple Rearrangements

In many organisms, including humans, individuals with complicated chromosome rearrangements have been found. Thus, Palmer et al. (1976) described a rearrangement involving chromosomes 3, 11, and 20, in the mother of a chromosomally unbalanced child. They also listed 14 previously published multiple-break cases. Bijlsma et al. (1978), who described an exceptional family with two reciprocal translocations in three generations leading to the birth of one unbalanced individual, also mentioned a few more complex rearrangements. Later cases have been collected by Meer et al. (1981), who described the segregation of a complex rearrangement between chromosomes 6, 7, 8, and 12 through three generations. In a more recent paper, Kousseff et al. (1987) described a phenotypically abnormal boy with seven aberrant chromosomes resulting from eight breaks, and cited over 50 cases of multiple rearrangements from the literature.

A phenotypically abnormal child, with five structurally aberrant chromosomes 1, 4, 7, 12, and 15, was born to a woman who, during pregnancy, developed malignant melanoma, which was not treated before the child was born (Fitzgerald et al., 1977). One cannot help wondering whether the same unknown agent might have been responsible for both the malignant disease in the mother and the chromosome aberrations in the child.

Based on present evidence, it is impossible to decide whether such complex chromosome rearrangements, although rare, might still be more common than expected if breaks occurred independently. Obviously, publication bias is a significant factor, since the more complicated a chromosome rearrangement is, the more likely it is to be published. However, it is also true that many agents, such as cosmic rays, viruses, or mutagenic substances, affect cells nonrandomly.

The reproductive risk for carriers of complex chromosome rearrangements is high. In a study of 25 families, there was 53.7% incidence of abnormal pregnancy outcome (Gorski et al., 1988).

Phenotypes of Balanced Translocation Carriers

The overwhelming majority of persons with balanced reciprocal translocations are phenotypically normal. However, some observations indicate that at least certain reciprocal translocations may affect the phenotype. This evidence comes from studies in which the frequency of apparently balanced reciprocal translocations is compared in mentally retarded and control populations. For instance, Funderburk et al. (1977) found, in 455 retarded children, seven reciprocal translocations, whereas the corresponding number, in 1679 non-retarded children with psychiatric problems, was four ($P < 0.05$). By pooling the results of various surveys on mental retardates, the authors concluded that these patients have five times more balanced, mainly de novo, reciprocal translocations than consecutive newborns do. Interestingly, the incidence of balanced Robertsonian translocations does not seem to be increased in mentally retarded patients.

Another related phenomenon is represented by families in which the same balanced chromosome abnormality, translocation or inversion, is present in the phenotypically normal parent and the abnormal offspring.

This may result from the apparently balanced abnormality, in reality involving a small deletion, or at least the destruction of a gene that would give a recessive gene on the homologous chromosome the opportunity to express itself. A family that would fit this idea had both parents (first cousins) heterozygous carriers of the same paracentric inversion. One normal son had a similar chromosome constitution, whereas an abnormal son was homozygous for the inversion (Price et al., 1987). Nullosomy for one or more genes may have caused the abnormal phenotype of the homozygous son. Another hypothesis is that a position effect exists in which a gene functions differently in a new cytogenetic environment. However, very little is known about position effect in humans, although this phenomenon may play an important role in malignant transformation (Chapter 29).

Phenotypes of Unbalanced Translocation Carriers

An unbalanced translocation involves partial trisomy for one chromosome and partial monosomy for another, although the deleted segment may be very small or almost nonexistent if one of the breaks lies at a telomere. Trisomy and monosomy effects practically always include mental retardation and multiple congenital anomalies. The analysis of the symptoms is often made difficult by simultaneous monosomy and trisomy. By now, the chromosomes and phenotypes of thousands of unbalanced translocation carriers have been described. The reader is referred to the compendiums of Borgaonkar (1984), de Grouchy and Turleau (1984), and Schinzel (1984).

Even if breaks occurred exclusively in the Q-dark bands, the number of random interchanges would be enormous. However, the range of combinations that allow the birth of a live child is much more limited, since most sizable deletions are lethal, as are many duplications. It is obvious from any survey of the literature that this strong selection has led to a relatively high incidence of certain partial trisomies and monosomies, whereas others are extremely rare or nonexistent. The following parameters probably determine this unequal distribution: (1) the length of the segment involved; (2) the Q-darkness versus brightness of the segment; the more Q-dark a region is, the more severe are the effects of imbalance; (3) individual genes that may act as trisomy or monosomy lethals; and (4) special "hot spots," short Q-dark bands, which have been assumed to contain a high density of genes and which may also act as trisomy and monosomy lethals (Kuhn et al., 1987).

The observations made on partial 11q trisomy (Pihko et al., 1981) serve as an illustration of the last point. In 20 cases in which the trisomy ranged from most of 11q to 11q23→ter11q, there was no difference in the quality or quantity of the symptoms. The inevitable conclusion is that most—

possibly all—the symptoms are caused by trisomy for the short segment distal to 11q23. Similar studies on partial trisomies and monosomies for other chromosome arms would be of interest.

Minute duplications and deletions may be more important than thought earlier. In Fig. 26.1, the relevant chromosomes of a family with a very small reciprocal translocation, 3p;21p, are illustrated diagramatically (A Drewry, unpublished). Indeed, this exchange is so small that, but for the satellites on 3p, it would never have been discovered. The family had three carriers and four affected members in three generations. The symptoms that were caused by the minute deletion of 3p included mental retardation, sacral dimple, and abnormal ears and teeth (A Drewry, unpublished). In the carriers, the chromosomes 3 and 21 obviously form two bivalents, resulting, for once, in 1:1:1:1 segregation (normal: carrier: one type of unbalanced: another type of unbalanced). However, a family member with partial trisomy for 3p could not be cytologically ascertained, and such a minute duplication probably would not cause any recognizable symptoms.

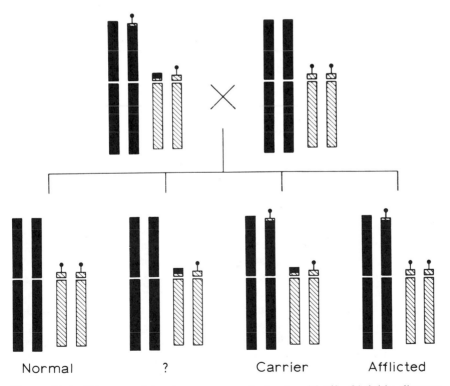

Figure 26.1. Diagram of the chromosomes of a family with t(3p;21p) (the diagram was drawn before the identity of the acrocentric was known). It is not known whether individuals with partial trisomy for 3p exist (courtesy of A Drewry).

Fetal Death

In many translocation families, the lethal effects of the various trisomies and/or monosomies are reflected in the increased rate of spontaneous abortions and stillbirths. Often a very early abortion remains unrecognized. Thus, a sizable translocation, 3q−;4p+, in the father, apparently resulted in his ultimate sterility after the birth of one normal carrier son (Sarto and Therman, 1976). In another family, Nuzzo et al. (1973) found a maternal translocation in which the entire 2q was attached to 1p, resulting in four recognized abortions and no live births.

The best data come from chromosome analyses of couples with repeated spontaneous abortions. Depending on the basis for selection of couples for such studies (the number of abortions, habitual abortion combined with abnormal offspring, whether other causes for abortion have been ruled out, etc.), from 0 to 31 percent of the couples had reciprocal translocations (Ward et al., 1980). In a review of studies on 1,331 couples, the incidence of Robertsonian and balanced translocations was 6.2 percent (Davis et al., 1982). Fryns et al. (1984), in a study of 1,068 couples with recurrent fetal loss, reported 33 (3.09%) reciprocal translocations, 20 (1.87%) Robertsonian translocations, and six (0.56%) other chromosome aberrations; a total of 59 (5.5%) abnormalities. Usually, the number of Robertsonian and reciprocal translocations found are about equal, and to these can be added a similar number of cases with X chromosome mosaicism.

Examples of Translocation Families

Families in which one parent is a balanced translocation carrier fall into the following classes: (1) those in which none of the possible abnormal offspring is viable; (2) those in which one type of offspring, usually the one with the smaller deletion, is born alive; and (3) those in which two types of abnormal offspring are viable. Only a few, rather arbitrarily chosen, translocation families are presented here, as examples.

Families in which all pregnancies end as spontaneous abortions have been mentioned in the previous section (for example, Nuzzo et al., 1973).

A typical representative of the second group was studied by Pihko et al. (1981; Fig. 26.2). The abnormal daughter was severely retarded mentally and showed diverse congenital anomalies. Chromosome analysis revealed a too-long 4q, whereas the mother and sister were balanced carriers of t(11q−;4q+). The spontaneous abortions were not available for cytogenetic studies, but it is possible that they represented other types of unbalanced chromosome constitutions. Since the segment from 11q is apparently attached to the very end of 4q, the symptoms of the proposita are probably caused mainly by trisomy for about one-half of 11q. Another

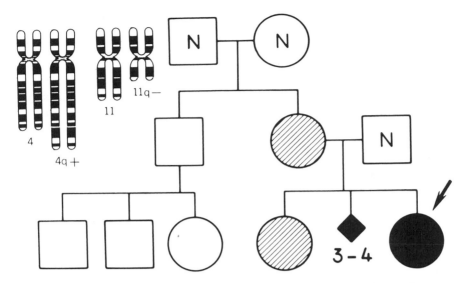

Figure 26.2. A family in which the mother and one daughter (shaded) were balanced carriers of t(4q+;11q−), one daughter (black) had the unbalanced translocation chromosome 4q+, and abortions possibly had 11q− in unbalanced state; N, chromosomes normal (Pihko et al., 1981).

similar family has been presented by Centerwall et al. (1976); here the segregation of t(9p−;14q+), in four generations, resulted in six affected individuals with partial trisomy 9p and four phenotypically normal carriers. Another typical result of a reciprocal translocation, 7q−;21q+, in a male was the birth of an abnormal daughter trisomic for the end region of 7q and a spontaneous abortion whose chromosome 7 displayed the corresponding deletion (Bass et al.,1973).

Fortunately, it is rare that more than one type of unbalanced offspring is born alive in the same translocation family. The occurrence of cri du chat syndrome and its trisomic "countertype" is discussed in Chapter 25. For a number of other translocations, a similar segregation has been described. To take a random example, Jacobsen et al. (1973) analyzed three generations of a family in which 14 normal carriers had t(11q−; 21q+), two abnormal segregants showed partial monosomy for 11q, and one had trisomy for the same segment. As might be expected, the monosomic individuals were more severely affected than was the trisomic one.

A 1:3 segregation (one of the four chromosomes goes to one pole while three go to the other) in a translocation carrier gives rise to unbalanced offspring with 45 or 47 chromosomes. Such disjunction is discussed in more detail in connection with the risk of abnormal offspring in translocation carriers. Eight kinds of offspring are possible from such a segregation. These include monosomy or trisomy for a normal chromosome.

An extra translocated chromosome combined with an otherwise normal complement (47 chromosomes) has been termed *tertiary trisomy*, and a 45-chromosome complement that includes an abnormal chromosome is *tertiary monosomy*.

Interchange trisomy implies that the two translocated chromosomes are present together with an extra normal chromosome (47 chromosomes) (Lindenbaum and Bobrow, 1975). A rare situation in which two different types of abnormal offspring resulted from 1:3 segregation is represented by a woman with t(9q−;21p+) who gave birth to one daughter with an extra 9p chromosome and to another who was 21-trisomic, in addition to a chromosomally normal daughter (Habedank and Faust, 1978). Her translocation had features that are known to promote this type of disjunction, namely, the chromosomes were of different size, one was acrocentric, and the breaks were near the centromere. Another reciprocal translocation that agrees with these rules and practically always segregates 1:3 is t(11;22)(q23;q22). In 72 families the mother was the carrier; in two, the father (Fraccaro et al., 1980; Zackai and Emanuel, 1980). Normals and balanced carriers were equally frequent in the offspring.

An interesting family with five abortions was studied cytologically by Kajii et al. (1974). Segregation in the father, who had a t(13q−;18q+), led to three chromosomally analyzed abortions; 47,+13(tertiary trisomy), 46,13q− (unbalanced translocation), and 47,t(13q−;18q+)+18 (interchange trisomy). The abortion with 46 chromosomes resulted from an adjacent-1, 2:2 disjunction (Fig. 26.3); the other two, from 1:3 segregations.

Meiosis in Translocation Carriers

Since homologous chromosome segments tend to pair in meiosis, even when one of them is translocated to another chromosome, the two normal and the two translocation chromosomes often form a group of four, which in some organisms can be seen as a cross-like figure in pachytene (Fig. 26.3). Very small translocated segments may remain unpaired or fail to form a chiasma. This results in the formation of two bivalents, or a group of three and a univalent. However, if one terminal chiasma is present in each arm of the pachytene cross, the metaphase configuration will be a ring of four (Fig. 26.3); or if a chiasma fails to form in one arm, the result will be a chain. A ring or chain of four may orient itself in different ways on the spindle.

An alternate orientation (Fig. 26.3) gives rise to one cell with normal chromosomes and to another with the translocation chromosomes. Adjacent-1 orientation (Fig. 26.3) leads to the formation of two unbalanced cells, each with one translocation chromosome. Adjacent-2 orientation (Fig. 26.3) gives rise to two cells that are usually even more unbalanced. Various types of 1:3 segregation are also possible, as dis-

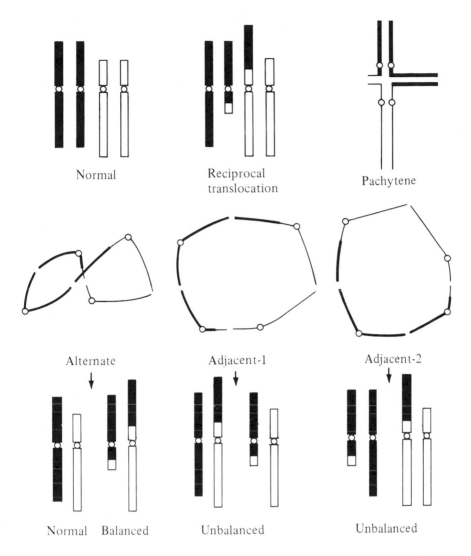

Figure 26.3. Reciprocal translocation between two chromosomes, pachytene configuration of the four chromosomes, and modes of orientation of a ring of four in metaphase I: alternate, adjacent-1, adjacent-2 (1:3 and 0:4 segregation, not shown). The gametes formed are: normal, balanced, two types of unbalanced (zygotes possibly viable), and two types of even more unbalanced (zygotes presumably nonviable). In adjacent-1 segregation, homologous centromeres separate; in adjacent-2 segregation, homologous centromeres go to the same pole.

cussed above. Sometimes two bivalents are formed, and their independent segregation produces equal numbers of normal, carrier, and two types of unbalanced gametes (Fig. 26.1). It should be stressed that there is no theoretical expectation for the segregation ratios of human reciprocal translocations, since the relative frequencies of the different orientations of a specific ring or chain are unknown, so we have to rely on empirical risk figures. Usually, however, complementary classes from the same orientation are equally frequent.

Genetic Risk for Translocation Carriers

One of the most important unbiased sources of reciprocal translocations is provided by studies of the newborn (Hook and Hamerton, 1977). In 56,952 infants, 51 balanced reciprocal and insertional translocations were found, which happens to be the number of balanced Robertsonian translocations in the same material (Table 26.1). This amounts to one balanced translocation per 1000 neonates. A much smaller number of unbalanced translocations or insertions, that is, seven (0.1/1000), was encountered in the same newborn population. Other findings of this study are given in Table 26.1.

It has been obvious for a long time that the risk figures for balanced translocation carriers having a subsequent chromosomally abnormal offspring are very different for translocation carriers ascertained by chance compared with those found through an unbalanced offspring. Trunca and Mendel (unpublished), in their analysis of 828 translocations, give the following figures. In the unbiased group, the risk for a chromosomally unbalanced child was 1.5 percent, and that for miscarriage or stillbirth,

Table 26.1. Chromosome abnormalities in 56,952 newborn infants.[a]

Abnormality	Incidence (per 1000 neonates)
Aneuploidy (including mosaicism)	
Sex chromosomes[b]	
Males	2.61
Females	1.51
Autosomes	1.44
Structural abnormalities	
Balanced Robertsonian translocations	0.90
Balanced translocations	0.90
Unbalanced Robertsonian translocations	0.07
Unbalanced translocations	0.12
Other structural abnormalities	0.55
Total	6.05

[a] Modified from Hook and Hamerton, 1977.
[b] Numbers apply to infants of the relevant sex.

25.0 percent. On the other hand, when the reciprocal translocation was ascertained through a chromosomally unbalanced child, the risk for further chromosomally unbalanced offspring was 16.2 percent, and for a miscarriage or stillbirth, 25.1 percent. Whatever the ascertainment of the reciprocal translocation, the ratio of normal to balanced carrier offspring is about 1:1 (Trunca and Mendel, unpublished), since these are complementary and usually both are normal.

The risk figures for different types of translocations depend on the pachytene configuration that the four chromosomes form. This again is determined by the shape of the chromosomes, the distances of the breakpoints from the centromere (interstitial segment) and from the telomeres; these distances, in turn, affect the probability of crossing-over in the exchanged and the interstitial segments. The orientation of a translocation quadrivalent has been directly studied in the meiosis of many organisms, but not in humans (Lewis and John, 1963).

In humans the orientation can be concluded from the empirical risk figures obtained from a large number of translocation families (Trunca and Mendel, unpublished). According to Trunca and Mendel, the types of segregation taking place in the variously constructed pachytene configurations are the following:

1. The interstitial segments are so short that they do not form chiasmata. Of ten abnormal children, six were the result of adjacent-1, and four of adjacent-2 segregation.
2. In the families in which at least one interstitial segment was expected to have a chiasma, 390 of 395 abnormal offspring resulted from an adjacent-1 segregation.
3. When the translocated segments are very short, the four chromosomes will form a chain or two bivalents. In such families, of 530 unbalanced offspring, 525 were the result of an adjacent-1 segregation.
4. When the non-exchanged part is very short, thus being unable to form a chiasma, the resulting chain is expected to undergo an adjacent-2 segregation. Indeed, 30 of 36 children in this group resulted from this type of segregation.
5. The following factors seem to favor 1:3 over 2:2 segregation: one of the chromosomes is acrocentric, at least one break is near the centromere, and the participating chromosomes are very unequal in size; in other words, the pachytene configuration is highly asymmetrical (Lindenbaum and Bobrow, 1975; Trunca and Mendel, unpublished). In this group, 77 chromosomally abnormal children were found, of whom 50 had 45 or 47 chromosome constitutions. When the pachytene cross was relatively symmetrical, only 19.8 percent of the chromosomally abnormal children resulted from a 1:3 segregation.

The translocations for which 1:3 segregation has been observed involve the chromosomes very nonrandomly. Thus, interchange trisomy has been found only for chromosomes 18, 21, and 22, whereas 9p seems to be preferred in tertiary trisomy (Lindenbaum and Bobrow, 1975).

About 90 percent of the chromosomally unbalanced children resulting from 1:3 disjunction have been born to carrier mothers. The risks for further unbalanced liveborn offspring when the family has been ascertained through a 1:3 segregant are in the same range as for families that have been detected through an unbalanced 2:2 segregant, that is, 10 to 20 percent for a carrier mother, and 0 percent for a carrier father (Lindenbaum and Bobrow, 1975).

The overall risks of abnormal offspring for male and female carriers are different (Trunca and Mendel, unpublished). For males (996 carriers), the risk was 6.6 percent; for females (1539 carriers), 11.9 percent.

The highest and the lowest risks are found in the following translocation groups (Trunca and Mendel, unpublished). If the exchanged segments are so short that crossing-over rarely takes place in either side-arm of a pachytene cross, resulting in a chain or two bivalents, the risk for a live-born abnormal child is 21.0 percent, and for a miscarriage or stillbirth, 25.7 percent. The low-risk group consists of carriers of translocations in which the exchanged segments are relatively long, and the interstitial segments short, leading to the formation of a ring. The risks in this group are 2.5 percent for a live-born, chromosomally abnormal child, and 33.7 percent for a miscarriage or stillbirth.

The risk of abnormal offspring in the high-risk group was 17 percent for male carriers and 19.7 percent for females. In the low-risk group, the corresponding numbers were 0 percent for the males and 4 percent for the females. The risk for stillbirths and miscarriages in the high-risk group was 28.9 percent for the males and 24.5 percent for the females, whereas the corresponding numbers in the low-risk group were 28.3 percent for the males and 40.2 percent for the females (Trunca and Mendel, unpublished).

Sperm Chromosomes in Meiotic Segregation Analysis

In the last few years, the study of sperm has greatly increased the accuracy of meiotic segregation analysis. The most important groups of balanced carriers are those of reciprocal translocations, Robertsonian translocations, and inversions. Sperm chromosomes are made visible by fertilizing hamster eggs with human sperm (Martin, 1988b). This technique allows a direct analysis of the results of the meiotic process, whereas fetal or newborn chromosomes have undergone severe selection before they come under study. A disadvantage of the sperm technique is that, since it requires a great deal of work, only a limited number of sperm from a still more limited number of carriers can be analyzed (Martin, 1988a; 1989). In 1989, the sperm chromosomes of 13 translocation carriers (one had two reciprocal translocations) had been investigated (Martin, 1989;

Pellestor et al., 1989). In addition, chromosomes from carriers of four Robertsonian translocations and two inversions, as well as from five other males, had been analyzed. Since that time, a few more carriers have been added to the list (Martin et al., 1990; Templado et al., 1990; Martin, 1991).

In the 13 translocation carriers, all segregation types (alternate, adjacent-1, adjacent-2, 3:1, and 4:0) were found, whereas the 4:0 segregation has never resulted in a fetus or live-born child (Martin, 1988a, 1989). The segregations that give rise to unbalanced gametes are found much more frequently than in observations on fetuses or newborns, although the results vary greatly (from 19% to 70%) among different translocation carriers.

Interchromosomal effects mean that the behavior of one chromosome affects the behavior of a non-homologous chromosome. The possible occurrence of this phenomenon in humans will be discussed in Chapter 27.

References

Bass HN, Crandall BF, Marcy SM (1973) Two different chromosome abnormalities resulting from a translocation carrier father. J Pediatr 83:1034–1038

Bijlsma JB, deFrance HF, Bleeker-Wagenmakers LM, et al. (1978) Double translocation t(7;12), t(2;6) heterozygosity in one family. A contribution to the trisomy 12p syndrome. Hum Genet 40:135–137

Borgaonkar DS (1984) Chromosomal variation in man: a catalog of chromosomal variants and anomalies, 4th edn. Liss, New York

Burnham CR (1962) Discussions in cytogenetics. Burgess, Minneapolis

Centerwall WR, Miller KS, Reeves LM (1976) Familial "partial 9p" trisomy: six cases and four carriers in three generations. J Med Genet 13:57–61

Davis JR, Weinstein L, Veomett IC, et al. (1982) Balanced translocation karyotypes in patients with repetitive abortion. Am J Obstet Gynecol 144:229–233

Fitzgerald PH, Miethke P, Caseley RT (1977) Major karyotypic abnormality in a child born to a woman with untreated malignant melanoma. Clin Genet 12:155–161

Fraccaro M, Lindsten J, Ford CE, et al. (1980) The 11q;22q translocation: a European collaborative analysis of 43 cases. Hum Genet 56:21–51

Fryns JP, Kleczkowska A, Kubien E, et al. (1984) Cytogenetic survey in couples with recurrent fetal wastage. Hum Genet 65:336–354

Funderburk SJ, Spence MA, Sparkes RS (1977) Mental retardation associated with "balanced" chromosome rearrangements. Am J Hum Genet 29:136–141

Gorski JL, Kistenmacher ML, Punnett HH, et al. (1988) Reproductive risks for carriers of complex chromosome rearrangements: analysis of 25 families. Am J Med Genet 29:247–261

Grouchy J de, Turleau C (1984) Clinical atlas of human chromosomes, 2nd edn. Wiley, New York

Habedank M, Faust J (1978) Trisomy 9p and unusual translocation mongolism in siblings due to different 3:1 segregations of maternal translocation rcp(9;21) (p11;q11). Hum Genet 42:251–256

Hook EB, Hamerton JL (1977) The frequency of chromosome abnormalities detected in consecutive newborn studies—differences between studies—results by sex and by severity of phenotypic involvement. In: Hook EB, Porter IH (eds) Population cytogenetics. Academic, New York, pp 63–79

Jacobsen P, Hauge M, Henningsen K, et al. (1973) An (11;21) translocation in four generations with chromosome 11 abnormalities in the offspring. Hum Hered 22:568–585

Kajii T, Meylan J, Mikamo K (1974) Chromosome anomalies in three successive abortuses due to paternal translocation, t(13q–;18q+). Cytogenet Cell Genet 13:426–436

Kousseff BG, Nichols P, Essig Y-P, et al. (1987) Complex chromosome rearrangements and congenital anomalies. Am J Med Genet 26:771–782

Kuhn EM, Sarto GE, Bates B-J G, et al. (1987) Gene-rich chromosome regions and autosomal trisomy. A case of chromosome 3 trisomy mosaicism. Hum Genet 77:214–220

Lande R (1979) Effective deme sizes during long-term evolution estimated from rates of chromosomal rearrangement. Evolution 33:234–251

Lewis KR, John B (1963) Spontaneous interchange in *Chorthippus brunneus*. Chromosoma 14:618–637

Lindenbaum RH, Bobrow M (1975) Reciprocal translocations in man. 3:1 meiotic disjunction resulting in 47- or 45- chromosome offspring. J Med Genet 12:29–43

Martin RH (1988a) Abnormal spermatozoa in human translocation and inversion carriers. In: Daniel A (ed) The cytogenetics of mammalian autosomal rearrangements. Liss, New York, pp 319–417

Martin RH (1988b) Human sperm karyotyping: a tool for the study of aneuploidy. In: Vig BK, Sandberg AA (eds) Aneuploidy, Part B: Induction and test systems. Liss, New York, pp 297–316

Martin RH (1989) Invited editorial: Segregation analysis of translocations by the study of human sperm chromosome complements. Am J Hum Genet 44:461–463

Martin RH (1991) Cytogenetic analysis of sperm from a man heterozygous for a pericentric inversion, inv(3)(p25q21). Am J Hum Genet 48:856–861

Martin RH, McGillivray B, Barclay L, et al. (1990) Sperm chromosome analysis in a man heterozygous for a reciprocal translocation 46,XY t(12;20)(q24.3;q11). Hum Reprod 5:606–609

Meer B, Wolff G, Back E (1981) Segregation of a complex rearrangement of chromosomes 6, 7, 8 and 12 through three generations. Hum Genet 58:221–225

Nuzzo F, Giorgi R, Zuffardi O, et al. (1973) Translocation t(1p+;2q–) associated with recurrent abortion. Ann Genet 16:211–214

Palmer CG, Poland C, Reed T, et al. (1976) Partial trisomy 11, 46,XX,–3,–20, +der3, +der20, t(3:11:20), resulting from a complex maternal rearrangement of chromosomes 3, 11, 20. Hum Genet 31:219–225

Pellestor F, Sèle B, Jalbert H, et al. (1989) Direct segregation analysis of reciprocal translocations: a study of 283 sperm karyotypes from four carriers. Am J Hum Genet 44:464–473

Pihko H, Therman E, Uchida IA (1981) Partial 11q trisomy syndrome. Hum Genet 58:129–134

Price HA, Roberts SH, Laurence KM (1987) Homozygous paracentric inversion 12 in a mentally retarded boy: a case report and review of the literature. Hum Genet 75:101–108

Sarto GE, Therman E (1976) Large translocation t(3q−;4p+) as probable cause for semisterility. Fertil Steril 27:784–788

Schinzel A (1984) Catalogue of unbalanced chromosome aberrations in man. De Gruyter, Berlin

Templado C, Navarro J, Requena R, et al. (1990) Meiotic and sperm chromosome studies in a reciprocal translocation t(1;2) (q32;q36). Hum Genet 84:159–162

Trunca C, Weiner D, Kaplan A (1981) The meiotic behavior of reciprocal translocations. Am J Hum Genet 33:124A

Ward BE, Henry GP, Robinson A (1980) Cytogenetic studies in 100 couples with recurrent spontaneous abortions. Am J Hum Genet 32:549–554

White MJD (1978) Modes of speciation. Freeman, San Francisco

Zackai EH, Emanuel BS (1980) Site-specific reciprocal translocation, t(11;22) (q23;q11), in several unrelated families with 3:1 meiotic disjunction. Am J Med Genet 7:507–521

27
Robertsonian Translocations

Occurrence

Robertsonian translocations (RTs) refer to the recombination of whole chromosome arms. Such translocations take place most often between acrocentric or telocentric chromosomes. They have played an important role in the evolution of both plants and animals, as demonstrated by organisms within a population, a species, or in closely related species that have different chromosome numbers but the same number of chromosome arms. Searle (1988) has mentioned many studies on the occurrence of RT in various mammals, including mouse, shrew, antelope, vole, mole rat, and lemur. In particular, the common shrew (*Sorex araneus*), in which 14 chromosomal races have been found, has been extensively studied. These races, which differ in number and combination of RT, range geographically from Aberdeen, Scotland to Krasnoyarsk, Siberia.

Although RTs are the most common structurally abnormal chromosomes in humans, whole-arm transfers between human chromosomes other than the acrocentrics seem to be extremely rare; only a couple of cases have been reported. One reason for this scarcity may be that such translocations are not ascertained through abnormal offspring, since monosomy for one chromosome arm combined with trisomy for another would be lethal (Schober and Fonatsch, 1978; Niikawa and Ishikawa, 1983). However, whole-arm transfers between nonacrocentric chromosomes are not found in unselected populations either. In the following discussion, the term Robertsonian translocation (RT) will be used to describe a whole-arm transfer between acrocentrics.

RTs, as a rule, do not affect the phenotype of a balanced carrier, apart from occasional male sterility. Individuals with 45 chromosomes including an RT between two long arms are called balanced. That the deletion of the short arms of the acrocentrics does not have any damaging effects is an indication that, apart from the rRNA genes, they are heterochromatic.

The relatively high observed frequency of RTs probably reflects their high population incidence. On the other hand, the probability of their ascertainment is increased by their familial occurrence. For instance, in unselected material, 85 to 95 percent of DqDq translocations are familial (Nielsen and Rasmussen, 1976).

The different modes of formation of RTs between two acrocentric chromosomes are shown diagrammatically in Fig. 9.5. One chromosome may break through the short arm and the other through the long arm near the centromere, or both may break through the centromere. In both cases, the result is one long and one short monocentric chromosome. If both chromosomes have a break in the short arm, one dicentric and one acentric chromosome are formed. One or both acrocentrics may also break through the satellite stalk, in which case the translocation chromosome has a nucleolar organizing region in the middle (Mikkelsen et al., 1980). The mechanics of the formation of RTs are discussed, for instance, by John and Freeman (1975).

Monocentric and Dicentric Chromosomes

Banding techniques demonstrate unequivocally that both monocentric (Fig. 27.1) and dicentric RTs exist (Niebuhr, 1972). However, in individual cases it is often difficult to distinguish between the two. This is not made easier by the fact that one centromere in a dicentric is often inactivated, which means that its site is not marked by a constriction (Niebuhr, 1972). However, even if both centromeres are functioning this does not, as a rule, lead to aberrations in mitosis, since there is almost never a twist between them.

The small chromosome consisting of the short arms of two acrocentrics is usually, but not invariably, lost. The occurrence of such small bisatellited chromosomes, in addition to the normal chromosome complement, was mentioned in Chapter 25. Among 11,148 Danish newborn infants, six with such chromosomes were found, giving a frequency of 0.54/1000 (Nielsen and Rasmussen, 1975). Palmer et al. (1969) described a rare family with both a DqDq and a DpDp chromosome. Four family members had both, whereas two had only the longer chromosome. Furthermore, Abeliovich et al. (1985) reported a family in which the balanced mother and a daughter with Down syndrome had both the long and the bisatellited small chromosome.

Isochromosomes resulting from misdivision of the centromere cannot be distinguished from RTs between two homologous chromosomes on morphological grounds. However, the history of the chromosome often

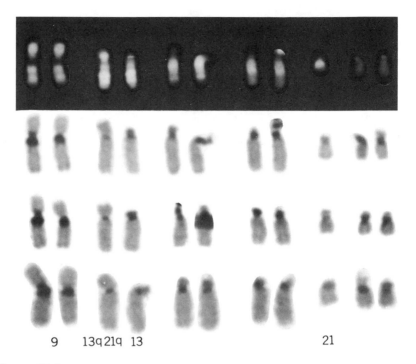

Figure 27.1. Partial karyotypes of a woman with 45,XX,t(13q21q), representing a family with many carriers and several Down syndrome children. One chromosome 9 has a large, partially inverted C-band. The translocation chromosome, 13q21q, has one short C-band and is monocentric (Sarto and Therman, unpublished).

allows a determination to be made. If a person has one normal cell line and another with 46 chromosomes including one free 21 and a metacentric consisting of two chromosomes 21, the latter is obviously an isochromosome. On the other hand, in a mosaic with a normal cell line and another with 45,t(21q21q), an RT can be taken for granted. In a family studied in our laboratory, in which three children had Down syndrome, the father was such a mosaic, and the affected children had 46,t(21q21q). Mosaics with a telocentric and an isochromosome for a Dq or a Gq, which arise through misdivision of the centromere, have been discussed in Chapter 19.

Even more complicated mosaics involving RTs have been encountered. Thus, in two children with features of Down syndrome, one cell line had 45 chromosomes with a 15q21q translocation, whereas the other showed 46 chromosomes, including a 21q21q chromosome (Atkins and Bartsocas, 1974; Vianna-Morgante and Nunesmaia, 1978). A few individuals with two RTs have been described (for example, Orye and Delire, 1967; Cohen et al., 1968). Also, a therapeutically aborted fetus had 44 chromosomes, including two t(14q21q) chromosomes (Rockman-Greenberg et al., 1982). However, one normal woman with two RTs has been described (Morgan et al., 1985). Furthermore, in a family in which the parents were first cousins and heterozygous carriers of a t(13q14q), three of the children had 44 chromosomes, including two such translocation chromosomes (Martinez-Castro et al., 1984). Both the heterozygotes and the homozygotes were apparently normal in this family. In cases in which heterozygous or homozygous carriers do have abnormalities, one cause could be a scarcity of rRNA genes since the incidence of transcribed regions varies between six and ten even in normal persons (Mikelsaar et al., 1977).

Nonrandom Participation of Acrocentric Chromosomes in RTs

Therman et al. (1989) collected RTs from the literature through August 1987 (Table 27.1). When more than one family member had the same translocation, it was counted as one translocation. All possible acrocentric combinations were found, but the chromosomes took part in RT in a highly nonrandom way. The 1266 translocations with clear ascertainments were classified: unbiased (column 1), trisomy 21 (column 2), trisomy 13 (column 3), infertility and repeated abortions (column 4), unspecified mental retardation (column 5), and Prader-Willi syndrome (column 6). In the combined material (column 7), the RTs most frequently found were 13q14q and 14q21q, with 21q21q the third in frequency.

Unbiased ascertainment

The unbiased cases (Table 27.1) were found in consecutive newborn surveys, in controls of various population studies, in amniocenteses performed because of maternal age or some other unrelated reason, and by chance. In this group, also, 13q14q was the most frequent combination, with 14q21q and 21q21q second and third, indicative that these RTs arise more often than the others.

Ascertainment through trisomy

In the group ascertained through 21 trisomy (column 2), the leading combination is 14q21q, whereas 13q21q and 15q21q are much rarer. The second group in frequency is 21q21q. In cases found through 13 trisomy (column 3), the predominant combination is 13q14q, and a smaller group consists of 13q13q. It should be noted that to our knowledge no individual with 22 trisomy has been found through an RT.

Table 27.1. Robertsonian translocations by chromosome type and ascertainment bias[a]

Chromosome	(1) Unbiased	Ascertainment Bias					(7) Totals with ascertainment	(8) Totals all cases
		(2) Trisomy 21	(3) Trisomy 13	(4) Infertility	(5) Mental retardation	(6) Prader-Willi		
13/13	4	0	26	9	1	0	40	43
14/14	0	0	0	9	0	0	9	9
15/15	0	0	0	12	3	9	24	24
21/21	5	231	0	1	2	0	239	245
22/22	0	0	0	13	3	0	16	16
13/14	147	0	61	149	45	0	402	479
13/15	4	0	4	10	5	2	25	28
13/21	2	19	1	1	1	0	24	32
13/22	4	0	3	0	0	0	7	11
14/15	9	0	0	7	11	1	28	34
14/21	16	323	0	18	11	0	368	447
14/22	4	0	0	8	2	0	14	18
15/21	1	30	0	3	1	0	35	46
15/22	3	0	0	4	1	1	9	9
21/22	1	23	0	2	0	0	26	30
Totals	200	626	86	246	95	13	1266	1471

[a] Modified from Therman et al., 1989.

Ascertainment through infertility

The patients in this group (column 4) fall into two classes: those ascertained through repeated abortions and those ascertained through infertility, the latter especially affecting males. Of the 246 cases, 56 were found through infertility, and in 51 of these chromosome 14 was involved. It was proposed that the male infertility is caused by a small deletion at the breakpoint in 14q (Therman et al., 1989). If this hypothesis is true, these RT chromosomes should be monocentric. Previous studies have also established that RTs may cause male infertility. In their review, Zuffardi and Tiepolo (1982) reported that, in patients at infertility clinics, RTs were about ten times more frequent than in the newborn population. One mechanism that might account for this phenomenon is the tendency of RTs to attach to the sex vesicle, which might prevent the inactivation of the sex chromosomes in male meiosis (Luciani et al., 1987; Guichaoua et al., 1990). The most frequent RT combination in column 4 is 13q14q, with 14q21q the next most frequent. Carriers of t(14q14q), t(15q15q) and t(22q22q) have had only abortions. A number of 21- and 13-trisomic embryos also end as abortions.

Ascertainment through unspecified mental retardation

This group (column 5), ascertained through unspecified mental retardation and/or other anomalies not representing known trisomies, is obviously heterogeneous. The anomalies probably are often incidental to the RT.

Ascertainment through Prader-Willi syndrome

In all 13 cases (column 6) ascertained through this syndrome, one or both participating acrocentrics were chromosome 15. Other studies have pinpointed the Prader-Willi factor to the pericentric region of this chromosome. About half the observed Prader-Willi patients have chromosome abnormalities. Of these, most are a deletion in the centric region of chromosome 15; reciprocal translocations or duplications involving this region are also found (Ledbetter et al., 1982; Mattei et al., 1984 Butler, 1990).

Causes of Nonrandom Participation of Chromosomes in RTs

Robertsonian translocations display features that distinguish them from other reciprocal translocations: (1) Ionizing radiation and chromosome-breaking substances do not seem to increase the incidence of RTs. On the other hand, certain substances, such as mitomycin C, preferentially cause whole-arm transfers (Hsu et al., 1978). (2) Unlike other translocations, which take place more or less randomly between different chromosomes, the participation of the acrocentrics in RT is extremely nonrandom (Table 27.1).

Most of the differences between Robertsonian and other translocations can be explained on the assumption that the former, as a rule, are the result of exchange in meiosis or mitosis, and not of breakage and rejoining. Possibly the repeated sequences in the centric regions have an indiscriminate tendency to pair, and crossing-over in a reversely paired segment or a U-type exchange would lead to whole-arm transfers. This would be the mechanism producing the baseline number of RTs in the different classes (Table 27.1). The behavior of chromosomes 13, 14, and 21, on the other hand, is understandable if we assume that they have a homologous segment in common (A–B in Fig. 27.2), which is inverted in chromosome 14 relative to the two others. Crossing-over in the inverted region between chromosomes 13 and 14, and chromosomes 14 and 21, respectively, would give rise to t(13q14q) and t(14q21q), which are the common types of RT. However, since RTs between chromosomes 13 and 21 are not increased, the segment that is inverted in 13 and 14 is probably different from the inverted segment common to 14 and 21.

Although satellite associations probably constitute the mechanism that brings acrocentric chromosomes together, they do not seem to play a role in the nonrandomness of the chromosomes participating in RTs (Jacobs et al., 1976; Therman et al., 1989).

Results of molecular studies on pericentric regions of acrocentric chromosomes have been reviewed by Choo et al. (1988), Therman et al. (1989), and Cheung et al. (1990). So far, such analyses have not explained

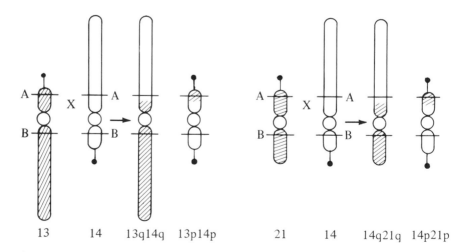

13   14   13q14q   13p14p   21   14   14q21q   14p21p

Figure 27.2. Origin of Robertsonian translocations 13q14q and 14q21q through crossing-over in segment A–B that is inverted in chromosome 14 relative to chromosomes 13 and 21.

the nonrandom acrocentric combinations in RTs. However, they map the road that may lead to a more accurate understanding of this phenomenon.

Segregation in Carriers of Robertsonian Translocations

The existing information on segregation ratios in DqDq and DqGq carriers is summarized in Table 27.2. All the offspring of a 13q13q and 21q21q carrier are 13 trisomic and 21 trisomic, respectively. Even a family with eight Down syndrome children, in which the mother was a 21q21q carrier, has been described (Furbetta et al., 1973).

It should be stressed that a carrier of a translocation between two homologous chromosomes can have only abnormal offspring or spontaneous abortions. Thus, in a woman who was ascertained because she had four spontaneous abortions, the two chromosomes 7 had formed a t(7p7p) and a t(7q7q) (Niikawa and Ishikawa, 1983). Furthermore, practically all carriers of t(14q14q), t(15q15q), and t(22q22q) have been identified because they have had only spontaneous abortions. However, an unexpected outcome was observed in two families (Kirkels et al., 1980; Palmer et al., 1980). In both, a phenotypically normal woman with 45,XX,t(22q22q) gave birth to a daughter with the same chromosome constitution. In these extremely rare cases, either the sperm was monosomic for chromosome 22 or the extra 22 in the daughters was lost at a very early stage.

The risk figures for producing unbalanced offspring are somewhat different, depending on the mode of ascertainment. Whatever the ascertainment bias, the probability of producing a healthy carrier is 50 percent for 13q14q, 14q21q, and 21q22q translocation carriers (Table 27.2). Surprisingly, in the European Collective Study of Parental Diagnosis, a surplus of paternally derived balanced t(13q14q) carriers was found (Boué and Gallano, 1984). In families found in unselected populations, such as newborn infants, the risk for unbalanced offspring is less than in families ascertained through an affected member. There is general agreement with the statement by Evans et al. (1978, p. 112): "In conclusion, this and

Table 27.2. Segregation in carriers of Robertsonian translocations[a]

Translocation	Risk of Unbalanced Offspring (%)		Probability of Healthy Carrier (%)
	Female carrier	Male carrier	
13qDq (mostly 14)	<1	Very low	50
13q13q	100	100	0
Dq21q (mostly 14)	10	Very low, estimated 2.4	50
21q22q	6.8	Upper limit 2.9	50
21q21q	100	100	0

[a] Data from Hamerton, 1970; Mikkelsen, 1971; and Chapman et al., 1973.

other similar studies suggest that when ascertained in a family by chance, both balanced reciprocal and Robertsonian, except t(14q21q), translocations carry a low risk of producing a congenitally malformed offspring."

For any carrier of a 13q14q translocation, the risk is very low. Hamerton (1970) estimated the risk for a 13qDq carrier to be 0.67 percent, usually quoted as less than 1 percent. Low as this figure is, it is still higher than the risk for the general population, in which estimates of the incidence of 13-trisomic children range from 0.005 percent to 0.02 percent. It should also be remembered that this risk figure (<1 percent) is based on one 13-trisomic offspring, who was not a proband (Hamerton, 1970).

Most information on segregation of Robertsonian translocations comes from families ascertained through an individual with Down syndrome (Table 27.2). The risk figure for a female Dq21q carrier is about 10 percent. The risk for a male carrier is much lower. It has been estimated by Hamerton (1971) to be 2.4 percent, but this figure is based on a very small number of cases. The latest risk figure, 6.8 percent, for a female carrier of a t(21q22q) has been determined by Chapman et al. (1973). For a male carrier, the estimated upper limit for the risk is 2.9 percent.

The considerable difference in the risk of 13qDq and Dq21q carriers producing unbalanced offspring is assumed to depend on an alternate meiotic configuration, being symmetrical for the former and asymmetrical for the latter (Fig. 27.3). Segregation in the configuration formed by a DqDq translocation would, as a rule, result in one cell with the translocation chromosome and another with the two free chromosomes. In the meiotic configuration formed by Dq21q, the free 21 would be near the same pole as the translocation and would, therefore, sometimes undergo adjacent segregation. Probably also because 21 is smaller than a D chromosome, it would more often fail to form a chiasma and drift at random in the first meiotic anaphase. This may explain the observation that, although the alternate meiotic configuration formed by 21q22q is symmetrical, the risk for unbalanced offspring is much higher than for a DqDq carrier. Another factor that may influence the empirical risk figures is the possibility that more 13-trisomic than 21-trisomic zygotes end as abortions.

Segregation in Sperm Cells of RT Carriers

Pellestor (1990) has reviewed the segregation of chromosomes in carriers of RTs, studied by using in vitro sperm penetration of hamster eggs. The five carriers included two males with t(13q14q) and one each with t(13q15q), t(14q21q), and t(21q22q). The ratio of normal and balanced chromosome constitutions does not differ from 1:1 except in the t(14q21q) carrier. This may depend on the small number of sperm analyzed or on the fact that this translocation is asymmetrical, in contrast to the others, which are

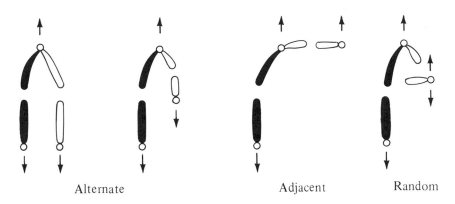

Figure 27.3. Different modes of meiotic orientation and segregation of Robertsonian translocations. Alternate segregation of t(DqDq) or t(DqGq) results in normals and carriers (1:1); adjacent segregation of t(DqGq) in trisomy and monosomy of G (1:1), and random drifting of univalent G in all four types (1:1:1:1).

symmetrical. The unbalanced chromosome constitutions range from 7.7 percent to 27.0 percent, with a mean of 15.8 percent. This is considerably higher than the frequency, 5.1 percent, of unbalanced embryos found in prenatal diagnoses performed when one parent is a known RT carrier (Boué and Gallano, 1984). Apparently, there is a strong selection against unbalanced carriers in the time, between sperm and embryo, as well as between embryo and live-born child.

Interchromosomal Effects

By *interchromosomal effects* are meant the influences certain abnormal chromosomes may have on the behavior of nonhomologous chromosomes. Such effects have been established, for instance, in *Drosophila* (Oksala, 1958).

In the human, interchromosomal effects have been claimed for various structurally abnormal chromosomes. Thus, very large heterochromatic blocks, for instance in chromosome 9, have been thought to promote nondisjunction of other chromosomes (Verma and Dosik, 1980). A similar claim has been made for inversions (Kaiser, 1980). Reciprocal translocations have also been reported to increase the risk of nondisjunction of other chromosomes. Thus, Lindenbaum et al. (1985) found that when a family was selected through a 21-trisomic child, the parents had a significantly higher frequency of balanced reciprocal translocations but not of RTs, unrelated to chromosome 21. Martin (1988), who reviewed the evidence for interchromosomal effects in sperm, found that only in a carrier of two balanced translocations were unrelated chromosome abnormalities significantly increased (Burns et al., 1986). These observations may mean that only some exceptional chromosome aberrations have interchromosomal effects.

Reports of interchromosomal effects exerted by RTs have all but vanished from the literature. In 1971, Mikkelsen claimed that a carrier of a t(DqDq) has a 2 percent risk of having a 21-trisomic child. On the other hand, Harris et al. (1979), who analyzed segregation in 86 families with t(13q14q), found no chromosomally unbalanced offspring. In Table 27.1, in all cases ascertained through 13- or 21-trisomy, the relevant chromosome was involved in the RT, which excludes interchromosomal effects in this material (Therman et al., 1989). This is borne out by the sperm chromosome analysis in five carriers of RTs, discussed above (Pellestor, 1990). Chromosome abnormalities not related to the translocations were not increased, compared with males with normal chromosome constitutions. RTs, thus, do not seem to exert interchromosomal effects (Therman et al., 1989; Pellestor, 1990). For reciprocal translocations, there is more evidence for such effects (Lindenbaum et al., 1985; Couzin et al., 1987). However, the evidence is, in part, anecdotal, and more studies are needed in this field.

Conclusions

The nonrandom participation of acrocentric chromosomes in RTs depends on an originally nonrandom formation of RTs and the mode of ascertainment (Table 27.1). The hypothesis that best fits the observations presumes that a basic frequency of the different RT types arises through adjacent chromatid exchanges, corresponding to mitotic chiasmata. The predominance of t(13q14q) and t(14q21q), even in unbiased material, is explained by the assumption that chromosome 14 has different inverted segments relative to each of the other two chromosomes. Crossing-over between two inverted segments gives rise to an RT.

High-resolution chromosome banding, quantitative banding studies (Drets et al., 1990), exact determinations of centromere number, and molecular studies should contribute to a better understanding of RT formation. An interesting problem is how the different acrocentrics are able to retain their specific structures in spite of unequal exchanges.

RTs do not seem to have interchromosomal effects. Whether extreme heterochromatic variants, reciprocal translocations, and inversions exert such effects are still open questions.

It is also not clear whether a monocentric RT and the corresponding dicentric RT have similar segregation ratios, or whether t(13q21q), t(14q21q), and t(15q21q), for instance, have the same probability of causing the birth of 21-trisomic offspring.

Still another question is whether the scarcity of rRNA genes, which may be the result of RT formation (especially the formation of two RTs), induces phenotypic abnormalities and even prenatal death.

References

Abeliovich D, Katz M, Karplus M, et al. (1985) A de novo translocation, 14q21q, with a microchromosome—14p21p. Am J Med Genet 22:29–33

Atkins L, Bartsocas CS (1974) Down's syndrome associated with two Robertsonian translocations, 45,XX,−15,−21, + t(15q21q) and 46,XX,−21, + t(21q21q). J Med Genet 11:306–309

Boué A, Gallano P (1984) A collaborative study of the segregation of inherited chromosome structural rearrangements in 1356 prenatal diagnoses. Prenat Diag 4:45–67

Burns JP, Koduru PRK, Alonso ML, et al. (1986) Analysis of meiotic segregation in a man heterozygous for two reciprocal translocations using the hamster in vitro penetration system. Am J Hum Genet 38:954–964

Butler MG (1990) Prader-Willi syndrome:current understanding of course and diagnosis. Am J Med Genet 35:319–332

Chapman CJ, Gardner RJM, Veale AMO (1973) Segregation analysis of a large t(21q22q) family. J Med Genet 10:362–366

Cheung SW, Sun L, Featherstone T (1990) Molecular cytogenetic evidence to characterize breakpoint regions in Robertsonian translocations. Cytogenet Cell Genet 54:97–102

Choo KH, Vissel B, Brown R, et al. (1988) Homologous alpha satellite sequences on human acrocentric chromosomes with selectivity for chromosomes 13, 14, and 21: implications for recombination between nonhomologues and Robertsonian translocations. Nucleic Acids Res 16:1273–1284

Cohen MM, Takagi N, Harrod EK (1968) Trisomy D_1 with two D/D translocation chromosomes. Am J Dis Child 115:185–190

Couzin DA, Watt JL, Stephen GS (1987) Structural rearrangements in the parents of children with primary trisomy 21. J Med Genet 24:280–282

Drets ME, Folle GA, Monteverde FJ (1990) Quantitative detection of chromosome structures by computerized microphotometric scanning. In: Obe G, Natarajan AT (eds) Chromosomal aberrations:basic and applied aspects. Springer, Berlin, pp 1–12

Evans JA, Canning N, Hunter AGW, et al. (1978) A cytogenetic survey of 14,069 newborn infants. III. An analysis of the significance and cytologic behavior of the Robertsonian and reciprocal translocations. Cytogenet Cell Genet 20:96–123

Furbetta M, Falorni A, Antignani P, et al. (1973) Sibship (21q21q) translocation Down's syndrome with maternal transmission. J Med Genet 10:371–375

Guichaoua MR, Quack B, Speed RM, et al. (1990) Infertility in human males with autosomal translocations: meiotic study of a 14;22 Robertsonian translocation. Hum Genet 86:162–166

Hamerton JL (1970) Robertsonian translocations. In: Jacobs PA, Price WH, Law P (eds) Human population cytogenetics. Williams and Wilkins, Baltimore, pp 63–80

Hamerton JL (1971) Human cytogenetics I. Academic, New York

Harris DJ, Hankins L, Begleiter ML (1979) Reproductive risk of t(13q14q) carriers:case report and review. Am J Med Genet 3:175–181

Hsu TC, Pathak S, Basen BM, et al. (1978) Induced Robertsonian fusions and tandem translocations in mammalian cell cultures. Cytogenet Cell Genet 21:86–98

Jacobs PA, Mayer M, Morton NE (1976) Acrocentric chromosome associations in man. Am J Hum Genet 28:567–576

John B, Freeman M (1975) Causes and consequences of Robertsonian exchange. Chromosoma 52:123–136

Kaiser P (1980) Pericentrische Inversionen menschlicher Chromosomen. Thieme, Stuttgart

Kirkels VGHJ, Hustinx TWJ, Scheres JMJC (1980) Habitual abortion and translocation (22q;22q): unexpected transmission from a mother to her phenotypically normal daughter. Clin Genet 18:456–461

Ledbetter DH, Mascarello JT, Riccardi VH, et al. (1982) Chromosome 15 abnormalities and the Prader-Willi syndrome:a follow-up report of 40 cases. Am J Hum Genet 34:278–285

Lindenbaum RH, Hultén M, McDermott A, et al. (1985) The prevalence of translocations in parents of children with regular trisomy 21: a possible interchromosomal effect? J Med Genet 22:24–28

Luciani JM, Guichaoua MR, Delafontaine D, et al. (1987) Pachytene analysis in a 17;21 reciprocal translocation carrier: role of the acrocentric chromosomes in male sterility. Hum Genet 77:246–250

Martin RH (1988) Human sperm karyotyping: a tool for the study of aneuploidy. In: Vig BK, Sandberg AA (eds) Aneuploidy, Part B: Induction and test systems. Liss, New York, pp 297–316

Martinez-Castro P, Ramos MC, Rey JA, et al. (1984) Homozygosity for a Robertsonian translocation (13q14q) in three offspring of heterozygous parents. Cytogenet Cell Genet 38:310–312

Mattei MG, Souiah N, Mattei JF (1984) Chromosome 15 anomalies in the Prader-Willi syndrome: cytogenetic analysis. Hum Genet 66:313–334

Mikelsaar A-V, Schmid M, Krone W, et al. (1977) Frequency of Ag-stained nucleolus organizer regions in the acrocentric chromosomes of man. Hum Genet 37:73–77

Mikkelsen M (1971) Down's syndrome. Current stage of cytogenetic research. Humangenetik 12:1–28

Mikkelsen M, Basli A, Poulsen H (1980) Nucleolus organizer regions in translocations involving acrocentric chromosomes. Cytogenet Cell Genet 26:14–21

Morgan R, Bixenman H, Hecht F (1985) Human chromosome variation with two Robertsonian translocations. Hum Genet 69:178–180

Niebuhr E (1972) Dicentric and monocentric Robertsonian translocations in man. Humangenetik 16:217–226

Nielsen J, Rasmussen K (1975) Extra marker chromosome in newborn children. Hereditas 81:221–224

Nielsen J, Rasmussen K (1976) Autosomal reciprocal translocations and 13/14 translocations: a population study. Clin Genet 10:161–177

Niikawa N, Ishikawa M (1983) Whole-arm translocation between homologous chromosomes 7 in a woman with successive spontaneous abortions. Hum Genet 63:85–86

Oksala T (1958) Chromosome pairing, crossing over, and segregation in meiosis in *Drosophila melanogaster* females. Cold Spring Harbor Symp Quant Biol 23:197–210

Orye E, Delire C (1967) Familial D/D and D/G₁ translocation. Helv Paediatr Acta 22:36–40

Palmer CG, Conneally PM, Christian JC (1969) Translocations of D chromosomes in two families t(13q14q) and t(13q14q) + (13p14p). J Med Genet 6: 166–173

Palmer CG, Schwartz S, Hodes ME (1980) Transmission of a balanced homologous t(22q;22q) translocation from mother to normal daughter. Clin Genet 17:418–422

Pellestor F (1990) Analysis of meiotic segregation in a man heterozygous for a 13;15 Robertsonian translocation and a review of the literature. Hum Genet 85:49–54

Rockman-Greenberg C, Ray M, Evans JA, et al. (1982) Homozygous Robertsonian translocations in a fetus with 44 chromosomes. Hum Genet 61:181–184

Schober AM, Fonatsch C (1978) Balanced reciprocal whole-arm translocation t(1:19) in three generations. Hum Genet 42:349–352

Searle JB (1988) Selection and Robertsonian variation in nature: the case of the common shrew. In: Daniel A (ed) The cytogenetics of mammalian autosomal rearrangements. Liss, New York, pp 507–531

Therman E, Susman B, Denniston C (1989) The nonrandom participation of human acrocentric chromosomes in Robertsonian translocations. Ann Hum Genet 53:49–65

Verma RS, Dosik H (1980) Human chromosomal heteromorphisms: nature and clinical significance. Int Rev Cytol 62:361–383

Vianna-Morgante AM, Nunesmaia HG (1978) Dissociation as probable origin of mosaic 45,XX,t(15;21)/46,XY,i(21q). J Med Genet 15:305–310

Zuffardi O, Tiepolo L (1982) Frequencies and types of chromosome abnormalities associated with human male infertility. In: Crosignani PG, Rubin BL (eds) Genetic control of gamete production and function. Academic, London, pp 261–273

28
Double Minutes and Homogeneously Stained Regions

What are DMs and HSRs?

Double minutes (DMs) and homogeneously stained regions (HSRs) provide good examples of phenomena that were originally regarded as cytological oddities but that have turned out to be expressions of a fundamental process, gene amplification. Evidence for the structure and behavior of DMs and HSRs comes from two sources: human and animal cancers and cell lines subjected to selective pressure for drug resistance. As a rule, they have not been observed in normal untreated cells.

DMs are small spherical structures that occur in pairs, their number varying greatly from cell to cell. They were first described in the 1960s in solid human tumors and in induced mouse sarcomas (Cowell, 1982). Many of the early findings were in children's neurogenic tumors, but gradually observations of their occurrence in most types of solid tumors and many leukemias have accumulated (Sandberg, 1990).

HSRs are, as the name indicates, chromosome segments that are increased in length and stain uniformly with banding techniques. They were first described by Biedler and Spengler (1976) in human neuroblastoma cells and in methotrexate-resistant hamster cell lines. Since then, HSRs have been found in an increasing number of human and animal cancers. Both HSRs and DMs occur in addition to the usual chromosome complement of the cell.

Structure of Double Minutes

DMs vary from very small double dots (Fig. 28.1a), which resemble diplococci, to larger spherical or fragment-like structures and rings (Fig.

302

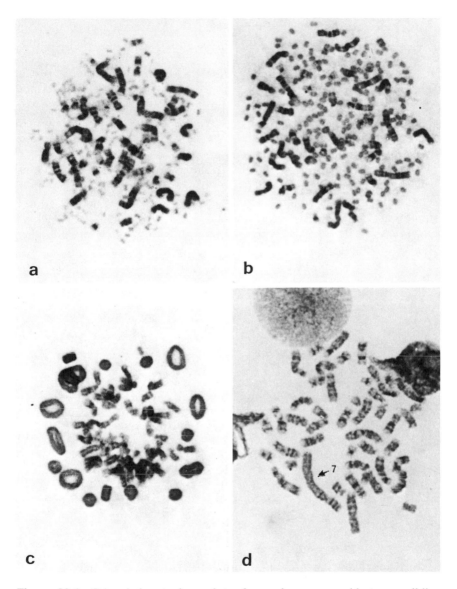

Figure 28.1. G-banded metaphase plates from a human neuroblastoma cell line. (a) Small double minutes; (b) medium-sized double minutes; (c) large rings; (d) long, homogeneously stained region on chromosome 7 (Biedler JL, Ross RA, Shanske S, et al., 1980. Human neuroblastoma cytogenetics: search for significance of homogeneously stained regions and double minute chromosomes. In: Evans AE (ed) *Advances in Neuroblastoma Research*. Raven, New York, pp 81–96).

28.1b,c). Recent molecular studies suggest DMs contain circular DNA molecules that lack telomeric sequences (Lin et al., 1990). Their staining properties show them to consist of chromosomal material that stains evenly with banding techniques. They also resemble chromosomes in their chromatin structure (Bahr et al., 1983). This has been confirmed with scanning electron microscopy (Fig. 28.2) (Jack et al., 1987). The number of DMs is highly variable among different lines of the same cancer, as well as among cells within the same tumor, ranging from none to several hundred per cell (Levan et al., 1981).

DMs were originally thought to be centric chromosome regions. However, they have been shown to lack centromeres, since they do not stain with C-banding or Cd-banding, and are not attached to the mitotic spindle (Barker and Hsu, 1978; Levan and Levan, 1978). Finally, the lack of centromeres in DMs has been confirmed with anti-kinetochore antibodies (Haaf and Schmid, 1988).

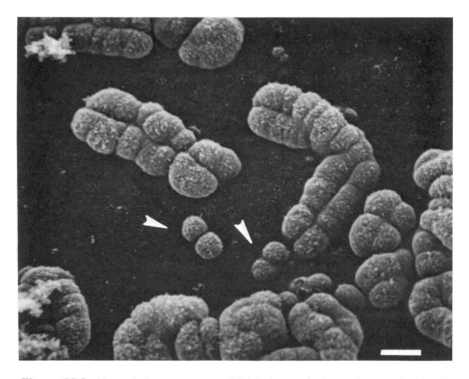

Figure 28.2. Normal chromosomes and DMs (arrows) photomicrographed in the scanning electron microscope. The structure of the DMs, which vary in size, is identical with that of normal chromosomes (Figure 2, p. 50 of Jack EM, Waters JJ, Harrison CJ, 1987. A scanning electron microscopy study of double minutes from a human tumour cell line. Cytogenet Cell Genet 44:49–52, Karger, Basel).

DMs replicate once in every mitotic cycle during early S phase (Barker et al., 1980a). In metaphase they do not lie in the middle of the plate, as small chromosomes usually do, but are embedded in persisting, presumably nucleolar, material, which is mostly attached to the ends of chromosomes (in cancer cells nucleolar material often persists to meta-anaphase) (Levan and Levan, 1978). In anaphase, the DMs get a free ride attached to the chromosomes, their two parts going to the same pole. Part of them may remain between the anaphase groups, forming micronuclei and being eventually lost. This type of segregation is naturally highly inaccurate and explains the wide variation in the number of DMs. Their survival and frequency in cells derived from the same tumor seems to depend on the conditions under which the cells grow. Thus, in the SEWA mouse sarcoma, the DMs are retained in 90% of cells in vivo. In culture, most cells lose the DMs, which, however, reappear if the cells are retransplanted into a mouse (Levan et al., 1977).

The mode of segregation of the large fragment-like or ring-shaped DMs is not known and should certainly be studied.

Homogeneously Stained Regions and C-Minus Chromosomes

Since HSRs segregate normally in mitosis, they are much more stable than DMs. However, they, too, may increase or decrease in length as a reaction to the environment or undergo other structural changes.

HSRs stain, as a rule, uniformly with G- or Q-banding (Fig. 28.1d), their staining intensity being in the intermediate range. Similar to DMs, they replicate within a short period during early S phase. However, in some cases they display a pattern of thin G-bands or they show C-bands, which obviously means that an additional segment has been coamplified with the repeated gene (Cowell, 1982). Even a whole HSR, in a human breast carcinoma cell line, was intensively Q-bright, similar to Y-heterochromatin, and stained darkly with C-banding (Barker et al., 1980b), an interesting finding in originally female cells. HSRs may be of considerable length, the DNA content of the chromosome involved being increased from 30 percent to 250 percent of the cell's DNA (Balaban-Malenbaum et al., 1979).

HSRs may involve different specific regions in the chromosome complement (Biedler and Spengler, 1976). Interestingly, several of the points in human neuroblastomas coincide with the hot spots for mitotic chiasmata in Bloom syndrome (Kuhn et al., 1985). This probably means that these regions are especially liable to undergo unequal crossing-over. Unequal SCE has, indeed, been observed within HSRs in the human melanoma cell line, MeWo (Holden et al., 1987).

HSRs involving the ribosomal RNA genes (satellite stalks) on chromosome 14 were observed in two families (Cowell, 1982). Similar HSRs occurred in three chromosomes in a rat hepatoma cell line (Miller et al., 1979). These structures consisted of unstained satellite stalks alternating with typical HSRs. Instead of the some 200 copies of ribosomal RNA genes present in normal rat cells, the hepatoma cells contained some 2000 (Miller et al., 1979).

Levan et al. (1981) found that, in certain SEWA mouse sarcoma lines, the DMs were gradually being replaced by homogeneously stained telocentric, or metacentric, chromosomes, which varied in number from zero to fifteen per cell. These chromosomes did not show a C-band and were accordingly called C-minus or CM chromosomes. Obviously, CMs are independent HSRs that have gained a centromere. They have a clear primary constriction, but the centric region has not so far been studied with more sophisticated banding techniques.

DMs and HSRs as Expressions of Gene Amplification

It is now clear that DMs, HSRs, and CMs are expressions of the same process: gene amplification. This was first proposed by Biedler and Spengler (1976), who observed that the HSRs appeared in hamster cells during an increase in their methotrexate resistance. This assumption has been amply confirmed.

The cancer drug, methotrexate, is a folic acid antagonist that is bound by the enzyme dihydrofolate reductase. Resistance to methotrexate can be induced in cultured mammalian cells by first exposing them to a low concentration of the drug, which kills most of them. The few survivors are grown out and exposed to a higher concentration. This process is repeated several times, the cells becoming stepwise more and more resistant to methotrexate (Schimke, 1980). Correspondingly, the number of dihydrofolate reductase genes increases. Simultaneously, the HSRs and DMs, which have been shown to consist of repeats of this gene, become longer or more numerous (Schimke, 1980).

Cells resistant to several other substances, such as colchicine, vincristine, phosphonacetyl-L-aspartate (PALA), and cadmium, to mention a few, have also been observed to develop HSRs and DMs (Cowell, 1982).

Apart from such experiments, gene amplification has been seen almost exclusively in malignant cells. It can also be determined with molecular techniques in cases where no DMs or HSRs are visible, perhaps because they are, in size, below the resolution of the light microscope. Eight of the 30 oncogenes known in 1987 were found amplified (Alitalo et al., 1987). The same oncogenes, for instance, oncogenes of the *myc* family, may be amplified in a whole spectrum of malignant diseases. The number of repeats ranges from a few to several hundred.

DMs and HSRs are Interchangeable

A variety of observations show that DMs and HSRs (or CMs) represent the same phenomenon in different guises—DMs reflecting an unstable, and HSRs a more stable state. First, as described above, they display similar staining and replication characteristics. Even more convincing is their behavior: they occur often in the same cancer, but not in the same cell. During the development of the SEWA mouse sarcomas, HSRs may vanish, to be replaced by DMs (or CMs). Or conversely, when DMs disappear, HSRs or CMs make their appearance (Levan et al., 1981). This has also been demonstrated convincingly in cell hybrids, between a human neuroblastoma and mouse fibroblasts, in which HSRs, on the two human chromosomes 1, were replaced by DMs (Balaban-Malenbaum and Gilbert, 1980).

Origin of DMs and HSRs

The origin of HSRs and DMs raises some intriguing questions. How does either type originally arise? And how do HSRs break up into DMs? An even more puzzling phenomenon is the integration of DMs into a chromosome to form an HSR. Nor is it known how the CMs pick up their C-bandless centromeres.

The mechanisms either for the break-up of HSRs or for the integration of DMs are at present completely unknown, as is the origin of CM centromeres.

Significance of HSRs and DMs

As discussed above, DMs and HSRs (and CMs) are different expressions of gene amplification. The role played by them in the development of cells resistant to various drugs is obvious. The idea has also been proposed that this could be the mechanism inducing resistance in whole organisms to various agents, such as insecticide resistance in insects (Schimke, 1980).

In the development of malignant disease, amplification plays a dual role. First, it may be a step in oncogenic transformation. DMs and HSRs may also be involved in the progression of many tumors from fairly benign to highly aggressive (Alitalo and Schwab, 1986). Selection pressures clearly play a decisive role in such processes. These obscure processes may create other weird chromosomes, not resembling DMs or HSRs. For instance, in mouse cell lines, chromosomes with several C-bands, in one case with 14, have been observed (Bregula and Levan, 1985).

The most probable explanation for gene amplification is repeated unequal crossing-over, either between sister chromatids or homologous chromosomes (Chapter 12; Therman and Kuhn, 1981). This clearly applies to the amplification of ribosomal RNA genes described above (Miller et al., 1979), since unequal crossing-over between satellite stalks is not too uncommon (Therman et al., 1981). Whether unequal crossing-over, alone, suffices to account for the amazingly fast appearance—and disappearance—of HSRs is not clear.

An alternative mechanism that has been assumed to lead to gene amplification in microorganisms is saltatory replication (Schimke, 1982). This means that a chromosome segment replicates more than once during an S period, and the additional copies are either integrated into the chromosome or become independent DMs. The mechanics of this type of amplification have been reviewed by Alitalo and Schwab (1986).

References

Alitalo K, Schwab M (1986) Oncogene amplification in tumor cells. Adv Cancer Res 47:235–281.

Alitalo K, Koskinen P, Mäkelä TP, et al. (1987) *Myc* oncogenes: activation and amplification. Biochim Biophys Acta 907:1–32

Bahr G, Gilbert F, Balaban G, et al. (1983) Homogeneously staining regions and double minutes in a human cell line: chromatin organization and DNA content. J Natl Cancer Inst 71:657–661

Balaban-Malenbaum G, Gilbert F (1980) The proposed origin of double minutes from homogeneously staining region (HSR)-marker chromosomes in human neuroblastoma hybrid cell lines. Cancer Genet Cytogenet 2:339–348

Balaban-Malenbaum G, Grove G, Gilbert F (1979) Increased DNA content of HSR-marker chromosomes of human neuroblastoma cells. Exp Cell Res 119:419–423

Barker PE, Hsu TC (1978) Are double minutes chromosomes? Exp Cell Res 113:457–458

Barker PE, Drwinga HL, Hittelman WN, et al. (1980a) Double minutes replicate once during S phase of the cell cycle. Exp Cell Res 130:353–360

Barker PE, Lau Y-F, Hsu TC (1980b) A heterochromatic homogeneously staining region (HSR) in the karyotype of a human breast carcinoma cell line. Cancer Genet Cytogenet 1:311–319

Biedler JL, Spengler BA (1976) Metaphase chromosome anomaly: association with drug resistance and cell-specific products. Science 191:185–187

Biedler JL, Ross RA, Shanske S, et al. (1980) Human neuroblastoma cytogenetics: search for significance of homogeneously stained regions and double minute chromosomes. In: Evans AE (ed) Advances in neuroblastoma research. Raven, New York, pp 81–96

Bregula U, Levan A (1985) Double minutes in a cell line from mouse fibroblasts grown under nonselective conditions. Suppression of a double minute-free sideline by in vivo environment. Hereditas 102:259–276

Cowell JK (1982) Double minutes and homogeneously staining regions: gene amplification in mammalian cells. Annu Rev Genet 16:21–59

Haaf T, Schmid M (1988) Analysis of double minutes and double minute-like chromatin in human and murine tumor cells using antikinetochore antibodies. Cancer Genet Cytogenet 30:73–82

Holden JJA, Hough MR, Reimer DL, et al. (1987) Evidence for unequal crossing-over as the mechanism for amplification of some homogeneously staining regions. Cancer Genet Cytogenet 29:139–149

Jack EM, Waters JJ, Harrison CJ (1987) A scanning electron microscopy study of double minutes from a human tumour cell line. Cytogenet Cell Genet 44:49–52

Kuhn EM, Therman E, Denniston C (1985) Mitotic chiasmata, gene density and oncogenes. Hum Genet 70:1–5

Levan A, Levan G (1978) Have double minutes functioning centromeres? Hereditas 88:81–92

Levan A, Levan G, Mandahl N (1981) Double minutes and C-bandless chromosomes in a mouse tumor. In: Arrighi FE, Rao PN, Stubblefield E (eds) Genes, chromosomes, and neoplasia. Raven, New York, pp 223–251

Levan G, Mandahl N, Bengtsson BO, et al. (1977) Experimental elimination and recovery of double minute chromosomes in malignant cell populations. Hereditas 86:75–90

Lin CC, Meyne J, Sasi R, et al. (1990) Apparent lack of telomere sequences on double minute chromosomes. Cancer Genet Cytogenet 48:271–274

Miller OJ, Tantravahi R, Miller DA, et al. (1979) Marked increase in ribosomal RNA gene multiplicity in a rat hepatoma cell line. Chromosoma 71:183–195

Sandberg AA (1990) The chromosomes in human cancer and leukemia, 2nd edn. Elsevier Science Publishing Co., New York

Schimke RT (1980) Gene amplification and drug resistance. Sci Am 243:60–69

Schimke RT (1982) Summary. In: Schimke RT (ed) Gene amplification. Cold Spring Harbor Laboratory, Cold Spring Harbor, New York, pp 317–333

Therman E, Kuhn EM (1981) Mitotic crossing-over and segregation in man. Hum Genet 59:93–100

Therman E, Otto PG, Shahidi NT (1981) Mitotic recombination and segregation of satellites in Bloom's syndrome. Chromosoma 82:627–636

29
Chromosomes and Oncogenes

What Is Cancer?

There are two types of neoplasms, both of which are expressions of
abnormal growth. Benign tumors are outgrowths that are self-limiting;
that is, they grow to a certain size and then stop or regress. Most of us are
acquainted with benign tumors, such as polyps or warts. Malignant tumors,
on the other hand, usually show unlimited growth; they escape the rules
of differentiation and grow wild. They also have the ability to infiltrate
and destroy normal tissues, and most malignant tumors are also capable
of spreading to new sites by metastasis. Tissue cultures of cancer cells are
immortal, whereas normal cells divide only a limited number of times in
vitro. Furthermore, normal cultured cells stop dividing when they make
contact with each other, whereas malignant cells are able to grow in
several layers. The histological structure of cancerous tumors usually
differs greatly from the original normal tissue and often appears to be
anaplastic. Advanced cancer may display a varied cytological picture;
cells with small and large, often giant, nuclei exist side by side with cells
having several or weirdly shaped nuclei. Cancer mitoses also exhibit a
wide spectrum of abnormalities, such as multiple poles, disorganized
metaphases, anaphases with laggards and chromatid bridges, endomitoses,
and endoreduplications. These phenomena indicate that the mitotic processes of chromosome replication and division, usually so orderly, have
been dramatically disrupted (Therman and Kuhn, 1989).

Malignant tumors are by no means specific to man but are found
throughout the animal kingdom, from ants to whales. Corresponding
phenomena also occur in plants. The so-called crown gall, for example,
which affects a wide variety of plant species, resembles animal cancer.

The induction of crown gall requires that a wound in a suitable host plant be inoculated with *Agrobacterium tumefaciens*. After enough cells have been transformed into crown gall cells, the tumor continues to grow even after the bacteria have been killed. The transformation occurs when a segment of a plasmid is transferred from the inducing bacterium and is incorporated into the host cell genome.

Cancer Induction

Cancer is caused by mutation in the broadest sense of the word. There is convincing evidence that the overwhelming majority of malignant tumors have a clonal origin (Nowell, 1976); a change takes place in a single cell from which the entire tumor is derived. In primary tumors all cells may display the same abnormal chromosome constitution. Enzyme studies of women with different alleles of an X-linked gene show that the same X chromosome is active in all the cells of a tumor. The immunoglobulin chain produced by a plasma-cell tumor nearly always confirms the assumption of a clonal origin of the disease.

That an organism's genetic constitution may have a decisive effect on its probability of developing cancer is borne out by many observations. For instance, there are inbred mouse strains in which most animals develop malignant tumors. A definite tendency to develop malignant disease seems to be inherited in some human families. In many such "cancer syndrome" families, about one-half the members eventually develop one or more malignancies. In one family (Lynch et al., 1977), 20 of 88 relatives studied had been affected with carcinoma of the colon and/or endometrium (uterine epithelium). Other types of tumors were also found in the family, and 16 individuals had more than one primary malignancy. For offspring of affected parents, the risk of colon/endometrial cancer was 52.8 percent in the 20- to 60-year age group, whereas none of the children of unaffected parents or the unrelated spouses developed cancer.

Miller (1967) reviewed populations with especially high risks of leukemia. In Caucasian children under 15, the incidence of leukemia is 1/2880. If one identical twin has leukemia, the risk of leukemia for the other twin is 1/5. In persons who have been exposed to ionizing radiation, which is mutagenic, the risk is also greatly increased. Thus, in Hiroshima survivors who were within 1000 meters of the hypocenter, the probability of developing leukemia is 1/60.

Especially interesting are the chromosome instability syndromes (Chapter 11), of which the most extensively studied are ataxia telangiectasia, Fanconi anemia, and Bloom syndrome. The homozygotes, who show a greatly increased rate of chromosome breakage, also have a greatly increased risk for malignant disease; for instance, in Bloom syndrome it is 1/4 of patients, and in ataxia it is 1/8.

It is obvious that malignant disease depends to a great extent on genetic factors. It is also known that most, possibly all, carcinogens are mutagens; however, not all mutagens necessarily induce cancer. There is also a direct connection between the carcinogenicity of various agents and their ability to break chromosomes. Examples of such agents include ionizing radiation, a great variety of chemicals, chromosome breakage syndromes, and viruses.

Two main types of genes play a role in cancer induction. The first is a set of growth-stimulating genes, called *proto-oncogenes*, whose normal alleles may mutate into *oncogenes*. The (mutant) gene products of oncogenes are positive stimulators of malignant cell growth, and their genetic effects are dominant. The second is a set of tumor suppressor genes, called *anti-oncogenes*, whose normal function is to prevent overgrowth of cells. When these genes are inactivated by mutation, the absence of their products allows malignant growth to occur. Mutants of this sort are recessive (except in gene *p*53): the malignant transformation of the cell occurs when the mutant allele of the anti-oncogene is homozygous or hemizygous or when both copies of the chromosome region containing the gene are lost.

One of the fastest growing fields in biomedical research is the molecular biology of oncogenes and oncogenesis. This field has been reviewed in many articles (for instance, Alitalo and Schwab, 1986; Cole, 1986; Haluska et al., 1987; Sandberg et al., 1988; Sager, 1989) and books (for instance, Heim and Mitelman, 1987; Cavenee et al., 1989a; Pimentel, 1990; Sandberg, 1990).

This chapter attempts a short survey of the chromosomal aspects of oncogenesis. This field, too, has been widely reviewed, for instance, by Yunis (1986), Heim and Mitelman (1987), Pimentel (1990), and Sandberg (1990).

Oncogenes

So-called proto-oncogenes are normal genes present in all metazoan cells. What role they play under normal circumstances is mostly unknown. It is likely—and for a couple of oncogenes there is evidence for this—that they are involved in cell division, growth, and differentiation (Bishop, 1983).

Viruses for a long time have been known to cause cancer in animals. The Rous sarcoma virus, a retrovirus (RNA virus) that induces malignant tumors in chickens, was discovered in 1911. An association between virus infection and several human malignant diseases has been assumed. Such diseases include various leukemias, Hodgkin's disease, Burkitt's lymphoma, and cervical, hepatocellular, and nasopharyngeal cancers. Possibly virus infection constitutes one step in the multistep process of malignant transformation in these diseases.

Genes homologous to cellular proto–oncogenes are found in retro-viruses known to cause cancer in various animal species. They transform cells, either by being inserted into the host genome, or by being present in multiple copies in the host cell (Bishop, 1983). It is thought that the retroviruses originally picked up these oncogenes from the metazoan cells they infected. A normal cell is transformed when one or more proto–oncogenes in it are activated, which can occur through mechanisms such as point mutation, position effect, or amplification.

The oncogene of the Rous sarcoma virus is called v–scr, and its normal homolog in a metazoan cell, c–scr. The versions of this gene in fishes, birds, and mammals are closely related to the viral gene.

Some 60 human proto–oncogenes have by now been localized to a specific chromosome band or at least to a specific chromosome.

These types of oncogenes are dominant in their effects, as shown by transfection experiments. Purified DNA fragments from a variety of can-cers, when transferred to recipient cells (a process called transfection), transform nonneoplastic cells with high efficiency. DNA fragments from normal cells also accomplish transformation, although with a very low frequency, which has been interpreted to mean that the fragmentation itself may sometimes activate an oncogene (Cooper, 1982).

Reciprocal Translocations and Oncogenes

It has long been thought that if a particular chromosomal aberration is found consistently in a certain type of malignant disease, the aberration must be involved in causing the malignancy (Sandberg, 1983). The search for such chromosome aberrations has been made difficult by the tendency of malignant cells to accumulate chromosome abnormalities *after* trans-formation has taken place (Chapter 30). Real progress in this field began only after 1970, when banding techniques were developed, and especially after high-resolution banding came into use (Yunis, 1981). Other impor-tant technical improvements include short-term culture and synchroniza-tion of cancer cells (Yunis, 1981, 1984).

The list of chromosome aberrations characteristic of specific types of malignant disease is continuously growing. In leukemias and lymphomas, these are mostly balanced reciprocal translocations; in solid tumors, they are deletions and sometimes trisomies (Mitelman, 1988; Sandberg, 1990).

The first chromosome aberration consistently associated with malig-nancy, the Philadelphia chromosome (Ph[1]) (a G chromosome with about half of its long arm missing), was described in chronic myelogenous leukemia (CML) by Nowell and Hungerford (1960). Banding showed this chromosome to be 22, and a careful analysis by Rowley (1973) revealed that, in 90% of the cases, the abnormality was a translocation between 9q and 22q. With prophase banding, the breakpoints were defined as q34.1 and q11.2, respectively (Fig. 29.1; Yunis, 1983).

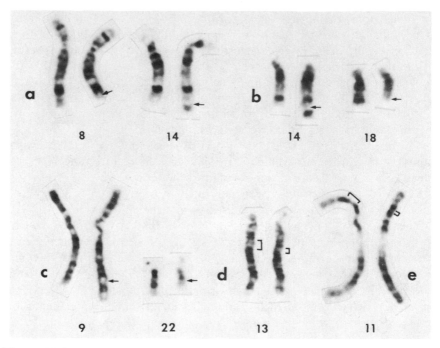

Figure 29.1. Selected Giemsa-banded chromosomes prepared by high-resolution technique at the 850 and 1200 band stages from patients with (a) non-Burkitt small cell lymphoma and t(8;14); (b) follicular small cleaved cell lymphoma and t(14;18); (c) chronic myelogenous leukemia and t(9;22); (d) constitutional retinoblastoma and partial loss of band 13p14; and (e) constitutional Wilms' tumor and partial loss of band 11p13. Arrows indicate breakpoints involved in the translocations, and brackets illustrate band deletion (Yunis JJ. The chromosomal basis of human neoplasia. Science 221:227–236. Copyright 1983 by the AAAS).

With recombinant DNA techniques, the oncogene c–abl has been localized to the part of 9q that is translocated to 22, where it has come to lie next to the immunoglobulin light chain lambda gene.

Even more intensively studied has been the c–myc oncogene, which is involved in the origin of the highly malignant Burkitt's lymphoma. The most common chromosome finding in malignant cells of patients with this disease is t(8;14)(q24;q32.3) (Figs. 29.1, 29.2). The c–myc has been mapped to 8q24, and the immunoglobulin heavy chain locus to 14q32.3. The new location of the c–myc gene, next to the broken immunoglobulin gene, changes the regulation of the c–myc gene (Robertson, 1984). In a minority of cases, the end of 8q is translocated to 2p11 or to 22q11, which contain the genes coding for kappa and lambda light chain immunoglobulins, respectively.

The same chromosome abnormality may occur in several malignant diseases, and a spectrum of abnormalities may be characteristic of one

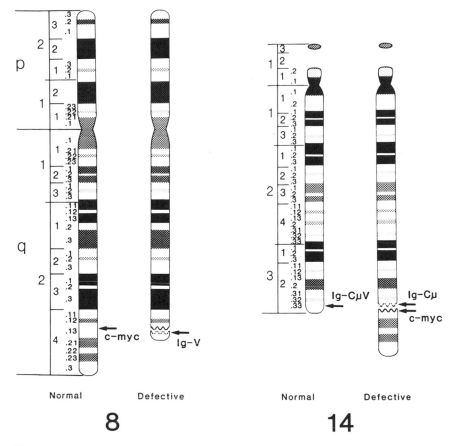

Figure 29.2. Location of c–*myc* oncogene and heavy chain immunoglobulin variable (V) and constant μ (Cμ) genes on normal and defective chromosomes 8 and 14 in Burkitt's lymphoma, represented at the 1200 Giemsa band stage. The defective chromosome 8 loses the c–*myc* and gains V genes. The defective chromosome 14 gains c–*myc* from chromosome 8, becoming contiguous or near to Cμ. Arrows point to the normal and rearranged locations of these genes. Broken ends of defective chromosomes indicate breakpoint sites (Yunis JJ. The chromosomal basis of human neoplasia. Science 221:227–236. Copyright 1983 by the AAAS).

type of malignancy (Mitelman, 1988). Furthermore, translocations that appear identical in the light microscope may have different breakpoints on the molecular level. Ironically, as observations concerning the relationships of oncogenes to the constant chromosome breaks become more and more accurate, the interpretation of these observations becomes more and more difficult (Robertson, 1984). In other words, at present there exists no unified theory to explain the role of chromosome aberrations in the activation of oncogenes.

In some cases, the oncogene is moved next to a promoter sequence. In others, the oncogene may come into the vicinity of a transcriptional "enhancer" region. Oncogenes may also be activated through a point mutation, or the transformation may involve their amplification (Land et al., 1983).

In many primary tumors, as well as in cultured malignant cells, homogeneously stained chromosome regions (HSRs) and double minutes (DMs) have been observed (Chapter 28). The amplification often happens during tumor development and is not involved in its origin. However, in colon carcinoma the HSRs and DMs reflect the amplification of the c–*myc* gene (Alitalo et al., 1983). In this cancer and in others, gene amplification may be the mechanism of transformation (Marx, 1984), or at least constitute one step in it. Trisomy, for a chromosome or chromosome segment, may naturally have the same effect (Gilbert, 1983).

Interestingly, constant chromosome aberrations have also been observed in benign tumors, for instance, in meningiomas, lipomas, leiomyomas, and mixed salivary gland tumors (Sandberg et al., 1988; Sandberg, 1991). In meningiomas, chromosome 22 or, more rarely, part of 22q may be missing (Zankl and Zang, 1980; Maltby et al., 1988). Even in normal brain tissue, an X chromosome in females or a Y in males may be lacking, whereas chromosome 7 may occur in triplicate (Heim et al., 1989). Thus, an abnormal chromosome constitution, in itself, is not a sure sign of malignancy.

Cancer Suppressor Genes or Anti-Oncogenes

In the 1970s, experiments fusing normal and malignant cells showed that the cells resulting from the fusion were, in many cases, nonmalignant. Later, it became clear that this was dependent upon the addition of specific chromosomes, or even single genes. Chromosome 11 has proven especially effective in this respect. These observations have led to the realization that the normal alleles of certain genes control cell division and differentiation, and prevent formation of metastases. This tumor-suppressing activity of the anti-oncogenes is lost when a recessive allele becomes homozygous, hemizygous, or when the locus is nullosomic (Sager, 1989; Cavenee et al., 1989a; Weinberg, 1991). Thus, the suppressor genes are recessive on the cellular level (except many mutants of $p53$), but the tendency in certain families to develop cancer is inherited in a dominant manner because the frequency of somatic mutations is high enough to produce homozygosity or hemizygosity in at least some cells of a person who has a heterozygous genotype at the start.

The most extensively studied of the diseases caused by suppressor genes is the childhood tumor, retinoblastoma (cancer of the retina). The gene involved is Rb, and the genotype of a normal person is Rb/Rb. A prerequisite for tumor development is homozygosity or hemizygosity for the allele rb, or nullosomy for the locus. The possible genotypes of retinoblastoma cells thus are rb/rb, rb/–, or –/–. Deletions have placed the gene at 13q14 (Fig. 29.1; Cavenee et al., 1983, 1989b).

Retinoblastoma may occur as an isolated case, usually involving only one eye; or the tendency to it may be inherited as a dominant trait, in which case both eyes are usually affected. The genotype of a person with inherited retinoblastoma is either Rb/rb or Rb/–, and mutation or deletion of the Rb gene results in malignant transformation of a retinal cell. In persons with the genotype Rb/rb or Rb/–, the risk of developing retinoblastoma is some 100,000 times higher than in the population in general, and the risk for other types of cancer, especially osteosarcoma, is also increased (Murphree and Benedict, 1984).

Several mechanisms leading to retinoblastoma in persons with the genotypes Rb/rb or Rb/– have been established. The gene may mutate. Chromosome 13 may be lost, or a segment including 13q14 may be deleted, or the chromosome with Rb may be lost and the homologue duplicated. Other possibilities include mitotic recombination or the loss of the Rb allele through a translocation break (Cavenee et al., 1983).

In a few persons who have developed retinoblastoma, all cells have a congenital heterozygous deletion of 13q14. These individuals are slightly retarded and have other physical anomalies (Francke and Kung, 1976).

Observations similar to those in retinoblastoma have been made in more than 30 malignancies, such as small-cell lung cancer, breast and colorectal cancers, children's neurogenic cancers, endocrine neoplasia type 2, and Wilms' tumor (Sager, 1989; Weinberg, 1991). Tumor suppressor genes have been localized to 13 chromosome arms. A missing chromosome or band has often given the first clue to the localization of such a gene.

Multistep Carcinogenesis

The changes in a cell that play a role in cancer transformation fall into different groups. A gene mutation, or an integration of a virus into the genome of the host cell, involves a qualitative change in DNA. Gene activation through position effect is usually brought about by a balanced translocation or by an inversion. The mechanisms that cause duplication or amplification of genes are nondisjunction or the largely unknown processes leading to DMs and HSRs. Deletions may come about through nondisjunction or the loss of a chromosome or chromosome region or the destruction of a gene when a break goes through it.

The thought that malignant transformation involves more than one step is not new (for reviews, see Knudson, 1973; 1986; Fialkow et al., 1981; Klein and Klein, 1985). It began with the two-step hypothesis for retinoblastoma and has now reached claims that 10–15 changes may be needed in some malignancies for transformation (Marx, 1989).

The idea of a multistep carcinogenesis is supported by several lines of evidence. Malignant disease often appears 10 to 30 years after a person has been exposed to a carcinogen. Precancerous conditions, such as papillomas, adenomas, and preleukemic disorders, may precede transformation. Substances that alone do not induce cancer but promote the effect of carcinogens are known. Furthermore, it is now obvious that the activation of one oncogene, as a rule, is not enough to transform a cell, but is only one of several necessary steps (Gilbert, 1983). Thus, Burkitt's lymphoma may require three or four steps, including activation of two oncogenes and infection with Epstein-Barr virus (Land et al., 1983). Also, unlike normal cells, which are able to divide only a limited number of times, cultured cell lines with unlimited growth potential can be transformed to malignant cells in a single step. This means that such cell lines may already have undergone the other necessary changes (Cooper, 1982). The observations on "cancer syndrome" families also agree with the multistep hypothesis and have been helpful in identifying suppressor genes. One of the diseases studied most extensively in this respect is colorectal cancer (Vogelstein et al., 1989). Initially, in normal epithelial cells a suppressor gene on chromosome 5 is inactivated, or lost. Next comes hypomethylation of DNA, which is followed by a mutation of the *ras* proto-oncogene. The losses of chromosomes 18 and 17 complete the transformation into a carcinoma cell. Further chromosome losses provide the tumor with the ability to form metastases. As will be discussed in Chapter 30, a tumor may undergo additional constant chromosome changes after transformation, which makes the distinction between transformation and progression possibly meaningless.

References

Alitalo K, Schwab M (1986) Oncogene amplification in tumor cells. Adv Cancer Res 47:235–281

Alitalo K, Schwab M, Lin CC, et al. (1983) Homogeneously staining chromosomal regions contain amplified copies of an abundantly expressed cellular oncogene (c–*myc*) in malignant neuroendocrine cells from a human colon carcinoma. Proc Natl Acad Sci USA 80:1707–1711

Bishop JM (1983) Cellular oncogenes and retroviruses. Annu Rev Biochem 52: 301–354

Cavenee W, Hastle N, Stanbridge E (eds) (1989a) Recessive oncogenes and tumor suppression. Current communications in molecular biology. Cold Spring Harbor Laboratory Press, Cold Spring Harbor, New York

Cavenee WK, Dryja TP, Phillips RA, et al. (1983) Expression of recessive alleles by chromosomal mechanisms in retinoblastoma. Nature 305:779–784

Cavenee WK, Scrable HJ, James CD (1989b) Molecular genetics of human cancer predisposition and progression. In: Cavenee W, Hastle N, Stanbridge E (eds) Recessive oncogenes and tumor suppression. Current communications in molecular biology. Cold Spring Harbor Laboratory Press, Cold Spring Harbor, New York, pp 67–72

Cole MD (1986) The *myc* oncogene: its role in transformation and differentiation. Annu Rev Genet 20:361–84

Cooper GM (1982) Cellular transforming genes. Science 217:801–806

Fialkow PJ, Martin PJ, Najfeld V, et al. (1981) Evidence for a multistep pathogenesis of chronic myelogenous leukemia. Blood 58:158–163

Francke U, Kung F (1976) Sporadic bilateral retinoblastoma and 13q− chromosomal deletion. Med Pediat Oncol 2:379–385

Gilbert F (1983) Chromosomes, genes, and cancer: a classification of chromosome abnormalities in cancer. J Natl Cancer Inst 71:1107–1114

Haluska FG, Tsujimoto Y, Croce CM (1987) Oncogene activation by chromosome translocation in human malignancy. Annu Rev Genet 21:321–345

Heim S, Mitelman F (1987) Cancer cytogenetics. Liss, New York

Heim S, Mandahl N, Jin Y, et al. (1989) Trisomy 7 and sex chromosome loss in human brain tissue. Cytogenet Cell Genet 52:136–138

Klein G, Klein E (1985) Evolution of tumours and the impact of molecular oncology. Nature 315:190–195

Knudson AG (1973) Mutation and human cancer. Adv Cancer Res 17:317–352

Knudson AG (1986) Genetics of human cancer. Annu Rev Genet 20:231–251

Land H, Parada LF, Weinberg RA (1983) Cellular oncogenes and multistep carcinogenesis. Science 222:771–778

Lynch HT, Harris RE, Organ CH Jr, et al. (1977) The surgeon, genetics, and cancer control: the cancer family syndrome. Ann Surg 185:435–440

Maltby EL, Ironside JW, Battersby RDE (1988) Cytogenetic studies in 50 meningiomas. Cancer Genet Cytogenet 31:199–210

Marx J (1989) Many gene changes found in cancer. Science 246:1386–1388

Marx JL (1984) Oncogenes amplified in cancer cells. Science 223:40–41

Miller RW (1967) Persons with exceptionally high risk of leukemia. Cancer Res 27:2420–2423

Mitelman F (1988) Catalog of chromosome aberrations in cancer, 3rd edn. Liss, New York

Murphree AL, Benedict WF (1984) Retinoblastoma: clues to human oncogenesis. Science 223:1028–1033

Nowell PC (1976) The clonal evolution of tumor cell populations. Science 194:23–28

Nowell PC, Hungerford DA (1960) A minute chromosome in human chronic granulocytic leukemia. Science 132:1497

Pimentel E (1990) Oncogenes, 2nd edn. CRC Press, Boca Raton, Florida

Robertson M (1984) Message of *myc* in context. Nature 309:585–587

Rowley JD (1973) A new consistent chromosomal abnormality in chronic myelogenous leukemia identified by quinacrine fluorescence and Giemsa staining. Nature 243:290–293

Sager R (1989) Tumor suppressor genes: the puzzle and the promise. Science 246:1406–1412

Sandberg AA (1983) A chromosomal hypothesis of oncogenesis. Cancer Genet Cytogenet 8:277–285

Sandberg AA (1990) The chromosomes in human cancer and leukemia, 2nd edn. Elsevier Science Publishing, New York

Sandberg AA (1991) Chromosome abnormalities in human cancer and leukemia. Mutat Res 247:231–240

Sandberg AA, Turc-Carel D, Gemmill RM (1988) Chromosomes in solid tumors and beyond. Cancer Res 48:1049–1059

Therman E, Kuhn EM (1989) Mitotic modifications and aberrations in cancer. CRC Crit Rev Oncogen 1:293–305

Vogelstein B, Fearon ER, Baker SJ, et al. (1989) Genetic alterations accumulate during colorectal tumorigenesis. In: Cavenee W, Hastle N, Stanbridge E (eds) Recessive oncogenes and tumor suppression. Current communications in molecular biology. Cold Spring Harbor Laboratory Press, Cold Spring Harbor, New York, pp 73–80

Weinberg RA (1991) Tumor suppressor genes. Science 254:1138–1146

Yunis JJ (1981) New chromosome techniques in the study of human neoplasia. Hum Pathol 12:540–549

Yunis JJ (1983) The chromosomal basis of human neoplasia. Science 221:227–236

Yunis JJ (1984) Clinical significance of high resolution chromosomes in the study of acute leukemias and non-Hodgkins lymphomas. In: Fairbanks VF (ed) Current hematology, Vol 3. Wiley, New York, pp 353–391

Yunis JJ (1986) Chromosomal rearrangements, genes, and fragile sites in cancer: clinical and biologic implications. In: DeVita VT Jr, Hellman S, Rosenberg SA (eds) Important advances in oncology 1986. Lippincott, Philadelphia, pp 93–128

Zankl H, Zang KD (1980) Correlations between clinical and cytogenetical data in 180 human meningiomas. Cancer Genet Cytogenet 1:351–356

30
Chromosomal Development of Cancer

Chromosomes and Cancer

It has been known since the beginning of the present century that the number of chromosomes in cancer cells often deviates greatly from the usual number in healthy cells of the host organism. The prominent German biologist Theodor Boveri observed that multipolar mitoses in sea urchin eggs led to abnormal chromosome numbers, and these in turn resulted in abnormal development of the larvae. Since cancer cells often display multipolar divisions, Boveri concluded that the resulting deviant chromosome numbers were the cause of cancerous growth. Boveri's book *Zur Frage der Entstehung maligner Tumoren* ("On the problem of the origin of malignant tumors") appeared in 1914 (Wolf, 1974). However, Boveri had put the cart before the horse. It is now clear that multipolar divisions appear only *after* the cells have undergone a malignant transformation (Therman and Kuhn, 1989). But Boveri's basic hypothesis, that chromosome aberrations may cause cancer, is very much alive today, as shown by the discovery of the relationship of chromosome structural changes to oncogenes (Chapter 29). It is now clear that, although certain constant chromosome anomalies are involved in the origin of cancer, most of the observed aberrations, both numerical and structural, arise during the progression of a malignant disease and that they in turn affect the further development of the tumor or leukemia. The difficulty has often been to distinguish the primary chromosome changes from the secondary ones, and even now it is often unclear whether a certain abnormality is a step in carcinogenesis or is only making the already transformed cells more malignant.

Chromosome Studies in Ascites Tumors

Cancer cytology was launched in the 1950s with the study of transplantable ascites tumors of the mouse and the rat (Yosida, 1975). These tumors were also the first mammalian tissues from which satisfactory chromosome preparations were obtained. Bayreuther (1952), who seems to have been the first investigator to apply a colchicine derivative to mouse ascites tumors, observed that both the chromosome number and morphology deviated from those of normal mouse cells.

Subsequent studies have shown that many mouse ascites tumors are near-triploid or near-tetraploid and that the karyotype shows many morphologically abnormal chromosomes. For example, the hypotetraploid Ehrlich tumor, so widely used in various experiments, displays only a couple of chromosomes that can be matched even approximately with any normal mouse chromosome.

Primary tumors in man sometimes induce the development of ascites fluid, in which dividing tumor cells can be studied. Such cells also show striking abnormalities, both in chromosome number and structure.

Chromosome Studies in Cancer

The earlier studies on the chromosome constitutions in malignant diseases have been repeatedly reviewed, for example, by Atkin (1974), Sandberg and Sakurai (1974), Makino (1975), Sandberg (1979), and Nowell (1982).

In the third edition of his *Catalog of Chromosome Aberrations in Cancer* Mitelman (1988) lists 9,069 cases of malignant disease in which banded chromosomes have been analyzed. Only about 15% of these are solid tumors, the rest consisting of leukemias and lymphomas. This probably resulted from the greater difficulty of obtaining satisfactory chromosome preparations from solid neoplasms. In the 9,069 cases, the total number of chromosomes involved in abnormalities is 28,179. These chromosome aberrations represent a wide spectrum of phenomena (Mitelman, 1988; Sandberg, 1990). The chromosome numbers may range from near haploid to polyploid, or the cells may have gained or lost individual chromosomes. Structural changes may lead to partial trisomy or monosomy, as in unbalanced translocations, isochromosomes, isodicentrics, or ring chromosomes (Tables 11.1 and 30.1). Amplification may be expressed as homogeneously stained regions or double minutes (Chapter 28). The number of genes may not change, but the genes may be relocated through balanced reciprocal translocations, insertions, or inversions. Many tumors are characterized by highly abnormal *marker* chromosomes, which often are the results of multiple breaks and not amenable to analysis.

Table 30.1. Mitotic modifications and aberrations in cancer and their cytogenetic effects (Therman and Kuhn, 1989).

Mitotic modification/aberration	Cytogenetic effect
Increased Metaphases/Prophases	Unknown
Faulty alignment of chromosomes	Aneuploidy
Multipolar mitoses	Aneuploidy; multinucleate cells
Endoreduplication	Polyploidy
Endomitosis	Polyploidy
C-mitosis	Usually cell death
Restitution	Polyploidy or cell death
Mitosis without cell division	Polyploidy; cells with two or more nuclei
Cell fusion	Polyploidy; binucleate or multinucleate cells
Segregation after mitotic crossing-over	Amplification/underreplication; homozygosity
Allocycly of chromosomes	Chromosome loss
Misdivision	Isochromosomes, telocentrics
Changes in constitutive heterochromatin	Unknown
Changes in facultative heterochromatin	Gene activation/inactivation
Lack of Barr bodies in female tumors	Unknown

Stemline and Tumor Development

Most tumors have a *stemline*, which consists of cells with the same chromosome constitution, often including striking marker chromosomes. One or more cell lines with other chromosome constitutions may also be present. A stemline often responds to a new environment, for instance, transplantation into an alien host species, by a change in its chromosome constitution. (Some tumors have lost their immunological specificity to the extent that they are able to grow even in a different host species.) Chemotherapy may also affect the karyotype of a stemline (Yosida, 1975). Finally, the stemline usually changes spontaneously during the progression of a tumor.

Chromosome changes in malignant diseases fall into three groups: (1) So-called constant changes that play a role in the origin of the malignancy. These are highly nonrandom (Chapter 29). (2) Aberrations that characterize the stemlines of specific types of cancer. These aberrations still seem to be nonrandomly distributed, but the nonrandomness is not as extreme as in the first group. (3) Aberrations found in dividing cells that have been "pushed out" from the stemline and show a wide range of variation even within a tumor. In this group, the aberrations appear to be more or less random (Mitelman, 1990).

Although breaks, and especially nondisjunction, may involve the chromosomes more or less randomly, selection, both during cancer transformation and progression, leads to the observed nonrandomness in human and animal (Levan et al., 1977) malignancies. This means that a more-or-less predictable series of chromosome changes takes place during the development of a cancer. One of the first diseases analyzed in this respect was chronic myelogenous leukemia (CML), in which the primary aberration is t(9q;22q), other anomalies appearing during the progression of the disease. Mitelman et al. (1976) (Fig. 30.1) listed additional chromosome changes in 66 of 200 CML patients who had the Ph[1] (22q−) chromosome. In 88 percent of the cases, the chromosomal development took what the authors called the major route. In 18 patients, a second Ph[1] chromosome appeared; in seven, an extra chromosome 8; and in nine patients, an i(17q) was found. In nine patients, both two Ph[1] chromosomes and an extra 8 occurred, whereas in six others the extra 8 was combined with an i(17q). Finally, in six patients, the cells showed, in addition to two Ph[1] chromosomes, both an extra 8 and i(17q). The same type of development is often observed when the disease is followed in individual patients (de Grouchy and Turleau, 1974).

Mitotic Aberrations in Cancer

Apart from structural changes, abnormal chromosome constitutions are caused by mitotic aberrations (Chapter 15) whose incidence is greatly

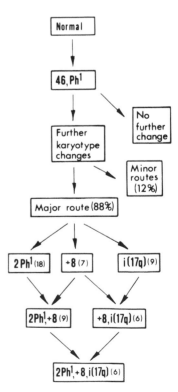

Figure 30.1. Chromosome abnormalities, in addition to the Ph[1] chromosome (22q−), in 66 cases of chronic myeloid leukemia. Numerals in parentheses in the lower part of the diagram indicate the number of cases showing the chromosome abnormality (Mitelman et al., 1976).

increased in cancer. However, relatively little attention has been given to these phenomena, although they constitute the bridge between the newly transformed cancer cell and the variety of chromosome constitutions observed in the cells of advanced tumors.

The wide range of chromosome number in cancer is reflected in the size (Fig. 30.2), DNA content, and shape of the nuclei. Malignant tumors often have characteristic patterns of heterochromatin, varying from almost none to prominent chromocenters (Fig. 6.2). Moreover, giant nuclei in any tumor may be devoid of either constitutive or facultative heterochromatin, including X chromatin bodies. An interesting phenomenon in many female tumors is the complete absence of Barr bodies in all cells (for instance, 20–40 percent of cervical cancers are X-chromatin negative). However, it is not clear whether this depends on the loss or reactivation

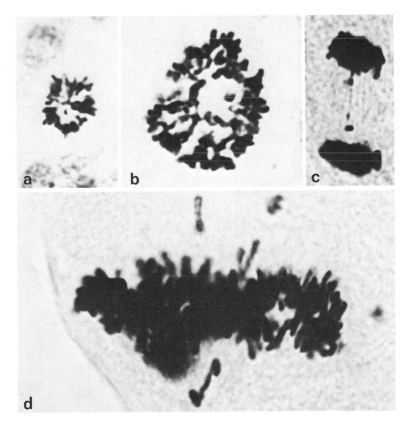

Figure 30.2. Mitotic stages from normal human placenta (a) and cervical cancer (b–d). (a) Diploid metaphase (polar view); (b) metaphase in octoploid range (polar view); (c) anaphase with a bridge; (d) giant metaphase (side view) (Therman et al., 1984).

of the inactive X chromosome, or possibly on the loss of the inactive X and the duplication of the active one (Therman et al., 1985).

The first mitotic change in a malignant tumor is that the ratio of metaphases to prophases, which in normal cells is about 1 or less, is increased, sometimes to values of 35 and higher (Fig. 30.3). This ratio naturally reflects the relative durations of the stages (Timonen and Therman, 1950; Therman et al., 1984, 1985; Therman and Kuhn, 1989). However, in cancer it is not clear whether the prophase is shortened, the metaphase lengthened, or possibly both.

Another abnormality, which is seen in almost all cancers, is a faulty alignment of the chromosomes in metaphase or anaphase. This results in chromosome laggards outside the metaphase plates or in chromosomes not included in the anaphase groups. This may in turn lead to nondisjunction, chromosome loss, or misdivision.

The presence of multipolar mitoses (Fig. 30.4) is characteristic of many malignant tumors. Thus, in a study of 82 cervical cancers, 61 displayed them (Therman et al., 1985), whereas they are practically nonexistent in untreated normal tissues. Therefore, the finding of even one multipolar division is highly indicative of malignancy (Therman and Kuhn, 1989).

Endoreduplication and endomitoses are also more frequent in malignant than in normal tissues, and the resulting endopolyploidy may reach high levels (Figs. 15.2, 30.2d, 30.4d; Therman et al., 1983). Other mitotic aberrations are rarer (Table 30.1) and play a less important role in the creation of abnormal chromosome constitutions.

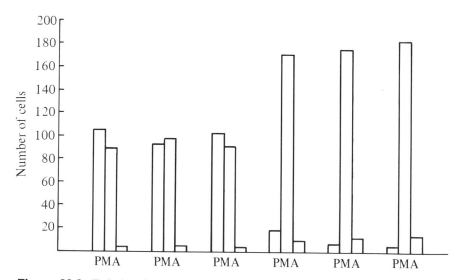

Figure 30.3. Relative frequencies of prophases (P), metaphases (M), and anaphases (A) in three biopsies of normal epithelium of human fetal tubes (left) and in three cases of cancer in adult fallopian tubes (data from Lehto, 1963).

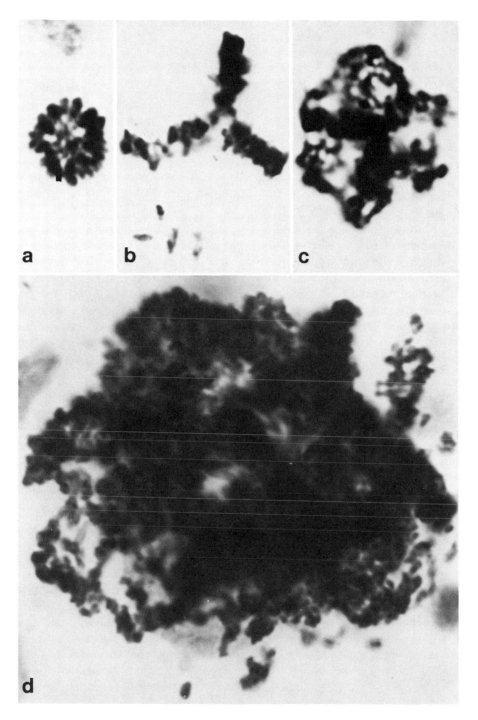

Figure 30.4. Metaphases from normal trophoblast (a), and from cervical cancer (b–d). (a) Diploid metaphase in polar view; (b) side-view of a tripolar metaphase with laggards (Therman et al., 1984); (c) six-polar metaphase; (d) highly polyploid metaphase with numerous poles (Therman and Kuhn, 1989, reprinted with permission from CRC Press Inc.).

Mitotic aberrations were first analyzed systematically in neoplasms of the human female genital tract (Timonen, 1950; Timonen and Therman, 1950), and later in other human and animal tumors (Oksala and Therman, 1974; Therman and Kuhn, 1989). All of these studies have yielded similar results, as have investigations on transplantable (Oksala, 1956) and induced (Scarpelli and von Haam, 1957) mouse tumors. The ubiquitous presence of mitotic aberrations in animal and human cancers indicates that they reflect some basic step in cell transformation. Most of these aberrations involve a disturbance in the coordination of the chromosomal and spindle mechanisms; this coordination is highly accurate in normal cells.

Mutations in the gene NM23 (*No Metastasis*) allow a tumor to develop metastases (Marx, 1990). Such mutations may also give rise to disturbances of the mitotic spindle. An interesting question is at which point in the transformation process mitotic aberrations first appear.

Attempts have been made to apply observations on mitotic disturbances to cancer diagnosis (reviewed in Therman and Kuhn, 1989), although more systematic studies are needed in this area.

Selection and Tumor Progression

Table 30.1 (see also Table 11.1) lists the different mitotic aberrations whose incidence is increased in cancer, together with their cytogenetic consequences. The combination and frequency of aberrations vary greatly among different tumors, but such aberrations are extremely rare or even nonexistent in normal untreated cells.

Mitotic aberrations, together with changes in chromosome structure, create the almost unlimited variety of chromosome constitutions found in malignant disease. The nonrandomness of the primary cancer-inducing changes and of those characteristic of the stemlines owes its origin to cell selection. The role of selection in promoting cells with changes needed in transformation is self-evident. After transformation, selection continues to further the fastest-dividing cell type(s), which will form a new stemline. This process obviously involves the accumulation of cancer-promoting genes and the loss of anti-oncogenes. A new stemline is thus always more malignant than the previous one. This leads to a stepwise development of a more and more aggressive neoplasia. Such changes are also reflected in the clinical behavior of a cancer, in that a slow-growing cancer may at one jump become more malignant. Similarly, a malignant disease, which to a certain point has responded satisfactorily to radiation or chemotherapy, may suddenly become resistant to the treatment.

References

Atkin NB (1974) Chromosomes in human malignant tumors: a review and assessment. In: German J (ed) Chromosomes and cancer. Wiley, New York, pp 375–422

Bayreuther K (1952) Der Chromosomenbestand des Ehrlich-Ascites-Tumors der Maus. Naturforsch 7:554–557

Grouchy J de, Turleau C (1974) Clonal evolution in the myeloid leukemias. In: German J (ed) Chromosomes and cancer. Wiley, New York, pp 287–311

Lehto L (1963) Cytology of the human Fallopian tube. Acta Obstet Gynecol Scand Suppl 42:1–95

Levan A, Levan G, Mitelman F (1977) Chromosomes and cancer. Hereditas 86:15–30

Makino S (1975) Human chromosomes. Igaku Shoin, Tokyo

Marx J (1990) New clue to cancer metastasis found. Science 249:482–483

Mitelman F (1988) Catalog of chromosome aberrations in cancer, 3rd edn. Liss, New York

Mitelman F (1990) Patterns of chromosome variation in neoplasia. In: Obe G, Natarajan AT (eds) Chromosomal aberrations: basic and applied aspects. Springer, Berlin/Heidelberg, pp 86–100

Mitelman F, Levan G, Nilsson P, et al. (1976) Non-random karyotypic evolution in chronic myeloid leukemia. Int J Cancer 18:24–30

Nowell PC (1982) Cytogenetics. In: Becker FF (ed) Cancer: a comprehensive treatise, Vol 1, 2nd edn. Plenum, New York, pp 3–46

Oksala T (1956) The mitotic mechanism of two mouse ascites tumours. Hereditas 42:161–188

Oksala T, Therman E (1974) Mitotic abnormalities and cancer. In: German J (ed) Chromosomes and cancer. Wiley, New York, pp 239–263

Sandberg AA (1979) The chromosomes in human cancer and leukemia. Elsevier North-Holland, New York

Sandberg AA (1990) The chromosomes in human cancer and leukemia, 2nd edn. Elsevier Science Publishing, New York

Sandberg AA, Sakurai M (1974) Chromosomes in the causation and progression of cancer and leukemia. In: Busch H (ed) The molecular biology of cancer. Academic, New York, pp 81–106

Scarpelli DG, von Haam E (1957) A study of mitosis in cervical epithelium during experimental inflammation and carcinogenesis. Cancer Res 17:880–885

Therman E, Kuhn EM (1989) Mitotic modifications and aberrations in cancer. CRC Crit Rev Oncogen 1:293–305

Therman E, Sarto GE, Buchler DA (1983) The structure and origin of giant nuclei in human cancer cells. Cancer Genet Cytogenet 9:9–18

Therman E, Buchler DA, Nieminen U, et al. (1984) Mitotic modifications and aberrations in human cervical cancer. Cancer Genet Cytogenet 11:185–197

Therman E, Denniston C, Nieminen U, et al. (1985) X chromatin, endomitoses, and mitotic abnormalities in human cervical cancer. Cancer Genet Cytogenet 16:1–11

Timonen S (1950) Mitosis in normal endometrium and genital cancer. Acta Obstet Gynecol Scand Suppl 31:1–88

Timonen S, Therman E (1950) The changes in the mitotic mechanism of human cancer cells. Cancer Res 10:431–439

Wolf U (1974) Theodor Boveri and his book "On the problem of the origin of malignant tumors." In: German J (ed) Chromosomes and cancer. Wiley, New York, pp 3–20

Yosida TH (1975) Chromosomal alterations and development of experimental tumors. Handb Allg Pathol 6:677–753

31
Mapping of Human Chromosomes

Gene Mapping

The mapping of human chromosomes is progressing so rapidly that it is no longer possible to maintain an up-to-date catalog in book form. The standard listing of human genes, Victor A. McKusick's *Mendelian Inheritance in Man*, has been published in nine editions since its first appearance in 1966. The first edition contained just over 1000 entries; the ninth edition, which appeared in 1990, contained more than 5000. The catalog now cites more than 36,000 references and 56,000 authors. *Mendelian Inheritance in Man* is now available to geneticists as an on-line computerized database known as OMIM—the only form in which the rapidly burgeoning body of information can be kept current (McKusick, 1990, 1991).

Virtually every issue of *Science* now contains at least one paper reporting the assignment of a new gene to a particular chromosome or the cloning and sequencing of a new gene. The same is true of *Nature*, *Cell*, *Genomics*, and a horde of other journals. The mass of accumulating data has been kept under control through the efforts of researchers who have participated in frequent International Workshops on Human Gene Mapping: in New Haven in 1973; Rotterdam, 1974; Baltimore, 1975; Winnipeg, 1977; Edinburgh, 1979; Oslo, 1981; Los Angeles, 1983; Helsinki, 1985; Paris, 1987; New Haven, 1988 and 1989; and Oxford, 1990. The results from the Oxford conference are published in the 786 pages of *Human Gene Mapping 10.5* (1990), which reports the mapping of about 1900 genes and more than 5000 DNA segments.

A useful progress report appeared in *Science* (Stephens et al., 1990) along with a beautiful wall chart of the Human Genome Map, 1990. The map right now is only about 1% complete. The Human Genome Project, recently launched by the National Institutes of Health and the Department of Energy, aims at producing a complete sequence of the 3×10^9 base pairs of DNA in the human genome within the next 15 years (*U.S. Genome Project: The First Five Years FY 1991–1995*, 1990).

Identifying Map Sites

A map is a picture on which the locations of objects are shown in relation to the overall pattern. In genetics, the picture may depict:

1. A summary of *recombination* frequencies resulting from two- or three-factor crosses. This is a *linkage map*. Two genes that are linked to each other are on the same chromosome. The lower their frequency of recombination, the closer they are to one another on the chromosome. A complete linkage map shows the one set of linked genes for each chromosome and shows the correct order of the genes on the chromosome. However, because of localized differences in the intensity of crossing-over, the distances shown on the linkage map may differ markedly from the physical distances between the markers on the chromosome.
2. The chromosomes as they appear on a microscope slide. The picture that one sees will depend, of course, on the method used to prepare and stain the chromosomes. The map is a *chromosome map*. The aim of mapping is to be able to point to the spots on the picture of the chromosome at which specific genes are located.
3. A representation of the chromosomal DNA. The resolution may be a fairly coarse picture of *fragments* of DNA whose lengths have been measured and whose relative positions have been discovered by determining the positions of endonuclease break points (Chapter 5). On the other hand, it is now possible to determine fine structure at the level of *nucleotide sequence*. Any map representing the structure of the DNA is a *molecular map*. One goal of the Human Genome Project is to define the relationship between the molecular map and the chromosome map.

The astonishing advances in gene mapping demonstrate the value of applying many different techniques to the solution of a single, central problem. These range from family studies to somatic cell genetics and from cytogenetics to biochemical and molecular studies. Table 31.1, taken from McKusick (1991), summarizes the methods that have been used for mapping human autosomal genes and the number of genes successfully mapped by each method. Most of these methods will be described briefly in the remainder of this chapter. Often a gene assignment based on one method has been confirmed with another. The traits for which loci

Table 31.1. Numbers of autosomal loci mapped by various methods.[a]

Method	Number of loci mapped
Somatic cell hybridization	1148
In situ hybridization	687
Family linkage study	466
Dosage effect	159
Restriction enzyme fine analysis	176
Chromosome aberrations	123
Homology of synteny	110
Radiation-induced gene segregation	18
Other	143

[a] From McKusick VA (1991) Current trends in mapping human genes. FASEB J 5: 12–20.

have been mapped include inherited diseases (such as cystic fibrosis), enzymes (such as tyrosine aminotransferase), serum proteins (such as α-haptoglobin), ribosomal RNA genes, fragile sites (such as the fragile-X site), and many positively and negatively acting oncogenes (such as the *ras* gene, which is involved in producing cancers of the bladder, lung, and colon; and the *RB1* gene, whose product is required to prevent retinoblastoma) (Shows, 1978; Magenis, 1988; McKusick, 1991; Pimentel, 1990; Cavenee et al., 1989).

In chromosome mapping, as in many other branches of cytogenetics, chromosome banding provided a breakthrough. Natural variations in banding patterns provide a means by which genes can be assigned not only to individual chromosomes, but also to specific chromosome regions. In situ hybridization of DNA and RNA probes (Chapter 5) to banded chromosomes has provided a valuable method for equating points on the molecular map with points on the chromosome map. The accuracy of gene localization has been further improved by the use of prophase banding.

Gene assignments are classified as *confirmed* when at least two studies have come to the same conclusion; *provisional* when only one determination exists; and *controversial* when different studies provide contradictory assignments (Donald and Hamerton, 1978).

Family Studies

It is usually easy to decide, on the basis of family studies, whether a gene lies on an autosome or on one of the sex chromosomes. An X-linked gene is never passed from father to son, whereas a Y-linked gene always is, and cannot be passed from father to daughter. The first human gene to be assigned to a specific chromosome was red-green color blindness, which was assigned to the X chromosome in 1911 (McKusick and Ruddle, 1977). Now, more than 200 X-linked genes are known (Davies et al.,

1990). Even a "non-gene"—the DNA sequence corresponding to the fragile-X site—has recently been characterized at the molecular level (Oberlé et al., 1991; Yu et al., 1991). Very few genes have been assigned to the Y chromosome, the most important being SRY on Yp. This gene, which seems to be the single gene responsible for determining maleness in XY individuals, has recently been cloned and sequenced (Sinclair et al. 1990).

For autosomal genes, studies of linkage and crossing-over show whether or not two or more genes are on the same chromosome (*syntenic*). The first demonstration of linkage between two autosomal genes was in Jan Mohr's 1954 Ph.D. thesis, which demonstrated linkage between the Lutheran blood group and the secretor gene (McKusick, 1991). However, such data show only that two genes are on the same chromosome; they do not reveal *which* chromosome.

The assignment of a gene or a linkage group to a specific chromosome can be done on the basis of family studies only if a suitable marker chromosome, readily distinguishable from its normal homologue, is available. Typical markers consist of long or short heterochromatic regions, fragile regions, structurally rearranged abnormal chromosomes, or, more recently, polymorphic cut sites recognized by specific restriction endonucleases. The first gene assigned by means of a marker chromosome was the Duffy blood group locus, which segregated with a large variant of chromosome 1 (Donahue et al., 1968). The extra length of this chromosome turned out to be due to an abnormally large region of centric heterochromatin. In another early linkage study, it was shown that the gene for α-haptoglobin was inherited together with a fragile site on 16q (such a fragile site is illustrated in Fig. 9.6 a and b) in 30 family members and was separated from it in 3 (Magenis et al., 1970). The recombination frequency of only 9.1% indicates that the α-Hp locus lies near the fragile site on 16q. ("Near" is an imprecise term. Two genes separated by 1 million base pairs give about 1 percent recombination.) In one case, a chromosomal marker—an abnormal fragile region near the distal end of Xq (Fig. 22.2 d)—seems in itself to produce a mutant phenotype: fragile-X mental retardation (Howard-Peebles and Stoddard, 1979).

The major histocompatibility complex (HLA) was assigned to chromosome 6 by demonstrating linkage to a pericentric inversion segregating in a family (Lamm et al., 1974). Reciprocal translocations involving chromosome 6 made the further localization of this gene to 6p21 possible (Breuning et al., 1977; Francke et al., 1977). This assignment was, in turn, confirmed through a study of partial trisomy for the segment distal to 6p21 that resulted from crossing-over in a pericentric inversion (Pearson et al., 1979).

We noted in Chapter 5 that the impossibility of arranging experimental matings in humans is no longer an impediment to measuring frequencies of recombination, at least in the male. With the advent of the polymerase chain reaction, it has become possible to amplify DNA from single cells, including sperm cells, and to detect new associations of DNA sequences (Li et al., 1988). If homologous chromosomes of a male subject can be distinguished from one another by two (or more) restriction sites or other sequence differences, the frequency of recombination between the two sites can be measured directly by examination of gametes.

Somatic Cell Genetics

Although refinements in banding techniques have made many visible chromosome markers available (it is claimed that by now every human being can be distinguished by them), gene mapping owes its greatest advances to other methods, especially somatic cell hybridization. All cell hybridization techniques are based on the observation that somatic cells of the same species or of two different species will fuse under certain conditions. For purposes of human chromosome mapping, human cells are usually hybridized with rodent cell lines—generally mouse or Chinese hamster—capable of unlimited growth in culture. The following criteria should be considered when the cell types are chosen for human gene mapping (Creagan and Ruddle, 1977):

1. The cells grow rapidly in culture.
2. The cells are easy to hybridize, and the hybrid cells divide in culture.
3. The chromosomes of the parent cells can be identified without difficulty (Fig. 31.1).
4. Human chromosomes are unilaterally lost from the hybrid cells (see following paragraphs).
5. The human genetic markers can be easily determined and are distinguishable from those of the other parent cell.

Spontaneous fusion of somatic cells is an extremely rare phenomenon, which probably occurs only when one cell type is malignant. (An exception is provided by cells of Bloom syndrome patients, as described in Chapter 8). The incidence of cell fusions can be increased considerably by treating cultured cells with inactivated Sendai virus or a chemical agent such as polyethylene glycol (Ruddle and Kucherlapati, 1974). When two cells fuse, the hybrid at first has two nuclei; it is a *heterokaryon*. After nuclear fusion, the cell is called a *synkaryon* (Fig. 31.2).

In order to study hybrid cells, one must be able to propagate *selectively* those cells that contain chromosomes from both parents. Generally the human cells used in the mixture have limited capacity for growth in culture; they will quickly be swamped out by the growth of the parental rodent cells and of the rodent-human hybrid cells. The selection procedure must distinguish, therefore, between rodent cells and rodent-human hybrid cells. Typically, the rodent cell line used in these experiments

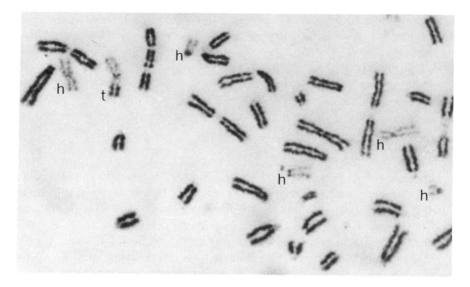

Figure 31.1 Part of the metaphase plate from a man-mouse hybrid cell stained with G-11. Mouse chromosomes, from an aneuploid cell line, are dark with light centric regions, human chromosomes (h) are light with dark centric regions, and the translocation (t) between the two species is part dark, part light (courtesy of RI DeMars).

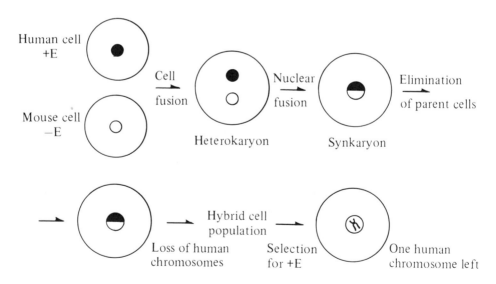

Figure 31.2. Assignment of the gene coding for the enzyme E to a specific human chromosome (black) through fusion of a human cell (nucleus black) with a mouse cell (nucleus outlined), followed by cell selection.

carries a recessive mutation—a nutritional deficiency, for example—that can be complemented by a wild-type gene in the human cells. By growing the cells in culture medium devoid of the required nutrient, one selects against the parent rodent cells and allows selective growth of hybrid cells containing a specific chromosome or chromosome segment from the human parent cells. In practice, selection may be positive or negative, relative or absolute. The means used include culture media in which a certain cell type cannot grow or grows preferentially, or selective killing of one cell type with toxins, antibodies, or viruses to which the other cells are resistant.

Even an artificially increased cell fusion rate is so low that the hybrid cells have to be enriched relative to the parental cells (Ruddle and Kucherlapati, 1974). Sometimes hybrid cells divide faster than the parent cells, but usually selection for the hybrids involves suppression of the parental cells. In the example in Fig. 31.2, the mouse cells can be eliminated by a medium in which only cells that produce the enzyme E are able to grow. If one wishes to do so, the human cells can be killed with diphtheria toxin or the cardiac glycoside ouabain, to which the mouse and hybrid cells are insensitive. Figure 31.2 illustrates the steps in the assignment of the gene coding for a hypothetical enzyme E to a specific human chromosome. As the hybrid cells multiply in culture, they begin to lose human chromosomes in a more or less random fashion. Cell hybridization can be regarded as a parasexual process in which meiotic segregation is replaced by random chromosome loss. Neither the reason for nor the exact mechanism of the process of chromosome elimination is understood, although it plays an important role in the gene mapping procedures.

Chromosome elimination leads to the formation of hybrid clones that differ in their human chromosome content. At this point, selection for or against a certain phenotype in the hybrid cells is an important tool in the gene mapping process. In our example (Fig. 31.2), a selection system is used that allows only those cells producing enzyme E to survive. Naturally the clearest result is obtained when cells with phenotype E have only one human chromosome left, which must therefore be the site of gene E. The first human enzyme to be assigned in this way was thymidine kinase (TK) to chromosome 17 (Ruddle and Creagan, 1975).

In our example, we selected directly for the enzyme produced by the gene we wanted to map. However, the same selectively grown hybrid cells could have been used to map some other enzyme. Normally, the hybrid cells that grow under the selective conditions are a mixed population. The usual result of random chromosome elimination is a collection of clones with different combinations of human chromosomes. To map some other *unselected* gene, say the one that produces enzyme H, one merely looks among the selected hybrid cells for those that produce enzyme H and determines which human chromosomes are present in all of the H-producing cells. If there is only one chromosome that is common to all of the H-producing cells, the assignment of the gene to its chromosome is unambiguous.

A *clone panel* of cultured hybrid cell may be established in which each chromosome has a unique pattern of presence or absence among the clones in the panel. A panel of only five cloned cultures is sufficient to identify each of the 24 human chromosomes (See Table 31.2). Mapping is done by testing each clone in the panel for the presence or absence of a particular identifiable gene product (or DNA sequence). The summary of +/0 reactions with the members of the clone panel produces a binary pattern that uniquely identifies the human chromosome that is the site of the gene (Ruddle and Creagan, 1975). With the clone panel technique, it is also possible to determine whether or not two or more genes are syntenic.

Chromosome Rearrangements

It is often possible to determine the order of genes on a chromosome and their location within specific chromosome segments by studying rearrangements, such as translocations, involving the relevant chromosome. The occurrence of a particular phenotype in hybrid cells that have retained *partial* chromosomes restricts the location of the gene to the part of the chromosome that is present in the cell. By the use of several, partly overlapping translocations, the assignment of a gene can be limited to a smaller and smaller chromosome segment—the so-called SRO (smallest region of overlap)—in chromosomes that have *lost* the genetic function.

This was done for three X-linked genes by means of a translocation in which almost the whole Xq was attached to the distal end of 14q

Table 31.2. Demonstration of a clone panel. Five hybrid clones A–E are selected for the presence (+) or absence (0) of the 24 human chromosomes shown across the top. When these clones are tested for the presence or absence of any particular human gene product or DNA sequence, the +/0 pattern for the particular gene product, emphasized in the table by shading, produces a pattern that allows the product to be assigned to a specific chromosome.[a]

	1	2	3	4	5	6	7	8	9	10	11	12	13	14	15	16	17	18	19	20	21	22	X	Y
A	+	0	+	+	+	+	0	+	+	+	0	+	+	0	+	0	0	0	0	0	+	+	0	0
B	+	+	0	+	+	+	0	0	+	+	0	0	+	0	0	+	0	0	+	+	+	0	+	+
C	+	+	+	0	+	+	+	0	0	+	0	0	0	0	0	0	+	0	+	0	0	+	0	+
D	+	+	+	+	0	+	+	+	0	0	+	0	0	0	0	0	0	+	0	+	+	+	+	+
E	+	+	+	+	+	0	+	+	+	0	+	+	0	+	0	0	0	0	+	+	0	0	0	0

[a] From Ruddle and Creagan (1975); modified and reproduced, with permission from the Annual Review of Genetics Vol. 9, © 1975 by Annual Reviews Inc.

(Allderdice et al., 1978). Cell hybridization studies showed that the genes for HGPRT (hypoxanthine-guanine phosphoribosyl-transferase), PGK (phosphoglycerate kinase), and G6PD (glucose-6-phosphate dehydrogenase) segregated with the long translocation chromosome as did the autosomal gene NP (nucleoside phosphorylase). The three X-linked genes could thus be assigned to Xq and the autosomal gene to 14q (Ricciuti and Ruddle, 1973). By means of other X-autosomal translocations, it was possible to demonstrate that the order of the three genes was: centromere-PGK-HGPRT-G6PD, and to determine the limits of the segments within which each of them must be situated.

Other Uses of Deletions and Translocations in Mapping

A number of single genes (or, in some cases, syndromes apparently caused by a few genes) have been mapped by prophase banding to determine deletion or translocation break points. Thus, the gene for Duchenne muscular dystrophy was mapped to Xp21, when in several affected females the translocation break point coincided with this band, and a few other X-linked genes have been assigned in the same way (de Grouchy and Turleau, 1988). Wilms' tumor-aniridia syndrome has been found to be caused by a deletion of 11p13. On the other hand, the connection of the Prader-Willi syndrome and 15q11–q13 is less clear, since virtually all cases appear to be de novo mutations, and the cytogenetic abnormalities associated with the syndrome are diverse. They include deletions, duplications, and translocations, but not all Prader-Willi patients have discernible chromosome abnormalities (Ledbetter et al., 1982; de Grouchy and Turleau, 1988). Furthermore, the Prader-Willi syndrome seems to be affected by *imprinting*: in a normal diploid, only the allele inherited on the paternal chromosome 15 is expressed (Little et al., 1991). As discussed in Chapter 29, retinoblastoma was first mapped by showing its correlation with the hemizygosity of 13q14.

In Situ Hybridization

We discussed in Chapter 5 a powerful method for unifying the molecular map and the chromosome map: the use of labeled DNA probes to identify regions of complementary DNA on chromosomes fixed to microscope slides. A single-stranded DNA (or RNA) probe may be labeled with a radioactive isotope or a side group such as biotin that can be used as a target for fluorescence staining (Chapter 5). If a radioactive probe is hybridized to a chromosome preparation in which the chromosomes have been treated to separate the DNA strands, the location of the complementary sequence in the chromosomal DNA will be surrounded by silver grains after autoradiography (Pardue and Gall, 1975). In this way, the human satellite DNAs have been localized to the centric and Y heterochromatin (Yunis et al., 1977). The repeated genes, which occur in 100 to 200 copies in the human chromosome complement, have also been mapped by direct hybridization (Evans and Atwood, 1978). They include the genes coding for the ribosomal proteins 18S and 28S, which are situated on the satellite stalks of acrocentric chromosomes. The genes producing the 5S ribosomal protein have been assigned to 1q42–q43 (Steffensen, 1977). The assignment of the histone genes, repeated about 40 times, to 7q32–q36 was confirmed by direct hybridization on prophase-banded chromosomes (Chandler et al., 1979).

Single genes were first localized with in situ hybridization to the polytene chromosomes of *Drosophila*, in which a band may consist of thousands of copies of a gene (Fig. 31.3). The first human single genes were localized with this technique in 1981. These were α-globin genes, assigned to chromosome 16 (Gerhard et al., 1981), and β-globin genes, to 11p (Malcolm et al., 1981).

In situ hybridization has opened up completely new possibilities for gene mapping. Any gene or DNA sequence that has been cloned can now be mapped (Harper and Saunders, 1984; and Chapter 5). The great

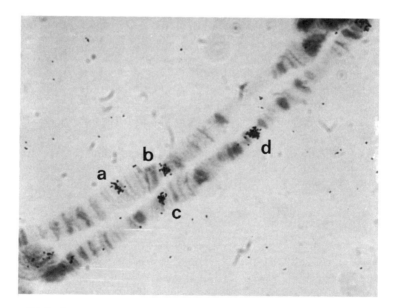

Figure 31.3. In situ hybridization to *Drosophila* polytene chromosomes. The chromosomes were hybridized with ³H-labeled RNA homologous to a *Drosophila* transposable element known as the *P* element and autoradiographed. The silver grains reveal the chromosomal sites of insertion of this element. At several sites (a and c) it can be seen that only one of the paired homologues contains an insert. Site c is the location of a new mutation caused, in this instance, by insertion of a *P* element there (courtesy of K Loughney and B Ganetzky).

advantage of this technique, apart from accuracy, is that a gene need not be expressed, which is a prerequisite for gene mapping with the cell hybridization technique. Single-gene mapping differs from the assignment of longer DNA sequences in that information from a number of auto-radiographed metaphases has to be pooled to localize the gene to the region that contains the highest total number of silver grains. Alternatively, one can use fluorescence labeling and computer-assisted microscopy to detect a weak signal from a labeled site on the chromosome.

McKusick (1991) reports that almost 700 autosomal genes have now been mapped by *in situ* hybridization methods (Table 31.1). The number will surely be close to 900 by the time this book is printed. New techniques have been developed for multicolor fluorescence labeling of chromosomes, which allows two or more specific probes to be identified in a single nucleus. Even interphase chromatin in hypotonically swollen nuclei can be stained with these fluorescent probes, and the distance between the bands in such fluorescence-labeled chromosomes has been shown to be directly proportional to the molecular distance (up to about 1 million base pairs) separating the two binding sites (Lichter et al., 1990; Trask, 1991). It is reasonable to expect that these new techniques will improve the diagnostic power of cytogenetics, allowing chromosome abnormalities to be detected even in non-dividing cells. The use of double- and triple-fluorescence labeling to detect subtle changes in structure, copy number, and physiological state can be expected to shed new light on chromosome structure and function (Trask, 1991).

Recombinant DNA Gene Mapping Methods

Recombinational mapping of a genome requires the identification of a large number of mutations that have observable phenotypes. "Saturation" of the recombinational map can almost be achieved in microbial systems, where the experimental organisms can be treated with mutagens to induce high frequencies of mutations, where culture conditions can be varied at will to select for interesting phenotypes, and where matings can be arranged without concern for the rights and feelings of the experimental organisms. In humans, of course, the investigator must take the phenotypes and matings that come along and make the best of them. Because humans are such diverse creatures and because we are acutely aware of their variations—especially those that compromise health—the pure Mendelian approach to genetic characterization of the species has produced an extensive and useful map. It is, however, far from saturated (Stephens et al., 1990).

Cytogenetics—the union of chromosome mapping with Mendelian genetics—has yielded a great deal of information about the location of genes on chromosomes. The correlation of chromosome anomalies with mutant phenotypes has helped to pinpoint the positions of genes on the human chromosomes, and the use of somatic cell genetic techniques has greatly accelerated progress in placing the known genes in their proper places on the chromosome map. But these methods, for all their power, cannot produce a complete map of the human genome (de Grouchy and Turleau, 1988).

The tools of molecular biology, described in Chapter 5, have finally given us the ability, at least in principle, to produce a map of the human genome that shows *everything*! The availability of highly specific restriction endonucleases that cut DNA into fragments of manageable length has made it possible to clone pieces of DNA that can be used as markers for specific locations on the genome. Even randomly collected fragments can be useful. In a large collection of random fragments, some will be found, by in situ hybridization methods, to bind specifically to chromosome bands already known to be associated with genetic disorders. Others will specifically identify locations that are polymorphic in the human population—that show variation with respect to the presence of an endonuclease cut site or that differ with respect to the number of tandem repeats of some simple-sequence element that they contain (*Human Gene Mapping* 10.5, 1990).

The polymerase chain reaction (PCR) provides a method by which DNA in the region flanking a given marker fragment can be amplified and cloned (Erlich et al., 1989), so that overlapping sets of clones ("contigs") that cover a large region of the genome can be isolated and sequenced. By "walking" from a site known to be close to an interesting gene and sequencing overlapping fragments in a collection heading toward the target gene, it is possible eventually to get the entire DNA sequence of the gene, even if the structure of its product is entirely unknown. That method has been used recently to clone the genes for cystic fibrosis (Kerem et al., 1989; Riordan et al., 1989); for familial adenomatous polyposis, a condition that leads ultimately to colon cancer (Kinzler et al., 1991; Nishisho et al., 1991); and SRY, the male-determining gene on the Y chromosome (Sinclair et al., 1990; Gubbay et al., 1990).

The development of the yeast artificial chromosome (YAC) cloning system has provided a method for cloning much larger fragments of DNA than had previously been possible (Schlessinger, 1990), and the invention of pulsed-field gel electrophoresis (PFGE) has provided a technique for separating and characterizing DNA fragments that were too large to be studied with the standard methods (Cantor et al., 1988). These methods for handling large pieces of DNA will expedite the construction of contigs and increase the speed at which geneticists can walk, skip, and jump along the human genome to find genes of interest.

A further procedure that has also found use in gene mapping is the isolation and sorting of chromosomes with a fluorescence-activated cell sorter. Each fraction, which consists of one to three chromosome types, can be purified further and used to obtain DNA from a specific chromosome (Lebo, 1982; Yu et al., 1984; and Chapter 5).

Conclusions

The total number of human genes is still a matter of guesswork. Presumably it is much larger than the number found in the *Drosophila* genome, which is believed to contain 5000–6000 genes. The prevailing crude estimate of the number of human genes is 1×10^5. Obviously only a fraction of them are known. McKusick (1990) lists approximately 4900 autosomal genes, of which about a third are mapped to specific chromosomes. Because of the easy detection of X-linkage, about 200 genes are known to be on this chromosome.

The combined application of classical cytogenetics and molecular genetics is allowing clinical geneticists to dissect complex genetic disorders. Down syndrome is an example (Fig. 31.4). Korenberg (personal communication) has analyzed numerous cases in which short duplications have resulted in *partial* 21-trisomy—cases with triplication of short segments of chromosome 21. Cytogenetic and molecular techniques make it possible to identify the ends of the triplicated regions within about 400 kb pairs of DNA—less than 1 percent of the length of the chromosome.

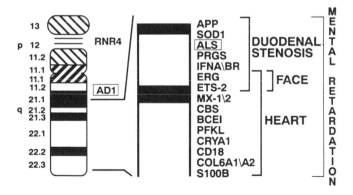

Figure 31.4. Mapping of Down syndrome phenotypes to regions of chromosome 21. Small duplications leading to partial trisomy for chromosome 21 have been studied by molecular and biochemical techniques to determine the endpoints of the triplicated segments. The map shows the phenotypic effects—duodenal stenosis, facial characteristics, heart abnormalities, and mental retardation—produced by triplication of various segments of the chromosome. Also shown are the locations of various genes: for example, APP = amyloid beta (A4) precursor protein; SOD1 = Cu-Zn superoxide dismutase 1 (soluble); CBS = cystathionine beta synthase; and COL6A1\A2 = collagen type VI, alpha 1 and alpha 2 (courtesy of JR Korenberg).

Korenberg has mapped the various phenotypes associated with Down syndrome to different regions of chromosome 21 by determining the phenotypic effects associated with trisomy for short regions of the chromosome. As the resolution of such mapping increases, the chances of identifying the underlying biochemical causes of the multiple abnormalities in Down syndrome will increase.

More than half of the localized genes have been mapped by means of cell hybridization. However, it seems safe to assume that the future belongs to in situ hybridization and other molecular approaches. We should, however, remember that, as so often before, techniques as yet unknown may revolutionize gene mapping in the years to come.

One of the goals of human genetics is the development of a complete gene map. This task is daunting, since the overwhelming majority of the genes are still unknown, but the Human Genome Project should be able to provide the money and the organizational support needed for such a massive effort. One of the tasks ahead is the coordination of the results of formal genetics, somatic cell genetics, and molecular studies of chromosome structure. The crowning achievement at the molecular level will be the base sequencing of the total DNA of the human genome and the correlation of such data with the functions of different parts of the chromosomes.

References

Allderdice PW, Miller OJ, Miller DA, et al. (1978) Spreading of inactivation in an (X;14) translocation. Am J Med Genet 2:233–240

Breuning MH, Berg-Loonen EM van den, Bernini LF, et al. (1977) Localization of HLA on the short arm of chromosome 6. Hum Genet 37:131–139

Cantor CR, Smith CL, Matthew MK (1988) Pulsed-field gel electrophoresis of very large DNA molecules. Annu Rev Biophysics Biophys Chem 17:41–72

Cavenee W, Hastie N, and Stanbridge E (eds) (1989) Current communications in molecular biology: Recessive oncogenes and tumor suppression. Cold Spring Harbor Laboratory, New York

Chandler ME, Kedes LH, Cohn RH, et al. (1979) Genes coding for histone proteins in man are located on the distal end of the long arm of chromosome 7. Science 205:908–910

Creagan RP, Ruddle FH (1977) New approaches to human gene mapping by somatic cell genetics. In: Yunis JJ (ed) Molecular structure of human chromosomes. Academic, New York, pp 89–142

Davies KE, Mandel JL, Monaco RL, et al. (1990) Report of the committee on the constitution of the X chromosome. Cytogenet Cell Genet 55:254–313

Donahue RP, Bias WB, Renwick JM, et al. (1968) Probable assignment of the Duffy blood group locus to chromosome 1 in man. Proc Natl Acad Sci USA 61:949–955

Donald LJ, Hamerton JL (1978) A summary of the human gene map, 1973–1977. Cytogenet Cell Genet 22:5–11

Erlich HA, Gibbs R, Kazazian HH Jr (eds) (1989) Current communications in molecular biology: polymerase chain reaction. Cold Spring Harbor Laboratory, Cold Spring Harbor, New York

Evans HJ, Atwood KC (1978) Report of the committee on in situ hybridization. Cytogenet Cell Genet 22:146–149

Francke U, George DL, Pellegrino MA (1977) Regional mapping of gene loci on human chromosomes 1 and 6 by interspecific hybridization of cells with a t(1;6)(p3200;p2100) translocation and by correlation with linkage data. In: Sparkes RS, Comings DE, Fox CF (eds) Molecular human cytogenetics. Academic, New York, pp 201–216

Gerhard DS, Kawasaki ES, Bancroft FC, et al. (1981) Localization of a unique gene by direct hybridization in situ. Proc Natl Acad Sci USA 78:3755–3759

Grouchy J de, Turleau C (1988) Mendelian disorders and autosomal structural rearrangements. In: Daniel A (ed) The cytogenetics of mammalian autosomal rearrangements. Liss, New York, pp 769–801

Gubbay J, Collignon J, Koopman P, et al. (1990) A gene mapping to the sex-determining region of the mouse Y chromosome is a member of a novel family of embryonically expressed genes. Nature 346:245–250

Harper ME, Saunders GF (1984) Localization of single-copy genes on human chromosomes by in situ hybridization of ³H-probes and autoradiography. In: Sparkes RS, de la Cruz FF (eds) Research perspectives in cytogenetics. University Park Press, Baltimore, pp 117–133

Howard-Peebles PN, Stoddard GR (1979) X-linked mental retardation with macro-orchidism and marker X chromosomes. Hum Genet 50:247–251

Human gene mapping 10.5 (1990) Cytogenet Cell Genet 55, Nos 14

Kerem B-S, Rommens JH, Buchanan JA, et al. (1989) Identification of the cystic fibrosis gene: genetic analysis. Science 245:1073–1080

Kinzler KW, Nilbert MC, Su LK, et al. (1991) Identification of FAP locus genes from chromosome 5q21. Science 253:661–665

Lamm LU, Friedrich U, Petersen GB, et al. (1974) Assignment of the major histocompatibility complex to chromosome no. 6 in a family with a pericentric inversion. Hum Hered 24:273–284

Lebo RV (1982) Chromosome sorting and DNA sequence localization. Cytometry 3:145–154

Ledbetter DH, Mascarello JT, Riccardi VM, et al. (1982) Chromosome 15 abnormalities and the Prader-Willi syndrome: A follow-up report of 40 cases. Am J Hum Genet 34:278–285

Li H, Gyllensten UB, Xui X, et al. (1988) Amplification and analysis of DNA sequences in single human sperm and diploid cells. Nature 335:414–417

Lichter P, Tang, C-J C, Call K, et al. (1990) High-resolution mapping of human chromosome 11 by in situ hybridization with cosmid clones. Science 247:64–69

Little M, Heyningen V Van, Hastie N (1991) Dads and disomy and disease. Nature 351:609

Magenis RE (1988) Application of structural rearrangements and DNA probes to gene mapping. In: Daniel A (ed) The cytogenetics of mammalian autosomal rearrangements. Liss, New York, pp 855–893

Magenis RE, Hecht F, Lovrien EW (1970) Heritable fragile site on chromosome 16: probable localization of haptoglobin locus in man. Science 170:85–87

Malcolm S, Barton P, Murphy C, et al. (1981) Chromosomal localization of a single copy gene by *in situ* hybridization—human beta-globin genes on the short arm of chromosome 11. Ann Hum Genet 45:135–141

McKusick VA (1990) Mendelian inheritance in man, 9th edn. Johns Hopkins University Press, Baltimore

McKusick VA (1991) Current trends in mapping human genes. FASEB J 5:12–20

McKusick VA, Ruddle FH (1977) The status of the gene map of the human chromosomes. Science 196:390–405

Nishisho I, Nakamura Y, Miyoshi Y, et al. (1991) Mutations of chromosome 5q21 genes in FAP and colorectal cancer patients. Science 253:665–669

Oberlé I, Rousseau F, Heitz D, et al. (1991) Instability of a 550-base pair DNA segment and abnormal methylation in fragile X syndrome. Science 252:1097–1102

Pardue ML, Gall JG (1975) Nucleic acid hybridization to the DNA of cytological preparations. In: Prescott DM (ed) Methods in cell biology 10. Academic, New York, pp 1–16

Pearson G, Mann JD, Bensen J, et al. (1979) Inversion of chromosome 6 with trisomic codominant expression of HLA antigens. Am J Hum Genet 31:30–34

Pimentel E (1990) Oncogenes, 2nd edn. CRC Press, Boca Raton, Florida

Ricciuti FC, Ruddle FH (1973) Assignment of three gene loci (PGK, HGPRT, and G6PD) to the long arm of the human X chromosome by somatic cell genetics. Genetics 74:661–678

Riordan JR, Rommens JM, Kerem B-S, et al. (1989) Identification of the cystic fibrosis gene: cloning and characterization of complementary DNA. Science 245:1066–1073

Ruddle FH, Creagan RP (1975) Parasexual approaches to the genetics of man. Annu Rev Genet 9:407–486

Ruddle FH, Kucherlapati RS (1974) Hybrid cells and human genes. Sci Am 231:36–44

Schlessinger D (1990) Yeast artificial chromosomes: Tools for mapping and analysis of complex genomes. Trends Genet 6:248–258

Shows TB (1978) Mapping the human genome and metabolic diseases. Birth Defects, Proc 5th Internat Conf: 66–84

Sinclair AH, Berta P, Palmer MS, et al. (1990) A gene from the human sex-determining region that encodes a protein with homology to a conserved DNA-binding motif. Nature 346:240–244

Steffensen DM (1977) Human gene localization by RNA:DNA hybridization *in situ*. In: Yunis JJ (ed) Molecular structure of human chromosomes. Academic, New York, pp 59–88

Stephens JC, Cavanaugh ML, Gradie MI et al. (1990) Mapping the human genome: current status. Science 250: 237–250

Trask BJ (1991) Fluorescence *in situ* hybridization. Trends Genet 7:149–154

U.S. Genome Project: The First Five Years FY 1991–1995 (1990) U. S. Department of Health and Human Services and U.S. Department of Energy. National Technical Information Service, Springfield, Virginia

Yu L-C, Gray JW, Langlois R, et al. (1984) Human chromosome karyotyping and molecular biology by flow cytometry. In: Sparkes RS, de la Cruz FF (eds) Research perspectives in cytogenetics. University Park, Baltimore, pp 65–73

Yu S, Pritchard M, Kremer E, et al. (1991) Fragile X genotype characterized by an unstable region of DNA. Science 252:1179–1181

Yunis JJ, Tsai MY, and Willey AM (1977) Molecular organization and function of the human genome. In: Yunis JJ (ed) Molecular structure of human chromosomes. Academic, New York, pp 1–33

Index of Names

Subject Index